Related Books of Interest

Do It Wrong Quickly
How the Web Changes the Old Marketing Rules

by Mike Moran
ISBN: 978-0-13-225596-7

For decades, marketers have been taught to carefully plan ahead because "you must get it right — it's too expensive to change." But, in the age of the Web, you can know in hours whether your strategy's working. Today, winners don't get it right the first time: They start fast, change fast, and relentlessly optimize their way to success. They do it wrong quickly...then fix it, just as quickly!

In this book, Internet marketing pioneer Mike Moran shows you how to do that — step-by-step and in detail. Drawing on his experience building ibm.com into one of the world's most successful sites, Moran shows how to quickly transition from "plan then execute" to a non-stop cycle of refinement.

You'll master specific techniques for making the Web's "two-way marketing conversation" work successfully, productively, and profitably. Next, Moran shows how to choose the right new marketing tools, craft them into an integrated strategy, and execute it...achieving unprecedented efficiency, accountability, speed, and results.

 Listen to the author's podcast at:
ibmpressbooks.com/podcasts

Mining the Talk
Unlocking the Business Value in Unstructured Information

by Scott Spangler and Jeffrey Kreulen
ISBN: 978-0-13-233953-7

Two leading-edge IBM researchers introduce a revolutionary new approach to unlocking the business value hidden in virtually any form of unstructured data—from word processing documents to websites, e-mails to instant messages.

The authors review the business drivers that have made unstructured data so important– and explain why conventional methods for working with it are inadequate. Then they walk step-by-step through exploring your unstructured data, understanding it, and analyzing it effectively.

D0357564

Related Books of Interest

Search Engine Marketing Inc.
Driving Search Traffic to Your Company's Web Site
Second Edition

by Mike Moran and Bill Hunt
ISBN: 978-0-13-606868-6

In this book, two world-class experts present today's best practices, step-by-step techniques, and hard-won tips for using search engine marketing to achieve your sales and marketing goals, whatever they are. Mike Moran and Bill Hunt thoroughly cover both the business and technical aspects of contemporary search engine marketing, walking beginners through all the basics while providing reliable, up-to-the-minute insights for experienced professionals. Includes Bonus DVD with more than 2 hours of exclusive how-to video presentations, plus audio interviews and whitepapers on cutting-edge search engine marketing topics.

 Listen to the author's podcast at:
ibmpressbooks.com/podcasts

Reaching The Goal
How Managers Improve a Services Business Using Goldratt's Theory of Constraints

by John Arthur Ricketts
ISBN: 978-0-13-233312-2

Managing services is extremely challenging, and traditional "industrial" management techniques are no longer adequate. In *Reaching The Goal*, John Arthur Ricketts presents a breakthrough management approach that embraces what makes services different: their diversity, complexity, and unique distribution methods.

Ricketts draws on Eli Goldratt's Theory of Constraints (TOC), one of this generation's most successful management methodologies... thoroughly adapting it to the needs of today's professional, scientific, and technical services businesses. He reveals how to identify the surprising constraints that limit your organization's performance, execute more effectively within those constraints, and then loosen or even eliminate them.

 Listen to the author's podcast at:
ibmpressbooks.com/podcasts

Related Books of Interest

The New Language of Business
Carter
ISBN: 0-13-195654-X

Executing SOA
Bieberstein, Laird, Jones, Mitra
ISBN: 0-13-235374-1

Enterprise Master Data Management
Dreibelbis, Hechler, Milman, Oberhofer, van Run, Wolfson
ISBN: 0-13-236625-8

Inescapable Data
Stakutis, Webster
ISBN: 0-13-185215-9

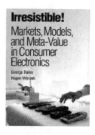

Irresistible! Markets, Models, and Meta-Value in Consumer Electronics
Bailey, Wenzek
ISBN: 0-13-198758-5

Can Two Rights Make a Wrong?
Reger
ISBN: 0-13-173294-3

Praise for *The New Language of Marketing 2.0*

"Many books tell marketers what to do, but this one shows them. With the changes now sweeping marketing, global marketers should not ignore the real-life examples and rich case studies in this resource."
—Mike Moran, coauthor, *Search Engine Marketing, Inc.*, and author,
Do It Wrong Quickly: How the Web Changes the Old Marketing Rules

"B2B marketers learning from B2C marketers and vice versa is a critical best practice. With more than 50 case studies, this book embodies the mandate to explore, learn, and grow from best practices around the world. This is a must read for marketers and business owners alike."
—Karen Vogel, Founder and President, The Women's Congress

"To succeed in this rapidly changing environment, businesses must adapt their marketing strategies accordingly. *The New Language of Marketing 2.0* provides practical, proven, and prescient tools to do exactly that."
—Dr. Steve Moxey, Research Fellow,
High-Tech Marketing, Manchester Business School

"I loved the customer examples. They gave me a number of ideas of how a company might expand its marketing portfolio by better leveraging the new social media world."
—Ron Williams, Professor, Kenan-Flagler Business School,
University of North Carolina at Chapel Hill

"This is a great collection of cutting edge marketing and insightful case studies. It offers the latest thinking in the field of marketing, showing you how to take advantage of the new world of Web 2.0 thinking."
—Nigel Dessau, Chief Marketing Officer, AMD

"If you are trying to shift the focus of your business to better serve and retain your customers, part of that must be the new Web 2.0 marketing strategies and learn how to be part of the conversation. *The New Language of Marketing 2.0* will help you find a way to combine your vision for the future with creative approaches."
—Mike Lackey, President, AIT Global and Special Advisor to the Executive
Director for the United Nations Global Alliance for ICT and Development

"*The New Language of Marketing 2.0* makes sense of new media vessels such as virtual worlds, blogging, wikis, social networking communities, and gaming and clearly describes how these new vessels can work for us."
—Jennifer McClure, Executive Director,
Society for New Communications Research

"The goalposts may not have moved—business goals remain fairly constant—but the field of play is completely different. *The New Language of Marketing 2.0* is your playbook to outmaneuver, outscore, and consistently beat your competition."

—Betty Spence, Ph.D., President, NAFE

"IBM's marketing of SOA is a best practice. IBM's ability to focus on how customers can get started and providing education and guidance is tremendous. There is a lot to learn from the IBM team in B2B marketing."

—Judith Hurwitz, President & CEO, Hurwitz & Associates,
and coauthor, *Service Oriented Architecture For Dummies*

"The landscape has changed, and new techniques leveraging Web 2.0 have changed the dialogue in the marketplace. Those who learn these global and dynamic dialogues fastest will drive growth. *The New Language of Marketing 2.0* teaches you how with more than 25 case studies."

—Don Tapscott, coauthor, *Wikinomics: How Mass
Collaboration Changes Everything*

"Today's business environment is completely different: interaction, communication, and information exchange have expanded to include virtual worlds, wikis, blogging, gaming, and online communities. *The New Language of Marketing 2.0* will provide insight into how to adapt your marketing strategies to engage your customers where they really are, and where they are going to be tomorrow."

—Carolyn Leighton, Founder/Chairwoman,
WITI (Women in Technology International)

"This book doesn't just 'tell' how to achieve success in the new Marketing 2.0 world: it shows how. Sandy has done breakthrough work with her team, and is sharing best practices. Not only does this book guide the reader to the next level of business development, it provides case studies that begin to bring the future of marketing into focus."

—Rod Baptie, Managing Director, Baptie & Co., Ltd.

"The landscape has changed, and new techniques leveraging Web 2.0 have changed the dialogue in the marketplace. Those who learn these global and dynamic dialogues fastest will drive growth. *The New Language of Marketing 2.0* teaches you how with more than 25 case studies."

—Don Tapscott, coauthor, *Wikinomics: How Mass Collaboration Changes Everything*

"This is a great collection of cutting edge marketing and insightful case studies. It offers the latest thinking in the field of marketing, showing you how to take advantage of the new world of Web 2.0 thinking."

—Nigel Dessau, Chief Marketing Officer, AMD

The New Language of Marketing 2.0

The New Language of Marketing 2.0

How to Use ANGELS to Energize Your Market

Sandy Carter

IBM Press
Pearson plc

Upper Saddle River, NJ • New York • San Francisco
Toronto • London • Munich • Paris • Madrid
Cape Town • Sydney • Tokyo • Singapore • Mexico City

www.ibmpressbooks.com

IBM Press Program Managers: Tara Woodman, Ellice Uffer

Cover design: IBM Corporation

Associate Publisher: Greg Wiegand
Marketing Manager: Kourtnaye Sturgeon
Publicist: Heather Fox
Development Editor: Kevin Howard
Managing Editor: Kristy Hart
Designer: Alan Clements
Project Editor: Chelsey Marti
Copy Editor: Deadline Driven Publishing
Indexer: Cheryl Lenser
Compositor: Nonie Ratcliff
Proofreader: Karen Gill, San Dee Phillips
Manufacturing Buyer: Dan Uhrig

Published by Pearson plc
Publishing as IBM Press

IBM Press offers excellent discounts on this book when ordered in quantity for bulk purchases or special sales, which may include electronic versions and/or custom covers and content particular to your business, training goals, marketing focus, and branding interests. For more information, please contact:

U. S. Corporate and Government Sales
1-800-382-3419
corpsales@pearsontechgroup.com.

For sales outside the U. S., please contact:

International Sales
international@pearsoned.com.

Library of Congress Cataloging-in-Publication Data

Carter, Sandy, 1963-
  The new language of marketing 2.0 : how to use ANGELS to energize your market / Sandy Carter.
    p. cm.
  ISBN 978-0-13-714249-1
  1. Internet marketing. 2. Communication in marketing. 3. Web 2.0. I. Title.
  HF5415.1265.C37 2008
  658.8'72—dc22

                              2008035861

  Pearson Education, Inc
  Rights and Contracts Department
  501 Boylston Street, Suite 900
  Boston, MA 02116
  Fax (617) 671 3447

  ISBN-13: 978-0-13-714249-1
  ISBN-10: 0-13-714249-8

Text printed in the United States on recycled paper at Courier Stoughton in Courier, Massachusetts.
First printing October 2008

To my Guardian Angel from above, my parents for their encouragement of bold and creative thoughts, my angel daughters, Maria and Cassie, and the love of my life, Todd!

Contents

N   Nail the Strategy

L   Leads and Revenue

Putting It All Together

The following materials can be found on the companion Web site at ibmpressbooks.com/angels

Foreword
by Bruce Harreld

A s I write this foreword, we are facing changes of epic proportions. A global economic slowdown seems imminent, rapidly rising energy and commodity prices are forcing global citizens to alter how we conduct our everyday lives, financial markets are in turmoil, and socio-political unrest has many countries in gridlock.

Yes, the world is changing, but what else is new? Change is a constant in today's world just as it was when first written in hieroglyphics by an ancient Egyptian several millennia ago. The bigger news is that we are learning from the past and are, thus, more capable of dealing with change than ever before.

Constructively embracing change is what separates winning marketing executives from the losers. Winning marketers look upon change as an opportunity to reposition offerings to meet shifting customer needs. Simply put, change is something great marketers seize. As Winston Churchill once remarked, "To improve is to *change*; to be perfect is to change *often*." Hence, the most important challenge for today's marketer is how to keep pace with and take advantage of change.

This book is all about helping you do just that...successfully deal with change. If you want to be a winning marketer you must read it. Ignore it at your own peril! It offers insights into the most recent developments in marketing as well as how to adapt more traditional marketing approaches to today's changing environment. Inside you'll find new perspectives on how to develop creative marketing strategies. Plus, it is full of real-life examples of how to successfully execute winning marketing plans.

In writing this book, Sandy Carter conducted interviews with many of today's most successful marketing leaders. She presents their insights in a crisp, easy-to-read style and offers many new ideas, tools, and practices for enabling companies to succeed, change, and thrive in the 21st century.

Equally important are the insights Sandy gleans from our experiences within IBM. The global shifts mentioned earlier have required us to augment our bag of old tricks with new ones. For example, in the past we might have relied merely upon direct mail or e-mail to announce a new offering. Today, while we will still do a mailer, we'll also post our announcement via viral marketing sites, blogs, social networks Google News, and videos on You Tube. Another example is our 2008 IMPACT conference for which we created Google blogs and You Tube video "Sneak Previews" to create enthusiam and interest well before the event actually kicked off. While we held the conference in real-time in Las Vegas we also broadcast the conference in Second Life to another audience via the Internet. Thus, while 6,500 attendees listened to our executives and customers at the convention hall, thousands more listened to the conference from the convenience of their homes or offices via video streaming on the Internet. We then followed up with MySpace, Facebook, and AOL pages to continue marketing the conference well after it was over. These new Marketing 2.0 techniques expanded our reach and extended the life of the conference well beyond the few days of the actual event. All this enabled more customers, business partners, and IBM'ers all over the world to participate in the conference than ever before. Over and over again we have learned that effective syndication of our marketing messages through these new Web 2.0 media maximizes our reach and responsiveness.

As I have witnessed first hand, Sandy Carter is truly a remarkable marketing executive. Sandy has excellent insights into all elements of marketing from strategic planning to tactical execution. Thus, it is no surprise she has written such an excellent guide on how the emerging Web 2.0 techniques can help marketers dynamically and successfully use change to their advantage. It's a pleasure to recommend her book and work with her organization within IBM. Enjoy!

—Bruce Harreld, Senior Vice President, IBM Corporation

Foreword
by Roy A. Young

As we close out the first decade of the new millennia, business has entered a revolutionary age in marketing, one in which the traditional strategies and rules no longer apply. Largely because of the overwhelming power and influence of the Web and other electronic communications, consumers are now in control. They can easily research all available choices through dialogues with suppliers, vendors, experts, and other consumers; they can ignore your irrelevant communications and turn their attention elsewhere; and they can often quickly switch to the competition to get their needs met. Consequently, marketing is no longer about pushing messages to convince prospects to take action, but instead, it's about conducting *conversations* to engage prospects with relevant content that will ultimately lead them to take the action you need for business impact.

Service Oriented Architecture (SOA), Web 2.0, mash-ups, "green" technologies, and even video games are part of the new rules of marketing, and it is essential that all business professionals have a command of these and other new tools if they want to continue to generate demand for their companies' products and services.

In her new book, Sandy Carter weaves the new tactics and technologies of this new age in marketing with real-world examples of their successful implementations. As a practitioner who works in the trenches to generate business results—not an ivory tower academic or consultant who merely tells companies what to do without having to implement strategies or projects—she skillfully breaks down the modern marketing process into its base components, and then she shows the best means to *execute* each of these.

As a leader of MarketingProfs, today's largest publisher of actionable know-how to keep marketers effective and current, I know our readers worldwide will find value from Carter's insights. Her new book opens my eyes to the ways businesses use what she calls industry "influencers" to drive key performance indicators. This key group—including groups such as investors, industry experts, thought leaders, students, and teachers—should be the focus of targeted marketing efforts. By connecting with the industry influencers, you illuminate a willing audience on the use and capabilities of your products and new technologies while at the same time constructing a pipeline of future business leaders, customers, and investors.

I was fascinated to read about one example of how this is executed successfully in the new "serious video game" developed by IBM known as INNOV8. This technology appeals to a generation raised on Nintendo, Playstation, and Xbox by providing an interactive graphic interface that actually teaches real-world business scenarios. These scenarios can be updated and modified to meet the needs of business and can—for example—show how student x would deal with a resource action at a phone bank or construct a datacenter to ensure that it has the lowest possible carbon footprint...along with other skills that are in high demand by today's employers.

Filled with practical case studies and best practices, *The New Language of Marketing 2.0* shows practitioners, consultants, academics, and students how the new rules of marketing can drive business impact. If you study and apply the lessons in the book, you will become a champion in your organization.

—Roy A. Young, president, MarketingProfs, and coauthor of *Marketing Champions: Practical Strategies to Improve Marketing's Power, Influence, and Business Impact* (John Wiley, 2006)

Preface

There are hundreds of books on marketing in stores today. Why this book and why now? The answer has to do with global megatrends that drive marketing today, as well as a technology-driven revolution in the world of marketing. This preface explains the context that helped shape this book by surveying these megatrends. We touch on the Web 2.0-related changes that quarter by quarter change how to define what marketing can do and how companies execute marketing tactics. This Web 2.0 revolution has reshaped consumer behavior and redefined the relationship between the enterprise and its customers.

The most effective marketers today employ a rigorous marketing methodology across both traditional and recently developed techniques. I call this approach "hybrid marketing." My team and I at IBM execute hybrid marketing via a methodology called ANGELS, which is described in the introduction. The essential goal of this book is to provide a blueprint for effective hybrid marketing in a changing world. Following are the megatrends that deem this new marketing essential.

Change as a Way of Life–Experiment

Given the quickness with which markets change, to retain its value, marketing must evolve. According to the BM Global CEO Study: The Enterprise of the Future (IBM, 2008), since 2006, the *change gap tripled*. More CEOs than ever before—eight out of ten—anticipate significant change in the next three years, up from six out of ten in 2006. What this means is that change is becoming more difficult, the pace of change is quickening, and many companies struggle to keep up.

The capability to be nimble and move quickly in the market is *the* key element in successful marketing. Organizations must have the capability to literally "turn on a dime" to keep pace with change. Marketing organizations need to ensure they are not reactive to change, but driving and leading change in a proactive way. Web 2.0 enables companies to be more nimble. It encourages free-flowing experimentation. Think about it: You can test an idea online at breakfast, and by lunch, you can see the response.

Technology Rules

At least two major trends in technology will impact the marketing profession in the future: experience and personalization. The basic question is, "How do you leverage technology and innovation to provide people with the most compelling quality of experience possible?"

Evolution of New Marketing Enablers

Web 1.0: Access information, purchase online

Web 2.0: Share and collaborate

Web 3.0: Experience, participate, and co-create

Yesterday's Web 1.0 world brought the capability that helped customers access information and purchase online. Today, Web 2.0 pushes sharing and collaborating, whether that is product reviews or asking for help on LinkedIn for how to market a product. For those leaders, today is also the day of Web 3.0. It is a world of a visual, immersive experience, and its goal is participation and co-creation. It will have elements of 3D and will offer to those bold marketers a way to create an experience that is a breakthrough.

The recent National Retail Federation (NRF) gave a glimpse into the future with an exhibit at which you stand in front of a mirror while shopping and your friends rate your outfit. The digital generation loved it. The common theme among the online, mobile, and physical environment—the 3D Internet—will continue to evolve into a community-like setting. Web 3.0 comes alive.

The second technology change is about the ability to personalize. The concept of individualism will evolve, and technology will enable products to be customized to your company or to a consumer.

What is exciting are the brands that are already starting to get this trend. They do not think only in terms of integration, but they think in terms of optimization. They view every interaction with a customer as an opportunity to learn from those interactions to make customers' experiences more personal, whether it be B2B or B2C. Ron Williams, an adjunct professor at the University of North Carolina in the entrepreneur department, highlights Best Buy as a great experience-based company. Per Williams, "What Best Buy did was to break its store model before it was broken. They went out and began building stores around customer experience."

Marketing organizations need to imagine their companies' experiences either in 2D or 3D. They need to ask, "What is the experience my clients have today and what do I want that experience to be?" Successful marketers deliver service, cater to customers, and position their products to meet customer needs; but they will do so in an experiential mode. Implications for marketers are a segmentation that is not based on the size of a company or even the role. It is a segmentation based on required experience in the marketplace. Successful marketers revolutionize the "customer experience" with dynamic marketing, whether through the Web, face-to-face contact, or traditional marketing mechanisms.

Web 2.0 is driving change in the marketing world. It changes how you listen to your customer. Blogs, for instance, enable you to listen to watercooler discussions you never had access to before. Change occurs in how you communicate to the customer; communication is more of a dialogue versus a broadcast message. Messages meant for one type of audience are being read by all audiences, so authenticity and focus must change. Influencers are evolving so that one wiki post or viral tactic can impact your brand, which is now jointly managed by the customers and you as marketer. Both groups are now brand facilitators, not owners.

Globalization Is Here

The Internet has leveled the playing field for companies of all sizes in all geographies. A small company in Cambodia can get attention in the United States using the right tactics, whereas five or ten years ago, this would have been impossible.

Ray Hammond, a world-renowned futurologist and author of more than 19 books, comments about the challenge, "Companies have to learn to be both global and local. An understanding at a local level about the culture and about the way people react is absolutely vital to international strategy. Advertising teams have known this for a long time because most advertising needs to be tailored for local consumption. In marketing, there has been less attention paid to it, but the most competitive companies will figure it out and pay attention to it strongly." According to the IBM Global CEO Study: The Enterprise of the Future, IBM, 2008, 75 percent of CEOs are actively entering new markets around the world in pursuit of new customers and scarce talent. Marketing now must agilely balance the local and global concepts.

How do you take advantage of this trend? First, examine and explore your global opportunities. Is your company ready to take your product or offering across borders? Are you ready to market effectively and with a unique approach, nation by nation, to the BRIC countries—Brazil, Russia, India, and China? If your answer is yes, then select specific global initiatives. If you are not ready, get ready now!

The Collaborative and Informed Customer

The customer is continually changing, and marketers need to constantly reevaluate customer needs to best influence their decisions. In addition to traditional shifts in taste and style, customers change in more fundamental ways, such as how they prefer to gather information, how they make decisions, and who they trust as influencers and advisors. With the rise of the Internet and social connectivity, there is now a more informed and demanding customer who is capable also of influencing peers' buying decisions. According to the IBM Global CEO Study: The Enterprise of the Future, IBM, 2008, more than 75 percent of the survey respondents see these savvy customers not as a threat but as an opportunity to differentiate.

These shifts in customers need to be factored into the marketing plans. To achieve success in the future, companies need to develop collaborative relationships and capabilities (B2B as well as B2C) to create innovative services, products, and experiences. Some are getting sophisticated at collaborative development as well; one CEO uses the term "prosumer," a consumer who is a coproducer of your product or service. The tried and true marketing and the new marketing 2.0 approaches must reach this new prosumer. This hybrid marketing approach is one that must be leveraged.

Corporate Social Responsibility (CSR)

One common trend is the growing focus on corporate responsibility. Why? First, the climate crisis is taking priority across the world. Incentives, government regulations, and cultural expectations are increasing the consciousness about the environment. According to IBM Global CEO Study: The Enterprise of the Future, IBM, 2008, more than 66 percent of CEOs see rising corporate social responsibility (CSR) expectations among their customers as an opportunity to differentiate themselves against their competitors, to grow market share, and to gain access to new markets and geographies.

Marketing must conduct business in an environmentally conscious way. In fact, any marketing in the next few years that does not pay attention to energy and environmental needs will be at a disadvantage. Joining the CSR trend is a part of the new-world marketing, which is here to stay. Make your CSR marketing strategy a genuine one.

The Fundamentals Are Still Critical

As a professional marketer (and reader of this book!), now is the time to embody and understand the new world. The bar has been raised. To perform, you must understand the Marketing 2.0 world. Education and experimentation are the name of the game because there are no rules, and breakthrough thinking and techniques will separate the winners from the losers. Because the bar is now raised, people need to execute on a hybrid model that mixes old and new approaches with both approaches united under a consistent framework for execution. This hybrid model is ANGELS.

You might not find books about marketing in this hybrid world. You might find books on new marketing techniques, but they neglect the tried-and-true marketing methods. You might find books on foundational elements that neglect recent innovations. This book reflects the complexity of the marketing world as it truly is today, and it includes case studies of companies that are experimenting successfully today. These companies combine new and old techniques. This book is the result of the new language of marketing, which leverages the learning of more than 14 marketing awards based on Marketing 2.0 best practices and the learning from our customers and partners. See Figure Preface.1.

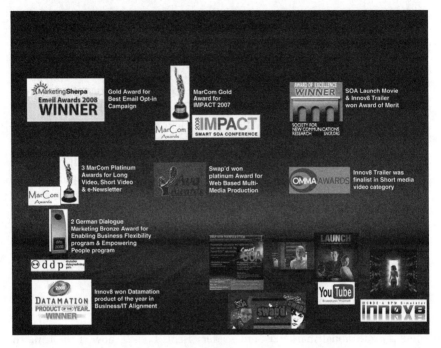

Figure Preface 1   Fourteen marketing awards for marketplace innovation.

The new language of Marketing 2.0 is born!

For an additional CEO study on factoids, go to
ibmpressbooks.com/angels.

Acknowledgments

T his book represents two passions of mine: marketing and technology. Marketing is a discipline that drives and motivates me to figure out how to create more value for my customers and how to help them seize their dreams. Technology powers better dialogues, listening, and demand generation. It powers the entire marketing lifecycle!

Hopefully, you will love the stories as much as the facts in this book. I learn from stories and love telling stories. In fact, my favorite quote is from an old Indian proverb: "Tell me the facts and I'll learn. Tell me the truth and I'll believe. But tell me a story and it will live in my heart forever." Stories are the heartbeat of life.

This story would not have been possible without the help of many people.

First, God, who blessed me with creativity and a love of numbers—especially pipeline numbers—so that I was able to persevere and write this book and learn from so many phenomenal people.

Second, my family: Todd, Cassie, and Maria, who supported my weekends of writing, and my parents, who inspired my bold ideas, and to my in-laws who cheered me on!

Third, key members of my team who were deeply involved through all stages of the book: Liz Markiewicz, Becky Michel, Sarah Duffy, John Gordon, Tara Woodman, Ellice Uffer, Ayalla Goldschmidt, and Michael Holmes.

Fourth, to my customers for the great sharing of their learnings: Forrester Research, Inc.; Rubicon Consulting; Rackspace; Midwest Airlines; University of North Carolina at Chapel Hill; KDPaine & Partners, LLC; EepyBird.com; Nortel; Object Management Group (OMG); Ascendant Technology, LLC; Prolifics; Ray Hammond; Unilever Dove; Harley-Davidson Motor Company; Staples; *CMO Magazine*; Market Strategies

International; The Coca-Cola Company; Communispace Corporation; Nielsen Online Digital Strategic Services; Collective Intellect; RedMonk; Mezzanine Consulting, LLC; FastStartPR; Baptie & Co Ltd; BrandGames; Irving Wladawsky-Berger; Corporate Executive Board; Gartner, Inc.; Google, Inc.; MarketingNPV LLC; Society for New Communications Research (SNCR); IDC; Rohit Barghava; ConAgra Foods; Tellabs, Inc.; SiriusDecisions, Inc.; CARMA; adidas Group; Lenovo; nGenera Corporation; MyVirtualModel; Dell; Hurwitz & Associates; Harris Ginsburg; IMS Health Incorporated; MarketingSherpa Inc.; DBC PR+New Media; Louis Vuitton; Nintendo; Eli Lilly and Company; Alfred Karcher GmbH; Rolls-Royce; Marks and Spencer; Li & Fung Limited; MarketingProfs; Chatsworth Communications; Technorati; Harvard Business School; Manchester Business School; Nielsen Online; The Women's Congress; Geoffrey Moore; Women in Technology International (WITI); AMD; AIT Global; The Kaplan Thaler Group, Ltd; and Moosejaw Mountaineering and Backcountry Travel, Inc.

Fifth, my entire Websphere and SOA marketing team and all the IBMers around the world who also contributed to the book: John Collins, Mike Sagalyn, Craig Merrigan, John Kennedy, Miroslav Hofbauer, Natasha Kudrey, Ferdinand Kolcak, Tina Zmuc Reflak, Oliver Nickels, John Soyring, Rich Lechner, Steve Cole, David Parker, Susan Schiffler, Jon Iwata, Ed Brill, Jeff Schick, Nancy Pearson, Dan Powers, Ken Creary, Ian Hughes, Cheryl Elliman, Scott Hebner, Kathy Mandelstein, Todd Watson, Dave Laverty, Buell Duncan, Errol Denger, Gina Poole, Paraic Sweeney, Karla Norsworthy, Arwinder Kaur, Richard Smith, Karen Keeter, Peter Korsten, and Bob Guidotti.

Finally, to my new friends at Pearson Education: Kevin Howard, Cindy Teeters, Chelsey Marti, and Greg Wiegand!

About the Author

Sandy Carter is IBM's vice president of SOA and WebSphere marketing, strategy, and channels. She is responsible for IBM's cross-company, world-wide SOA initiatives and is in charge of one of IBM's premier brands, IBM WebSphere. Carter is known for her great business results; IBM WebSphere has realized 15 consecutive quarters of growth at constant currency. She is also known for her outstanding innovative Marketing 2.0; she has led the brand to win 14 industry marketing awards in the past year.

Embracing the new global world, Carter has traveled to more than 59 countries to meet with customers and partners while assisting IBM's SOA initiatives to earn third-party validation and top leadership rankings by analysts and pundits alike. She has combined her marketing prowess with her love of technology by being a constant student of the new world and leveraging the new Web 2.0 tools of social networking, serious gaming, twitter, viral, and blogging. Please visit Carter's blog at http://www-03.ibm.com/developerworks/blogs/page/SOA_Off_the_Record.

Carter is an active member of Women in Technology International (WITI) and a member of the WITI Executive Advisory Council, the Marketing Focus Advisory Council (where she was named winner of the Best Speaker Award), the chief marketing officer (CMO) Inner Circle, and the American Management Association (AMA). She also serves as a board member of the Grace Hopper Industry Advisory Committee and is the co-lead of IBM Partnership Executive at Duke University. Carter is listed in Madison's Who's Who and is a founding member of the WITI Global Executive Network (GEN) program for senior executive women.

Carter is a frequent speaker at industry events sponsored by *Infoworld* magazine, Gartner Group, IDC, Forrester, and the WITI. She is the best-selling author of the book *The New Language of Business: SOA and Web 2.0*. Twice she has won the AIT Global's most valuable member of the year award for the United Nations ICT for Sustainable Development. She holds a bachelor of science degree from Duke University and an MBA from Harvard Business School.

Introduction

*In matters of style, swim with the current; in matters of
principle, stand like a rock.*
—Thomas Jefferson

What is marketing? For me, it is the heart and soul of every business.
Marketing is a game changer for competitive advantage and helps companies
make better decisions, create and drive better strategies, and have better execution. In today's world, in which CEOs are focused on growth and profit,
marketing can be one of the winning ingredients that help to propel a company forward. As Peter Drucker, management expert and author, wrote,
"Because its purpose is to create a customer, a business has two basic and critical functions: marketing and innovation. Marketing and innovation produce
results; the rest are "'support.'"

Marketing has evolved, and the Thomas Jefferson quote is applicable
today—marketing requires marketers to swim in the "current" of social networking and other new techniques and to focus on some of the basics. The
old world is the marketing basics such as customer-requirements management, value-based pricing, segmentation, value propositions, and measurements. The new world brings in new media, new channels, and new markets.
In today's environment, the combination of the two worlds win, and the help
of technology strengthens both of those worlds. Throughout this book, we
talk about when to adopt new techniques, when to hold firm on the basic
principles of marketing, and when to combine the two!

The following introduces you to the ANGELS marketing framework and the key trends that you need to understand before we start on the concepts that combine both worlds.

Focus on the ANGELS Framework

Today's market is fast, challenging, and energizing. You have to fight for your place in the information overload. As I look at the way to do great marketing that truly adds client value, I find myself working with my team on six steps: Analyzing the market, Nailing the strategy, Go-to-Market execution, Energizing the channel and community, and of course, focusing on the Leads and revenue. Finally, last but not least, leverage technology to Scream your message to the market. (See Figure 0.1.) This ANGELS model allows the combination of traditional and Marketing 2.0 techniques. I believe it is this hybrid approach that leads to success.

Analyze Here, There, and Everywhere
- New Research Methods
- Globalization
- Segmentation

Nail the Strategy
- Role Based
- Branded & Lightly Branded
- Corporate Social Responsibility
- Category Creation

Go to Market
- Value Proposition
- Influencers
- Word of Mouth
- Relationships

Energize the Ecosystem and Market
- Social Networks & Communities
- Gaming
- Widgets and Wikis
- Blogging (including Twitter)
- RSS
- Podcasting and Videocasting
- Virtual Environments

Leads and Revenue
- In Process Metrics
- Leads & VLR
- Dashboards

Scream
- Technology
- Digital Citizen

Figure 0.1 The ANGELS model—this is the model we use throughout the book!

A = Analyze and Ensure Strong Market Understanding

Analyzing and ensuring market understanding helps in the process of making the best decisions possible by understanding the marketplace and your customers. In the new world, listening and analyzing has become a function of not only market research, but of the online dialogues as well. We can now peek into customers' conversations, thoughts, and feelings expressed in blogs, wikis, virtual environments, and other new arenas. The more you know about your customer, the more market-focused your strategy.

Obtaining customer insight is best done by combining the proven methodologies with the new-world techniques. The facts are needed, and the process that you use is shown in Chapter 1, "Listening and Analyzing in the Global World."

In this section, the process of traditional + Marketing 2.0 techniques, or hybrid marketing, is shown through a combination of discussion and case studies on this topic including

- Listening and Analyzing in the Global World and traditional research methods
- Segmentation
- Globalization

N = Nail the Relevant Strategy and Story

Innovation-centric marketing is about establishing the right strategy—one with sufficient focus—and then innovatively telling a story that matters. An old Indian proverb states, "Tell me the facts and I'll learn. Tell me the truth and I'll believe. But tell me a story and it will live in my heart forever." Marketing is about affecting the emotions of the buyer. It is about creativity and about connecting powerfully with your customers through value that matters to them. Marketing enables innovation through collaboration and agility. Think of agility as responsiveness to change—the heart of innovation—and the ability to move fast, with all the requisite first-mover advantages.

Business strategy and vision are part of a continuous process that one might call the strategic cycle. The strategy needs to be supported by levels of detail so that the strategy can be executed. Properly managed, the strategic cycle enables communication throughout your company or division about your direction. This, in turn, supports coordination of all the elements needed to be successful, including marketing. You might have multiple strategies depending on your size of business. At IBM, for example, we have business-unit plans, segment-business plans, and offering/solution business plans.

The strategy cycle, of course, is driven by the marketing discipline but cannot be done in isolation. In Figure 0.2, the framework from Oliver Wyman Consulting shows how to view the whole picture, from framing of customer selection and the value proposition, to the value capture and understanding of how marketing can help drive profit. In addition, it enables for a discussion of how your culture and organization structure will support your strategic shifts and advances.

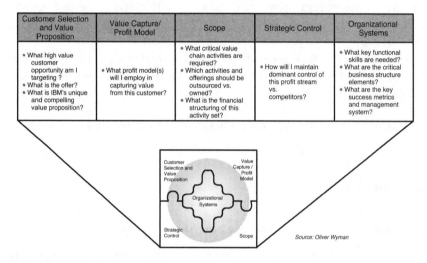

Figure 0.2 Model for business design.

One of the areas I spend a lot of time on is taking the strategy and figuring out how to lay it out in the marketplace. The story is the key. Telling the story is about finding the relevant item that appeals to the buyer's interest. Here the market must speak; it is an iterative process of testing the waters and aligning the key influencers around the story. However, a story alone is not good enough. The proof the story must be real in your customers, partners, and offerings. (See Figure 0.3.)

For example, when IBM began to talk about a new business-driven approach called service oriented architecture (service oriented architecture is simply an easier way of doing business and connecting your applications), we introduced the extreme makeover to showcase customer stories that were based on our key messages and storyline. Why? Customers believe other customers. Period. We leveraged easily understood metaphors from current pop culture to communicate the value of our invention, and we leveraged the expertise and strength of the storytelling experience: a beginning, a middle, and an end! Storytelling helps you take the strategy to a place where you can evoke a strong, positive feeling. At times, the right story moves us beyond rational and functional criteria toward a deeper, sustainable connection. The more powerful it is, the more you can make it directly applicable to the customer as a person, based on a role. This concept of person-to-person marketing, not just business-to-business (B2B) marketing is where trust is a key element.

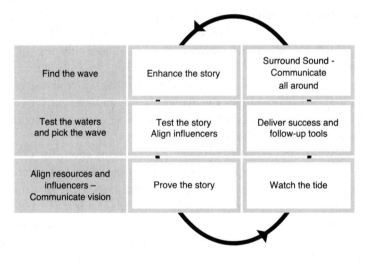

Figure 0.3   The storytelling model.

The right strategy told through the right story will have elements of personalization to them. This requires an understanding of the role that your customers play, and recognition that they might play different roles at different times. For instance, a chief information officer (CIO) might play the role of innovation change agent sometimes and cost cutter in other instances. In addition, because telling the story involves your brand, the new world requires that you not just brand, but also lightly brand with customers playing an active role in the shaping of your brand identity. Finally, in today's world, no story or strategy is complete without discussing and recognizing the importance of corporate social responsibility (CSR).

In this book, we go into more detail on the following strategic elements that are most impacted by the new Marketing 2.0 world:

- Relevance and roles
- Branding and lightly branded
- CSR

G = Go-to-Market Plan

The go-to-market (GTM) plan is how you plan to take the story and the offerings to the market. Your integrated marketing communications strategy articulates your key benefits, that is, the promise of value for each target audience. The strategy also conveys the reasons why customers should believe your promise. This step involves thinking through what stage of the buying cycle the clients are in and what their key decision criteria are. Major elements include which dimensions of your promise of value most influence the buying decision.

Influencers have been changing over time, and the source and scope of the message after it is released into the marketplace is no longer under your control. Communities and blogs, where companies have no control over the message, have influence over the buying decision, too.

In addition to the content of marketing communication, the GTM plan covers the tactics that are placed in market by segment and agreed to by sales, marketing in both global roles and field marketing, or geography-based roles. The point becomes clear when you see these huge lists of tactics: You need an integrated plan and strategy. One example is shown in Figure 0.4. The secret is two-fold. You must have an end-to-end GTM plan, and you must leverage both new and traditional marketing methods.

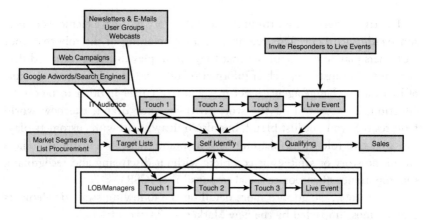

Figure 0.4 The GTM plan.

In this book, we go into more detail about the following:

- Influencers
- Relationships
- Word of mouth

E = Energize the Channel and Community

Energizing your channel (both directly and indirectly) and the appropriate communities (universities, online groups, governments, and so on) needs to happen for marketing to succeed. Your plan needs to include the overall distribution strategy and how it will provide effective and efficient coverage. Understanding the specific channel wants and needs, channel objectives, selection criteria, channel mix, and channel costs—especially with the new world of channels you didn't anticipate—will help drive better results. Such elements of your marketing mix can provide a sustainable advantage against existing and emerging competitors.

Identifying the specific activities, costs, critical dates, and responsibilities that support the overall strategy will require thoughtfulness of when to use the basic blocking and tackling such as sales training and when to supplement with new Marketing 2.0 techniques like enablement "widgets" or wikis. Also, a new critical question is what influencer groups or communities are needed. The discussion will center around when a company should facilitate the community versus using those communities that already exist.

A new area that IBM has been piloting is gaming to enable the education of new ideas or new technology areas. So far, the energy and the results of this use of "serious gaming" has been well worth the time and dollars associated with it. Again, however, it is the way that all these activities are orchestrated and not just across one channel, but the channel and community as an integrated whole. Many marketing organizations ignore this step and do this at their own peril.

In this book, we go into more detail about the following:

- Social networks with virtual environments
- Online communities including Facebook
- Participation with Viral and Serious Gaming
- Collaboration through Widgets and Wikis
- Blogging including Twitter

- RSS
- Podcasting
- Videocasting

L = Leads and Revenue

Leads and revenue are usually the key measures of marketing's success. Tom Rosamila, a general manager with IBM's WebSphere division, likes to say that marketing is sales one quarter out. The approach to executing, managing, and evaluating marketing's effectiveness by analyzing results to improve planning capabilities and business results is mandatory in any successful marketing management system. Leads and revenue associated with those leads are the end result. In addition to those metrics, a dashboard of in-process metrics is usually the best way to ensure you are headed in the right direction and taking appropriate corrective actions along the way. For instance, understanding your response rate to your marketing mix while your tactics are in-flight can help you fine-tune your approach and improve results. With Marketing 2.0, there are new metrics you need to evaluate and those metrics you will need to prune.

In this book, we go into more detail about the following:

- In-process metrics
- Leads and validated lead revenue
- Dashboards
- Engagement Metrics

S = Scream! Don't Forget the Technology and Passion!

Marketing is about showing and sharing your passion. That's what makes the best of everything, so don't forget to wear your passion on your sleeve and scream your differentiation and value. Companies need to learn how to embrace the energy of a scream in their marketing at the right time to the right people. The essence of screaming is that it needs to be full of energy, leveraging technology applied to today's customer in an agile fashion but in a personalized way. It is about shifting from broadcast mode to dialogue mode. (See Figure 0.5.)

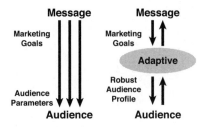

Figure 0.5 "Screaming" shift from broadcast to dialogue.

In this book, we go into more detail about the following scream accelerators:

- Timing
- Technology
- Digital citizen

We then close with a case study about IBM's WebSphere Brand story and how the brand was revitalized by setting a new agenda in the marketplace.

Let's Get Started!

Enjoy this book and let me know your feedback and other great case studies you know of at scarter@us.ibm.com!

Analyze **Here, There, and Everywhere**
■ New Research Methods
■ Globalization
■ Segmentation

I

Listening and Analyzing in the Global World

A moment's insight is sometimes worth a lifetime's experience.
—Oliver Wendell Holmes Jr.

You are not alone. And neither are your customers. These basic facts are all too true for those of us in marketing who work tirelessly to get our message into the market. It's too bad. If we were all alone—or at least the only one attempting to influence our customers' decisions—our jobs would be a lot easier. Unfortunately, the trend is moving the other way. With increased competition coming from all corners of the globe, and customers learning just as much from each other as they are from any product or service vendor, the job of a marketing professional requires creativity and innovation to address potential customers through their most important sources of influence. And those sources change from country to country and customer to customer.

One of the major trends that marketers of the twenty-first century must be adept at is the new global world. The emerging global economy introduces a vast, complex, and competitive landscape. Firms must deal with new opportunities and pressures to survive and succeed. Although there is no one formula for success, companies must integrate into the fabric of the new global economy to understand and leverage the economic value it offers.

This requires a change in mindset that mandates marketers act locally while thinking globally. As one customer told me, "Developing countries grow gradually at first, then suddenly emerge as large markets. We must be prepared to respond quickly. This will require us to make fundamental changes to our business now, rather than implement event-driven reactions." Analyzing this global (yet local) market is one of the most important jobs that a marketing team can do. The market changes quickly and unpredictably.

Changes in regulation, government, and competitors' actions can have disastrous effects on business if they are not quickly identified, anticipated, and evaluated. A maniacal focus on what's happening and who is gaining influence over your portfolio takes time, but it is well worth the effort if your business's results improve, especially as you grow globally. A marketer's job is to think about the future, or, as my chief marketing officer says, "Do a lot of forward thinking" to provide insight into the business. That insight must now expand beyond a round world to a new flat world, as articulated so notably by Thomas Friedman.

Listening and Analyzing in Both Old and New Ways

This chapter discusses how to keep abreast and anticipate the market in a global way with a local view. How to achieve the mergence of old and new approaches is of interest to Michael Sagalyn, a manager of market intelligence segment analysts in IBM's software group: "An organization's adoption of social computing techniques for marketing does not happen automatically. Leaders need to clearly communicate the vision of a new hybrid model for doing business; your staff needs to buy into the evolution; you'll want to engage in skill building to achieve mastery of Web 2.0 technologies and techniques; and finally, the organizational structure might need to change in response to new processes and new functional disciplines."

As you gain experience, you should consider how best to fold marketing innovation into the day-to-day operations of your firm. Figure 1.1 illustrates three ways the new world and the old world of marketing are required to work together to provide the insight needed for a glimpse into the future.

Figure 1.1 Analyze with three key focuses.

Although these are not the only ways to look at your market, *outside in*, they should provide the framework that enables you to see your world through a new lens. This chapter is followed by a set of case studies that bring to life the key points made. We look at Nortel's segmentation and how the company has localized its segmentation by markets, and then learn the lessons of Lenovo, Dove, and IBM in leveraging insight, segmentation, and global-local lessons that drive growth.

Outside in is the new term for ensuring you are not focused on internal views but continuously looking outside your four walls. From the IBM CEO Study discussed in the Preface, CEOs identified that collaboration is the foundation of most innovative business models, and collaboration with groups outside of a company is the best source of innovative ideas. However, even CEOs see a collaboration gap as teams leveraging the outside view try to make better business decisions. There are many barriers, which, as expected, are tied to culture. Others are tied to deficiencies in existing processes and systems that inhibit them from extending outside the four walls of the firm. We discuss what you can do to overcome these challenges.

Every company needs to have forward-looking insight to compete in today's 2.0 world. Whether it is exploring pools of profit, the competitive landscape, client needs, or the wisdom of crowds, companies need to see the world for themselves. *Seeing the world today involves multiple perspectives and requires not just data but insight from multiple angles.*

Discovery

One of the important questions that starts a market discovery is, "How big is your market?" Market discovery is a continuous process. As customers change, markets change, and as new markets in the global world enter your vision, you have to reevaluate the size of the market.

Market size and growth are key elements to determining your company's investment strategy. Although some markets might be ready for rapid growth, they might also start from a small base of interest. Growing that market can require a significant investment in awareness activities to help build the market overall and the presence in the market. Be prepared for competitors who enter the market as well; they will attempt to capitalize on your market development efforts. Determining the best time to enter a market is a critical decision for success. Even with the new 2.0 world, this is required to target your markets correctly.

How do you get the insight you need for these market dynamics? As shown in Table 1.1, depending on the maturity of the market—Nascent, Emerging, or Established—the methods will vary. For instance, if you are in a mature market, there are usually several industry reports on size and growth trends. However, if it is a beginning or Nascent market, you have to be more creative in your sizing and look at things like comparable market segments and your prospect base. In analyzing growth, you might need to look at other substitute products.

Table 1.1   Estimating Market Size and Growth

Market Size	Suggestions
Nascent	Comparable market segments Prospect base Pricing models for substitute products
Emerging	Average transaction sizes Size of customer segments Adoption rates
Established/Mature	Comparison with complementary markets Vendor revenues Analyst reports Customer spend data

Equally important is the capability of the market to warrant sustained investment. By evaluating market size and market growth, you can access the factors that determine overall attractiveness. Before entering any new marketplace, always size the market, growth, and concentration of competitors in the space. Also important is studying the industry concentration and profitability. Markets are not good opportunities just because they are big. Some large, mature markets have one or two strong competitors with the overwhelming majority of the market share. For instance, in computer chips, Intel® and AMD are formidable competitors. Although these markets might appear attractive due to their shear size, it is critical to figure out how to establish a niche to enable future growth instead of going directly after a behemoth.

In addition, the profitability of an area is important to note. For instance, what are the typical margins for someone in the business? If they are low, and you do not have a new business model, it is better to reevaluate the opportunity. In some developing countries, to enter, you need to invest in the national interest or in its partner ecosystem. The cost might be prohibitive to your business model.

Now, why does this matter in a global, local world? There are many factors that go into deciding where to focus. Size and growth are factors, but others depend on local competitors and government stabilities as you investigate the BRIC countries (Brazil, Russia, India, and China).

The analysis in Figure 1.2 is always part of my decision making.

Criteria	Weight	Range			Score
		Low (1)	Medium (3)	High (5)	
Future Market Growth	30%	<5%	5-12%	>12%	○
Market Size	30%	<$250M	$250 - $700M	>$700M	●
Industry Concentration	20%	Top 3 > 50%	Top 3 30 – 50%	Top 3 < 30%	●
Industry Profitability Proxies	20%	Score varies by stock price to sales (5%), profit margins (5%), beta (5%), and financial analyst recommendation (5%).			●
Information is for illustration purposes only.					

Figure 1.2   Critical elements for sizing a new or current market.

Insight is not just about size and opportunity but about people. Whether you are in business to consumer (B2C) or business to business (B2B), you are marketing to customers—people. Customers around the world are changing, and new customers are coming into play. Purchasing power is increasing in rapidly developing economies, and prosperity is increasing in Western economies. China and India will add one billion customers to the global economy in 5–10 years (new economy), and retiring baby boomers will spend their accumulated wealth and will pass it on to the "inherited" generation X (old economy). In addition, with the speed at which the world is changing, to not get left behind, you must look ahead. This means to do this analysis successfully, a combination of traditional and Marketing 2.0 techniques are required.

The Traditional Methodology

Traditional research is still valuable today. Use of traditional market research methods (such as quantitative survey research) or qualitative methods (such as direct observation, ethnography, focus groups, and others) helps you to make better decisions based on facts, opinions, and perceptions from the market place. How do you leverage traditional methodologies? You start by engaging a traditional market research firm to identify customer needs, wants, requirements, expectations, and perceptions to ascertain your most attractive market segments. Depending on the nature of your business, this is done with a representative sample from either the market segments that you already know exist or from a global, national, or regional sample of buyers and influencers.

For example, a research engagement typically begins with a qualitative research to determine key issues from a market perspective and to establish clear terminology for a quantitative survey instrument. To accomplish this task, a firm conducts a few focus groups. Alternatively, if for an advanced understanding of latent needs; ethnography can also be considered. In an ethnographic study, one person, or a small group of people, is observed interacting with the environment.

Peter Kowalski, director of Research Strategy at KDPaine & Partners (located in New Hampshire), explains it as, "...so, for example, if your company was a grocery store, and your goal was to determine how people are shopping for groceries, we would start with one or two people. We would go over to their house. We would have them walk us around their kitchen, show us their grocery list, and then we would go to the grocery store and follow them around. To understand how they interact, we would ask them some different questions while they're making different decisions and observe them in their kind of native environment. That sounds a lot more like anthropology than business, but it has its application because definitely people are more comfortable in their environment and we can see how they're interacting with different people, different things, and where they are making certain decisions." This is a 2.0 trend within the traditional methodology. Not just asking customers what they think but observing what they do. This is a critical insight in the new world.

Research findings are then used to evaluate your company's current understanding of its target market segments. A gap analysis, done by your company or the market research company would ensue. This step is valuable because it can show you major types of gaps in your customer insight. The gaps include

- Gaps in what your customer says they want and what they express would be ideal given their current workplace situation and what they would be willing to purchase. For example, at IBM, we did a research project where more than 80 percent of customers said they wanted a function, but when we delivered it, purchases were low. We missed the key question: "Would you be willing to pay for it?"

- Gaps between what your product and company offer and what your consumers want. This one is straightforward.

- Gaps in terms of what your customers or potential customers think about your company from a brand-equity perspective—reputation, image, and value—and customers' willingness to do business with your firm. These intangible attributes are important because they underpin most tangible decision drivers in a purchase situation.

An end-to-end example is the one we did for IBM's service oriented architecture (SOA) movie, a tactic to get our message out to the market in a fun way. (See Figure 1.3.)

Figure 1.3 SOA movie example.

In this example, we identified our own market segment and did focus groups with key customers to share our first movie production. Then we did mini ethnographies, where we watched people go to our "theater" (which was a room in a hotel!), and how they decided to go to a movie and why. Then we did a small survey of one segment (loyal customers) and some further research to determine how that segment behaves. We tested movie trailers to precisely determine what this segment likes and dislikes and observed how they responded and their reactions—not just asked them about them. This enabled us to review the responses and the surveys to precisely determine how the segment would respond in terms of numbers and research. This approach doesn't have to be expensive. We used our own existing brand user groups and client board of advisors.

If you take the traditional approach and supplement it with some of the emerging research methodologies that leverage social media, you can further refine your research. The human mind is a complicated animal. As Michael Sagalyn, manager of IBM Market Intelligence, explains, "So, to be able to say that all of these things—both traditional and new methods—yielded the same or close to the same result, that becomes compelling in terms of making a business decision, especially if it's a large business decision." In other words, when old and new methods yield the same results, your level of confidence in the data rises.

What's the timeframe for a qualitative ethnographic research to be completed? You can do a Web-based quantitative national survey in an afternoon or dive deeper in a matter of months. Thus, a typical survey utilizing both qualitative and quantitative methods to identify and validate a market segmentation takes about four to five months. Adding an ethnography takes longer (an additional two or three months) because you actually have to use highly trained surveyors for that methodology. It can always be done in less time with more researchers and more budget.

In summary, we are witnessing an inflection point in the evolution of market research. In my talks with Brad Bortner, a principal analyst at Forrester, observed that when new technologies drive change in how we conduct research, conventional wisdom about "what works" is often set aside. "The transition to using social media as a resource for market research is the third of the major changes to have hit the market research industry," Brad says. He goes on to explain that "...in the '70s, it was the move from face-to-face interviewing to the phone. The feeling at the time was that the phone would never replace the face-to-face experience. And then it happened again in the '90s with the advent of online panels and with the concomitant concern about sample quality. Now, almost 50 percent of surveys use online panels. Qualitative research had not been affected much by previous major changes in the industry until now."

New Trends in Research

Web 2.0 has transformed market research, giving companies access to the voice of their customer in a way never before possible.
—*Diane Hessan, CEO, Communispace*

Let's discuss ways to augment traditional research through a couple of gold mines for this new research:

- Online communities
- Online reviews
- Blogs

Online Communities for Insight

In my conversation with Diane Hessan, CEO of Communispace, she neatly sums up the potential of online communities to directly impact your business—often in real time. "Online communities eliminate the need to find new customers each time you have a set of new questions that require you to set up discrete research projects," she explains. "They have fundamentally changed the way companies listen to their customers. These communities can be run like a utility—when you come to work in the morning, you turn on the heat, the lights, and the voice of the customer. It's always there for you, whenever you need it."

The development of online communities have afforded us an opportunity to observe people interacting with one another, expressing their own opinions, forming relationships, and breaking relationships. These relationships are with other consumers, with just friends, and with companies, products, or logos. People today form relationships with anything. We can now directly observe this within the rules of online communities. It is not exactly the same as the real world because if someone asks you to be his friend on Facebook, you are more likely to agree than if someone in the real world said, "Can I call you my friend?"

As Diane Hessan explains it, "Setting up online communities for customer insight does not have to be a daunting exercise. There are firms that specialize in that work. One of the reasons clients outsource to set up and manage the communities is that clients are swamped and don't have the time to pay attention to it. We recruit based on criteria established by client companies.

Our B2B clients typically have names of customers from which to recruit, but in 70 percent of situations, clients don't have the names. Hence there is a fairly structured recruitment process to get customers into the community and to keep them participating. We keep the communities small and intimate. This ensures that members' voices are really heard."

So, we can leverage these online communities—how the constituents express their opinions and how they behave. We can also now observe how they form interconnected relationships. For example, did you post it to your MySpace page, did you put something on your blog, or did you link to a particular person? Research teams can now observe these actions, and they can analyze all of the text, speech, and video interactions. Pete Blackshaw, executive vice president of Nielsen Online Digital Strategic Services, conveys the importance of conducting market research through the multiple forms of online expression: "The migration from consumer expression from text to multimedia has enormous anthropological value; customers are bringing front and center their behavior in full rich media right to our laps. The Web is becoming an unprecedented looking glass into human behavior."

Supplementing in-person focus groups and ethnographies, a great research company can analyze the data and determine what the "customers" think. With the nature of the online community to express their own opinions, what research is able to do is to absorb conversation that previously was held behind closed doors or at the proverbial water cooler. It also avoids issues of potential biases in traditional research, as respondents sometimes provide answers they believe their interviewer prefers. "Observations in online communities have this added benefit where we aren't concerned that someone might be changing their behavior because they feel they are being watched," said Peter Kowalski of KDPaine & Partners. "But there are privacy concerns. We strongly believe that each of our clients who work with us to gain insight from social media-based research programs should have a clear privacy policy that lists appropriate and inappropriate research methods and uses so that we can be sure stakeholders are heard when they want to be. As an example, in the offline world, it is a great practice to attend town hall meetings and take note of concerns that might affect your organization, but it would be frowned upon to use microphones to listen to conversations that people are having in their living rooms. The same goes with online."

With the advent of all of this content that's constantly updated 24x7 online, we can segment online communities and use traditional and online observations to triangulate each other. If you know your market segment, you can find those same market segments online and see precisely what they save about your company and what recommendations they might make. For instance, on one of the online communities for the IBM WebSphere product line, we found information about what would make our product better than another product, and structured review sites helped us understand precisely how to make better products. Even for new segments, such as Web 2.0 products that IBM sells, we leveraged the online community to determine when and if a product would result from something we called Project Zero.

These overheard conversations are just as compelling as having a focus group. I love to learn from reviews where my customers say, "This product is great except for this." It provides me insight and a way to have constant analysis without potential bias that's being brought in by the researchers, not to mention the opinions of introverts who don't openly express their opinions and leave them open for public interpretation. People are more truthful when they are in those communities than when they are face-to-face with a researcher whose presence is going to impact what that person says that brings about validity concerns.

Online communities enable you to find and interact with that "smart consumer," the one who is progressive about technology use while still being pragmatic. (An equivalent to this is the market research firm that identifies style and trend setters in major cities, such as the kid in Tokyo who is the first to hang charms on his cell phone or the girl on the lower east side who is the first to bring Puma sneakers back.) One of the keys to market research is finding that progressive consumer so that your vision is not watered down by the masses. This is aspiration versus status quo reflection, and online communities can assist in this area.

Last but not least, community-based research can be an efficient. As Brad Bortner of Forrester writes, "Online communities for research have a short ROI. One traditional focus group can cost $8,000 to $15,000. A five-to-eight city qualitative project can cost upward of $100,000. If you replace only three physical world qualitative projects with your online community, it has paid for itself." Bortner reaffirms such efficiencies: "Putting much of your qualitative research into that community has a large capacity. You could be running five or six activities in the one community. Essentially, utilizing online communities for market research changes the whole economics, whereby you are moving qualitative research variable costs into a fixed cost asset."

Blogs for Insight

Blogs are similar to online communities. Tracking and understanding what influential bloggers are writing is invaluable, but you first have to know which ones matter to your business and which ones have the biggest set of followers.

Pete Blackshaw, executive vice president of Nielsen Online Digital Strategic Services, describes how to get started in monitoring blogs: "The best way to start out to do that is to do blog searches using key terms that define your market. These can be the same terms that are used for search marketing in your organization. After you've done that, you can start identifying the blogs that are the dominant ones by using one of the search engines (for example, Google or Technorati). You can review the people who pop up; then, after you have the feel for that, you have to measure the conversation. Measuring conversation is more sophisticated, and unless you have in-house capabilities, you should engage with a vendor who has the text-mining tools to do that. After you have ascertained where people are talking about your brand, start to engage in a conversation with them and begin to track your impact. Is the buzz or sentiment about your brand changing? Is it more positive than negative? We try to comprehensively look at all the social media that would matter to our set of clients. We monitor the gist of the conversation of the zeitgeists of their industries or of a product area. We pull out the concepts they are talking about and watch as the concepts shift over time."

In addition, your own blog can provide insight. I have one of the top blogs at IBM on SOA. I receive comments from customers asking questions about products or offerings, and it provides me insight on what is working and where people are going for information.

Blackshaw gave a great example from one of the companies he works with: "Our client had undergone a major brand shift. They had changed the nature of their business in a very substantial way. They had engaged us to track in print media and in blogs how they are being described (again, a combination of new and old media). So, company XYZ wanted to keep track of how that brand shift was taking place, and what we found was actually that the brand shift took place a lot faster in traditional media because the journalists were referencing corporate materials and were in contact with corporate public relations professionals. They were able to say, 'Okay, this is what the company is calling itself now.' But, what we observed in the blogosphere was much slower and that they were a little more skeptical about the new positioning of the company. So, in terms of an actionable result, for them, it showed that although XYZ did a great job communicating to the traditional media, they didn't reach all the critical influencers to completely move the needle on their brand position. It took a lot longer in terms of actual people who are engaged with the company on a consumer level."

Our advice is to start with the basics—are you being referenced by blogs? Twitter feeds? Are you relevant to the discussion? Are you more relevant today than before? Are you conversational? Then start to drill down—are they making positive or negative comments? This is important because a small volume of negative comments can sneak into other media that might influence consumer opinion. How are these opinions trending?

Some consumers are more important than others. Learning to focus on this community, which communities to place your time with and how to interpret the information, takes time to learn, but it is worth the effort. According to Tim Wolters, CTO of Collective Intellect, "An automaker wanted to test a campaign for one of its vehicles. They conducted a test marketing campaign aimed at the online gaming demographic. They informally produced a video showing the vehicle with the context of a popular online multiplayer game. We first identified the top 50 bloggers and sources of YouTube gaming videos. Our client chose to promote its vehicles in a game to the top 20 bloggers— and YouTube videographers. Twelve of the 20 wrote about the automakers campaign, which in drove three million views of the placement in just a few days. This was so successful that the automaker ran a campaign based on this approach during a major sporting event." Collective intelligence is part of a trend toward comprehensive monitoring of brand performance on the Web; the firm conducts real-time text mining and presents its findings through a dynamic dashboard.

Online Product Reviews

In terms of reviews, what's most compelling is what aspects of products are discussed. One needs to determine what is negatively or positively discussed, and whether this is something that will stop customers from making a purchase decision. As Blackshaw points out, "So, what we found there in terms of a predictor for sales and in terms of what has a really good relationship with sales is that reviews, especially reviews on the structured review sites, have a good relationship in terms of [deciding] if it eventually becomes the popular product."

For example, the insight and discovery of our online products reviews (see Figure 1.4) for WebSphere are invaluable in our requirements process. In this example, the areas of positives and the areas of concerns provide us with a new form of listening.

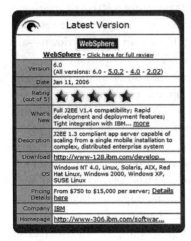

Review

IBM WebSphere Application Server is a conglomeration of software. At its most basic, WebSphere is a J2EE 1.3 compliant application server that handles the usual tasks and provides the necessary administrative tools. On top of this functionality, however, sits an enormous stack of support and related software that sets WebSphere apart in this demanding and highly competitive space.
Read Entire Review

From Soup to Nuts With IBM WebSphere

IBM WebSphere: J2EE 1.3 compliant app server capable of scaling from a single mobile installation to complex, distributed enterprise systems

An application server has many masters, often in the guise of architectures: client/server, Web applications, Web services, and (certainly in the case of IBM) services for various mainframe systems. They busy themselves with plugging holes in the architecture of the Web (session and state preservation, anyone?), connecting with voluminous far-flung data, and, to a certain extent, performing the services of a security cop.

Is it any wonder then that application servers themselves are complicated pieces of software or that they may require a virtual army of support software?

This preamble is relevant to reviewing IBM WebSphere Application Server because it is a particularly **BIG** piece of software, or more accurately, a conglomeration of software. At its most basic, WebSphere is a J2EE 1.3 compliant application server that handles the key Java containers (i.e., EJB, Web, Application, and Applet), monitors and preserves Web status, performs transaction control, and provides the necessary administrative tools.

However, such a description is like saying a house is a cubic structure with doors and windows. For IBM, WebSphere Application Server is a cornerstone, not only of the WebSphere brand but also of its entire Java-Web (e-business) line. On top of the application server is an enormous stack of support and related software, and that is what puts WebSphere Application Server at the top of its class.

It's in the Stack ...

By convention, products are reviewed on their own merits and more or less in isolation. We feel that with application servers this is misleading. Application servers are designed to serve many masters, so the "stack" of supporting software is at least as important as the application server itself. While IBM's server can plug in out with any similar product in terms of performance, basic features, and general polish -- its integration with other software is what most distinguishes it.

Figure 1.4 WebSphere product reviews.

The conclusion here is that traditional forms of research are not going away, but marketers' jobs are now harder because they cannot control the user-generated content prevalent on the Web. Therefore, they must evaluate and triangulate all the market insight provided from both types of information. That is, marketers correlate online and offline data to see if these data mutually confirm a point of view on the market.

Matt Collins, vice president of Software Group Market Intelligence at IBM, has seen the value of social computing in his work. He says, "To adequately support the market intelligence requirements of business, it's essential that we leverage the dynamic, accessible wisdom that the social computing environment can provide. If we use the Internet to monitor the 'heartbeat' of our clients and prospects, companies can more closely match the responsiveness of smaller competitors while retaining our advantages of scale. Not leveraging this medium would be like tying one hand behind our back."

This is very similar to what we used to do in the old world. We'd have someone clip all the press reports and news happening to try to decipher market trends. Now this is much easier, but need to be managed by watching and learning each day.

Segmentation

A segment is where you identify the markets that you might serve. You should describe the market by size, growth and trends, and analysis by

customer group—size, function, industry, geography, and other key elements. For example, retailers in Europe with more than 500 employees are
considered a segment. A segment can also be loyal IBM customers who have
a certain type of application. Some of the key questions to ask are What
makes a segment attractive (size, growth, profitability, or others)? Where are
the profitable customers? It is a continuous process of reviewing where the
marketing is today and where the market is heading. Over two-thirds of
best-of-breed companies segment their customer sets.

Determining which parts of the market your company can serve profitably
(see Figure 1.5) involves identifying the most attractive customers and what
and how they buy. Critical is the business value they require. A key part of
segmentation is to review the viability of selected segments with respect to
value and the ability to execute. You have to determine which segments you
can add real value to and where you can create strategic control points to
drive market leadership. What is a strategic control point? It might be an
install base, brand, patent, or copyright, or it might be a cost advantage.
Depending on your budget and skills, this aspect of defining a market can be
done by a research firm. Based on what you are selling, you might need to
identify the partners and channels necessary to meet the needs of the target
customer segments.

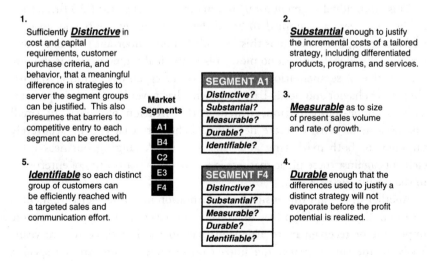

1.
Sufficiently *Distinctive* in cost and capital requirements, customer purchase criteria, and behavior, that a meaningful difference in strategies to server the segment groups can be justified. This also presumes that barriers to competitive entry to each segment can be erected.

2.
Substantial enough to justify the incremental costs of a tailored strategy, including differentiated products, programs, and services.

3.
Measurable as to size of present sales volume and rate of growth.

4.
Durable enough that the differences used to justify a distinct strategy will not evaporate before the profit potential is realized.

5.
Identifiable so each distinct group of customers can be efficiently reached with a targeted sales and communication effort.

Market Segments

A1
B4
C2
E3
F4

SEGMENT A1
Distinctive?
Substantial?
Measurable?
Durable?
Identifiable?

SEGMENT F4
Distinctive?
Substantial?
Measurable?
Durable?
Identifiable?

Figure 1.5   Market segmentation.

This approach ensures the ability to execute. Many psychographic profiles are useful for messaging, but somewhat less useful for go-to market decisions. One big test is to think about how real the segment is—meaning, is it too narrow and esoteric? If so, that is a key sign that marketers are being a bit too academic.

However, with the new world, how does this segmentation process get modified? I spoke with one of IBM's segmentation experts, Steve Gessner, market intelligence principal consultant, to learn more about this crucial task.

First, the act of segmentation and targeting is a fundamental marketing activity. It is the first step of marketing. You must establish targets and how to measure success. This has not changed and will not change. What's changing is how we answer these questions in the global, electronic, personalized landscape of the future.

Segmentation used to be about segmenting buyers into groups with homogeneous needs, and the fundamentals of segmentation have not changed in 30 years. However, as technology, client insights, and customer expectation regarding personalization have improved during the last ten years, segmentation has followed suit and become less about the practice of fundamentals and more about driving segmentation down to the individual client company and more recently to the individual decision maker within the company.

This "individual segmentation" is a distinct challenge for B2B firms that, in the past, were accustomed to broad demographic segments and generalized targeting, but nowhere is this capability more important than in competition in the globalizing economies. This individual segmentation is moving the practice of segmentation to a new level of capability. Linking specific clients to behavior and needs-based segments has never been more important. This is niche-segmentation, which is the creation of relatively small microsegments with discrete needs and behaviors that can be accurately targeted for both marketing and sales actions. Arranging business value elements against these niche markets is an important capability of enterprises in the twenty-first century.

Another important dimension of segmentation in this new environment is measurability and trackability. Marketing effectiveness has never been more important or received more attention than in the last three to five years. Tools for measuring marketing impact on revenue streams around specific client target spaces are critically important as firms move forward in the global economies. So, not only must these "microsegments" be identified, they also must be measurable and their responses trackable. This is a challenge for firms that have historically created market segmentation definitions that are broad and difficult to measure impact around and are certainly not measurable at the client level.

Finally, the advent of social media marketing is changing the face of what we consider segmentation. Segmentation approaches during the next five years will include attitudinal groupings of buyers in the blogosphere, and firms will determine how to impact such attitudes using techniques and technologies only just being developed. We refer to these segments as blogsegments; influencing them will become a critical component that will accompany the new marketing capabilities required around segmentation in general.

Globalization

Today's flat world has profoundly redefined the economics of distance. Companies of every size are taking advantage of nimble global networks to create new capabilities and capture new opportunities. In its 2008 study, "The Enterprise of the Future," IBM found that 85 percent of CEOs plan partnerships to capitalize on global integration opportunities.

The globally integrated enterprise is a step beyond what has been known as the "multinational corporation" that has its hub and outposts and costly replication of functions in many locations. Instead, the globally integrated enterprise locates and connects operations and functions anywhere in the world based on the right skills and the right business environments. In doing so, it deploys a business design that can respond efficiently and effectively to pervasive and constant global economic change and the global competition for talent.

The globally integrated design enables organizations to grow and innovate competitively by undertaking dynamic reconfiguration of business processes and operations at high speeds. These processes can then support rapid reconfiguration of capabilities, knowledge, and assets for use in innovative business models. Companies constrained, for example, by an aging workforce are learning to access, attract, and maintain talent from around the world.

Forces driving the global integration of business include the following

- **Economics:** Global competition drives the relentless pursuit of better economic solutions.
- **Talent:** Local, regional, and national gaps have led to global marketplace for talent, with work moving to the best locations for both cost and quality.
- **Standards:** Open standards and interfaces make it possible to quickly connect organizations around the world.

In a globally integrated enterprise, reconfiguration takes place across the enterprise ecosystem as well as within its own organizational boundaries. In making the decision to become globally integrated, businesses need to

- Define how value gets created in their businesses and ecosystem.
- Thoroughly map relationships among and between people, processes, and technology using techniques such as component-business modeling.
- Become engaged with social, regulatory, and government issues in every area where they seek to have business operations.

In an industry where supply-chain transformation has pointed the way to large-scale, global integration, IBM is transforming its operations from service delivery and manufacturing and virtually all support functions, from research and development to sales and marketing. It uses global centers of excellence to tap global talent who provide innovative solutions for clients everywhere.

The globally integrated enterprise is skilled in attracting talent, connecting and leveraging sources of production, and creating value, regardless of the physical location or the organizational ownership of these resources. It fosters close interaction across its ecosystem of internal and external stakeholders, including employees, customers, partners, government agencies, and others.

In my travels to more than 59 countries, I have observed how the emerging global economy introduces a new competitive landscape. To win in this new world, companies have to understand and leverage the economic value and innovation possibilities that this new world introduces. In this era, firms must consider a set of choices that will define their businesses and operating models. In its research, IBM has defined six areas of focus (shown in Figure 1.6) or capabilities that all firms need to develop:

- **Leverage global assets.** Use global resources most economically and effectively.

- **Manage value in an ecosystem of increasingly specialized entities.** Continually assess where, when, and by whom value is created.

- **Build a specialized enterprise.** Enable modular business operations.

- **Enable collaboration.** Employ both collaborative and traditional innovation approaches.

- **Manage risk and control.** Take innovative approaches to risk management.

- **Serve distinct global markets.** Seek new clients and potential partners.

A Tool for Rethinking Business Practices

Figure 1.6 Six essential global competencies.

One of the key business steps is serving distinct global markets. To seek new clients and potential partners, you need to focus on the right set. You need to use global demographics to segment the market to understand developing versus emerging markets. To serve global markets, firms must think about new ways to segment the market without the constraints of geographical boundaries. Great marketing organizations will tap into, analyze, and leverage global demographical data to capitalize on new global market opportunities.

As you explore niche markets, you will discover global sets of small local markets. Can you supply the same niche market that occurs across multiple geographical locations? For the most part, the decisions that companies make are similar, but the way they talk and think through those decisions might change. How do you scale to take on those challenges? Understanding which products and services that can be applied across multiple local markets with minimal or no customization might be a potential market segment.

Each of those needs to be segmented for you to develop a deep customer intimacy and respond quickly to needs. Here, the use of technology, such as a CRM tool, might help you identify unique needs of diverse cultures and market segments across global markets. Globalization and specialization serve to fuel competitive intensity as new entrants can more easily bring tailored offerings to market. Operating in geographically dispersed markets increases the need to develop a deeper understanding of the local customer and develop capabilities to rapidly respond to their needs. All these factors affect the way you segment in a global world. For instance, you might find that you need to leverage a global ecosystem of partners to deliver customized solutions to win in a new space.

Table 1.2 shows these best practices of companies looking to explore segmentation on a global basis. It shows the steps to grow your capability in the market and your skills in understanding the flatter world. Through its intense research, IBM has been able to help you step through the competencies required from ad-hoc use of segmentation through to world-class segmentation in the global world.

Table 1.2 Serve Distinct Global Markets—Detailed Assessment Criteria

	Level 1 Ad Hoc	Level 2 Aware	Level 3 Capable	Level 4 Mature	Level 5 World Class
Practice 1: Use global demographics to segment the market; for example, developing versus emerging markets.	Minimal use of global demographics. Ad hoc and manual processes. Lack awareness of need for capability.	Starting to develop processes and capabilities. Seeking best practices. Learning from mistakes.	Sources for global demographics are identified and used. Data is understood. Staff are trained. Basic tools and systems are in place.	Global demographic data is standardized and interpreted. Tools and technology are in place to perform sophisticated analysis on data.	Analysis tools and techniques undergo review and continuos improvement. New and improved sources of data are identified.
Practice 2: Explore niche markets, global sets of small local markets.	Global markets are not well understood. Capabilities required to explore niche and small local markets are not understood.	Starting to develop tools and capabilities. Understand how existing product and services can be applied.	Capabilities and tools have been developed. Niche markets have been identified. New products and services are being developed.	New product development factors in global market opportunities. Ongoing education plans and support.	Intellectual capital relating to global niche markets is harvested. New methods of analyzing markets are developed and refined.

Table 1.2 Serve Distinct Global Markets—Detailed Assessment Criteria (continued)

	Level 1 Ad Hoc	Level 2 Aware	Level 3 Capable	Level 4 Mature	Level 5 World Class
Practice 3: Develop deep customer intimacy and respond quickly to needs.	Unique customer needs and wants are not easily understood. Methods and tools are ad hoc and lack standardization.	Starting to develop processes and capabilities. Seeking best practices. Learning from mistakes.	Systems are in place to analyze and understand unique customer needs. Capabilities to quickly respond to needs are being developed.	Organization sheds traditional "plan and push" approach to "engage and collaborate." Responsive delivery supported by a flexible and modular internal structure.	Tools and systems enable organizations to track customer lifecycle and predict key needs.
Practice 4: Leverage a global ecosystem of partners to deliver customized solutions.	No or minimal contact with global partners. Adhoc management of contracts.	Processes to engage global partners are being developed. Understanding of key capability gaps is developed.	Processes are well documented and understood. Database of partners that can fill organization's capability gap is established.	Catalogue of global partners is used to rapidly assemble teams. Processes are in place to assess and classify new partners.	Extensive catalogue of global partners is maintained. Processes to identify "best fit" combination of partners is established.

To make these concepts come to life, see Chapter 2, "Segmentation in Action: The Nortel Case."

Conclusion

We are not alone. And the increasingly global, dynamically competitive world in which we work is only getting faster. But in these changes, as in every turning point, lie opportunities for major growth, differentiation, and business success to the agile marketeer who is able to combine tested traditional approaches with innovative marketing tools.

Marketing is about helping your company make better decisions. To make better decisions, you need to understand your market and where it is going. In addition, it means listening to your customers more intimately and leveraging new and traditional methods for analysis. Market research combined with evaluating what needs are and are not met in the market and with your product are critical elements in understanding your customer better. New areas for research, such as ethnography, require that the decision-making process is evaluated. Online communities, bloggers, and product review sites will continue to flourish and are important insight into what your customers want. The new informed and collaborative buyer provides a peek into what used to be "water cooler" conversation. In fact, with this new buyer, individual segmentation needs to be investigated.

Explore these avenues to assist you in market leading segmentations and go global sooner than later. Assess your company's capability to be a player in the flat world!

2

Segmentation in Action: The Nortel Case

Nothing can add more power to your life than concentrating all your energies on a limited set of targets.
—Nido Qubein

The goal of customer segmentation is to know your customers better and to use that knowledge to drive revenue and profit. This basic concept of segmentation has not changed but in the Marketing 2.0 world, in addition to setting targets to measure success, you have to answer the segmentation questions in the global, electronic, personalized landscape of the future. In addition, segmentation enables you to focus on the relevant value for the customer. Segmentation is about a group of customers who have a set of characteristics that cause them to have similar product needs. Wikipedia states that "a true market segment meets all of the following criteria: it is distinct from other segments, it exhibits common attributes; it responds similarly to a market stimulus, and it can be reached by market intervention."

Companies that do great segmentation can experience rewards through the reach of profitable customers. In the Marketing 2.0 world, segmentation has become less about the practice of fundamentals and more about driving segmentation down to the individual client company and more recently to the individual decision maker within the company. Reaching profitable customers is not just part of marketing, but part of a successful business model, especially in the global-local world. In today's dynamic times, knowing your customers and growing a profit from them is a success factor. To get a full value from customer segmentation, a business must use a segmentation that is dynamic and global-local.

When you travel, you might note that the world is global and local at the same time. Each country is unique (local) but also has a touch of global to it. A personal example is that as I have traveled to more than 59 countries, I always stop for a Big Mac. Although the Big Mac is always the same, local items always appear on the menu. (Yes, this does allow me to claim that I have eaten in McDonalds in more than 59 of the countries—a fact my doctor hates, but my kids brag about!)

For marketers, the more global we are in terms of the footprint of our companies and marketing, the more local we need to become because the complexity of marketing intensifies at the local level. This makes segmentation tricky and more crucial as we see differences around the world. This global-local world requires that "microsegments" be identified, and be trackable. In this new environment, measurability and trackability is more important than in the last three to five years. Companies want to work with partners who can meet their specific needs and agendas. Ironically, in a global world, the expectation is a close personal relationship at the local level, thus, the essential need for a strong segmentation that is relevant in global-local markets. Additionally, differences in customs require the marketer to adapt to local preferences and norms that go beyond simple translation. To compete effectively in this environment requires global-local marketing!

Focus on Global-Local Marketing

As we discussed in Chapter 1, "Listening and Analyzing in the Global World," being able to explore the global market locally is a key to future success. Best-of-breed companies are able to

- Use global demographics to segment the market
- Explore niche markets or global sets of small local markets in pilot mode
- Develop deep customer intimacy globally and respond quickly to needs locally
- Leverage a global ecosystem of partners to deliver local customized solutions

In this chapter, we see Nortel in action as it progresses through the steps of global-local market segmentation. With the advent of Marketing 2.0, the view of segmentation is changing with the new technology approaches. Segmentation approaches during the next five years will include attitudinal groupings of buyers in the internet world. Influencing both external and internal constituents will become a critical component that will accompany the new Marketing 2.0 capabilities required around segmentation in general. We look at what successful market segmentation looks like and how to apply it around the world.

Focus on Nortel's Lauren Flaherty

Lauren Flaherty is the chief marketing officer (CEO) for Nortel Company. Her role is a global-local one and includes marketing communications and strategic decision making for the overall marketing execution. She is a member of the CEO's cabinet.

What Is Nortel?

For more than a century, people have looked to Nortel to make communication possible. Through identifying and harnessing innovation, Nortel has shaped the evolution of communications and changed the way the world connects. Today, Nortel drives the industry forward by addressing the challenges and delivering on the promise of hyperconnectivity: "a future in which every device and application that *can* be connected to the Internet *will* be connected." Nortel delivers intelligent and intuitive communication platforms that help its customers thrive in this new world.

Headquartered in Toronto, Canada, Nortel had revenues just shy of $11 billion in 2007. With customers in more than 150 countries, Nortel solutions power the globe's top 25 service provider networks, serve the foundations of world economies and financial centers, and drive communications that enrich rural and underdeveloped regions across the globe.

The Customers

Nortel delivers innovative hardware and software solutions designed to improve the way consumers and businesses around the world communicate—reducing complexity, increasing productivity, and making communications more cost effective. In delivering this business value, Nortel supports some of the world's largest and most successful public network carriers, including wireline, wireless, and cable operators. Nortel also provides solutions to newly established and growing service providers in emerging markets throughout the world.

The Product

Nortel's products in the communications space go across data, optical, wireless and voice technologies, and services. The company makes the promise of Business Made Simple. The next-generation technologies for both service provider and enterprise networks support multimedia and business-critical applications. Nortel's technologies are designed to help eliminate today's barriers to efficiency, speed, and performance by simplifying networks and connecting people to the information they need when they need it.

The Competition

The global hunger for connectivity is accelerating, and Nortel is at the center of an industry that is critical to our work, life, and economies. Nortel competes with companies such as Ericsson, Alcatel-Lucent, Motorola, Avaya, Nokia Siemens Networks, Huawei, ZTE, NEC, and Cisco. New market dynamics will separate those with the capability and vision to compete globally. Nortel aggressively partners with others to create a rich and broad ecosystem. Its partnerships include industry leaders such as Microsoft® and IBM, joint ventures such as the LG-Nortel joint venture, and relationships with other application providers and many of the largest carriers in the world.

The Global-Local Agenda at Nortel

As CMO, Flaherty wants to ensure she can impact two things: her brand and a drive to revenue. To do these two projects, she determined that the two were linked, and after strong analysis, she set out to make Nortel a world-class, global-local company.

Fish Where the Fish Are!

World-class companies get the best-performing market results when they have world-class segmentation. Flaherty wants to focus on the set of characteristics that are alike across similar product needs so that marketing is done based on that set of relevant factors. This makes a lot of sense. My father-in-law is a fisherman, and when he calls with good news on his fishing days, he makes an important statement: "It is so much easier fishing where the fish are." Nortel started the same way. Flaherty began her work at Nortel by updating its segmentation. As she says, "We saw something very obvious, which was where we had the best segmentation and the best line of sight to the opportunities—and the prospects—We got the best results."

Nortel started its journey of joining the new and traditional worlds of marketing with the basics. A whole orientation around a segmentation that was around odds, which as Flaherty describes it meant "...a segmentation analysis that was built around best possible odds, as opposed to just characteristics. So, which part of the market do we have the best odds of adding value to the client set? This is proving very innovative in the communications space."

Given that this segmentation is a competitive advantage, Flaherty shares her approach but not her secrets. The approach began with the profiling work. Nortel used the traditional views of attractive segments and growth. (See Figure 2.1.)

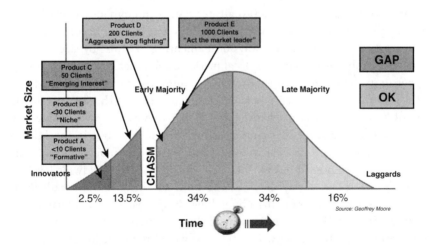

Figure 2.1 Example of traditional market segmentation.

However, then Nortel took those traditional profiles and leveraged algorithms to provide insight into its odds in those chosen segments and profiles.

As Flaherty comments, "It is not just a snapshot of who your normal segmentation studies would say, 'You've got your early adopters, you've got your leaders, your laggards, and so on.' This was based on historical spend patterns, an installed base, the entire mix. And then, with some deeper analysis on top of that, a view of the best possible odds."

Global-local businesses are those that can move from the view of "there are lots of fish in the ocean" to where a particular set of fish in a particular local market are most attractive to the company. The new segmentation work can provide you with detail down to a Google map level where you can be precise about local markets, such as in the New York metropolitan area or in the greater London area. The segmentation of knowing where the fish are that love your bait enables you to take your localized lists and drive better yield, not because the list is large, but because it is targeted more precisely at the best possible opportunities. This is like targeting a top fishing hole in a key market by using market information such as the sonar on a fishing boat.

Application to Your Company

You will hear it repeatedly. Doing it right at the start with strong segmentation and insight will lead to greater results throughout the marketing cycle. Be sure your segmentation can stand the test of value and relevance in your market. Look at the new ways of segmenting, not just by size and revenue, but as shown around odds, local markets, and other new ways of seizing opportunity. This new segmentation may require you to view the world in a new global, electronic, and personalized landscape of the future. In the global-local world, you need to see the global view while customizing at a local level. For example, banking is segmented globally, but in the Middle East, a customization takes us to local customs such as Arabic banking. This would have been missed if segmentation were only at the worldwide level.

Table 2.1 shows a way of gathering both the insight from traditional approaches and new thoughts about how to approach segmentation. For instance, in South Korea, where many of the cities have completely free wireless, there might be a new way to buy that would not exist in other areas or frustration in the way that others sell—not taking advantage of the wireless situation in South Korea. There is no formula for thinking "outside of the box," but as many companies skip through this step, or do not continuously update it, they miss major new and growing markets.

Table 2.1   Market Segmentation Requires New Global and Local Insights

What	How
Gather marketing intelligence	Customer surveys
	Multichannel intelligence
Identify your audience	Analyst subscriptions
	Competitor Web sites
Understand buyer behavior	Industry databases
	Focus groups
Analyze competitors	Brand tracking surveys
	Purchase driver analyses

The Global Brand Analysis

Part of analyzing your market is that you have to really understand how your brand stands up in the market. The traditional ways of looking at your brand are from brand positioning studies in the following list:

- **Unaided awareness:** When you think about xx, what companies come to mind?
- **Aided awareness:** Thinking of category, have you heard of Company X, Company Y, and so on.
- **Consideration:** Thinking of this category, which of the following companies would you consider purchasing or upgrading in the future?
- **Preference:** Thinking of this category, which of the following companies/products would you most prefer?

Traditionally, marketing professionals would give a brand-building assignment, and they would go through a series of tasks that build a brand in terms of consistency, look, tone, manner, and messaging, but typically it is done inside-out. Although companies do test their work, fundamentally the brand is architected from the inside-out.

However, Nortel sees that the new and traditional views must be combined. Flaherty comments, "We did early market intelligence work to get a read on Nortel's brand because Nortel had been through a roller coaster ride of ups and downs. The message from the market was clear and stunningly consistent for Nortel. We had to create a dialogue with the market on two fundamental pillars: The first concerned our reputation, especially around financial performance; for the second, we needed to show how Nortel delivered business value to its customers. Customers tell us, 'I want to work with a company that's reliable, who will be a good partner.' Their interest in reputation and the sources that most powerfully influence image are typically third-party and word-of-mouth. Customers today are smarter and better informed than ever before. We respect that at Nortel and plan to leverage it."

The brand must be looked at holistically—on the Web, on blogs, in your best customers' minds, in your employees' views, and in the traditional brand positioning studies. To drive her brand forward, Flaherty looked at the start of customer advocacy branding. She wanted the grassroots or "external shaping" of her brand, not just a brand shaped by the CMO. She realized that to do this, customer advocacy needed to be a major player and, therefore, needed to tightly link to her sales colleagues. (See Figure 2.2.)

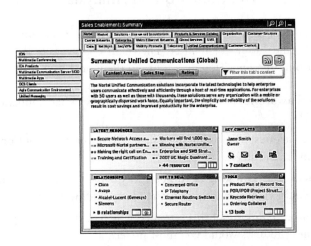

Figure 2.2   Nortel's sales portal based on brand analysis.

Flaherty comments, "We are even looking at our sales colleagues as marketing targets. Like customers, Nortel sales professionals have wants and needs; we've invested considerable time and effort to develop tools that will help them and keep them engaged and motivated." To grow the Nortel brand reputation with the sellers, Nortel developed a new portal with fresh and hip content. Flaherty excitedly explains, "We now have a CNN-like crawl on the portal so that I can tell them, 'Hey, here's what's fresh. Here's what's new and interesting.' And it's working! Adoption of the portal is at an all-time high and the usage rates we monitor for key content areas are on a steady and steep upward climb."

What Flaherty has done in this example is to link specific clients to behavior and needs-based segments. Her niche-segmentation and creation of relatively small microsegments allowed her to accurately target for both marketing and sales actions.

For brand reputation analysis, you have to check out what your competitors are doing and saying about your brand. A mentor of mine once said, "You should never be surprised by your competitors." You should always scout the competition to understand exactly what they are doing. Flaherty manages her brand reputation in a holistic fashion. She has collapsed many of the discrete pillars of activity that Nortel had into a more holistic set of programs based on the feedback.

However, the analysis showed that to impact her brand on a global basis, she also needed to go global, but be local, with the sales teams. That started Operation Tornado and a kickoff throughout the organization (shown in Figure 2.3).

Razor Sharp Targeting

1. Develop a segmented view of total addressable market.

2. Understand the cause and effect relationship between operational activities and financial outcomes.

3. Translate financial goals into integrated sales and marketing activities that are engineered to drive profitable growth.

4. Uncover opportunities and action through visualization of data patterns, trends and dependencies.

Figure 2.3 Operation Tornado kickoff material.

Operation Tornado

Operation Tornado is about leveraging the market segmentation based on the global-local view and turning it into execution. The innovative position here is that it takes into account the route map from day one. It is not about just looking at markets for their attractiveness from a revenue point of view, but also looking at what the channel execution capability is in those metropolitan markets.

One of the things Nortel learned from its analysis of the market was that it could not continue to execute in a textbook fashion. It had to continue to prime the market with the media and analyst relations, but for its particular view of the market, it learned that one of the gaps was in the enablement area of the complete channel. As Flaherty recalls, "We had to go to the direct seller and channel, and make sure those folks were fully trained, mobilized, activated, and understood the goals. A big part of this was to leverage customer advocacy, so the sales piece was fundamental." The other big fundamental is metrics. In Operation Tornado, the clear goal was to measure the progress and the results by sales cycle. In Figure 2.4, you can see the types of metrics that Flaherty and her team tracked around both the inputs and the outputs of the overall effort.

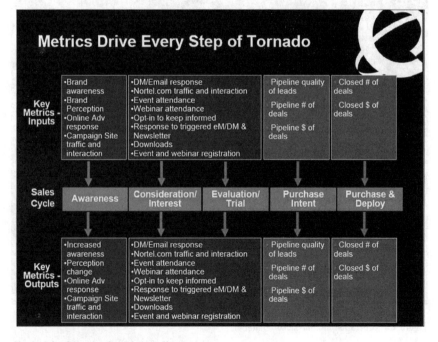

Figure 2.4 Operation Tornado kickoff material.

Table 2.2 illustrates that developing a plan of your routes to market is a key step, and you should ensure that your tactics line up on global and local lines. In addition, the enablement, which is an often missed step in marketing, is on the top priority list.

Table 2.2 Execution on a Market Segmentation

What	How
Identify routes to market.	Conduct routes to market analysis to identify primary routes for each offering.
Align the following to selected segments and routes.	Build multitouch campaigns with offers at every step of the way.
Offer value propositions and message.	Build and evangelize messaging guides throughout organization.
Integrated marketing program.	Leverage advertising, DM, events, Web, and tele-to generate leads.
Ensure major channel players are enabled and involved in the rollout.	Target key influencers to asses plan Set criteria for inclusion.

Now that Flaherty had her plan, she decided to take the global plan and do best-practice localized testing. One of the things that was radically different at Nortel in this project was it began by sharing the analyses with the teams executing in the local markets. To drive Operation Tornado, Flaherty identified four test markets globally based on the analyses: London, Singapore, Chicago, and Mexico City. Flaherty remembers sitting down in those four metropolitan markets with her sales colleagues, planning the campaign elements, and identifying key accounts, key prospects, and dormant accounts. In each of those four markets, they set a series of objectives that were related to demand generation and pipeline build that were jointly owned by the channel and by marketing. She wanted both to have a vested interest in the outcome of the new segmentation.

The metrics they tracked were those associated with return on investment (ROI)—actual campaign-dependent revenue objectives. The "team" carried a revenue target for the campaign initiatives in those four markets to see if the analyses and execution would lead them to success. As Flaherty explains, the work and research led to the conclusion that it needed better integration to succeed. She says, "Marketers talk about 360-degree integration, but fundamentally what they're often talking about is just the integration of the marketing discipline. So, it's often an interdisciplinary sort of focus from a marketing point of view. Here, our integration is deeper and needs to be in the new world to be successful. It combines direct sales, the channel, and the marketing teams together."

Application to Your Company

As we look back on the best practices in the making for the new global-local world in Chapter 1, we can see that Flaherty and her team have leveraged the best of the best. They leveraged global demographics to segment the market and started by developing that deep customer intimacy. They also focused on the time needed to effectively train and enable the local channel—the ecosystem. Flaherty quickly set up and trained a global ecosystem of partners to deliver customized solutions locally!

Flaherty notes that to do world-class work, world-class tools are needed. Nortel made many investments in segmentation technologies, and it works with a consultant to map the execution to the strategy by assisting Nortel with a new global-local dashboard.

For your company, make sure your teams are integrated through the required ecosystem that now varies in the changing world. Map your market: What is the structure? Who are the decision makers and who buys? Profile your customers and identify the purchase options. Marry the analyses to understand who buys to what their purchasing options are. As like-minded customers combine into segments, ask yourself the odds that they will buy but also, ask if you have the right ecosystem trained and measured correctly. If appropriate, also ask if you have the right tools to do this analysis on a continuous basis.

Finally, define key effectiveness measurements as the category is established:

- Market share
- Expense/revenue
- Awareness/consideration/preference
- Share of voice
- Leads
- Feed results into next cycle for continuous improvement

Nortel Lessons Learned

Flaherty articulated some of Nortel's most valuable lessons learned. Although there were many, the following sections review the top ones.

Skills

With the world becoming more digital, you must think about what implications that can have on your business. For Flaherty, there was an epiphany in her recent hires. She notes that, "Digital is just the vessel. What kind of talent do you need to have on the team? I think you have to have talented writers who can develop compelling and persuasive content—not just fluff. The market is becoming more editorial; it's more CNN-like than long-standing campaigns that we all used to drive. It is much more CNN-like in terms of how you have to reach out to your customers." Writing skills in the new world make a huge difference. What will set companies apart and showcase world-class marketing teams is the quality of the content and how effectively it is used.

Based on Criteria Only

For Operation Tornado, a lesson learned was to ensure that criteria for selection was set and adhered to before a market could become a "tornado" market. The upfront planning about what qualified a market to be in or out became a crucial way to manage success. Commenting on this aspect, Flaherty says, "They're in or out on the criteria that is assigned because the criteria is designed for success. So in other words, you don't lobby to be a tornado market. You qualify to be a tornado market. And many people you know might say, 'Hey, Lauren, I want to be a tornado market.' And the answer is, 'You have to qualify to be a tornado market and satisfy the criteria.' The overarching criteria of what it means to be a tornado market is the filter against which we can virtually ensure that we'll get the kind of results that we're looking for."

Speed, Baby!

The whole notion of customer-driven and market-driven marketing is here to stay. It is an enduring and important quality for us to preserve from the traditional world because ultimately marketing should be the voice of the customer. Therefore, marketing needs to understand what is relevant for the customer. However, the lesson learned from Nortel is in the speed at which things have to be managed. As Flaherty says, "What's different in the new world of marketing is the transaction speed or the duration of time. So, for example, I think there's more value now in touching prospects in many different ways and that keeping the dialogue fresh as opposed to just running something for seven months or a year is actually important, particularly in technology. As opposed to the traditional view of long, sustained initiatives over time, this whole thought of keeping the dialogue fresh, dynamic, new information, I think that's something that you're seeing from the marketplace. Speed is important."

The Outcomes

The appropriate question is: What's been the bottom line for Nortel with Tornado? From the onset, reputation metrics and ROI capture were integral to the campaign model, as was fundamentally reshaping the unfortunate, but commonly held, perception that integrated marketing means only integrated marketing communications. According to Flaherty, "By changing how we executed in the four launch markets, we demonstrated the positive impact a tightly aligned sales and marketing effort could drive. Lots of our regional folks now ask, 'How do I become a tornado market?'" The campaign drove the revenue objectives largely by driving up the transaction value of the deals closed—a by-product of doing more thorough segmentation upfront. As a result, Flaherty explains that the model is being expanded this year into 12 markets worldwide. Mission accomplished? "Not 100 percent," says Flaherty, "as reputation measures have proven tougher to budge." This is a reminder to all of the time and sustained investment required to build a strong brand and increase preference.

Conclusion

Segmentation is a continuous step in marketing. In this chapter, we saw that segmenting your market is a fundamental marketing activity. But with the Marketing 2.0 world, what has changed is how we determine the market on a global scale taking advantage of electronic and personalized concepts. Spend time upfront understanding your customer and the relevancy of the market you serve. Time spent here—both in the traditional view of segmentation and in opening your aperture to explore the new ways to see the world—pays off. Partnering on the way you attack the segments and how you enable locally is also a differentiator. In Marketing 2.0, segmentation has changed and become less about the practice of fundamentals and more about driving segmentation down to the individual client company and more recently to the individual decision maker within the company. At its heart, marketing activity is about doing activities that make the consumer want to greet the salesperson with a statement such as, "Oh good, I've wanted to talk to you for some time." Globalization means that companies have to learn to be global and local. And understanding the culture and the way people react at a local level is vital to international strategy. Applying these new hybrid marketing approaches to your segmentation and globalization strategies will pay off in the short and long term.

3

Globalization: Lenovo, Google, Unilever, and IBM

The world is flat.
—Thomas Friedman

In the last chapter, we discussed the importance of six factors of becoming a globally integrated enterprise. This new world is a tricky one; marketers need to understand it and study case studies and examples. A Price Waterhouse report on pharmaceuticals pointed out that diseases now take on different forms depending upon where you are around the globe. This means you can't package a drug and say that the drug works globally, because it actually has to be adapted. The same is true of marketing. The secret is to figure out when you need to change and when you need to manage elements globally. This chapter includes four case studies from Lenovo, Google, Unilever, and IBM to illustrate the concepts discussed in Chapter 1, "Listening and Analyzing in the Global World."

Focus on Unilever's Dove Brand

Oliver Engels is the European brand director for Dove, which is one of the key brands for Unilever. Unilever innovates at the global level through global innovation centers that drive the strategic brand development for Dove. The global team provides the regions with communication and marketing mix. Engels ensures that the innovations and the marketing mixes that are provided by the global teams meet the needs of Europe. The goal is to develop value propositions and consumer benefits that work globally but can be adjusted locally.

The Global-Local Concept at Dove

When you think about Dove, the essence of the brand is honest beauty. The brand value for Dove has been, since its infancy, to produce products that deliver real goodness to the consumer. Unilever wants to have a strong connection to real women and take that connection beyond being an ambassador of real beauty. Dove understands its customer inside and out. As Marti Barletta, the author of *PrimeTime Women: How to Win the Hearts, Minds, and Business of Boomer Big Spenders* wrote, "Contrary to popular opinion, Boomer women aren't in denial about aging. Advertisers are. And the women they're supposed to be trying to connect with are getting annoyed. One respondent said: "I really resent the notion that you can't grow old comfortably. You must *not* have wrinkles. The truth is, they are a natural part of aging." The Dove goal to make women feel more beautiful every day evolved over time. A new, bold plan emerged in the European office but became a global asset.

The history of Dove began in 1957 with a bar of soap and two basic parts of equity. The first was differentiation, which started with a different product experience—the soap was one-quarter moisturizing cream. The second was the connection to real women, which found its expression in Dove using testimonials in all its outward-facing material.

In 2004, Unilever realized that there was a juxtaposition in the market. Other companies said they were supporting beauty, but they showed only airbrushed, slim models. Dove wanted to truly connect with real women. As Barletta again writes, "Dove totally 'gets' this PrimeTime Woman. And the real story behind the success of this latest iteration of the Campaign for Real Beauty lies in the principle that this woman is comfortable in her own skin."

Dove sought to demonstrate that authenticity through a campaign that would feature real women without any kind of professional modeling background. This change would be bold and unchartered but would truly make Dove the ambassador of real women. The boldness grew as Ogilvy (Unilever's agency) came up with The Curvy Woman Campaign that was to be launched first in Europe.

The global team began the work and collaborated with the countries. The first challenge was to convince the countries that this campaign would work. Part of this convincing was a piece of marketing intelligence, executed on a global basis, in conjunction with Harvard Professor Nancy Etcoff and

Dr. Susie Orbach at the London School of Economics with StrategyOne. They found that more than two-thirds of women felt that the current media portrayed an unrealistic expectation and definition of what beauty was. The research also showed that only 2 percent of the women worldwide described themselves as beautiful. To use real women in ads was so groundbreaking that it invoked an intense debate within Unilever. It was a tough sell to convince everyone that this would be highly endorsed and appreciated by society in all countries.

For its global-local view, Unilever chose a few lead countries in which to first run the campaign—Germany, Netherlands, and the United Kingdom. After it received a positive response from these countries, Unilever made the decision to run the campaign in the United States one year later. The Curvy Campaign was the global ignition point. Let's explore how Dove drove this global concept successfully in these local markets.

We look at this campaign from the beginning point back in 2004 because it is significant to marketers that this campaign began locally as the teams discovered a gap in the market. The concept then emerged from a country to the global world. Second, it is a bold campaign that lives on even today. It has stood the test of time because of the way it understood the customer motivation, took that motivation, and used it to empower women throughout the world.

This Dove campaign unleashed the power of real women. It was followed by subsequent campaigns such as Tickbox and others. The Tickbox Campaign continued the theme of real women by having consumers vote on how they felt about the supposition of beauty. Provocative statements, one on the beauty stereotype and the other the "real" beauty view, were posed in the print and outdoor media. The Tickbox Campaign was another example of becoming more local as you become more global.

For example, in Russia, changes were made to the Tickbox Campaign based on the culture. As Engels comments, "Russia is a society with a different culture. The Russian women, for example, view the classic beauty game not as a burden but as a warmly embraced beauty contest. For Russian consumers, beauty products are the means to be competitive in the beauty game. The localization of the Campaign for Real Beauty in Russia was important; otherwise, our message would become less relevant. Winning in Russia for what we believe and what we stand for is significantly harder for Dove compared to other brands." For the local-global concept to be successful, the changes did not affect the core value, but the elements wanted to set the concept apart locally.

After the Tickbox campaign was created, a viral component of the campaign was unleashed. As Engels comments, "The viral campaign that was lead by the Canadian team where you see the transformation of ordinary women was drawn from this first power-packed global campaign. So, you see we are a global team working locally."

Although it began in Canada, the viral component quickly went global. Unilever did not expect the intense reaction, which turned out to be tremendous. Given the success, within two weeks, Unilever created many local versions of the viral campaign. Local customization was done as it entered the global market.

Today, the campaign continues. On YouTube, millions have viewed the videos associated with the campaigns have occurred. For example, the Dove Evolution shows how the pictures in the beauty magazines are changed. Unilever is leveraging technology to demonstrate the changes made in programs like Photoshop, makeup used, among other techniques used that create this unhealthy image of beauty.

There are also socially responsible blogs on beauty for teens. The Dove Self-Esteem forum (see Figure 3.1) has comments about the pressure young girls feel today. In fact, the film it did called "Little Girls," where young girls openly discuss how they feel about their bodies, evoked emotion around the world.

In the Self-Esteem forum, there is a "Moms and Mentors" forum to teach moms how to help young girls with self-confidence. The campaign has continued for more than four years—increasing and changing in the "container" of the message, now through YouTube and blogs, but living true to the initial global view.

Unilever elevated its social networking through co-creation by letting customers create ads. In 2008, Unilever had the clients vote on the ads, and then it announced the winners at its "Oscars." It included mobile voting on a global basis. The effect of these campaigns is that they are not the same campaign running in multiple countries, but tweaked and customized for the local markets.

Dove is an illustration not only of how a global company becomes local, but also one that analyzes the market and listens. As Marti Barletta writes, "Dove uncovered that there is a pent-up demand for a company to understand and acknowledge what women all over the world were feeling. It recognized there is no stronger way to build an intimate connection with a woman than to see into her real self, know her secret thoughts, show that you understand, and tell her that you love her anyway. And finally, it is a great example of understanding the value of a segment in the market." The women Dove has reached with its real beauty concept control, depending on whose figures you are reviewing, anywhere from 80 percent to 85 percent of the household spending. And Barletta and I agree on this great focus on a profitable segment as the "healthiest, wealthiest, most active, educated, and influential generation of women in history."

Figure 3.1   The Dove Self-Esteem forum.

Success Measured

One of the success drivers in Unilever's Campaign for Real Beauty was the fact that from the beginning, the campaign was solidly a global campaign with customization for local culture. This adaptation to local preferences has driven its longevity and results. According to Unilever, the results for the campaign in those early years were strong. The campaigns resulted globally in a 9.3 percent sales increase in 2005 across the entire Dove brand and a 9 percent increase in 2006. The specific campaign resulted in more than 50 percent sales increase in the respective category in the countries it ran.

It also touched on social responsibility and changed the Dove brand image to give it cultural relevance. In *Advertising Age*, Bob Garfield remarked, "You can't but help applaud marketers selling beauty products without trotting out the standard, impossibly gorgeous skinny young models." Rob Walker in *The New York Times* "Consumed" column called the campaign a "rare thing and pretty much a publicity bonanza for the Dove brand." *The Wall Street Journal* called it "groundbreaking." On top of this, the campaign has garnered countless awards around the world including four Clio Awards for print ads and a Cannes Lions Award for outdoor. Unilever's Dove brand has added $1.2 billion to its brand value over the past three years (2004–2007), according to Landor Associates.

In addition, Harvard Business School professors John Deighton and Leora Kornfeld, Unilever's Self-Esteem Fund and The Campaign for Real Beauty placed Dove at odds with its competitors. Consumers loved the conflict. They lit up the digital media, generating millions of pass-along clips for YouTube, clips such as Evolution and Hates Her Freckles. This campaign has stood the test of time. The campaign that started in Europe with controversy has become a global success.

Top Five Lessons Learned

Engels articulated some of Unilever's most valuable lessons learned. Although there were many, the following sections review the top ones.

1. **Global brand value:** Fundamental to the Dove success story is that it truly knew what it wanted the brand to stand for globally. As Engels described it, "We had a fundamental identity that survived as our lighthouse to provide us enough gravitation and reference to judge whether you do some things right and some things wrong." To actually stand out in the marketplace is difficult, and you must create something in the marketplace that actually adds value. You can't get away from that basic principle around the world.
2. **Risk taking:** You have to take risks based on facts. It takes courage to stand up for your ideas and beliefs. When reviewing the Curvy Women Campaign, when Unilever produced and tested it, the feedback told

them that it had tremendous energy; however, it did not predict the wild success and the tremendous impact it would have on society. The strong leadership at Unilever went with the facts plus their judgment.

3. **Consistency:** The Unilever campaign was about consistency. The campaign was run for the long term. As Engels describes, "What does that mean for Dove? When we created that Curvy Women Campaign, the implication was we would never, ever use any modeling in our communication again. Because we couldn't on one hand stand up for real women and at the same time do as the rest of the beauty industry in the rest of the communications."

4. **Cultural context:** Unilever learned that it had to respect the cultural context. There isn't a one-size-fits-all solution for that because if you want to portray real beauty and be an ambassador for real beauty, you have to do so in the appropriate cultural context. For example, as we discussed previously, Russia is a society with a different conditioning. When you look at the Dove campaigns from a Western European and North American perspective, the reaction was positive. However, Unilever didn't get that reaction in Russia. Nevertheless, they stuck to their global vision.

5. **It is not just product leadership, but the thought leadership:** Unilever's Dove recognized that it is not just about a product. Deighton and Kornfield wrote in their blog about the Dove success, "What we did not anticipate was that the technology that enabled intrusion would also enable defense against intrusion. From Tivo to Caller ID to social media, consumers have found ways to keep the invaders at bay. Marketers no longer rule the market. They are invited guests. If they are provocative, pertinent, and entertaining, they get to stay. If they are overbearing, there are ways to shut them out." And Dove turned into a brand that, through technology, had a product and a point of view of real women's beauty.

What's next for Unilever? This global campaign with a local flavor will continue to focus on the conversation through new innovation such as the Self-Esteem Fund.

Application to Your Company

There are three critical points to learn from this case study. First, a crucial step for Dove was market and client understanding. It got to the heart and soul of women. Everything it did rested on its customers' understanding and listening. Think about what criteria in your business matters to your customer.

Second, Unilever applied the global-local concept. In the future, it will not be about "can it be applied?" but it will be required in the new flat world. Evaluate your overall brand promise and determine the localization and customization that is required to make your brand a success around the globe. Like Dove, you don't have to give up the larger story, but given the local differences, those must be understood and adapted to. The value that Engels and his team provided locally, not just in execution but in knowledge and experience, was invaluable in the success of the work.

And third, branding in the Marketing 2.0 world is a radically different thing. The new world wants more. As Ogilvy comments, the brands of the new Marketing 2.0 world will be those that are focused on the following viewpoint: "Brand x believes the world would be a better place if...." For example, "Dove believes the world will be a better place if women knew what honest beauty really is." Think about the impact your brand has, not just on share of mind, but share of culture.

Taking risks on making your brand bigger than just the product is an important lesson. Dove determined to push thought leadership as prominently as product. It paid off for its revenue and results.

Focus on Lenovo

Craig Merrigan is the vice president of marketing at Lenovo, which is a publicly traded company that originated in China. It focuses on the personal computing market globally. Merrigan is an outstanding marketer who has worked at Proctor and Gamble, Quaker, and IBM. He went to Lenovo to explore a globally integrated enterprise. At Lenovo, one of the foundational elements of its positioning is the idea of a new world company.

As most companies today, the view is of the world as a duality emerging and developed. However, unlike other companies, for Lenovo, China, which is normally considered an emerging market, is a mature market because it has dominant market share there and a well-established business model. As Merrigan comments, "We have been number one for ten years in China and continue to expand our market share in a profitable way."

Lenovo focused on how to serve distinct global markets by leveraging global assets. It first applied the learning it amassed in China to India. Two years ago, it set a target of hypergrowth in India. It made a couple of key steps in leveraging its global assets and learning in the process.

First, it combined a team of Indians with experience in that market with a team in China. Given the similarities between China and India, it leveraged best practices. For example, China has a fragmented channel structure with a regional distribution and smaller resellers. Lenovo leveraged the investment and assets from China to India.

Second, it executed a marketing strategy in an integrated fashion that leveraged the China insights, but it also customized it to the local needs. For example, in Figure 3.2, Lenovo signed up a brother and sister Bollywood actor pair as spokespeople for the company.

Figure 3.2 Be differentiated in thought, action, and spirit.

The actors appear in their advertising, press, and other collateral. Obviously endorsement or celebrity-oriented marketing is something that the world has seen for a long time, but it had never been done in the PC category in India. As Merrigan describes, "Because we selected local people, we were able to display an international company that truly understood the local market."

Another example was the focus on local interests, such as Cricket. In India, the fans are wild about Cricket. Lenovo integrated its product around the matches as well as in the broadcasting. In addition, it integrated into the most popular television show in India. Lenovo placed its brand on the back of the monitors that the host and the primary contestant use and received a mass awareness installation every night of the week. These factors can be called empty awareness, but because they are coupled with and connected to the local culture, they enable rapid growth.

Finally, one of the global things that Lenovo did was anchor its business and brand in a single-driving principle. Much as Unilever did with "true beauty," Lenovo anchored its value proposition around the "engineered" PC.

Through market research, Lenovo found that the reason a customer buys from Lenovo is the promise of the best-engineered PC. It took that on as a brand promise globally and then instilled it in every discipline and region after testing its universal appeal. Lenovo wanted to do the diligence to ensure that it would work worldwide because it was positioning the company. It is not just a headline or a tagline but is the driving force that allows the teams to pull together for success at any level. The development team now uses this "best engineered" intent as it develops new products, and the countries use it in the way they take the product to market.

A Discussion of the Global-Local Concept with Wang Yong–Editor in Chief, CMO Magazine in China

To understand how the concept of being a global company is viewed in a local country, I spoke to Wang Yong, the editor in chief of *CMO Magazine* in China.

He shared his views on these concepts in four key points and he shared the differences and successes he sees in the China marketplace.

1. **Cultural positioning is a must:** Wang has observed that companies that focus on the culture are winners in the marketplace. This positioning involves understanding the culture of the local market and applying those lessons to the market in broad ways. He said, "I used to see companies translate beautiful English into beautiful Chinese. But now, best practice companies are touching the Chinese culture and getting the emotional linkage with the Chinese customers."

2. **Localization is a must:** Both on theB2B and on the B2C side of marketing, customizing for the local market must happen. For example, Kentucky Fried Chicken offers egg soup only in China. Some multinational B2B companies, such as Barco from Belgium, actually localize its product offerings.

3. **Channel understanding is a critical success factor:** The Chinese market consists of many small and medium businesses. Due to relationships and reach, to make an impact in the market, you must form and leverage relationships with local partners. He credits Lenovo for understanding, segmenting, and leveraging its channel relationships.

4. **Talent and team are mandatory:** An observation from China is that multinational companies perform marketing in China in a strategic way, whereas most local companies focus on tactics. Wang's view is that the talent gap needs to be worked through for a Chinese team to execute a complicated, nationwide campaign without compromise. Companies doing business in China need to invest in training.

Overall, Wang sees that the China market is maturing and the potential is huge. The focus on brands and branding is growing in China. Chinese clients are looking for brands they can trust.

Success Measured

Lenovo started off with zero percent awareness in India and within 18 months it achieved more than 80 percent awareness and about 75 percent consideration rate according to Merrigan.

Top Five Lessons Learned

1. **Team matters:** The first lesson learned from Lenovo was that of the formation of the team. The team worked successfully because it was made up of people in India who had experience in the market and from the team in China who had expertise achieving hypergrowth in emerging markets.

2. **Cultural positioning:** Lenovo learned cultural positioning. In some cases, it was the obvious use of a local focus, such as Cricket. However, in others, it was the way to go to market with channels and local relationships. Leveraging the knowledge was key to success. An example of how the knowledge was used by Lenovo was learning about the special needs of the aging population in China. Lenovo did a local promotion to working children about how a computer can benefit the elderly as a form of communication and respect. This year, Lenovo will take its knowledge through market research to the next level by investing in ethnographic research.

3. **Balance:** Lenovo learned to balance the localization. A trend in many emerging markets is the inexorable move of the markets from local brands to international brands. When the marketplace as a whole matures, the market develops an appreciation for international brands and less interest in the locally manufactured products. The interesting lesson was that focusing on competing against the other international brands, and not focusing on competing against the local brands was a key to success because the market forces shift the market share that way.

4. **A globally integrated enterprise:** Lenovo found value in being a globally integrated enterprise. It is not a local company with regard to where it is headquartered. It has employees in China, but as Merrigan would say, "Legitimately we can't tell you where our headquarters is. We have our CEO in Singapore and various functional leaders there. We have our North American headquarters in Raleigh, Durham, where we have a lot of development, quality, worldwide finance, worldwide marketing, and the Americas group. We run most of our Web operations out of Argentina. We've moved all of our agency and marketing production

resources to Bangalore in India. We are truly a globally integrated enterprise." The value is that Lenovo can leverage this expertise in different countries not just for cost savings but for efficiency, expertise, and cross-cultural insights.

5. **Learn what not to do:** The biggest lesson was learning that is it prohibitively expensive to build a custom segmentation for every single market. There are practical realities like consistency of worldwide deliverables around driving commonality of segmentation, but it is important to validate that segmentation locally, or at a minimum, allow it to be adjusted at a local level. For example, Lenovo has a segment called mouse potatoes. These are clients who use PCs primarily for entertainment purposes and tend to be higher income and optimistic about technology. That segment exists in every market, but for instance, in India, it does have differences. In India, downloading music is not as important as leveraging the DVD purchases. These adjustments of the segmentation show a unique understanding of the specific local market that is important. It is about blending the global and the local.

When Lenovo approaches a new market or country, it has a set of people with expertise in that culture. As Merrigan notes, "It's challenging on the one hand, but it's turning into a core competitive advantage for us. The more global you go, the more local you become."

Application to Your Company

The model of a globally integrated enterprise organizes work in different ways and requires varying skills and behaviors. You need to explore how to evolve your culture, policies, and programs to engage your employees at all stages of their careers, including how to attract, develop, and retain new generations of IBMers to become global-local citizens. By doing so, as the preceding example illustrates, you can create market access and opportunity for your company.

Focus on IBM

IBM has become a true multinational company with a view of global-local. We are focused on not just continuing our march to a globally integrated enterprise but also driving into global citizenship to ensure we have the skills and processes to be successful both globally and locally.

To really consolidate a view of IBM's use of the global-local concept in the setting of being a Globally Integrated Enterprise (GIE), I spoke with Miroslav Hofbauer, Central European marketing manager; John Kennedy, VP of Americas marketing, who has held positions marketing in Asia, Japan, and Latin America; and several of my local Service Oriented Architecture (SOA) team members. Overall the goal of our global-local strategy is to strike a balance between strategy and execution. The brand is the manifestation of the strategy, and a great brand is a differentiated brand. However, to relate at a local level, cultural positioning drives attention. Thus, the balance between the global strategy and the local needs are what will drive success in the market.

To illustrate, I wanted to use a category marketing example. At a global level, IBM had embraced SOA. A global strategy was laid out and marketing plays were called at a worldwide level. However, each country customized its marketing plays for SOA based on local requirements. The following are three examples of how that global category of IBM SOA was translated into local execution with its own adaptation:

- Leveraging local market opportunity but embracing global value of SOA
- Leveraging local customs to represent SOA global strategy
- Leveraging local "face" and technology preference to drive SOA penetration

For example, in Russia, the challenge was how to reach a country with eight time zones with a limited set of experts for a marketing event. Natasha Kudrey, IBM marketing manager in Russia, took this challenge on in real time as she was trying to make progress in educating the market on SOA. In December of 2007, the IBM Russia Software Team conducted a series of real-time online workshops for customers and business partners based throughout Russia. The only requirement for participation was Internet access. It leveraged technology from IBM called Lotus® Sametime®.

More than 210 customers and business partners took part in the workshops. Even though the seminars were done online, the clients could see live video transmission, could hear the speakers' voice, and could even submit online questions. They were even able to exchange ideas and collaborate over Sametime.

IBM Lessons Learned

1. Leveraging local market opportunity but embracing global value of SOA

In IBM Slovakia, it realized that Slovakia is moving from Slovak Crown currency to Euros on January 1, 2009. As Euro conversion becomes the highest priority for all IT departments, Ferdinand Kolcak, IBM marketing manager, used this as the main "reason for call" on the event invitation. It explained to potential participants that the currency move would include many challenges and proposed a method to drive a more productive environment. It began the two-way conversation by focusing on a local, cultural challenge. The results have been a lower expense to revenue ratio due to the targeting of the audience.

2. Leveraging local customs to embrace global strategy

In the Slovenian team, they localized by being creative with the SOA initials and their own local customs. (See Figure 3.3.)

Figure 3.3   Slovenia's tradition of gift boxes.

It sent potential participants the following three teasers three days in a row in a small box for SOA:

- Box with letter "S" (package with dried plum = Slovenian Sliva) with written positive words on "S" (Storilnost = efficency, Sodelovanje = cooperation, Stabilnost = stability, Strokovnost = expertise)
- Box with letter "O" (package with nuts = Slovenian Oreh) written words on box (Odgovornost = responsibility, Odlicnost = excellence, and Originalnost = unique)

- Box with letter "A" (package with dried pineapple = Slovenian Ananas) and written words on box (Aplikacija=application, Arhiv = archive, and Aktivnost = activity)

After Tina Zmuc Reflak, IBM market manager, got their attention with SOA teasers, she invited them to a local event at Ljubljana's castle, the highest point in Ljubljana that could be translated into the SOA story. Presentations were organized in different rooms to give these selected invitees a feeling of what SOA means in the real world—overview, control, connectivity, improvement, and processes. In each room, one piece of an SOA puzzle was collected, and at the end on the top of the castle, all pieces were put together to show the SOA story and how it can be integrated in each company to improve business. (See Figure 3.4.)

Figure 3.4 The SOA Event with local flavor.

3. Leveraging local technology preferences to drive SOA penetration

Oliver Nickels, IBM's SOA marketing leader in Germany, was faced with a challenge in the local region around the global strategy of SOA. Germany needed to provide a local face to SOA to start the dialogue with IBM. Peer-to-peer dialogue in Germany is the most effective way to bring to market new concepts in a country that is risk averse. Nickels wanted to provide its audiences with a "virtual" peer who could lead a discussion about local IT issues and how SOA helped his German company address those issues.

Nickels decided to make a fictitious IT-manager, Frank Bremer, the German star of a campaign that involved a peer-to-peer blog. The German team invited its customers to join his journey of change on a central URL, www.quovadis-bremer.de, which is an active blog known as the Bremer-blogposts. The campaign started with a book in which Bremer wrote about his experiences and thoughts about being the IT manager of Panta Rhei, a fictitious company.

The story in the blog, in the book, and in print was centered on the global IBM strategy but emphasized risk management and other key areas of focus from the German companies, including being told by a German. The results of going global-local were a response rate of 56 percent, overachieving by 30 percent the norm for German campaigns. It is also remarkable that 54 spontaneous customer comments were posted on the Web site about its value.

This is a great example of a campaign leveraging the global thoughts in a local way. In fact, this Quo Vadis, Bremer Campaign received the 2008 bronze DDP award, which is the annual award of the German Dialog Marketing Association, in the category of "best campaigns in IT industry." Although these items are part of larger tactics, the balancing between the protection of the global brand identify and the local flavor comes through in spades and makes these marketing techniques best practices in ensuring the concept that being more global means becoming more local.

Lessons Learned

1. **Local knowledge is required to capitalize on full market potential.**
   The more relevant your marketing strategy is to national agendas, the greater market access and freedom of action it achieves. Create and deploy a methodology to understand national agendas, identify and prioritize related opportunities, and allow local execution to implement the value of the global model.

2. **Don't forget country heritage.** Marketing strategies that leverage the local flavor prove to be successful because they speak to the audience. They can take the global strategy and adapt it to what is relevant and important to the local audience. This involves everything from the message to the execution elements of a marketing campaign.

3. **Skills are critical.** Ensure your marketing leaders have the ability to deeply understand and apply the full benefits of the global-local model to drive local execution. Skills are the battleground of the future, not just in the global-local concept but also in the flat world. Your people are your most valuable asset. In my SOA team, we have begun to focus on our skills in the global-local concept for a full day once a quarter.

Application to Your Company

For your company to be successful in marketing in the new flat world, you need to ensure a consistently high level of cultural adaptability. One idea you might want to apply to your company that IBM is leading is an online, annual "cultural literacy" program—including vignettes designed to reinforce the need for cultural adaptability and awareness. Setting up governance on what and how much can be changed will also assist in protecting the balance of the global and local concepts that must be delicately traded off.

Google

Andy Berndt, the managing director of the Google Creative Lab, walked me through one way Google is leveraging user-generated content for marketing goodwill locally. Doodle 4 Google is a competition where Google invites K–12 students to reinvent Google's homepage logo. In 2008, U.S. kids were asked to doodle around the theme "What if...?" The winners of the doodle contest show off their designs online! As Berndt explains, "We started out doing this in the U.K. and then we did it in Australia; now we're doing it in the U.S. It is a program package that we send out to schools. The kids extrapolate on, "What if you could do anything, if you could make anything, build anything, and imagine anything?" They can be the star of the Google logo. The kids draw an idea and Google selects a grand winner from a set of regional winners. The grand winner's design shows up on the Web site. (See Figure 3.5.) It is a type of local marketing that generates a lot of goodwill."

Figure 3.5   Doodle 4 Google.

How is Doodle 4 Google an example of taking a global thought local? Well, as Berndt explains, part of his job is to work with the Google brand and determine what gets people excited about Google. Although Google is a global brand, the contest brings in a local element and brings to life the brand attributes in a local way. For example, because Google likes to dream big, it instills the living brand promise into its local advocates by asking them to dream through the theme "What if...?"

Insights from Google

Small things make a difference. As Berndt explains, the impact of this locally has been larger than life. When he was recently interviewed on CNN, one of the first questions he was asked about was the local impact of the global brand Google.

Youth matters. Google's program begins in the schools and with teachers. Google's localization of the brand is a way to help them with what they do best.

Experiment with what works. Berndt calls this the "spirit that runs through Google." It experiments with tactics that work locally and those that they can extend globally, such as Doodle 4 Google.

Conclusion

Acting local in a way that the regional markets respect you is an element of globalism. There is an attractiveness of brands that can balance the global and the local factors. If a company was local and that was the advantage, it would be about positioning the company to be a local company. However, the research shows that the advantage belongs to the most global company that has the cultural positioning savvy. Cultural positioning is essential to localization and to gain the respect of the consumer, but demonstration of global capability and the sensibilities of the global markets ensures long-term success.

To win in the long term, a company needs to focus on its skills and its processes to ensure its localness is in sync with national agendas. It also must focus on balancing between the global and the local. Finally, becoming a globally integrated enterprise requires leadership from the marketing organization and a use of Marketing 2.0 techniques.

the Strategy
- Role based
- Branded & Lightly Branded
- Corporate Social Responsibility
- Category Creation

4

Fish Where the Fish Are
and Use the Right Bait

In strategy, it is important to see distant things as if they were
close and to take a distanced view of close things.
—Miyamoto Musashi

Finding the right place for your marketing focus is much like finding the right place to fish. Knowing where the fish are, what they like to eat, and what attracts them can turn your fishing trip into a meal! Making better business decisions comes from understanding your market and your customers more intimately in both today's view and tomorrow's prediction. You have to create something in the marketplace that adds value to the right set of people at the right time. Now that we have gotten the sneak peek into those "water cooler"–only conversations through the new forms of intelligence and know that to grow, there needs to be alignment with the emerging markets, we need to ensure we match our strategy and our messaging to the audience. In Figure 4.1, we see the ANGEL cycle. We explore four major areas of focus to ensure you nail your strategy and tell the story to the right audience in the right way with the right agenda.

Figure 4.1 Nail the relevant strategy and tell the story.

With the segmentation complete and the research on where demand exists (see Chapter 1, "Listening and Analyzing in the Global World"), our next questions relate to our relevancy in the market:

- Are the needs met by a category today or is the agenda set in the marketplace?
- Where and on whom should we focus our efforts on?
- How do we leverage our brand for customers?
- What's the corporate responsibility when taking a message to the market?

These four questions will help focus the strategy on what is relevant to the market, as shown in Figure 4.2.

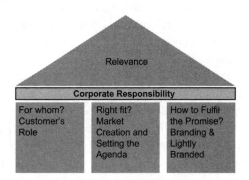

Figure 4.2 The key questions to answer.

The following questions encompass the new concepts that you should take away from this chapter. For each of these game changing points, there are case studies later in the book to help bring the points to life.

- **Who do we focus on for the best results?:** Role-based approaches can help you better target your potential customers at a lower cost. (See Chapter 5, "Relevance and Roles: Forrester Research.")

- **What is the right way to approach the target audience?**: Leveraging your listening both globally and locally enables you to set the agenda in the marketplace as a crucial goal of your strategy. (See Chapter 21, "End-to-End Example: IBM WebSphere and the SOA Agenda, Prolifics, Ascendant Technology.")

- **How do we fulfill the brand promise?**: A combination of both strong branding and light branding are relevant today and in the future. (See Chapter 6, "Lightly Branded: EepyBird.com, The Coca-Cola Company, and Mentos.")

- **Do we practice corporate social responsibility?**: Corporate social responsibility is not a trend. It is here to stay. The focus must begin with your strategy. (See Chapter 7, "Corporate Social Responsibility: IBM's Project Green, Marks, and Spencer.")

Answering these four questions correctly brings you to the most relevant story for your audience.

Where's the Best Fishing?

My father-in-law is a fisherman and he makes a profound statement when he takes my daughters fishing. He tells them, "We have to go and fish where the fish are and use the bait that those fish like!"

From our solid market analysis using both traditional and Marketing 2.0 techniques, we know our audience, how to find it, and how to ensure our messaging matches its needs. All good things in our business flow from relevance. When we are relevant, clients find us to be "need to have," not "nice to have." How can you be most relevant? Start by looking at the role that telling the story in language that the person in the role would understand. While this mission of targeting messaging has always been important in marketing, in today's Marketing 2.0 it is mandatory. Today, there is more noise in the system, and an expectation of more personalization from customers.

Which Fish? Role-Based Marketing

Role-based marketing is having a true understanding of the role a person plays before focusing your efforts, messaging, and offerings. Examples might include the role of chief marketing officer, chief financial officer, or business analyst. Talking to people by role is about understanding what makes them tick, what their challenges are, what they struggle with, and what they need to get to the next step in their careers. In essence, it is talking to them in terms of what keeps them up late at night. It has a personal dimension to it whether you are in B2C or B2B marketing.

Why is role-based marketing in a book about new-world marketing techniques? As the world becomes more global and local, the targeting that transcends global boundaries are roles. Roles are not titles, but the responsibilities that one holds. Industries do change throughout the world. For example, healthcare and banking are different by region. From our findings, roles seem to be a common denominator across the globe. Direct marketing or chief information officer are roles that have the same responsibilities whether you are in Vietnam or England!

Role-based marketing ensures you target the right audience with the right language and offerings. According to the 2007 Marketing Sherpa Study, 80 percent of customers find your offerings—not vice versa! That means in 80 percent of the cases, the right strategy is to determine what roles need to hear your story, determine what their language is, and understand where they go for their information.

How Do You Begin Your Role-Based Journey?

One of the first steps is to determine which roles you believe are most important for your offerings. The definition should be precise. Create a story around them in terms of their names, goals, genders, ages, geographies, and even personal histories. Think through their buying potential or power, their definitions of success, their goals, and their motivations. These personas should be a way to humanize your clients.

Some questions used at IBM to determine profiles include

- How do customers articulate their big picture needs and worries?
- Which needs and wants are most important?
- What are their past, current, and future priorities?
- Who are the users? What business problems are they trying hard to solve?
- What are the key drivers of customer satisfaction and loyalty?
- How well are offering/solution area wants and needs being met today?
- How do customers make purchase decisions? Who influences them?
- What are the buying patterns/attitudes? How might this change over time?

Figure 4.3 is a sample persona.

Brad Fisher
Senior Business analyst
29 Years Old, Engaged

"Business processes and activities need to be visible to me so I can provide the best recommendations to my team and management for how to optimize them."

Brad's Interests:

✓ Drives a VW EOS, owns townhouse in Chicago
✓ Heavy Internet user
✓ Reads *Wall Street Journal*, *Wired*, and *Business 2.0*
✓ Highly involved in social networking
✓ Hobbies include jogging, fantasy football & video games
✓ Enjoys watching Lost, The Simpsons, and The Office

Pet Peeves:

✓ Little organization, structure, and lack of quantifiable results
✓ Hates chaos and people who act without planning
✓ Gets frustrated with constantly shifting priorities and slow responsiveness

His Professional Goals:

✓ Aspires to fast track into management
✓ Improve analysis and communication of requirements for business processes and policies
✓ Membership in professional organizations, such as the International Institute for Business Analysis and BPM Institute

A Successful Day in the Office:

✓ Improve business models and processes
✓ Find ways to improve productivity and reduce costs
✓ Use existing application resources and services

Figure 4.3 A sample persona: Brad Fisher, senior business analyst.

This persona was built from several interactions, and our goal was to make it feel real and to personalize our customer. We learned that the more precise you can make it, the more relevant your marketing becomes. First, we looked at which roles controlled the budget and who had influence over the budget. Second, we worked with our sellers to determine which communities they sold to, and we even did mock sales calls to ensure that the questions were real and that we had differentiation in our answers. Third, we validated with our customer base.

What were some of the outcomes? For one of our roles, we learned that they played a heavier influencer role over the budget than we realized. We created a special offering Web site for collaboration and an event targeted just for them. For our IBM SOA initiative, this was the birth of our SOA Architect Summits, an in-person event led by Brian Safron, and our SOA Space, a community site for sharing best practices, as we understood the "person" and his needs and dreams.

The other great outcome was the knowledge that we had missed some white-space audiences (White space is the customer set you do not currently serve). We found that in the buying community, some of the important influencers were not being touched. In most cases, talking to multiple roles is required. Inside of IBM, our SOA success was driven by a strategy that was named "surround sound." What is surround sound? It is talking to multiple roles, in their languages, at the same time. Why is it important to talk to a number of roles? According to the 2007 Marketing Sherpa report, the number of people involved (in a greater than 1,000-person company) in a technology purchase decision over $25,000 is around 21 people!

In making our selection of purchase influences, we look to create sustainable competitive advantage for our business and outstanding value for the targeted roles. Above all, our personas must truly reflect how the market and the customer roles within it perceive value and, as a consequence, operate their purchasing. This process will make our message relevant.

Personalize Your Approach by Role

After you define your roles and determine "who" these customers are, the next step is to personalize the way you approach and what you approach them with. In Figure 4.4, you see that after the messaging workshops and documenting your personas, this insight needs to be leveraged for two things: where you present your product or service and what you present. Where do these customers meet your brand? What are the offline and online touch points?

Role-based marketing requires that you methodically review your offerings, advertising, Web sites, events, White papers, collateral, and your packaging and consumer activities to see if they are present in the right places and if they speak to the right role. All your tactics and demand generation should now reflect the role. For example, if your product targets merchandisers and category managers in retail, maybe the National Retail Federation conference is a great place to present your story that is now customized for merchandisers. It requires that you understand the nuances of the different roles and tailor the messaging that way. It requires that you operationalize your messaging and execute better versus execute differently.

For role-based marketing, you need to think about where your customers are today, but also think about where they are going in the future. In Figure 4.5, you see how we constant evaluate roles and decide which roles are the target ones in the future.

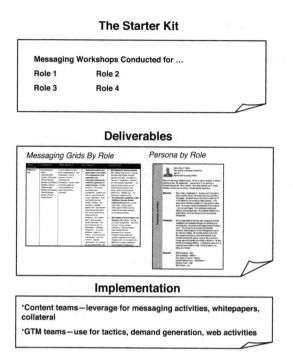

The Starter Kit

Messaging Workshops Conducted for ...

Role 1   Role 2

Role 3   Role 4

Deliverables

Messaging Grids By Role   *Persona by Role*

Implementation

•Content teams—leverage for messaging activities, whitepapers, collateral

•GTM teams—use for tactics, demand generation, web activities

Figure 4.4   Role-based marketing implementation.

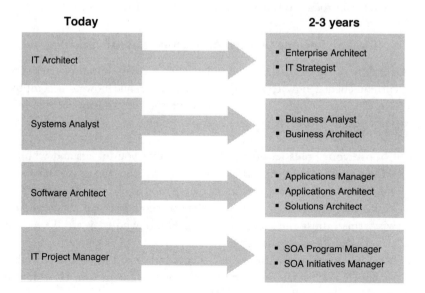

Today		2-3 years
IT Architect	→	• Enterprise Architect • IT Strategist
Systems Analyst	→	• Business Analyst • Business Architect
Software Architect	→	• Applications Manager • Applications Architect • Solutions Architect
IT Project Manager	→	• SOA Program Manager • SOA Initiatives Manager

Figure 4.5   Roles evolve over time—always revalidate.

In our business, new roles are created all the time, and touch points constantly change with the new media types emerging. Role-based marketing is a continual process. Needs, wants, priorities, attitudes, preferences, and behaviors lead to a tangible face for the role.

The Outcomes of Role-Based Marketing Done Right

The power of this marketing strategy is that it can help you improve your efficiency (expense/revenue, cycle time) and effectiveness (validated leads and validated lead revenue) of building demand through unique messaging to target audiences. It enables you to enhance your sales support and alignment with marketing by focusing on high-opportunity roles and using sales "tribal knowledge." If you do it right, role-based marketing actually enables you to save money in the way you execute. If you change nothing else about your tactic mix except targeting better, you will achieve better returns. For example, if you make 200 calls instead of 1,000 calls, then the conversion rates of your teletactics are better because the leads are more qualified.

Most importantly, role-based marketing helps you have a relationship with the person—your client. It enables you to redefine your target customer and meet the needs of the white space in a way you had previously not dreamed. Tensions do exist in the system, as we can see from Figure 4.6. The tension is in the breadth and depth of your offerings and how to balance targeting roles that are relevant today and those that will be relevant in the future.

Top Five Lessons Learned About Role-Based Marketing

Overall, role-based marketing enables us to identify how to better serve our current clients, how to target the white space, and how to accomplish these in the Marketing 2.0 world. Below are the top 5 ideas to focus role-based marketing efforts on:

1. **Choose your roles carefully:** Make sure that you understand who the influencer of the decision is and who the decision maker is. Make sure you include the sellers in the iterations as well as clients and partners.
2. **Make them real:** Your roles and personas should be real people; otherwise, this is just messaging matrices. Know who they are. Don't get theoretical; these are your customers.
3. **Message to the role, but don't forget surround sound:** Remember that there are few decisions today made by a single person. How do you enable a role to sell to other roles?

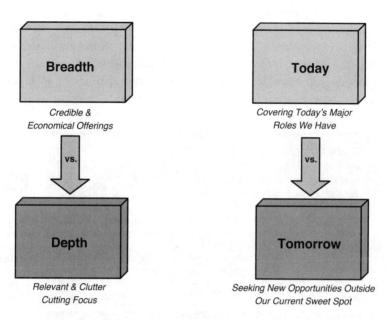

Figure 4.6   Role-based tension

4. **Measure the cost savings:** Role-based marketing saves you money because your conversations are more targeted and personal to the role.
5. **Obsess about your customer today and tomorrow:** At Boeing, customer-focus engineers have jobs that focus only on its customers' requirements. Remember that the market changes constantly, so be sure you continually reevaluate the roles you target.

How Big Is the Pond? Creating a New Market and Setting an Agenda

As you leverage the new methods of listening to determine if your customers' needs are met today and discover white space in your role-based approach, your action might be to rethink the market categories and agendas. A best-practice marketing company reconnects and stays connected to the marketplace. By staying close to its customers, Charles Schwab recognizes the need for discount brokerages, and it created one of the largest brokerage businesses in the world on that principle. In doing this, it created a new market. How and when do you create a new market in your industry?

Examining markets takes speed and some anticipation of your customers and your competitors' plays and strong execution. A market is sometimes a future state of how to meet a set of related customer needs.

How do you know if you need a new market definition? In Figure 4.7, there are three different ways to change your market.

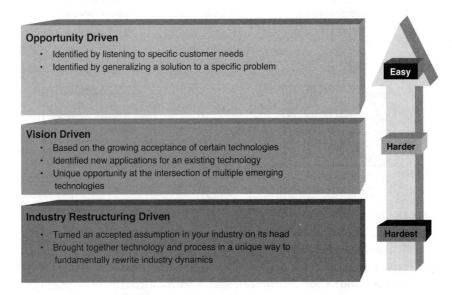

Figure 4.7 Actions to consider for new market creation.

When Do You Enter a New Market?

First, if you see a need that is not being met, your market definition can grow or alter. For example, an opportunity-driven change might be that you have identified a new or related customer need. For example, Gap added stores based on varying customer needs. The Banana Republic stores try to convey a more sophisticated image for an upscale customer. The Old Navy chain is designed to appeal to a younger generation of customers by emphasizing "fun, fashion, and value" through a store experience that delivers "energy and excitement."

Second, if you see new technologies that can change how needs are met, a new market might be on the horizon. Your new market might be vision-driven based on the growing acceptance of certain technologies or new applications for an existing technology. It might be based on the unique opportunity at the intersection of multiple emerging technologies such as Apple did with iTunes and its retail stores for the iPod and the iPhone. Steve Jobs focused on a fact about celluar phone usage—70 percent of cell phone owners use only 30 percent of the function. If they don't use the function within the first 48 hours, they will not use it!

Finally, there could be a complete change in a process as the market knows it today. It could turn an accepted assumption in your industry on its head by bringing together technology and process in a unique way that fundamentally rewrites industry dynamics. For example, eBay changed the process of buying with online auctions.

When Do You Know if There Is a Need for a New Market?

In Figure 4.8, I wanted to share a matrix that I use as I look out over markets.

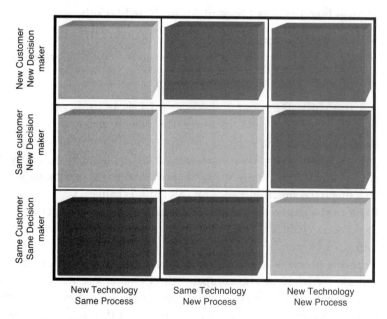

Figure 4.8 When do you know?

On the x-axis, you see the questions on technology and process change. On the y-axis, you can see a focus on the decision maker and whether you target a current customer. The shaded coding represents the degree of difficulty in creating a new market. Most people think that saying "new market entry" is specific enough; however, at IBM, we find that "new market entries" are quite broad and, in fact, the success factors and risks in the different types are different.

The closer you are to your current customer base, the less you change your technology, and the less change you demand from the customers' processes, the more chances you have to succeed. Before entering a market, you must understand your strengths and weaknesses—your ability to succeed as well as your goals. The level of your risk will be different depending on your goals and objectives.

For instance, if you look at your current customer with the same process and same decision maker and you are just changing technology, you have a greater chance of success than if all four are changing. Discovering which square you should focus on involves understanding the playing field you have today and where that playing field is going, which can yield great success.

Top Five Lessons Learned About New Markets

Creating a new market is challenging but very rewarding for a company. The top five ideas to remember about entering or creating a new market follow:

1. **See the shift:** From our ThinkForward Lab at IBM, we found that things change over time. However, the smaller and more gradual the change, the harder it is for us to see it. The difficulty in seeing small changes is that what was normal yesterday is replaced by a slightly different normal today. Only when you explore a period of time do you see how much the small shift adds up to a radical change.

2. **Explore the experience:** Put yourself in your clients' shoes and see how the process enables them. Even small things, such as calling support, sum up to a number of experiences—calling, how people are treated when the phone is answered, how many times they are passed around, and the attitude of the company throughout. For instance, Apple determined to make it easy for its iPhone users to understand the functions by "experiencing" the learning process for themselves. It ended up creating "show me how" for the iPhone—a set of simple videos to help cell phone users get more out of the phone. The videos made an impact, but yet were low cost, fast, and in sync with its overall branding.

3. **Enable your customers to lead their industries:** Everything comes back to this fundamental of the client. It goes beyond this thought. It means to obsess on your customers' businesses more than they do.

Boeing, for instance, a design and manufacturing company, has said that in 2016, its core competencies will be knowledge of the customer, integration, and lean operations. It doesn't say design. It doesn't say manufacturing. It says Boeing can make more money if it understands the customer and integrates the pieces and lets other people do design and manufacturing.

4. **Show, don't just tell:** When you test new ideas with customers, they most likely won't have thought about the new market area. For instance, from our IBM Research and Development lab, we show things in the future such as a 3D representation of the human body. Your doctor can "click" on a specific part of your avatar's body, such as the heart, and instantly see all of the available related medical history, including text entries, lab results, and MRIs. Testing these ideas might result in puzzled looks, but showing customers what might be evokes a strong reaction.

5. **Explore innovation in all fields:** To see the possibilities of the future, see how others do things. In the Green Space, IBM is looking at cellular technology to apply to green concerns. In the next five years, you might get this call on your mobile: "It's your air conditioner calling, you left me on, and nobody's home. I'm wasting energy. Would you like to turn me off?" IBM is working with CenterPoint Energy of Houston to install two million Internet-enabled electric meters that will enable consumers to control appliances via a Web browser or cell phone when they are away, saving time, money, and energy.

The Bait: Community and Lightly Branding

In a world of relevancy, branding is also changing. Customers are informed; they're online, and they orient in terms of communities of interest. In the digital world, an advocacy coming from the customers influences and shapes the formation of your brand. The characteristics of a brand remain the same, but the ownership of the brand is shared.

In today's new world, the brand matters more than it did before. For some, that seems like a paradox, but it is true. The crucial elements of the brand are image (perception), experience (end to end), trust (promise of consistent value), and relationship (motional connection). These attributes have not changed but the way those attributes are shaped has.

The brand is not your own. Image is now a dual play—online and offline. Bloggers, communities, and other digital-world technology shape the direction of your brand. Branding can no longer be controlled; now it needs to be fostered and nurtured in both the virtual and real worlds. This means that now your branding team is not just the team within your four walls, but also the team of "tippers" who influence others through community. Great branding means you have to form a relationship with them and unleash them with your brand promise.

Customers are now more informed and have high expectations and more porous boundaries between the customer and the provider. They are empowered to be independent through increased information availability enabled by technology advances. Before, we could target our brand messages to the audience; now, with the Internet, the branding intended for the investor is also in the hands of the consumer. In today's marketplace of the informed customer, you must continue to create things that are authentic to retain trust. Customers must believe that you will deliver what you say you will. Starting today, products and offerings, branding, and outward facing messages must be done through the listening and responding mechanisms that have become a part of our world. Finally, just like the old song, people do just "want to have fun." The experience online and offline makes it possible to create value not only in the product but also in the experience with the product and company. For example, Moosejaw is a company that specializes in providing its customers with outdoor, surf, skate, and snowboard apparel and equipment from the top-performing brands through its retail shops, catalogs, mobile phone, and online Web sites. With its commitment to shocking the customer with a unique, high-quality shopping experience, the company has earned a loyal following. Its brand loyalty is through an integrated customer experience from shopping, community, social networking, and mobile phone to create an amazing brand experience.

Community branding is not just about having a dialogue, but it's also about having the dialogue affect your brand. More people find out about a company's offerings through a Google search than the company's own branded Web site. Community branding can be basic, such as having an industry analyst or thought leader do a White paper for you and become your evangelist. Or it can involve having others talk about your brand.

It goes beyond these simple examples to the future of having jointly developed offerings that affect the brand, better known as co-creation. On our community site called Project Zero, we had multiple open communities share our IBM WebSphere Product called sMash. Everything from the features, to name testing, to the introduction at our major event was influenced by the community-branding concept.

Traditionally, marketing professionals are given a brand-building assignment, and they seek to build a brand in terms of consistency, look, tone, manner, and messaging but all in a controlled fashion. Fundamentally, the brand was architected from the inside out. Today, you see customers and partners outside your four walls becoming involved in developing your brand. It is much more of a grassroots external shaping of brands—community branding them in the market place. The exciting part is that customers are so informed, being online and in communities, they want to impact your brand.

Second, it is about lightly branding, which is leveraging other means to get your brand in the public eye in a positive, emotional way. It is about entertainment or providing a capability to enable customers to do something valuable (such as download a widget with the weather but also access your information) while affecting your brand positively. Some examples might include micro sites, games, tools, widgets, and other mechanisms that the technology now affords. Lightly branded is supporting your brand in a fun or valuable way.

A great example at IBM is in one area of our business called Business Process Management (BPM). We have a strong presence on an external micro site that is lightly branded for BPM. We leverage that micro site because there are many different players in the BPM space, and customers are not always going to come to www.IBM.com to find information on BPM. We leveraged some fun video problems, tools, and more to lightly brand our products and services on a third-party site. Again, this complements what we do on our www.ibm.com/bpm site as well. Lightly branding will continue to grow as we see more marketers leveraging third-party Web sites, syndication, YouTube, Yahoo, and so on. Customers today can select how, where, and when they want to become "aware" of something. This customer-controlled interaction is important, and in fact, it affects how we talk about awareness. interest, desire, and action. In the new world, there are no boundaries.

Note that branding today is broader than the mechanisms, methods, and techniques. It is about aligning the experience and the personality—both controlled and uncontrolled—to a set of attributes that make it special or unique. This personality is a combination of your "on purpose" work with the market-guided view of your brand. Each marketer now is not a brand guardian but a facilitator of his or her brand in the marketplace. And IBM is not the only company mastering lightly branding. Toyota gained success in its Scion brand through an entire strategy of lightly branding techniques to target a particular personality it wanted for this brand.

Pete Blackshaw, executive vice president of Nielsen Online Digital Strategic Services, explains the new world of branding. In Figure 4.9, we see his view of the six impacts of branding in the new world. He views the characteristics of trust, authenticity, transparency, affirmation, listening, and responsiveness as critical to branding.

The Six Drivers of Brand Credibility

Trust	Authenticity	Transparency
Confidence	As Advertised	Let the Sun Shine In
Consistency	Real & Sincere	Easy to Learn
Integrity	Real People	Easy to Discover
Authority	Informal	No Secrets
Affirmation	**Listening**	**Responsiveness**
Playback	Empathy	Follow-Up
Reinforcement	Welcome Mat	Invitational Marketing
Search Results	Humility (we can learn)	Solidifying the Solution
Community	Absorbing Feedback	Dignifying Feedback
Accountability		

Pete Blackshaw www.tell3000.com   Tell 3,000

Figure 4.9 Six drivers of brand credibility.

Blackshaw outlines three truths that impact branding:

- Businesses no longer hold absolute sway over the decisions and behavior of consumers.
- The longer companies refuse to accept the influence of consumer-to-consumer communication and perpetuate old ways of doing business, the more they will alienate and drive away their customers.
- To succeed in a world where consumers now control the conversation and where satisfied customers tell three friends and angry customers tell 3,000, companies must achieve credibility on every front.

As you look at your brand and guide its value and promise in today's market, combine the techniques available to you. In Figure 4.10, the constant refreshing of brands at IBM are done at least twice a year to reinforce their freshness and value in the marketplace.

We want to make sure that everything supports our branding, and that includes the lightly branded and community branding work that is happening in the marketplace with or without our permission!

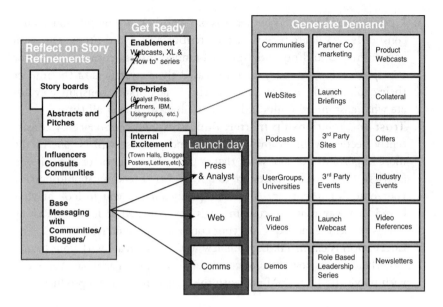

Figure 4.10   Major activity to revitalize the brand.

Top Five Lessons Learned About Community Branding and Lightly Branding

Branding is about the whole picture including community branding concepts, starting with inception of the story on the new news, through lightly branded, what are we going to do to entertain, shock, and amaze our customers beyond their imagination! Here are the top five ideas to remember about branding in the new world.

1. **Discover your communities:** The customer wants to play a role in your brand. Working with third parties, influencers, customers, and other market drivers, you can be a custodian of your brand. Make sure you extend your branding team outside your four walls.
2. **Learn how to dialogue:** Communities have their rules. They also can sniff out a marketing ploy. For examples, look at a few postings of corporate videos on YouTube and read the comments that follow. Make sure you understand and work with the community, not in your own world.

3. **Update your brand:** Whether it is old world or new world, you should constantly reevaluate how your top attributes and your promise in both community branding and lightly branded efforts comes across. For example, customers today have increased their awareness of the impact their choices make on the environment. Smart brands constantly evaluate what customers' wants and needs are by listening at all times.

4. **Trust and relationship matter:** Build trust and confidence by consistently keeping your promises. Your brand promise will be one of the most important pieces of work that you do. Be authentic online—if you aren't real, the consequences are tough! Lightly branding should portray your brand's authenticity. The concept encourages you to look at your brand in a way that the customer has never looked at it, but in a way that is authentic and expresses your company's personality.

5. **Cocreation is essential:** Explore new ways to co-create with your brand. Whether it is in new ways of customer service, such as what Apple did with its videos, or as IBM did with the actual creation of a product.

The New Fishing License: Corporate Social Responsibility (CSR)

Even Kermit the Frog talks about the value of being green! I am here right now in Washington DC and green is everywhere—in the Smithsonian, the hotel, and the list goes on. My friend just sent me an invitation to her "green" wedding, including a green invitation that I can plant. (The paper has seeds embedded in it!)

Social responsibility from companies today is expected. However, it is different from some of the eco-friendly initiatives in the past. Since 2004 through to 2008, three forces of change consistently rose on CEOs' agendas and all are linked to corporate social responsibility (CSR). CEOs plan their largest increases in customer investment to meet CSR expectations, and they develop new products and services to address those needs.

Today's initiatives are business-oriented and focused on incentives built around becoming green and the value it brings to the company as well. For example, companies convince customers to buy from them because they are greener; therefore, the customer can get more energy credits from the government. There is real value in the promise. Economic, regulatory, and consumer awareness all demand that companies address and take a stand on today's social issues.

So why is there a section in strategy around corporate responsibility? Because as business leaders and marketers, we need to address our customers' needs both today and in the future. Many of our customers and partners will want to do business with those who are socially responsible. For example, Whole Foods now has a full view of green throughout its supply chain. It looks for its business partners and suppliers to be green as well. As IBM approached Whole Foods to form a relationship with it, we had to engage with Whole Foods executives and explain what IBM does to minimize its impact on the environment and to design and develop our products to be as green as possible.

Ray Hammond, acclaimed futurogist comments, "I think the climate crisis is an important element for us to bear in mind because everybody in marketing must go about their business in an environmentally conscious way. And in fact, any marketing in the next few years that does not pay attention to energy and environmental needs, will actually shoot itself in the foot. It's clear to me that in the last couple of years there has been a gale force of change blowing. Even in the United States, and in Australia—which are countries that previously have been resistant to the idea of there being a major climate crisis—the wind of change is blowing. And, it seems to me that in all forms of marketing, awareness about consciousness for the environment, our emissions, and the problems of climate crisis will be central."

Social responsibility, and especially green efforts, will become a way of life. Carbon management is a boardroom issue with a wide gap existing between organizational rhetoric and actions. Businesses and consumers are unclear about actions to take for energy savings and reduced greenhouse emissions and are searching for guidance.

If you're a (marketer), how do you do leverage CSR in such a way that you are not viewed as taking advantage of it but are doing it in such a way that is real and authentic? One of the best steps in marketing, and something that IBM has taken seriously as early as 1971 with Thomas Watson, Jr.'s direction, is for companies to be role models in the community. How can your company and business really show its authenticity in this area? Green is not something that can be faked. With your seat at the table, make sure your company is viewing this not just as a marketing ploy but also as a strategic and serious issue for your company.

Given the incentives and tax credits that are available, determine how to quantify the value to your customers. Efficiency gains driven by new economics, information, and processes can be measured and managed. Chief financial officers (CFO) of today's organizations are in constant search of ways to measure the efficiency of their IT operations, and they're finding that vigilant control and reduction of energy use is actually a trigger to create savings in far more costly areas including people costs, facilities costs, and hardware acquisitions.

Leverage your supply chain strategy for green. Who are your partners and what requirements do you have for them? Are there key customers or partners that could switch to your company because of your efforts in this area?

Top Five Lessons Learned About Corporate Social Responsibility

CSR is a mandatory element now for every corporation. The important ideas to remember follow:

1. **Become a role model company:** The environment is important to all of us. It first starts, not with a marketing strategy, but a business strategy that sets your efforts into motion.
2. **Evaluate your partners and suppliers:** Both are critical drivers in the green world. The drive to become green often begins with the supply chain. Evaluate your key partners and suppliers as well as customers for their green efforts. Do you have green in your partnering and key supplier agreements today?
3. **Measurements matter to the business leaders:** In your green efforts, show the positive impact on the environment and on business with your products and services.
4. **Educate yourself and your company:** By choosing products and services yourself that yield green benefits, you can learn about what matters in the marketplace.
5. **Evaluate your brand:** Link your green efforts to your strong and lightly branded efforts.

Conclusion

Execution of your growth strategy requires several parts to work together. First, to know where the fish are and leverage the right bait, knowledge of the customer has to be a core competency. If you don't understand your customers, there will be no way to create an experience that makes your company unique and relevant.

Second, this means you must get out of the abstract and enter into the personal! You need to identify the right roles to "talk" to and to ensure you deliver value to customers' specific pain points. Whether you are B2B or B2C, role-based marketing requires that you know what makes your customers tick. Continuously evaluating the market is a requirement because you might miss new roles or needs as they develop and evolve.

Third, gaps create opportunities for setting the agenda and creating new markets in a global and local way. This agenda-setting task is one of the most important for marketers. The focus must be on making your clients industry leaders through your agenda and point of view.

Fourth, today's branding must link entertainment, conversation, and utility to create and fulfill the brand promise. You are not branding alone, but with a collaborative, informed client who wants a role in the brand definition and wants to have a great experience. The community branding aspect enables you to go beyond your four walls to influence your brand. Lightly branding provides a lift of entertainment and utility to the value that you portray in the market.

Finally, the new table stakes is corporate social responsibility (CSR), which is not just a marketing ploy, but it is here to stay for business reasons. Green has the economic foundations and awareness in the marketplace. For marketers, what is exciting is that the socially conscious world is different than in the past with motivations for customers to both obtain a good economic return on their investments and do well for the environment.

Nailing your strategy and telling your story are crucial to your growth and the greatness of your marketing play especially in the Marketing 2.0 world!

For a role-based demo, go to ibmpressbooks.com/angels.

5

Relevance and Roles: Forrester Research

Every individual matters. Every individual has a role to play.
–Jane Goodall

The world is flat today. Customers have locations around the world, and domain expertise has to be replicated region by region. Technology provides cost-effective alternatives to travel, and regional specialists are emerging for in-region support.

How do you create more relevant messaging and media outreach programs for regions and countries, languages and cultures, and areas with high-prospect density? You can target by size. However, relevance by size is an oxymoron because it is not a strategy for getting closer to customers' business problems or processes.

To understand business processes, you can message for relevance by industry. According to Forrester Research, 85 percent of the 100 largest technology vendors are already segmenting by industry, up 10 percent from last year. Vertical expertise is getting increasingly specialized. For example, financial services was a vertical split, but now we see more micro vertical markets such as U.S. high-volume private equity trading.

Role-based marketing, or finding relevance by the role that a person plays in a company, enables you to identify key stakeholders and the influencers behind the buyers. It communicates a distinct message about the value to individual roles and enables you to build a more personal relationship with your customer. It is a new marketing trend. Only one large technology firm targeted role-based marketing in 2006; and in 2007, 23 of the 100 largest technology firms had role-based messaging on their Web sites. Examples include UPS Logistics Technologies that focuses on making things easier for the person who ships the packages, and Cerner, which differentiates on roles within a specific industry concentration.

In this chapter, we discuss the value of and lessons learned about role-based marketing. Note: Roles are *not* titles. They describe responsibilities, objectives, and aspirations.

IBM believes in role-based marketing. (See Figure 5.1.) IBM reaches customers by talking to them about what matters the most to them at that time. The focus on role-based marketing, with the use of personas as the tool, is to nail who you are talking with in your dialogue. It is a best practice that is growing, especially with the emphasis of the digital generation growing up and the community trend. As part of the marketing team at IBM, we learned the value of this focus in our SOA efforts.

Note: SOA = Service Oriented Architecture

Figure 5.1 The IBM SOA journey with role-based marketing began in 2005.

IBM started as a pilot in 2005. A set of face-to-face events focused on two of our key roles—information technology (IT) directors and chief information officers (CIO). We offered targeted, face-to-face events with content tailored for the particular pains associated with these roles—in particular, a focus on return on investment (ROI) of their IT decisions. That led us to focus our events on helping CIOs learn how to do an effective ROI through techniques such as ROI assessments.

In 2006, we took this one step further with a focus on the enterprise architects. Although we continued the face-to-face events as well, our architect summits pulled in substantially more leads and revenue because we touched the audience in multiple ways. The presentations, speakers, demonstrations, and networking sessions were more personalized to this group because of the common thread among them—they were all enterprise architects! They had a "special space" on the Web site and materials targeted for them. We raised the bar, not only in terms of the number of roles we supported, but also in the touch points and deliverables.

In 2007, we took the next step to the business side by targeting a set of industry leaders and speaking their specific industry languages. No longer did we talk about technology, but to the language of the business— such as processing insurance claims, gift registries, and onboarding new customers, Again, we raised the bar on the number of touch points and deliverables.

To take this role-based approach even further, in 2008, we reviewed a number of best practices. The following section highlights one model from Forrester, Inc. Forrester has become a partner for IBM's future strategy around role-based marketing.

Focus on Forrester

For this particular case study, we talked directly with Charles Rutstein who oversees Forrester's global operations and works with chairman and CEO George F. Colony to implement the company's worldwide strategy. Working with the CEO, Rutstein managed the launch of the company's role-based strategy in the beginning of 2007 and leads Forrester's client group organizational structure. He continues to supervise the growth of Forrester's 18 role-based offerings to IT, marketing and strategy, and technology industry professionals. Through his tenure, Rutstein has managed almost all the company's primary offerings, including research, consulting, events, and peer-to-peer executive programs. He has been a member of Forrester's executive team since 2006.

What Is Forrester Research?

Forrester Research, Inc. (NASDAQ: FORR) is an independent technology and market research company that provides pragmatic and forward-thinking advice to global leaders in business and technology. It is based in the Boston area in the United States. For more than 24 years, Forrester has been making leaders successful every day through its proprietary research, consulting, events, and peer-to-peer executive programs. Forrester has been ranked in the top 75 on Forbes' 200 best small companies for five consecutive years running.

The Customers

Forrester's customers are vendors or developers of technology solutions and the business customers that purchase and deploy technology solutions from the vendors. Forrester provides research to assist in making effective business and IT decisions. Customers seek Forrester insight as a neutral source of information with an understanding of the key trends in the marketplace. Forrester has more than 2,400 end-user companies with which it does business on a worldwide basis.

The Product

Forrester's product is an interesting one. It provides intellectual capital. For the vendors it serves, the product is advice and council on how to improve their products, their positioning, and their messaging in the marketplace. Forrester encourages vendors to brief customers when they introduce a new product, change a business model, or form a new partnership. Forrester then writes a report upon which client users draw upon to make decisions. Think about it like consumer reports reviewing business-to-business technology companies. In 2007, Forrester will provide clients with more than 65 Forrester Wave evaluations; these are objective evaluations that use 50 to 200 criteria to evaluate competing products, services, and suppliers combined into a clear presentation of the findings.

For clients, Forrester provides an independent view into a comparison of choices available in the marketplace. This is based on its knowledge of what occurs in the marketplace. For instance, it conducts more than 280,000 consumer surveys worldwide to understand the consumer market, and almost 14,000 surveys on the business side. It is this expertise and breadth of knowledge that clients seek to leverage.

The Competition

There are several analyst firms in the IT and business market that compete with Forrester by offering similar market and vendor insight. Additionally, home-grown research projects that take place within business or IT vendor organizations serve as alternatives to Forrester's capabilities.

The Marketing Best Practice

The best practice from Forrester is role-based marketing through the use of personaes. This is a focused approach—not a broadcast but a dialogue with a set of customers who have things in common. As Rutstein says, "A role in our vernacular is not just a title, but it's a collection of a people with a shared set of challenges, opportunities, and aspirations ultimately. We go after 18 roles, 8 within IT, 5 within marketing and strategy, and 5 in the technology industry. Our charter is simple. Make those people successful."

A sidebar on role-based marketing is available on the companion Web site at ibmpressbooks.com/angels

The Role-Based Agenda at Forrester

Role-based marketing at Forrester started from the company's annual exercise of reviewing itself from an outside-in view (see Chapter 1, "Listening and Analyzing in the Global World"). As Rutstein says, "We undertook a look at what we call the fundamental truths where we said, 'Let's take an outside-in look at our business. We think we're good at some things, but are we good at those, objectively? Also, we think we're not so good at others. Are we maybe not so good at those objectively or compared to the market?' When you do that in an outside-in way, you learn some things about yourself. From that, we learned what we were passionate about, what we can be the best at in the world, and what will differentiate us."

This is a fundamental secret of successful companies: Marketing needs to be connected to the business strategy. In my view, marketing is the execution into the market of the business's core value. At Forrester, much like in IBM SOA, we began with the passionate side of how we provide more value to our customers because in the end game, that's what it is about.

Forrester evaluated different ways to provide value to its customers. They could have chosen to focus just on industry, but the industry view didn't get them personal enough to have a dialogue. Healthcare, for example, is different in the United States, Canada, the United Kingdom, and so on. Focusing by topical area also has challenges. "In the beginning, we found leading adopter vendors such as the Fortune 500 companies, early adopting users, and companies in Silicon Valley. However, a CIO in New York, a CIO in Paris, and a CIO in Tokyo, tell me about their issues, and when you go and you do the research," says Rutstein, "what you find is that their issues are almost identical around the world." This whole insight started a shift in Forrester strategy that began at the top with George Colony, the CEO.

The "Right" Number of Roles

To get started, Forrester leveraged its strong core base of 60,000 registered users. Its focus on the 18 roles came from its assessment of its current client base. It was committed to making this approach work—even if it meant massive changes to its company. As Rutstein says, "We decided that we were ready to walk away from current business if it made sense, but first we said, 'Let's take a holistic approach and see if it can all fit.' We were not seeking to bite off more than we had. So we first wanted to categorize what we had. So we ran through a process of looking at the entire client base, and we did a tremendous amount of research on those people. First, we did a title cut, and then we did a tremendous amount of detailed research. We did surveys, we did focus groups, and we asked people about their dreams, challenges, and aspirations. What dropped out the back of that filtering process were these 18 roles." If you look at the roles, you will see that the roles correspond to Forrester's customer set and the growth segments of the market, both locally and globally.

These roles were taken down a level to try to understand what mattered to that particular role, leveraging personaes (see Chapter 3, "Globalization: Lenovo, Google, Unilever, IBM" for more details on personaes). These persona requirements are what Forrester used to begin to humanize those to whom it provides products and services. (See Table 5.1.) By leveraging the aspirational goals of the persona, there is a personal aspect to role-based marketing. The focus on what is going to make "me" successful, what are the elements that "I" need to be a hero in my company, and other focused questions are a critical part of the marketing whether it is event tracks, articles, or skill building and education. Learning from the personal aspect of this concept occurs because it implies a partnership with the person, not just the company. The person then becomes the best brand ambassador you can have!

Table 5.1   Three Requirements for Effective Personas

Effective personas are:		
Based on ethnographic research	**Developed into archetypes that represent users' key behaviors**	**Used consistently throughout the design process**
Ethnographic research — like interviews and observation — conducted with representative users can reveal goals, attitudes, and behaviors that other techniques — like surveys and focus groups — can't.	When real users' goals, attitudes, and behaviors are embodied in a vivid description of a single "person" with a name and face, designers and stakeholders can get to know their target users — and make decisions that support their needs.	To ensure that personas get used, project teams must inform stakeholders about persona benefits and create an explicit plan for integrating personas into design and decision-making processes.

FORRESTER   Source: July 2007 "Best And Worst Of Personas, 2007"

Application to Your Company

Do you need massive amounts of money for research to start your view of what are the right roles? At IBM, we leveraged the tribal knowledge of our sales team to determine where to start. Even Rutstein says that in the beginning Forrester started the process with a small group of its executives to try to identify the roles. With its own experiences with customers and the market, they identified almost the exact set that its detailed research had revealed. "And so without any data whatsoever we drew 19 or 20 roles. After we finished the research, all the 18 that we picked were there. And we just eliminated a couple."

The application here is that you can start small with a pilot and your tribal knowledge and then leverage research on a need-to-know basis!

Also, Forrester teaches others the role-based approach through a set of evaluation criteria. Table 5.2 has some of the basics of doing great personaes for role-based marketing—ensuring you have usable, relevant language, and definitions to drive you along the way.

Table 5.2 Three Requirements for Effective Personas

Evaluation criteria	Why it's important	What to look for
Q1. Does the persona sound like a real person?	Personas remind stakeholders that they are designing for real people — not faceless, nameless users or stereotypes.	Elements that: • Sound believable individually. • Cumulatively create a well-rounded view of the persona's life. • Include rich details, create empathy, and make the persona memorable.
Q2. Is the persona's narrative compelling?	Engaging stories are easier to read and remember than a collection of data points.	Narratives that: • Include a series of events or actions that convey the persona's key goals, behaviors, and attributes in the form of a "day in the life" story.
Q3. Does the persona call out key attributes and high-level goals?	Short lists of key details help stakeholders focus on users' most relevant needs.	Callouts that: • Represent high-level goals and behavioral attributes that are consistent with the narrative. • Present this information in text or graphical formats, as appropriate.

FORRESTER Source: July 2007 "Best And Worst Of Personas, 2007"

Evaluation criteria	Why it's important	What to look for
Q4. Is the persona focused on enabling design decisions?	Personas play the role of the end user during the design process — so they should help design teams understand what users need and want.	Details that: • Help design teams decide what features and design elements would be useful, usable, and desirable for users. • Enable design decisions without being prescriptive. • Reflect user — not business —needs.
Q5. Is the persona usable?	When stakeholders can find and digest key details, they can more easily focus on the persona's needs.	Design elements that: • Make content easy to read and scan quickly. • Emphasize the most important information. • Help users navigate through multiple pages or sections of information.
Q6. Does the persona have appropriate production values?	When personas look like professionally produced deliverables, they are more readily accepted as important elements of the design process.	Design elements that: • Have professional polish. • Are free from typos, grammar mistakes, and sloppy layout practices.

FORRESTER Source: July 2007 "Best And Worst Of Personas, 2007"

Role-Based Products, Deliverables, and People!

Just defining a set of roles and personaes doesn't take you far if you don't leverage that knowledge in all that you do. If you decide that you need to reach a particular role, you need the right products and messages reaching them. For Forrester, that meant a change to the structure of its company, because its product is its intellectual capital. According to Rutstein, Forrester decided that "we would make sure that the structure of the company and all of the incentives all across the company would align with that go to market strategy. So formerly, for example, we had our research teams aligned by topics and industries. So the first thing we did was create 18 research teams, and slotted every single person in research into one of those teams."

This is not an easy step. Whether your product is a manufactured good or a service, this is a cultural shift. At Forrester, it already had mini pilots of this concept with its Affinity Networks, which did focus on roles such as CIO or security, before the entire company adopted the approach. Because that part of the business was role-based from the beginning, the teams and products for Forrester looked at this approach and concluded that it was a change that needed to be made. By the way, those areas of focus had been the fastest growing parts of Forrester's business.

However, for others in Forrester, the change was not that simple. Rutstein recalls working with the industry team and says, "Analysts who were on an industry-based research team had the biggest challenge. In the beginning, we basically went to them and we said, 'Look, we need you to pivot because we think you can be more relevant if you do.' Some of them said, 'Okay.' Others said, 'Oh I can't do that. I am a health care analyst or I'm a financial services analyst.' They had to transition to not having their whole purpose in life focused on, say, healthcare. But we had some people who just couldn't get past that and who said, 'You know what, that's what I want to be,' and so they departed." So, as Forrester did, make sure you think through the change that must be made when role-based marketing is adopted.

After Forrester aligned its teams around those roles and had deliverables based on those roles, it decided to change the role customers' experience end-to-end to focus on those roles. As Rutstein said, "We changed the Web sites, so it used to be if you went to Forester.com, you would see a spectrum of material. Right on that page on any given day you might see an item on the new iPod from Apple, you might see something on a big new storage array from EMC, a new release of WebSphere, something on online banking in Poland, you know, who's that page for? That page is for nobody. Or everybody."

Because much of its product distribution is done via the Web, it changed Forrester.com to have 18 Web experiences. It created a specific business site for each role. "We put somebody in charge of each of them. Again, with a mandate to simply make it relevant for that one person," discusses Rutstein. "We invited thousands of clients in to participate in the beta, and so our customers helped us to refine it. We did usability testing and focus groups because we had to make sure we had it right."

Forrester's end-to-end implementation began with a persona. Meet Michael Jacobs, a real person with goals and dreams and an IT infrastructure and operations professional. From this person, the deliverable of value to his role is shown in multiple ways. In Figure 5.2, we see a Web site with topics and materials specific to this role.

Figure 5.2 Web site synced with needs of role.

The key here is that this Web site mirrors the role profile shown in Figure 5.3, and it is also reflects in the sales collateral used in an engagement, as shown in Figure 5.4. The sellers are trained by role and focus on the needs of the role.

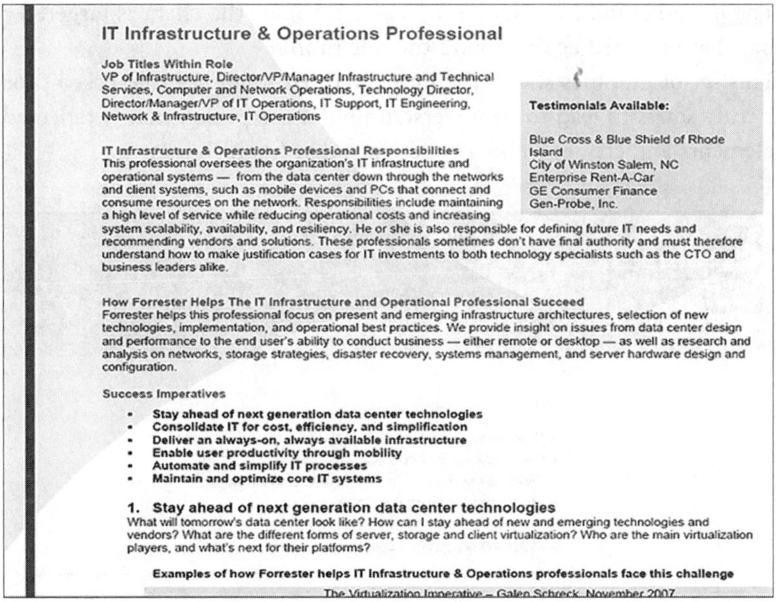

Figure 5.3   Mirroring the role profiles.

Figure 5.4   Sales material.

The leave-behind (see Figures 5.5a and 5.5b) for the client is targeted collateral that is geared again around the role profile.

This set of graphics shows the integrated nature of the role-based process that truly starts to lead to an understanding of the person that is reflected in all elements and creates a client experience that fits his goals.

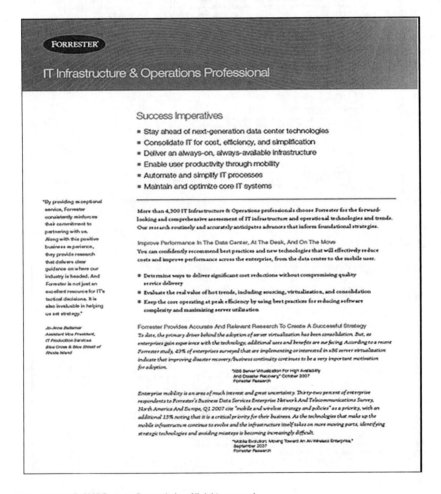

Figure 5.5a   Leave-behind for clients in role.

Figure 5.5b   Leave-behind for clients in role.

This focus on roles does not preclude the focus on key topics of the day. In Figure 5.6, the example is the focus on green. Themes can be applied across the roles, and in fact, it makes the theme more powerful. The green example allows focus on cost cutting to the CFO, but for the CIO, it focuses on what actions need to be taken.

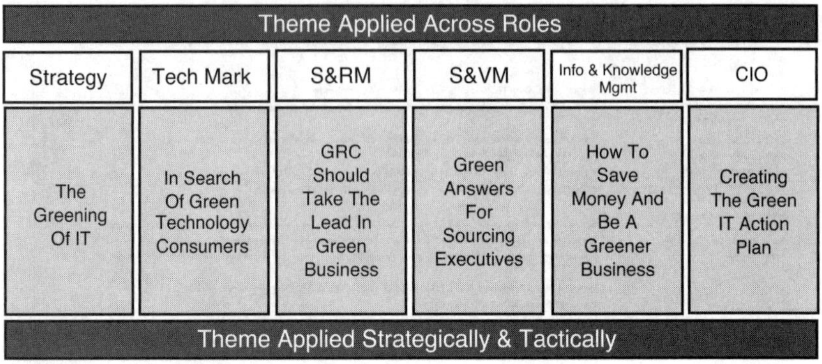

Theme Applied Across Roles					
Strategy	Tech Mark	S&RM	S&VM	Info & Knowledge Mgmt	CIO
The Greening Of IT	In Search Of Green Technology Consumers	GRC Should Take The Lead In Green Business	Green Answers For Sourcing Executives	How To Save Money And Be A Greener Business	Creating The Green IT Action Plan
Theme Applied Strategically & Tactically					

Figure 5.6 Roles cut across our traditional axis of "topics."

Application to Your Company

If you decide to go with role-based marketing and select a role, ensure that your company's products and services can meet the needs of that role. If not, your company needs to decide how to change the product, or not to try to start the dialogue with that customer role. Next, make sure that the total experience for the customer follows the role-based model. To have one element of your marketing strategy be role-based, and another element generic, defeats the purpose. Even if you have to focus on a single role and take it all the way through, you will be more successful than too many roles done half-way.

Communication Up and Down

A critical element that Forrester initiated for success was the clever way it communicated the role-based strategy. Because it tied directly to the segmentation for growth, it communicated the change in several ways.

First, it changed its entire company through the go-to market around role-based marketing so the profit and loss leaders were now grouped around these 18 roles and the 3 major categories of IT, marketing and strategy, and technology industry. Rutstein explains, "We pivoted all of the profit and losses (P and Ls) in the company to align with collections of roles. So the three major areas became where the P-and-Ls are now run. All the consulting businesses, leadership boards, and everything aligned to those P-and-Ls." For Forrester, it can measure the impact on its bottom-line growth directly to role-based marketing. It does not just own a single geography, but these leaders own the business around the world. They used to be geographically–based. They are now all global businesses. Each of these businesses by their design are global businesses and serve roles around the world in all the markets that Forrester serves.

Second, it declared a set of success metrics by role for the company. Although it cannot share the details of those metrics, Forrester did share the process. Rutstein used the CIO role as the example. He broke that role down and collaboratively defined success imperatives for it. And that was the same for each of the 18 roles. He and the teams set 4–7 imperatives per role that drove the sales team to the analyst. Each imperative was an absolute "must do" for success.

What did the imperatives look like and what value were they? First, they were framed in the language of Forrester's customers; they spoke their language. All employees say the success imperatives are framed in the words that their customers use. The value comes in enabling and communicating with the entire team. They became a great sales-force enabler. They drove the marketing collateral. They drove marketing and sales to work closer together. One of the pieces that was powerful was the "green" card. (See Figure 5.7.) It was given out at conferences and events to articulate publicly the focus.

IT Infrastructure & Operations Professional

▶ Stay ahead of next generation data center technologies

▶ Consolidate IT for cost, efficiency, and simplification

▶ Deliver an always-on, always-available infrastructure

▶ Enable user productivity through mobility

▶ Automate and simplify IT processes

▶ Maintain and optimize core IT systems

Figure 5.7   The green card.

Another was a big Forrester Technology Conference held in California. Connie Moore led the event and brilliantly architected it based on roles. (See Figure 5.8.) The sessions and tracks centered on what mattered most to those in attendance at the event.

Figure 5.8 Sample track from the Forrester Technology Conference.

Rutstein was big on the motivation of the imperatives through a simple example, "When a salesperson sits down with a CIO, he can take those success imperatives on a piece of collateral and push them across the table and say, 'Look, this is how we help people like you. Does that make sense to you? Are these the things that you struggle with?' And, of course, if we've done our research right, we know statistically speaking that almost all the things on that list are going to be things that that person is struggling with. That has turned out to be the case. Invariably, we get the response that says, 'Yes, it's exactly what my challenge is. Tell me how you help with these.' And so it really accelerates that conversation about how we can help provide more value."

The communication and overall success were felt by the internal team. Forrester is seeing an added benefit of employee retention. If you remember, Rutstein had some challenges with his analysts who did not want to change their products, their research, and their expertise. However, for those who stayed, one of the key metrics of success, especially in its industry and business, is analyst retention. Forrester saw its highest retention ever in 2007!

Application to Your Company

The biggest application learned from the communication plan is that the imperatives and communications are done around the role of "language." Defining how success looks is critical in determining not only end success, but also what changes need to be made along the way. Forrester communicated this internally and externally with the same diligence!

Forrester Lessons Learned

Rutstein articulated some of his most valuable lessons learned.

Outside In, Really!

One of the lessons learned for Forrester is that it has a greater understand of its customer. It was an eye-opening experience. Defining what makes people tick, what keeps them up at night, and what they need to do to take the next step in their careers, made what Forrester did so much more relevant. People talk about outside in, but doing it can be an experience that wakes up your business. Rutstein articulated it as, "It opens our eyes to things by role that seem 101 but are powerful. Like for chief marketing officers (CMOs), we write things like the marketing of marketing. How do you as a CMO convey to others in your company the value of marketing and the value your function provides? How do you create a language where you can communicate with them? This is just one example of the type of innovative thoughts that we would not have done in the past."

Change Slower Than It Appears in Your Mirror

Because of the real cultural shift in how you approach your business, role-based marketing might take longer than you think. If it is to be successful, it is not just a marketing change, but is also an end-to-end change. Changing products, or declaring that you don't have a needed offering for a role, can bring conflict into an organization. The advice is that the end result is worth it! As Rutstein explains, "This is classic change like what Kotter writes about. It's one of those classic undertakings where, you know, it's going to take a lot longer than you think it will. And there is going to be a lot more resistance than you ever anticipate. And you've got to just put your head down and keep going. It is well worth it." Another smart part of the Forrester story is its recognition of what it is already doing and its need to be explicit and build.

The GB: Governance and Best Practices

Governance is the consistent management, cohesive policies, processes, and decision rights for a given area of responsibility (from Wikipedia). Governance is required in how you work the topics that stretch across roles. Governance around the focus on roles includes establishing a clear process for proposing, approving, and implementing changes to the roles. For Forrester, its role governance process overview is annual, coordinated, and business case-oriented.

Forrester already had a collaborative society where the analysts would talk to one another in a structured, formal interaction, as well as, informal. So for Forrester, it was a sort of social norm, that if someone has written on a particular topic, that person would seek to share and collaborate across the organization. This social norm is one some companies will have to work on with a governance system to ensure sharing of the common themes. You don't want your chief supply officer to have a different point of view than your chief financial officer. The two languages must meet on a set of fundamental points.

However, for Forrester, one piece of the governance did turn out to be a little more challenging. "Analysts like to have a big megaphone," says Rutstein, "and write what they want to write and say this is relevant to everybody. Everybody needs to read my stuff. And, in fact, in the early days when we allowed analysts to tag their research and say what role the piece was targeted at, it shouldn't surprise that analysts would tag it with seven to eight of the eighteen roles. For example, they tag it to the CIO. And everybody in marketing tagged it to the CMO. And of course quickly you realize, 'Hey most of this stuff is not relevant. It's just not.' So, we instituted a rule that made me one of the least popular guys around here for a while called One Doc, One Role. That is to say every document can be tagged to one and only one role." This lesson of making sure that the material is speaking the right language is hard but critical for success. If the roles are different, you have to tune those messages accordingly!

Their role governance design principles consist of the following key points:

- Role changes will be made only if the changes contribute to long-term financial upside.
- Changes to roles must be approached with forethought and care because they impact
  - Our economics
  - The user experience
  - Other roles
  - Other products
  - Approaching change is a science and an art!
  - Science: process and questions
  - Science and art: interpretation and conclusion
- The science part must be well coordinated and batched.

One of the key lessons that Rutstein has had is a few surprise results that he is capitalizing on. Before, when Forrester had P-and-Ls by geography, best practices were not shared. So a great best practice from Amsterdam would never find its way to London or San Francisco. It would never find its way around the world. Now, with the global P-and-Ls, Forrester is finding that best practices are traveling around the world and making it more effective and efficient as a business and in marketing. As one of IBM's star marketers, Nancy Blum, comments, "This practice of sharing local best practices should be painted in bright red and hung as a commandment of role-based marketing."

Obviously this concept of roles can be leveraged online, with communities and social networks to emphasize the personal aspect.

Is It Working?

For Forrester, it sees results from its new companywide focus on role-based marketing. It looks at Web traffic in terms of the number of downloads, site visitors, and collateral downloads. It also measures Web traffic to role-specific content with analytic tools.

It sees increased growth in revenue and market penetration. From an in-process perspective, Forrester is viewing leads and new inquiries by role and by method of contact. Finally, it looks at the access and response to people in those roles.

Conclusion

Role-based marketing helps companies know their customers and prospective customers better—what are their challenges, who are they buying from, who are they not buying from, and why? This understanding down to the persona enables marketers to have more targeted events, deliverables, viral marketing, and so on to ensure greater success. In addition, role-based marketing demands a closeness between sales and marketing that is unprecedented in the market. Transforming your business to leverage role-based marketing will make you more successful with the selected roles. This creates profitability, which allows expansion into other areas. Because in the end, it is about having the dialogue that matters to your customers. Knowing what will make them successful and knowing their pains is what marketing is all about. And the Marketing 2.0 world demands more and more person-to-person marketing by role.

6

Lightly Branded: EepyBird, The Coca-Cola Company, and Mentos

A brand for a company is like a reputation for a person. You earn reputation by trying to do hard things well.
—Jeff Bezos

I just got back from my husband's basketball game. All night long I cheered for his team, which is one of many teams in a great men's basketball league in New York. During the evening, I started noticing a brand on the basketball jersey. It wasn't the focus of the jersey or the game. However, for a local group, it was a subtle, brand statement that the number-one team was associated with them. And, for me, it was a positive, local, and personal association with a global brand. As we discussed in Chapter 4, "Fish Where the Fish are and Use the Right Bait," lightly branding and brands driven by communities are growing in the market. The case study discussed in this chapter demonstrates how being a custodian of a brand is sometimes more powerful than owning it! While leveraging new media types to do it, Diet Coke and Mentos found themselves in a great lightly branded situation with a viral video whose goal was to entertain. In the end, the entertainment value was high and increased sales to Diet Coke and Mentos.

Focus on Lightly Branding

Customer-driven branding happens all around us. Companies today are custodians of their brands, not the owners. Companies have spent years building their brand equity. Now, in a global world, consumers take that brand equity and build their own stories. In 2006, a small two-person firm and physical theater company called EepyBird helped to place the mega brands of Diet Coke and Mentos into the hands of its customers. With a three-minute video called "Experiment #137," Stephen Voltz and Fritz Grobe made history.

First, let's go back. This video did not start as a marketing vision. It started in October, 2005, with a lawyer and a juggler who had heard from a fellow performer that dropping Mentos mints into Diet Coke creates a surprisingly powerful geyser of soda. For a show they had that night at the Oddfellow Theater, the small theater they work out of in Buckfield, Maine, they made a fountain using ten bottles of Diet Coke—that was the first "experiment." The effect on the crowd was amazing, and the people at the theater went crazy. These two performers thought they had something powerful! They then spent about six months working on creating over a dozen different effects. The concept was born.

This example illustrates that marketing is inspired in everyday situations, especially around the idea of having consumers "help" with your brand. It must relate to them. Now, we go into more depth about how this video was adopted by Diet Coke and Mentos. Since January, 2006, they've been through about 4,000 bottles of Diet Coke and over 36,000 Mentos, and in the process, they have worked with customers to strengthen these brands.

Focus on EepyBird's Grobe and Voltz

Fritz Grobe and Stephen Voltz are not your normal marketers. Grobe started out as a mathematician and dropped out of Yale so he could spend more time juggling. He is a five-time gold medal winner at the International Juggling Championships. He set a world record for juggling, and as he puts it, "way too many objects at the same time," and he toured with a Cirque du Soleil spinoff that he helped create called Birdhouse Factory. He has worked in theater and circus since he was a teenager. Voltz was a practicing litigator for more than 20 years in the Boston area. He is also an entertainer and was a street performer as a teenager in San Francisco, where he did magic, juggled, and was a fire-eater.

What Is EepyBird?

EepyBird is a small company that combines the power of entertainment and marketing to assist companies in lightly branding their products. Grobe and Voltz currently travel around the world performing Diet Coke and Mentos live shows and are now in the midst of creating new works using other consumer brands.

The Customers

EepyBird's primary customers are The Coca-Cola Company and the Perfetti Van Melle Corporation (maker of Mentos). It is expanding with other companies, and Grobe and Voltz continue to perform at their home base in Maine at the Oddfellow Theater.

The Product

The product is a creative use of products and entertainment in theatrical productions and videos. EepyBird explores how everyday objects can do extraordinary things.

The Marketing Best Practice

The marketing best practice is how EepyBird used a viral video for lightly branding two powerful brands. In Figure 6.1, you can watch the original version—Experiment #137. The video of two "scientists," 101 bottles of Diet Coke, and more than 500 Mentos that showed the reaction of the two products together in a huge fountain effect was virally passed around the world.

Grobe and Voltz put the video of this experiment on their Web site, EepyBird.com, and they told one person and went off to the theater to perform. That's all it took. As Fritz commented, "Stephen told his brother, that's it. One person, and so just a few hours later we were up to 4,000 views. By the end of the night, we were up to 20,000. On Monday morning, *The Late Show with David Letterman* called, and the producer had seen mention of it on a German blog. So it went from Voltz's brother to this German blog to the producer on Letterman." This was Experiment #137. As Voltz stated, "For Diet Coke and for Mentos, it was the moment when consumers took over the respective brands." Stephen and Fritz did two major Diet Coke and Mentos viral videos that year. The first one they did on their own, and The Coca-Cola Company sponsored the second one. The results were that Diet Coke saw significant sales of two-liter bottles and Mentos' sales went up more than 15 percent for the year.

Figure 6.1 Experiment #137: The Original.

Please see companion Web site at ibmpressbooks.com/angels for an interesting Diet Coke and Mentos experiment.

The Lightly Brand Agenda at
The Coca-Cola Company and EepyBird

The first video that EepyBird did was successful. Not just in the viral momentum but the effect on The Coca-Cola Company and Mentos brands. The reaction from Mentos was positive. Mentos called EepyBird within the first couple of weeks and asked how it might help and what it might do for EepyBird, especially because Voltz said that Mentos increased its sales by about 15 percent!

As Voltz commented, "One of the reasons that I think the Diet Coke and Mentos video was so effective was that it had a strong brand presence, but it wasn't about selling those brands, it was about having fun with those brands. We could have called it the extreme soda and candy experiment, and it came down to again an artistic decision to go with the powerhouse brands. In the end, we wanted people to understand that this is just soda and candy, and the way to do that is to call it Diet Coke and Mentos. It's a way for people to connect with these iconic brands. It's not so much about distinguishing between one similar brand and another. It's about making these brands fun and approachable."

As Voltz told me, "After The Coca-Cola Company saw what it was doing for sales of two-liter bottles of Diet Coke, the global interactive marketing team was asking, 'How we can help make the next video?'"

So The Coca-Cola Company and EepyBird formed a partnership after Michael Donnelly, director of Worldwide Interactive Marketing at The Coca-Cola Company, realized the potential from this viral video and its impact on The Coca-Cola Company brand and sales. As Donnelly says, "Our goals were to use this opportunity to celebrate creativity, self expression, and amateur artistry around the world. This is a great example of connecting people in a happy and positive way and a good representation of what we call living on the Coke side of life." For EepyBird, as Voltz comments, "We wanted to see where this viral success could take us. We wanted to apply our entertainment skills in a marketing context and do it with a powerful brand such as The Coca-Cola Company. The globalness of the venture was a huge plus." This highlights the savviness of The Coca-Cola Company and EepyBird engaging the everyday consumer to help in The Coca-Cola Company brand. This example is the essence of lightly branding. Consumers are helping in the creation of the brand attributes.

After Experiment #137, The Coca-Cola Company and EepyBird went on to Experiment #214. In addition to the experiment, The Coca-Cola Company ran Google Video's first ever online viral video advertising contest called "Poetry in Motion." The contest asked customers to produce and create their own videos. No press or push was done on the contest—it was simply done with the viral effect, and the winner was flown to Maine to work with EepyBird on the next video.

As Voltz explained, "Experiment #214 had over eight million views, was the #1 shared link among teens for three straight months, the #1 video on Google Video Top 100 for nine straight days, and the #31 viewed video of all time on Google Video." In Figure 6.2, you see the YouTube posting of this second video.

EepyBird's second viral video set a record as the contest promotion won Best in Show at OMMA Webby and was nominated for an Emmy. Coca-Cola doubled its site traffic and realized tremendous media efficiency. What made this so successful? As discussed in the following sections, there are three secrets to its success: edutainment, authenticity, and fans!

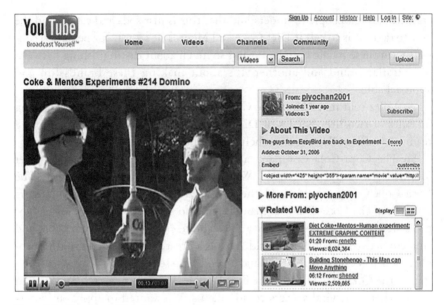

Figure 6.2 Experiment #214: the next round.

It Is Entertainment—Edutainment!

When I talked to both Grobe and Voltz, I discovered that their theater training, their clowning, and their juggling mindset came into play with their lightly branded video. I find this to be true across the board in marketing. The more fun that is combined with education or value, the more success you have. As Grobe comments, "We explored Diet Coke and Mentos in exactly the same way that I explore how balls can bounce off the floor, looking for ways in which you can discover something new, exploring some quirk about how the world works, and turning that into something that gets people excited."

I am fascinated with this story because Grobe and Voltz have combined marketing with entertainment. And I've found in my more than 15 years of marketing that the most entertaining videos move products. Marketing is part entertainment. Grobe and Voltz's focus going forward is not to deviate from this secret. They want to continue to create things that first and foremost are entertaining and look for the opportunities to use them to connect with brands. It's amazing to think that 40 million people watched that first video because it was fun, but it's even more amazing to realize that because of the way they lightly branded, sales significantly increased.

Application to Your Company

When you pull out your marketing plans, review them for their power of product value and fun. With the amount of information people have to deal with today, they are looking for something that stands out and captures their attention and imagination.

Marketplace patterns show that video consumption is huge. Sound bytes of information combined with entertainment are becoming more effective in the Digital Age. A CNN-like snippet combined with entertainment works in the digital marketplace. As Blaise Pascal said, "I have made this longer, because I have not had the time to make it shorter. Review your plans for an entertainment value that is short and to the point of value for your product or service.

Authentic

As Grobe explains, people on the Internet can sense when you're not being real. It's one of the biggest powers that customers now have—they can just click to something else. In the era of authenticity, bacyard experiments, wild and crazy ideas of building furniture out of FedEx boxes, and other ways that you can get people to look at your brand in a way that they've never looked at it before, create an authentic and fun look at your brand. It might not be the usual way that they use your product, but it creates a new context. Lightly branded is about combining existing brand attributes in new ways. The product shot is just that, a product, not a brand.

The powerful marketing effect here is that EepyBird stayed true to its mission—it did lightly branded shots that were real. Go back and rewatch the video. There is no real product placement. There are no Diet Coke logos, Mentos, or pictures showing and saying, "Isn't this refreshing or don't you love these mints?" There is no typical ad content hidden inside. As Voltz commented, "The second video we did had a little still frame at the end that said, 'Thank you to the folks at Diet Coke and Mentos for making this possible' or something light like that. If people thought they were watching a commercial and that someone was trying to sell them stuff, they wouldn't pass it onto their friends. They'd watch it and say, 'That's kind of cool.' The video had all these fans because we were using the product in a fun way. It was not a secret ad for The Coca-Cola Company. And the simple fact that we were honest got the very result The Coca-Cola Company wanted. The very light branding moved a lot of product."

Application to Your Company

In this type of marketing, you want your brand featured enough to be present so everyone knows what it is, but no more than that. Customers need to feel like they are experiencing your brand, not watching a commercial. In this mix of marketing, look for something people see that they enjoy and that has an emotional resonance. You want them to associate that feeling with the brand.

Be upfront with what you are doing in the market. If you want to advertise, advertise. However, if you want to use your product in a nontraditional way to show your brand personality, leverage that in your work. As Voltz says, "Our position to The Coca-Cola Company was that 'we can't take your money if we're going to betray our fans, your customers.' They're coming to us to see something that they think is authentic, that has a real feeling of authenticity. We can't betray that."

Fans and Friends

An interesting observation from Voltz was that he felt his video touched people on a 1:1 basis. Is it possible that a video that 40 million people watched was actually a 1:1 marketing tactic? Did that make these viewers not just customers, but fans? Voltz explains, "It's like having your own corner store. It's a personal presence where people can go and interact. And that's what's appealing to the digital kids. In the virtual world, it seems you can begin to approach a more interpersonal relationship with folks than through the TV or radio or print."

It is interesting to compare the different types of media that you can use to market. Obviously, 1:1 marketing has been talked about for awhile, but not in the context of making your customers your fans. Today, marketing is about having a multitude of conversations inside and outside the company. As we discussed earlier in this chapter, individuals now have a loud voice in the brand, so the more 1:1 situations you can manage in this complex world, the better. These conversations, however, are no longer in a controlled and polished messaging machine.

Voltz says, "They say TV is a cold medium and radio a hot medium. With radio, you feel like you know the people on the radio. They seem like your friend, and they're sitting in your car with you while you drive. Television is celebrity-based, and there's a wall between you and the glamorous people. Each works on their end of the spectrum."

However, the Web is a mixed medium. Like radio, you can get a sense of a personal connection. Even if millions of people watch a video, it feels like it's just you sitting there watching. With Experiment #137, there was a lot of personal stuff throughout the video. At least one path on the Web is to recognize the power of what it feels like in a 1:1 personal communication. As Voltz says, "When you are in the theater, you want to reach and touch each person in an individual way. That's the goal in the videos that we do. We place a small bit of us in each, and therefore, look for the one-on-one opportunities." Know that clients will buy more than your product or service; they also buy your personality and your values.

Customers want to do business with a company that has a human face on it, not just another big giant corporation. If you do your viral video correctly, you can make a personal connection with many corporate customers and fans. The point is to make them into fans, not just customers, and you create fans one at a time.

Application for Your Company

Explore where and how you let your company's personality shine to make your customers into fans. Your personality reinforces the idea that you want to have some kind of connection with customers. The ways in which you interact matter. Your company's personality can come through in the form of a shared enthusiasm or a reflection of its values. An emotional connection that occurs when you engage with your consumers is a requirement to make customers turn into fans.

What's the practical application here? Nilofer Merchant, CEO of Rubicon, made this a reality by changing the perception of one of her IT clients. Her view was that almost all IT ads can be written by the same person because they all claim high performance or high redundancy. To have her client's personality shine through, she went behind the scenes to give customers a sneak peek of the client's passion about its product. The video's goal is to shine the company's personality and passion for their product through their everyday actions portrayed in a fun way using the IT company's own programmers.

What activity could you do to show your true face and turn your customers into fans? Another example is from our IBM Impact conference in 2007. We had more than 25 percent of our conference session—that's 104 customer speakers—tell their story authentically! The impact for us was that customers left more fans than before because they heard the good and the tough and were able to see how loyal other customers were.

Similar to the way that people individually can be more transparent to their friends and, therefore, more engaging, companies can be themselves online and start to become more passionate about who they are and what they care about. People are more likely to share with their friends. That's what EepyBird did in their own way; they created both friends and fans.

EepyBird Lessons Learned

EepyBird and The Coca-Cola Company articulated some of their most valuable lessons learned.

Artists

Artists have opportunities there haven't been in 100 years—a poet or a musician or any artist. Artists can reach an audience now without having to be discovered. Grobe commented, "There's a chance with the Internet to get to your audience. And that's exciting. I think it's a time in history for everyone who creates as a living or as a hobby to take a chance. Because it's unique, I think, in history to be able to reach so many people with whatever little thing you find."

This creates the more personal challenge for people to not forget their inner talents. I was sitting next to a woman on a plane not too long ago; she's a visual video artist and sells her work on the Internet. Selling online is like having a gallery, but she didn't have to be discovered by a gallery first before reaching potential customers. She can begin to make a living while still pursuing shows in galleries. This is just one example. We live in an exciting time and people should go after their dreams!

The Model Is Changing

Voltz and Grobe envision many changes for marketing in today's culture. Going beyond the control of the message, other changes in the dynamic market exist. An example of the business model changes occurring with cocreation and action consumers is McAfee. McAfee offers customer lead support for technical problems. The internet has enabled a community of unpaid volunteers to assist each other via a set of archived questions and answers. Because there are other companies who make their living selling support, this era of the "prosumer"—or the proactive consumer—is going to change business models around the world.

Right-Brained, Left-Brained

An interesting discussion was around the approach of creativity and how much creativity should be present in your marketing. Russell Sawchuk wrote (based on Jay Conrad Levinson's excellent book called *Guerrilla Marketing*), "Your marketing can be twice as effective if you aim it at both right-brained (emotional, aesthetic) and left-brained (logical, sequential) people. The North American population is about evenly divided, so if you use only one approach, half your marketing budget will be wasted." The lesson learned from The Coca-Cola Company and Mentos is that this right-brained approach can't be your only touch point with the customer. There needs to be balanced marketing across the board to reach the mixed audience.

Conclusion

Lightly branding is about trusting your customer to see the value of your brand in an indirect, dynamic format. The concept encourages you to look at your brand in a way that the customers have never looked at it before, but a way that is authentic and expresses your company's personality. Fans and friends are not created overnight, but over time. The artist in you can come out in your marketing to the right-brained folks to drive a more dynamic form of lightly branded marketing. Clients have made the Internet a media of social and emotional connection. Differentiation is no longer about product or service, but about the concept of engagement, the level of engagement, and the degree to which a company succeeds in creating an intimate, long-term relationship with the customer. Lightly branding is one way to start that long-term relationship, while having fun.

For additional Coke and Mentos content, go to ibmpressbooks.com/angels.

To see the viral video, go to ibmpressbooks.com/angels.

7

Corporate Social Responsibility: IBM's Project Green and Marks & Spencer

It's not easy being Green.
—Kermit the Frog

As we discussed in Chapter 4, "Fish Where the Fish Are and Use the Right Bait," corporate social responsibility (CSR) and green initiatives are core tenets in today's society and in today's marketing. Even the American Marketing Association (AMA) has defined green marketing on Wikipedia.org. The reason is clear. According to Green Markets International, Inc., a recent survey discovered that 94 percent of all consumers prefer to do business with companies that demonstrate that they care about the environment. Almost 80 percent said they would pay more for environmentally friendly products.

Gartner, an industry analyst firm, forecasts by the end of next year that 50 percent of large- and medium-sized IT organizations in Europe will declare a green imperative due to financial, legislative, risk-related, and environmental pressures. However, less than 20 percent of organizations outside Europe will do the same.

Forrester, an industry analyst firm, has determined that clients submit roughly 20,000 analyst inquiries each year. In aggregate, these one-on-one interactions create a map of topical hotspots among Forrester's client base, with important insights for technology marketers. Since initiating research on green IT trends, Forrester analysts have fielded a steadily growing number of client inquiries on green topics, including corporate sustainability planning, data center energy efficiency, IT recycling, and green marketing tactics. This set of inquiries provides a window into the growing mindshare that environmental considerations have among IT professionals and their suppliers.[1] Given this strategic imperative of going green and corporate sustainability, how to market CSR is a top-priority topic.

In this case study, IBM's focus on CSR and the way it has taken its strategy to market will be summarized the case study on IBM's Project Big Green. IBM charted a course to redirect $1 billion in annual spending across its businesses toward the goal of dramatically increasing the level of energy efficiency in IT. The plan also included new products, services, and marketing for IBM and its clients that would sharply reduce data center energy consumption, transforming the world's business and public technology infrastructures into green data centers. When IBM premiered Project Big Green in May 2007, it did so out of the conviction that energy costs and climate changes are major issues confronting not only society but, more specifically, data centers. IBM was convinced that it had an important role to play in enabling data centers to become more efficient users of energy to reduce its carbon footprint.

Top Five Best Practices for CSR

To see how IBM's best practices shine through, we review the top five best-practice areas from Chapter 4 and show how IBM has effectively marketed the effort. As a reminder, those five areas are

1. Focus on becoming a role model company.
2. Evaluate your partners and suppliers.
3. Measurements matter.
4. Educate yourself and your company.
5. Evaluate your brand.

The following three key leaders address the details of IBM's marketing efforts: John Soyring, vice president of Industry Solutions and board member on IBM's Energy and Environment Board; Rich Lechner, vice president of Project Green; and Steve Cole, segment leader for one of the Green Solutions areas in IBM Energy Efficiency Technologies and Services.

Focus on Becoming a Role-Model Company

IBM has a longstanding involvement in the issues of environmental protection and conservation. In fact, going back to 1971, IBM's chairman at the time, Tom Watson, Jr., put in place the company's first corporate policy on environmental protection. Through the years, IBM has invested billions of dollars to develop new products, services, and technologies across the company to help its clients and the company achieve substantial energy conservation. Globally, IBM has around 850 specialists working on energy efficiency. For IBM, as you can see, the environment has been core to its business strategy for more than four decades.

When IBM started to focus on Project Green, it had a solid business strategy and history behind its marketing push. The tipping point for IBM's marketing focus was around the global crisis in climate and energy supply. As a reminder, just ten years ago, oil was $20 a barrel!

Recently, IBM's Boulder, Colorado, data center was expanded and retrofitted to meet the green-building rating standards, the Leadership in Energy and Environmental Design, developed by the U.S. Green Building Council. In addition to deploying energy-saving IT features such as virtualization of servers and storage in the Boulder data center, IBM has contracted with the local utility to be supplied with 1,000 megawatts of electricity generated by wind power.

Application to Your Business

Many companies today are accused of greenwashing. What is greenwashing? *Greenwashing* involves any scenario wherein a company issues false or misleading claims about a product's green attributes and its capability to provide an environmental benefit through use. The negative backlash and potential damage to the brand that can occur because of greenwashing can result in a public-relations nightmare. This is why, for any company, a green marketing campaign must be considered in a holistic manner, taking into account brand image, customer demands, and the overall strategy for the business. In short, there must be a credible link to your business in the environmentally sound way it delivers or produces goods and services before the green marketing campaigns are launched. As Rich Lechner comments, "Green is an area where it is incredibly important to have substantiation behind all claims. The market is experiencing greenwashing from companies in every industry, so having credible, documented proof of positive customer impact is critical."

You can read a sidebar on some important lessons learned in greenwashing at ibmpressbooks.com/angels.

You can be assured that if you begin marketing green or around the environment without a focus on your business strategy being solid, you will have a negative impact on your marketing. According to doorsofperception.com, the UK government is taking steps to discourage greenwashing. Consumer watchdog groups look for corporate bad behavior, particularly in the arena of greenwashing. Thanks to Web 2.0 technologies, these groups are empowered with the capability to quickly mobilize and raise awareness to brands accused of greenwashing through e-mail, blogs, and social networking sites. Nielsen Online suggests that the blogosphere can be treacherous territory when it comes to the announcements of corporate green initiatives. The report called greenwashing a "failed corporate strategy." Jessica Hogue, research director of Nielsen Online, says, "When it comes to the environment, consumers are insisting on both transparency and consistency from the corporations they patronize. Consumer support depends on action as well as perceived sincerity and commitment."

How do you evaluate your strategy and know what is the right approach to take in the name of showcasing your green initiatives, products, and services? First, determine where your company has focused its efforts, such as energy, carbon reduction efforts, and so on. Then see how integrated that focus on the environment is with your business strategy. Evaluate your integrated program of action and ensure that you have the investment behind the strategy. For instance, have you established effective green human resource (HR) policies for travel and remote working? Have you engaged with your employees on the green agenda and enabled sustainable behavior change across your business? Additionally, clear the way for innovation. The concept of "going green" is not only a strategic thought, but it also requires some cultural shift to thrive. Incorporate green thinking into not only business operations and processes but also into the way you think about designing, developing, and delivering products and services to your customers. Like any other strategic initiative, to be successful, your message and goal must resonate from the inside out.

Evaluate Your Partners and Suppliers

IBM continues to focus on ensuring that its own supply chain and that of its suppliers are committed to these areas of CSR. Again, for CSR and green, the preparedness before you make claims is paramount.

IBM is well positioned to be first to market with fresh new thinking and solutions on how companies need to tweak or reconfigure their supply chains to minimize their environmental impact. Of all major consultancies, we have the unique blend of a world-class supply chain management consulting practice, our internal supply chain (recognized as one of AMR's Top 25 Supply Chains in the world), and a great tradition of a leading innovative research group.

For example, with the market's enthusiastic reception for Project Big Green, IBM is already at work planning the next phase of what could be called Project Big Green 2.0. One feature of Project Big Green 2.0 is Energy Efficiency Certificates. Last year, IBM announced the first corporate-led initiative to assist clients, partners, and suppliers to earn Energy Efficiency Certificates for the power reductions achieved in their data center. The certificates are based on energy use reduction verified by a third party, Neuwing Energy, and provide a recognized way for businesses to attain a certified measurement of their energy use reduction. The certificates can be traded for cash on the growing energy efficiency certificate market or otherwise retained to demonstrate reductions in energy use and associated carbon emissions.

Application to Your Business

For your partners and suppliers, how do you ensure they are in support of your overall business strategy? This includes your marketing agencies. For instance, your agency could share their green standards with you through events. To market an environmental story, you must make sure that your strategy and the strategy of your partners and suppliers consistently and efficiently strive toward the same goal.

Measurements Matter to the Business Leaders–Market the Value

Speaking the language that is relevant to your clients is important. Focus on the right value proposition and messaging of value are critical. IBM adjusted its message according to the role. For example, for the CEO role, the message is about corporate sustainability. For the CFO role, the message instead focuses around financial implications, such as treating energy spend like other costs. In your green initiatives, show the positive impact on the environment and on business with your products and services.

In the latest press release on progress in the Project Green initiative, IBM discussed how to achieve energy efficiency and reduce carbon dioxide (CO_2) emissions with green solutions. The metrics used were both substantial and relevant. The typical 25,000 square foot data center can reduce its energy use up to 40 percent through energy efficiency projects. Assuming that the data center uses 22,000-megawatt hours (MWH) of electricity, this would represent savings of 8,700 MWH and one million dollars. The estimated energy efficiency savings would avoid the 6,700 metric tons of CO_2 emissions, which is the equivalent of 1,200 automobiles or seven million pounds of coal burned for energy generation.

As Rich Lechner comments, "This is a fast-moving market. A year ago, the primary drivers for clients being interested in green IT were financial (rising cost of energy coupled with dramatic growth in computer and data capacity requirements) and operational (customers literally could not deploy new servers or storage in support of new business opportunities or process changes because they could not get more power into their data centers or dissipate the heat that was in them). However, during the last six months, we have seen a rapid increase in environmental responsibility (sustainability, carbon footprint reduction commitments, and so on) as the driver for green IT projects."

From the February, 2008 report, "The Greening of Government," Janet Caldow (director of the Institute for Electronic Government®, IBM Corporation) found that "one third of respondents cited executive orders or regulations as the primary drivers of their green agendas. Twenty-five percent named economics. Nearly one-third cited ethics or sustainability as the key drivers. And, 10 percent identified energy independence. However, when queried further, almost 70 percent of respondents referred to economic factors, as they described reasons for their responses. For example, many executive orders were initially motivated by economics—cost savings associated with energy reduction. Those who named energy independence associated it with economic implications. Paradoxically, although study participants are motivated by different forces, they share common green priorities all related to energy reduction (green buildings, green transportation, and green procurement)."

As with any marketing project, ensure that you know what matters to your customer. Be sure you can articulate clearly the value that your project brings to the business leaders. At IBM, we find that green resonates across disciplines—from line of business leaders and CIOs, to the CFO and the board of directors. It is also grass-roots-driven and employees, shareholders, and customers ask companies what they are doing to be more energy efficient and environmentally friendly. For example, for IBM, we focus on case studies to show the value to the business.

Kalbe, a leading pharmaceutical and health company in Indonesia, teamed with IBM to deploy data center consolidation with an explicit goal of reducing energy consumption as well as reducing IT maintenance and space in its data center facilities, which are spread across different sites in Jakarta. IBM will help Kalbe to consolidate 5 data centers from its current 13 existing data centers during the initial phase, which will save the company space and reduce IT maintenance cost.

The bottom line is that your marketing needs to show that environmental investments are made for the same reason companies make other investments: because they expect them to deliver positive returns or to reduce risks.

Application to Your Company

There is no magic in green marketing. The basics make a difference. Understanding the value proposition by role and having solid references and offerings to back up the value statements are required, whether those statements are made to companies or to consumers. For example, Erik De Heus, CEO of Oxxio B.V, has leveraged smart meters in the Netherlands. It replaced the existing meters, which are typically the traditional meters, with smart meters. And on a daily basis, they collect all the 15 minutes of data throughout the day of each customer who has this meter installed. So customers can see on the Internet in an easy fashion their consumption, but also what have they done throughout the day to help reduce consumption. When you do something like smart metering, you can definitely have an impact on the way the end consumer ends up either thinking about or considering, not consuming, that last bit of electricity.

How can you apply this approach of giving your buyers and consumers a better line of sight? Helping all to understand the consequences of their actions must be one of the most powerful forces for change as we deal with this issue of climate, the environment, energy and technology, and how they intersect. Make sure you evaluate your references in this way.

Educate Yourself and Your Company

One of the interesting observations is that companies that do well with their various green initiatives educate their employees on green methods for both home and business. Again, being green means that it is embedded in your company's DNA. To be successful, it must be an embodiment of your business strategy. Your employees are the biggest evangelists you have. Ensure they are in sync with your strategy. IBM internally showcases, on its intranet, employees' personal green efforts. For example, Jochen Burkhardt, virtual worlds architect of IBM's Boeblingen Lab, built a smart house equipped with a monitoring system to control energy consumption. The house begins to warm up bath water when his alarm clock rings. As he locks his door on his way to work, the heating and cooling units start to run on minimum mode—all lights go dark. "I can turn up the heat from work right before I leave the office. When I get home, it's warm, and there is no unnecessary energy spent for heating when I'm away," said Burkhardt.

Steve Wilson, IBM team lead of the new product introduction team of Tucson, Arizona, clocks 32 miles in two hours on his bike every day—more than 70,000 miles since he began to advocate alternative modes of transportation in 2005. Steve says, "We're lucky in Tucson. There isn't much inclement weather. I have cold weather gear for the cold winter mornings, and I use insulated water bottles, so I always have ice water, even on the hottest summer days. And I always have my rain jacket with me, just in case."

IBM even encourages internal blogging on the best green ideas such as establishing a rebate program that rewards employees for being green and making environmentally sound and sustainable decisions. We even did a video contest for the employees looking for great Green Solutions and gave away cool prizes. (See Figure 7.1.)

Application to Your Business

How do you plan to assist the green movement throughout your marketing organization and the company? I view marketing as being the internal and external evangelists. On your intranet, highlight your green superstars. Train your teams on collaboration tools and telepresence services. Think about travel management policies and guidelines as well as how you run your conferences. For our IMPACT 2008 event, we had a green day and provided a reusable water bottle for attendances. However, we did not think through the recyclable bins and other elements of green that we will work through for IMPACT 2009. Even ideas such as employee engagement programs to support a carbon strategy can provide you credibility across the board.

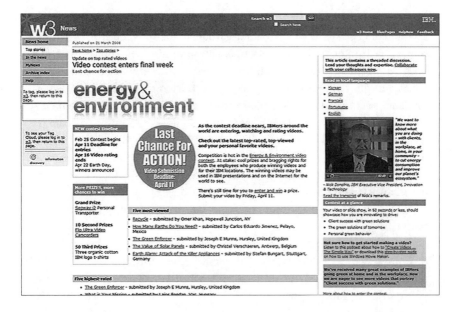

Figure 7.1 IBM's green employees.

Power Up Your Brand to Be Green–When You Think Green, Think Blue!

Well, it took us a while to get to the true marketing elements. However, in this space, it is crucial that you take the time to truly be green, not just market green. Without the basics laid, your company cannot be successful in this space.

GUILT-FREE MARKETING FOR
THE GREEN REVOLUTION

James Governor, Founder and CEO of Redmonk

If you're not a sustainability "true believer," one of the natural fears of marketing products with a green spin is that there is something hypocritical about it. However, there is nothing wrong with spin if the outcomes are positive. If your product makes a process more efficient, why not talk up the energy savings, and related carbon reductions, and provide customers with information to help make a more informed choice? There is nothing wrong with eco-rebranding. Great marketing isn't broadcasting a message, after all, it's engaging in a conversation that can change behaviors and make markets. When Nortel targeted Cisco in advertisements touting more power-efficient switches, some data center customers rethought their buying criteria. The result: lower electricity bills for customers, potentially providing Nortel with more marketing ammunition for the next round of competition. Cisco, of course, responded with product innovation and further market conversations.

Isn't that the kind of result that got you into marketing in the first place?

For the first time in my adult life, I am truly proud to be in the IT business. Why? Because of the leadership the industry is showing in terms of sustainability capabilities and narratives. The public sector is doing a lot of talking, while many industries desperately need help to prevent them from going underwater. I am not talking about rising sea levels, but rising oil prices. Ensuring energy supplies is perhaps the most profound risk facing many businesses today. Sustainability is about remaking an airline industry predicated on oil costing less than $80 a barrel. It's certainly not about sandals and tree hugging.

Green, though, is also aspiration. I mentioned pride. Well, we're seeing sustainability drive a powerful new alignment between corporations and employees. Employees can be deeply proud of who they work for, which also helps recruitment of the best and brightest. When green drives a sense of purpose *internally*, you're also likely to see better customer service and happier customers *externally*.

Isn't that the kind of result that got you into marketing in the first place? Don't fight a sense of purpose in others—tap into it. The best marketing is like pushing a snowball downhill. It's not spin; it's human nature.

Now for Project Big Green. How did we communicate our green credentials to our customers? The following list answers this question:

- **We helped customers get started based on our experience.** We established our passion and commitment to this space so clients want to know how we did it. Our marketing engine kicked off with a set of assessments to guide customers in their quest for becoming green based on our experiences with our clients but equally with ourselves.

- **We let the word-of-mouth marketing of customers lead the story.** In addition to IBM being a core reference, IBM wanted other clients to speak in the marketplace. Companies such as Nordcapital Holding GmbH & Cie. KG, Daito Trust Construction Co., First Data Corp., and MetLife were some of the first customers to speak out about IBM's green capabilities, according to Steve Cole.

- **We customized by industry pain.** For green, customization by role and industry is important. For instance, in the aerospace industry, it is important to help alleviate the pressure on the airline industry to reduce emissions. For automotive, the movement to green is about a move to alternative drivetrain technologies. BMW, General Motors, and Daimler Chrysler have all joined forces to look at hybrid electric vehicles. The construction industry is a big CO_2-emissions focus, and cement production is one of the biggest Greenhouse Gas (GHG) emitters. As you can see, each of these industries has an area of focus.

- **We focused on compelling, emotional, and business values.** The marketing and sales teams worked together to ensure that the emotional and business aspects of green were qualified in a set of sales kits. Qualifying questions for customers include

  - Are you under pressure to reduce energy costs?—Typically, they are 30 to 40 percent of your operating budget and growing by double digits!

  - Do you plan to build a new data center? Have you optimized your current IT architecture? Keep in mind, typical server utilization in a nonoptimized environment is only 5 to 15 percent.

  - Does your company have a "green" energy plan? Again, it is about your strategy.

  However, the marketing that Lechner did went beyond the business value and into the societal values of corporate responsibility. This decision was marketed as a head and heart decision. The emphasis on a company's role in the world is equally important as its bottom line.

- **Live the marketing!** The team took its mission of green seriously. For instance, instead of traveling, the team leverages Second Life for demos and to brainstorm ideas. The IBM Virtual Green Data Center was created as a realistic and immersive experience of what a green company is and actually simulates experiences for visitors to learn how to manage and improve energy efficiency. In Figure 7.2, you get a sneak peek of the second life view!

Figure 7.2 Going green in Second Life!

Application to Your Business

Questions you should ask about how you market your greenness include "What are the new green market opportunities and how do you leverage them? From a product-management perspective, how can you design your products to be more carbon-friendly? How do you optimise these benefits throughout the full product lifecycle? How do you ensure that your market-ing shows the world the green values you have, for instance at events, or in the way you travel to customers." Policies in the United States and other countries govern Environmental Marketing Claims in the United States such as the National Environmental Policy Act. Please see online Chapter 4 for the details of this act at ibmpressbooks.com/angels. Make sure you familiarize yourself with the right set of marketing tactics.

Project Green Results to Date

On the one-year anniversary of Project Big Green's launch, it's clear the project is making its mark on the data-center landscape. Arguably the biggest validation of these efforts came earlier in 2008 when IDG Computerworld selected IBM as the Top Green IT Company for 2008—an honor that was part of Computerworld's first Top Green IT Companies awards. Awards such as Computerworld's aren't handed out for just lip ser-vice to the cause of green computing. Rather, the award recognizes that IBM isn't simply "talking green" but is taking meaningful steps to reduce its CO_2 emissions inventory.

MARKS & SPENCER IS WELL POSITIONED FOR THE GREEN FUTURE

From IBM Global CEO Study: The Enterprise of the Future, IBM, 2008

To meet growing corporate social responsibility expectations, British retailer Marks & Spencer (M&S) has embarked on a €200-million, five-year plan that impacts almost every aspect of its operations.

When this effort launched in 2006, M&S knew it needed to engage customers in solving issues, not simply provide them with information. As one example, it gave shoppers bags "for life." If one wore out, its replacement was free. After four weeks, the retailer began charging for plastic bags, donating the proceeds to environmental charities. Quickly, customers began reevaluating whether they really needed a plastic bag. Even though the few cents didn't matter much financially, the fee made people stop and think.

Behind M&S's 35,000 products sit 2,000 factories, more than 20,000 farms, fisheries and forests, and an estimated 500,000 workers in the developing world. Through its recently established online supplier exchange, the company strives to simultaneously improve efficiency and sustainability. For instance, farmers who create biogases from farm waste are now selling green electricity to M&S—along with their beef.

M&S has proven it's possible to do well while doing good: the company's operating profit has increased at a compound annual growth rate of more than fourteen percent over the past five years.[2]

Conclusion

CSR is a requirement in today's business world. Green marketing has its challenges. Environmental and corporate responsibility must begin with the business formidable strategy, not just a set of messages. Your actions must come through in your partners, suppliers, and even employees. Only when the strategy is operational can you begin green marketing. AMR Research states, "We look at big companies like IBM as having a great influence on getting people to understand what the issues are and promoting those changes. IBM has been successful in this space first and foremost because of the groundwork laid. Secondly, it applied a set of powerful 'green-based' marketing strategies and tactics to drive its green credentials into the market with solid references, word of mouth, and influencers telling the story." Determine your corporate conscious and position and how you might play in the green world. With Project Big Green, IBM is leading by example. Clients are learning how they can reduce the CO_2 emissions associated with the operation of their data centers while at the same time simplifying and consolidating their data centers. The marketing journey has become one of assisting and encouraging change in others.

Endnotes

1. Source: February 29, 2008, "Forrester Clients Ask the What, Why, and How of Sustainable Computing," by Christopher Mines with Ellen Daley and Heidi Lo.

2. Marks & Spencer 2006 and 2007 Annual Reports.

For additional Green Marketing content, go to imbpressbooks.com/angels.

Go to Market
- Value Proposition
- Influencers
- Word of Mouth
- Relationships

8

Break Through the Noise

Things that upset a terrier may pass virtually unnoticed by a
Great Dane.
—Smiley Blanton

The Blanton quote is quite true, isn't it? Some things catch our attention and others don't. It has to do with several things—how many times you hear the message, how relevant the message is to you, how clever it is shown and discussed, and what your situation is. Noise can be defined as unwanted information. Advertisements on the Web, unwanted e-mails, or too much information can become noise in the Web 2.0 world. According to Wikipedia, noise can block, distort, or change the meaning of a message in both human and electronic communication. "Information Overload: We Have Met the Enemy and He Is Us," authored by Basex analysts Jonathan B. Spira and David M. Goldes, claims that interruptions from phone calls, e-mails, and instant messages eat up 28 percent of knowledge workers' work day, resulting in 28 billion hours of lost productivity a year. The addition of new collaboration layers force the technologies into untenable competitive positions, with phone calls, e-mails, instant messaging, and blog reading all vying for workers' time.

This chapter continues the discussion of the ANGELS framework, focusing on the new language of marketing. As shown in Figure 8.1, we look at how to break through the noise with a powerful go-to-market (GTM) plan that energizes the marketplace—including a defined geographical and local plan that supports the global objectives and use of the new Marketing 2.0 techniques.

Go to Market
- Value Proposition
- Influencers
- Word of Mouth
- Relationships

Figure 8.1   Go-to-market socially.

Operating as a globally integrated enterprise requires an understanding of the differing values that exist across various cultures and their potential impacts on the marketplace. Companies need to have a clearly defined set of goals that are integral to the business strategy, are well communicated throughout the global and local organization, and are leveraged to guide local actions. A strong global communications infrastructure achieves efficiencies by organizing and sharing best-of-breed, GTM plans and tactics across the globe, enabling local adaptation as required. The GTM plan must be built with relevance and value to defeat the noise.

With the strategy set and our story known, we have to prioritize the GTM elements necessary to break through the noise in the market, both traditionally and socially. The GTM plan is how you plan to take the story and the offerings to the market. You must have an integrated plan and strategy.

The following questions ensure you have the right plan for the intended audience despite the information overload:

- What are the execution priorities in the marketplace by country or geography from the segmentation?
- What is our value proposition foundation?
- Who do you take the priorities and value propositions to? What is the buying group and its role?
- How do you take the tactics to market?

To break through the noise, you must have a powerful message of relevance by local preference. The vessels matter only if you get the basics right.

Winning Prioritization

After you have laid out strategy, segmentation, and the high-level story, the winning priorities will vary and differ by geography, roles, and budget. Lack of prioritization drives unnecessary work and leads to integration issues internally. Externally, it leads to market confusion and focusing on unprofitable areas, as well as speaking the wrong language at the wrong time. In fact, it enables noise to continue because a company doesn't have the right focused mix or the right set of priorities to break through the marketplace noise.

Participation in setting priorities is critical to success so that all feel ownership of the actions. For example, it is about engaging sales early, so that you are not only building a plan that is credible in the marketing discipline, but you are also building a plan that is co-owned by sales. It is the combination of local sales and marketing priorities that need to factor into the marketing profile selection. For example, marketing might be setting an agenda for the future, but the market might need a simpler message that the sellers can sell today. Setting the priorities correctly would allow the dual set of goals but in a priority order.

Priorities can be suggested by the global team, but priorities need to have geography and local foundation. When problems occur, it is usually because no clear authority or accountability for prioritization is present. It is critical to prioritize for growth areas and for those core areas that supply ongoing revenue.

Ask the following key questions:

- At what level does marketing focus?
- How does marketing prioritize activities?
- Is there a framework for making decisions in the field?

Some of the core problems that we see are too many high priorities, too many teams trying to prioritize (worldwide, geographies, and sales), and lack of a process to prioritize. Best-practice companies provide a set of guidance to the geographies that enable for flexibility in their execution. The geography needs to work hand-in-hand with the worldwide team.

As shown in Figure 8.2, companies need to translate worldwide business and marketing priorities to local execution elements.

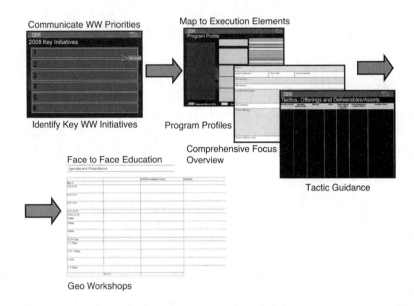

Figure 8.2   Geography guidance leads best practice.

The next section includes definitions of the key elements that IBM marketers use in their setting of guidance on priorities to the local teams, sales teams, and partners.

The elements of focus that we use at IBM are

- Local priorities
- Global priorities
- Program profile
- Focus Area guidance
- Tactical guidance
- Education

Local Priorities

The achievement of local geography targets is achieved through the mapping of offerings, value propositions, and key messages to tactical execution. These tactics are then placed into the mix in the marketplace, through a combination of traditional and Marketing 2.0 methods. The identification of all available assets and content to support local execution requirements should be done in face-to-face, comprehensive workshops, where each team can communicate its requirements and agree to a set of actions.

Global Priorities

Worldwide priorities are set in place by the headquarters or global team to drive the overall strategy. The best practice is to have tactic priorities and offer focus priorities. An example of a tactic priority is a focus on a certain number or type of roles in your role-based strategy or a set of goals for an emerging market or geography. For an offering focus, an example is a focus on a product category, such as SOA in the technology field or area.

Program Profile

A program profile addresses an area of market need or a category of solutions. The program profiles address broad customer needs as they occur at the business or division level. This means that a program profile might address multiple roles in either decision making or influencer roles. The creation of a standard messaging framework around the program profiles includes value propositions with supporting proof points. Those are then mapped to broad solutions. Where appropriate, offers and assets address the focus area level of the program profile. Program profiles must have longevity, which means that they must run at least four or more quarters.

Focus Area Guidance

Within each market need or category of solutions, specific ways and approaches to address business problems depend on the existing business environment and priorities exist. A focus area or play is a coordinated set of activities executed across direct marketing, business partner channels, communications, press, the Web, sales initiatives, and events to a select group of customers who would react to a market trigger and message. It is not a sequence of activities because all the activities can happen in parallel or in separate quarters. The key is the holistic view of the message across multiple GTM engines. For example, what you read on the Web is the same as what you see in the direct-mail piece, and both are consistent with what you hear at an event, what your sales rep or partner tells you, and what the press writes about. This surround sound enables you to go-to-market in a customer-centric way. It is a "natural" multitouch, surround strategy—not over-engineering in marketing flow charts.

In Figure 8.3, you see that the focus areas enable you to address these issues in a more granular, tactical way and from a marketing standpoint. They enable you to address the target-specific influencer and decision-maker roles in more defined market segments. They are likely to include not only the standard messaging framework but also a recommended approach to targeting market segments and roles. For example, your competitive customers worry about impending consolidation, architects in large enterprises look to get started with a new technology, business analysts in insurance companies look for ways to optimize processes, and application managers struggle to reuse existing applications. The focus areas should have assets that address the full marketing cycle. The focus areas and plays should be refreshed every quarter, and new focus areas should typically be introduced only when there is new messaging or market triggers that cannot be covered under existing plays. They should be constantly evaluated for effectiveness to see if they resonate in local markets.

Focus:		
Target Companies:	Target Titles:	Pains Addressed:
Play Scenario:		
IBM Solution:		
Top IBM Differentiators:		Proof Points:
Key Industries:		Key Competitors:
Primary Offerings:		Secondary Offerings:
Routes to Market: (OO):		

Figure 8.3 Focus area guidance for a local team.

Tactical Guidance

Within each focus area, apply tactical guidance. This tactical guidance leverages best-practice tactics that have worked across the world, but also what would be leading indicators in that region of the world. This tactical guidance recommends the right mix of tactics for a given focus area or play. For example, for some focus areas, there is a requirement for market education. The tactical guidance then recommends the marketing mix that is more focused on content syndication of White papers to provide education materials for potential customers. Compare that to a focus area or play where you need market presence where the recommendation is around visibility at third-party events. The guidance should make tactic recommendations based on the offer for that specific focus area and where the customer is in the adoption cycle and decision process.

We discuss more on the mix of the tactics in Chapter 11: "Energize the Channel with Communities: OMG, Adobe, and Rubicon Consulting, and Harley-Davidson." Finally, we provide a readiness worksheet for the geography as a way to have the local teams ensure they have covered all of their key areas. Shown in Figure 8.4, you see a sample checklist for a local team.

Ready for Q1?		Plan A - Momentum	Plan B - Expansion
Air Cover	Press and Analysts		
	Web Presence		
	Viral, Videos		
	Communications		
	Sales and Partner		
Program Execution	Events Strategy Enablement		
	X Brand Program Mgt Resources Incremental Budget		
	Q1 Geography Program Guidance		
	Q1 Geo tactical plans		
	Lead and Pipeline Targets Lead Management Plan & LGRs		
Deliverables	Demos and Videos		
	Sales Tools and Presentations		
	Collateral and Offers		
	Direct Marketing Deliverables		

Figure 8.4   Readiness execution scorecard.

Face-to-Face Education

Part of viewing great, best-practice companies is an in-person meeting to walk through the strategy, the segmentation, and the new story line so that the local team can ask questions and assimilate the guidance. At IBM, we do this in geography workshops. In these workshops, we have a two-way sharing of information and learn as much from the local team as it does from us.

For example, in a recent workshop, we learned that the geographies needed to shift resources from core marketing to winning new customers. This enabled our worldwide team to elevate the value of marketing to go beyond being a progression and assist engine to executing campaigns to grow in new accounts. It involved shifting funding from core activities to new customer assets.

This dialogue also enabled us to discover that for these new customers, a world-class, electronic nurturing machine was required. Based on that discovery, the marketing mix and investment to build a different kind of guidance was planned. It enabled us to funnel leads by interest area and continue the conversation with a new prospect, qualifying that prospect well before passing to our channel.

With the guidance in the hands of the local teams, they select what they will run based on local markets and budgets. As with most prioritization exercises, the guidance should consist of ways to review and focus on the geography plays. For example, as shown in Figure 8.5, we see a framework from David Parker, IBM GTS marketing executive. His best-practice model requires that the geography teams run only a specific number of plays across his portfolio, and he provides flexibility between small- and large-company plays. In the selection criteria, he has recommended a focus on the most attractive significant market potential, or gross margin, to drive a substantial portion of the revenue. In addition, because new acquisitions or new strategic growth plays might not meet the selection criteria, he works through the requested priorities with a strategic lens. He also provides guidance on how long to run plays, how often they are to be evaluated, and how the defining play priority must be done by targeted customer set and by the route to market.

Criteria	Unattractive	Attractive	Highly Attractive
Solution Differentiation	• Related service products lack clear differentiation	• Related products evaluated as market leading by Competitive Intelligence	• Related solutions recognized externally and internally as clearly differentiated
Revenue Plan	• Revenue target < $xM	• $xM < Revenue Target < $y0M	• Revenue target > $yM
Revenue Growth	• Planned revenue growth < a%	• a% < Planned revenue growth < b%	• Planned revenue growth > b%
Gross Profit Plan	• Related Products have GP < x%	• Related Service Products have x% <GP < z%	• Related Products have GP > z%
Market Share	• New entrant into market with < x% market share	• Recognized as leader in market with x% < Market Share < y%	• Market share leader with > y% share

Figure 8.5 Example of prioritization.

Top Five Lessons Learned for Prioritization of the GTM Guidance

Ensuring that your global priorities show up in the local markets guarantees that your strategy is executed to break through the noise. The following are the top five areas used as a checklist to prioritize for success:

1. **Identify global priorities and the guidance for geographies:** All teams around the world need to be guided by a set of priorities focused on the overall business strategy. You need to be crisp and clear in your communications of those priorities and guidance to provide direction for the local teams.
2. **Local priorities should be driven from global strategies:** Only then can you break through the noise on a country or even city basis. Guidance and a best-practice process to assist in making local priorities help drive greater success in each market.
3. **Two-way sharing:** Geography workshops helps clarify and share learning in a two-way fashion. We learn as much if not more from our geography teams.

4. **Checklist:** Provide the teams a checklist of all the items that team members need to think through to be successful. This assures quality of execution and a better mix going into the local market.

5. **Training and skills development:** This must be complete for products within the key focus areas. This sounds like basic advice, but sometimes a worldwide offering, for whatever reason, is not implementable at a local level.

Value Proposition

Now in the prioritization and guidance work, a core element in the focus areas is the value-proposition focus. A value proposition should be developed within the framework of our overall company's business strategy and segmentation. Figure 8.6 from Mezzanine Consulting, LLC, shows how it believes a value proposition fits with your business strategy and messages.

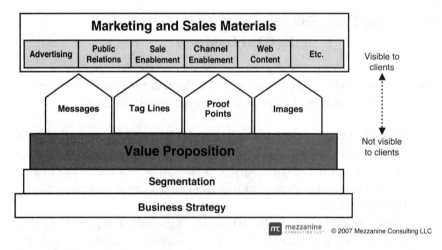

Figure 8.6   Value propositions are built on a company's segmentation and strategy.

The value proposition is one element of the overall marketing plan and is based on the overall business strategy. You should begin by thinking through your company's organization and your brand and develop a synergistic architecture. Value propositions sit on top of your business strategy. Generally, value propositions should be created when there's a need for a customer experience that sometimes requires customization at the geographical level. If you don't have a value proposition that is relevant to your client, no matter what else you do in the market, it will not be successful. The value proposition must matter in a significant way.

The key is where the customer is different, and if you can prove to yourself that the customer truly is different for a brand, geography, or a product area, you need a different or modified value proposition. For instance, I was recently in Dubai in the Middle East. We had a value proposition for the banking sector from a global basis that did not include Arabic Banking. Arabic Banking is an Islamic-based banking system that, among other principles, prohibits the collection and payment of interest. Because Arabic Banking was only 10 percent of the marketing opportunity worldwide, we had not added Arabic Banking as part of our overall value proposition. But in Dubai, it must be part of the local value proposition. This local knowledge required a modification of the value proposition and the offerings to truly be successful.

Value propositions are based on the target audience. Nima Parikh, a principal at Mezzanine Consulting, LLC, defines a value proposition as " what a business or offering stands for—a promise to deliver a specific benefit and the manner in which you will do so." She goes on to say that a value proposition is like the foundation of your house. Our value proposition is a promise to deliver a specific benefit. It's not visible to your neighbors any more than the value proposition is visible to your external clients, but everything rests on it. So, your neighbors can see your shutters and how you maintain them and even upgrade them for fashion, but it is the foundation that makes the house stand up strong.

Table 8.1 Four Characteristics of a Great Value Proposition

Differentiating	Relevant
Sets the offering apart from other direct and indirect competitive offerings	The offering and the point of differentiation truly matter to the customer
Compelling	**Enduring**
Gives the customer a credible reason to buy, following some sense of logic whether tangible or emotional	Long lasting, not easily duplicated by existing competitors or potential new entrants

There are four elements to a good value proposition. It should be tested as rigorously as possible across all four of these elements. The value proposition should be differentiating. You should set it apart from any of your direct and indirect competitive offerings that are in the marketplace. It should be relevant to the customers, meaning it should answer a desired benefit, want, or need they have. It should be compelling. Sometimes that causes a customer to want to take an action. Finally, it should be something that you are known for, and it should be enduring.

Why does a value proposition matter in breaking through the noise? At the basic level, you need a value proposition that the market likes. To keep your growth engine going and to set yourself up to strategically become a dominant force in your area of the world, the value proposition is the compelling reason that customers listen to your market message. The value proposition is your point of differentiation that is valuable to the market. If your value proposition can drive the positioning statement, the tagline, the GTM strategy, and the point of difference, then the rest of marketing matters. Whether a company is small or large is less relevant than whether you have a value proposition that works.

The value proposition needs to work for the specific region, channel, or customer that you are targeting. The differentiating points of why the customer should do business with you versus the competition set you apart and enable you to be heard above the noise. Thus, the value propositions must be targeted and real. There must be reasons to believe, overarching facts that support the credibility and proof points, which are examples that support the value proposition statement. The elements of a value proposition include the following:

- **Target customers:** Who specifically we want to have listen?
- **Defined market:** Who we are, understanding who else may be speaking to to the customer?
- **Differentiating points:** Why they should do business with us versus the competitive set?
- **Reasons to believe:** What overarching support do we offer to provide credibility?
- **Proof points:** Examples that support the value proposition statement.

We talk in terms of value proposition lasting at least three to five years. When you write a value proposition, you write in terms that stretch where you are today—words that are a bit future-looking. It's a bit aspirational so that it is enduring. It has to be the heart of your marketing to the outside world and inside world, too. It is what you build off of your value proposition that changes, whether it is in style or how the message reaches the market. So differentiating, relevant, compelling, and enduring are the four qualities that you should look for in a winning value proposition.

A value proposition can go beyond marketing. When I spoke with Craig Merrigan, VP at Lennovo, he told me about Lennovo's value proposition of "making the best engineered PCs." The value proposition started out as a marketing idea. However, now the value proposition is guiding development. As he explains, "I go to our quality meetings or engineering meetings and they each have their list of how they are going to make our PCs live up to this value proposition of best engineered."

The value proposition is a powerful unifying force. If you are going to succeed globally, this statement is a common core or positioning of brand. The power of authenticity will be perceived by the local market, if you make the value proposition customized to the local market. You can imagine the strength when product development has the statement that helps them understand who the target customer is, what the market is, what the desired wants and needs of the clients are, and what helps differentiate the product and company.

Take it one step further—if operations, finance, even legal, knew, understood, and had a clear idea of what your differentiating point in the marketplace is and how you should tailor all of the programs that they bring and use to touch customers and use to touch your internal organizations with the question, "Are we maximizing where we could make a difference?"

Top Five Lessons Learned for Value Proposition

The top five areas to think through while working on your value propositions include the following:

1. **Knowledge is crucial in multiple forms**: The global relevance, differentiation, and local flavor all matter. It is important to scour your organization for knowledge and insight through your market intelligence team, your product managers, sales people, channels, and strategy team. The upfront work is best done with a devoted, small team that can bring it together in a cohesive and efficient way.
2. **A team sport**: A value proposition is not developed by one person in his office, but it is a team effort. Mezzanine Consulting, LLC, recommends a multidisciplinary team, marketing management, product development,

sales, and strategy. Depending upon your GTM, you should also consider including channels, finance, and delivery.

3. **Use an external facilitator**: An external facilitator can help you focus on the process and the language to bring about a single view of how the product plays in the marketplace and ensure broad collaboration. For success, you need everyone to participate effectively. IBM has leveraged Mezzanine Consulting, LLC, in this respect and has further adopted its proprietary methodologies and processes to establish an internal value proposition practice with the sole purpose of focusing on IBM's many value propositions.

4. **Develop a synergistic architecture**: You will have more than one value proposition, and you want to ensure that they are all built in sync.

5. **Build upon it**: The hard work begins when you leverage the value proposition. Remember, the value proposition is what drives your deliverables and technically is not seen in public. The outcome of using it is what is visible. Start sharing it with people who need to use it and ensure that all of your images, sales material, channel enablement material, and your marketing materials leverage it as the base. Pull together a plan for who owns that value proposition—who is going to drive it forward, who is going to be responsible for communicating it, and how you are going to measure its performance effectiveness as you move forward.

The New "Who"

There is a new "who" in the marketplace since Marketing 2.0 has come into play. The new who is a broader and more informed group of constituents who collaborate before they buy. It looks for information but trusts a different kind of expert than in the past. Before we go into execution, your GTM plan needs to reflect the following three changes in the marketplace:

- The circle of influence
- The new buying group
- The new trusted who

The Circle of Influence

In the past, we could view audiences, stakeholders, or constituents, whether they're customers, clients, shareholders, future employees, neighbors, government officials, or a university as fairly discreet segments. We could segment them; we could target them and influence the channels of communication and interaction with them. To execute effectively today, you must see the market as a tightly coordinated view across all social media and traditional types of media because they are all aiming at the ultimate constituency or stakeholder called the client.

With Marketing 2.0 and Web 2.0, the message can't be segmented as done in the past. All audiences talk to each other and are interconnected. For example, when you communicate about pricing to a customer in one country, the knowledge of that immediately goes to all customers. What you communicate to the Wall Street analysts immediately goes to the press, employees, and retirees, and depending on the topic, it might go to clients and the world.

In the past, management of the message and value propositions could be done with some rigor. However, the world has changed, and it has to be rearchitected in our methods and how we manage our GTM plan. The diffusion of traditional media and the explosion of new media, such as blogs and Facebook, has changed not around just the quantity and nature of the media, but also around the people who consume and contribute to that. That changes the game significantly because now the customer or the other audiences are no longer recipients of messages or outbound tactics, but they contribute to them, create them, and talk to each other and to the companies. They work with each other in the new world.

For example, your Web site is not just for customers; it's also for the press, partners, analysts, and other constituents. This means that developing a Web site that is easy to navigate for those different influencers means clear offers for different influence groups and an organic search off the company's main page.

The New Buying Group

To complicate the matter more, in the new world of marketing, the buyer has also shifted. For example, for B2B technology companies, the buying group in B2B technology purchases is now up to 21 people.[1] How do you reach all of them in a trusted manner and know that they will share what you do and say? This new buying group, not an individual, that you are targeting requires significant changes in how you view the marketplace. In orchestrating your "who" for your tactics, you must reach this new form of buying group and do it in an effective manner.

The New Trusted Who

In addition to these new ways to communicate to the buying group, the focus on a marketing mix that includes heavy word-of-mouth marketing has increased. It has to do with who you trust. References and the power of others speaking for you have increased over the years and will continue to grow in importance. The shift is due to some of the containers, such as blogging, Facebook, wikis, widgets, virtual worlds; therefore, the reliance on others who have "been there and done that" has now increased.

Because the marketing mix for success has shifted, things such as white-paper syndication, PR, and "client satisfaction campaigns" have a more dramatic impact on the market. With the number of participants growing in the buying process, the need to look at account-based viral marketing (going beyond e-mail forwarding) has increased in importance. This thought process of how and who do you include in your "buying circle of friends" demands action-role-based marketing.

A case study on a best practice in go-to-market strategy for word-of-mouth is shown in Online Chapter 1, "Relationship and Word of Mouth: Rackspace" and can be found at ibmpress.com/angels.

Top Five Lessons Learned on the New "Who"

Understanding the new buying client is going to reduce the noise pollution. The top five tips for working through this new "who" include the following:

1. **The new buying group is a larger circle than before:** Be sure you are touching and talking to all people in the buying group with a message that is targeted just for them.
2. **The new buying group is more connected than ever:** These people listen to blogs, leverage proof in references, online case studies, and return on investment (ROI) calculators that were recommended to them via a friend. Be sure you are in the connected group!
3. **Get over it:** Determine where people are being influenced by social networking, such as blogs, and "get over" the fact that they don't have credibility or they don't really know what is happening. This is a new way for people to be heard and to share and create information and knowledge, so consider how you can leverage them thoughtfully.

4. **Think through the strategy of influence:** Don't just accept it but take advantage of it; acknowledge that it's not just about technologies and Web 2.0, but marketing! Determine your strategy and desired business outcomes to make Marketing 2.0 part of your GTM plan.

5. **Alter your marketing mix:** Given this chapter is about creating a GTM plan in the spirit of a globally integrated business, be sure you alter your mix to apply to the customers and markets around the world.

Conclusion

This chapter focused on the evolution of the GTM planning exercise in light of the new global-local world that exists. The planning, priorities, and value propositions no longer can be handed down from a global perspective, but wisdom has to be applied throughout the process of the local markets. This involves a more detailed and flexible approach from the global team down to the local teams.

An understanding of what drives your company's differentiation and value creation in a rapidly evolving business environment is core to success in breaking through the noise. Having well-established processes to understand and develop competitive differentiation, supported by a process and criteria for prioritization of investment, is part of a best-practice company. Key questions to address include "How do you determine your sources of differentiation globally and locally? Do you have a process in place for aligning your business strategy with your local decisions? What are your criteria for prioritization and investment decisions? What are your processes for prioritization and investment decisions?"

These decisions go hand-in-hand with the new circle of influence, the new buying group, and the new trust that is formed with others. These changes in the target audience impact all GTM decisions from the marketing mix to the tactical planning to a focus on a collaborative group of buyers. Reaching your local buying group in the right language and method with the right priorities enables you to break through the noise in the market.

Endnotes

1. From "MarketingSherpa Business Technology Marketing Benchmark Guide 2007-08," MarketingSherpa, Inc.

To view the SOA movie integrated example, go to ibmpressbooks.com/angels.

9

Influencer Value: The IBM Case Study

Never doubt that a small group of thoughtful, committed people can change the world. Indeed, it's the only thing that ever has!
—Margaret Mead

In this case study on IBM, we focus on how the influencers in today's Marketing 2.0 world impact your go-to-market (GTM) plan, your priorities, and how you form your value propositions. How do you effectively use them to break through the noise that exists in the marketplace today? In this case study, you find a methodical approach to the many influencers in the marketplace and a way to adjust based on the geographical and influence differences that exist by particular focus areas.

Influencers are classified as those who can have an impact on the sale of your product and the perception of your company. Examples include the following:

Universities: Colleges, professors, and students represent both current and future influencers. Apple did this very well in its early years with its focus on education as it provided schools with computers. IBM also focuses on this audience through its Academic Initiative and the IBM Serious Game, Innov8 (see Chapter 15, "Serious Gaming: IBM's Innov8").

Analysts (both financial and industry-related): In the high-technology space, industry analysts influence almost 85% of the sales made.

Employees: Your best evangelists are your internal employees because they are your most visible and vocal advocates or detractors!

Media: The press writes headlines that impact your perception in the marketplace.

Government: In all countries, but some more than others, the government influences sales and perceptions of products and companies by enacting mandates and regulations that create compliance issues that can tip the playing field.

Partners: Part of your ecosystem that has a vested interest in your products and services and in many cases is the face of your organization that the end user actually sees.

Bloggers and social networks: The new group of people who have a loud voice in the marketplace.

Many more examples than this exist, but you should see that those who influence do so in a way that is in line with their interests. To break through the noise with each group requires a focus on the language that each group needs to hear.

Focus on Influencers in Marketing

As I travel around the world, I am surprised at how much time and how many dollars companies spend focused only on the customer portion of their marketplace. Market-leading companies think more broadly and focus on the larger view to include influencers, going beyond the customer and understanding who has a larger share of voice in the market based on the news, announcements, and relevancy. In this case study, I highlight IBM's best practice of a full 360 degree view of the marketplace and the impact each group has on virtually all of its products, services, and announcements.

The Influencer Agenda at IBM

In this chapter, we explore three elements that are critical for a solid GTM plan:

1. Use of the Wheel of Influence
2. The Jam: a collaborative platform to leverage the influencer's ideas
3. Activation of the internal influencers

The Wheel of Influence at IBM

IBM leverages the Wheel of Influence to graphically depict the interrelation and dependency between IBM and those who hold sway in the marketplace. The wheel, as IBM leverages it, shows the focus of our consumers, media, investors, communities, academics, investors, government, and partners. It also includes IBM employees and subsets of the employee population, managers and executives, and future employees. IBM has recently added IBM Alumni as a focus as well. In Figure 9.1, we see the wheel as currently used by the IBM team.

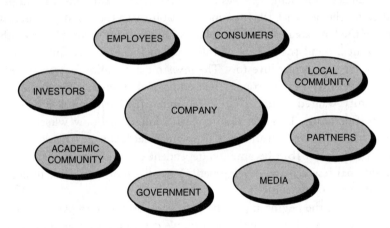

Figure 9.1   The Wheel of Influence.

The Wheel of Influence is a representation of the fact that IBM, like every enterprise and institution of import, is not an island. IBM is surrounded by different audiences and communities. It demonstrates that customers are important, but in addition to customers, many different audiences must be considered for business success.

IBM Marketing and Communications instituted the Wheel of Influence as a simple tool for the teams to understand all the influencer touch points during any announcement or campaign, or in light of hot topics facing the industry and society. For instance, if you sell a product, hire somebody, or advance a policy, the wheel reminds the team that it cannot be done in isolation in the context of any one audience. It might not involve every audience on that wheel, but chances are, it will involve or affect many.

It is worth noting that IBM encourages various influencer groups to work together. For example, we help connect industry analysts with reporters when they are writing about IBM announcements. Another example is that we connect university faculty members with the press.

The wheel is used to map a strategy for any given announcement or campaign or to address a societal issue such as corporate social responsibility and going green. The wheel is also used to anticipate responses and how to address those ahead of time. For example, how does IBM take to market the announcement of a new acquisition? At the writing of this book, IBM just acquired Cognos. In thinking through that acquisition, a plan to address each audience in its language was devised. For IBM customers, the language focused on the fact that IBM has more capability, so the GTM planning was done on the language of capability that is important to them. However, then IBM went around the Wheel of Influence to the next key influencer and planned for Wall Street investors. The investment community was interested in the capability but, of course, had additional interests. The investment community wanted to understand how much IBM paid, and if IBM used cash or financing. This community also wanted to know whether stock equity was considered. In addition, in its financial language, this community wanted to know if IBM became too dependent on acquisitions instead of its own internal research and development. Very different than those topics to a chief information officer (CIO)!

That is just the beginning. To be successful, you have to plan for the full view of the wheel. For example, how do we communicate the internal messaging to IBM employees? If you are in sales, the messaging would center around how much more you can sell, but to the software developer, you might want to understand why IBM didn't develop the software instead of buying it.

Another example is that of when IBM divested our PC business to the Chinese firm Lenovo. From an investment perspective, it viewed IBM as divesting in a commodity business. However, for the U.S. government, we had to ensure that we took time to go through the reasons IBM sold the technology business to a Chinese company partially owned by the Chinese government.

As Jon Iwata, senior VP of marketing and communications for IBM comments, "Think about the ripples that happen when you toss a pebble into a pond. When you toss a message, storyline, or program into the Wheel of Influence, you have to think carefully about the ripples that are sent throughout your entire ecosystem—the implications of it, the biases, the self-interest of all of these different audiences. With the explosion of social media, where basically the ripples become tidal waves, you have to be even more thoughtful and give it some critical thinking. Web 2.0, blogs, and other viral communications enable everyone to know everything, everyone to have a voice, and everyone to talk to everyone else. They can join arms, they have power, [and] they have influence, and companies have to take that seriously."

Application to Your Company

When you create your GTM plan, you need to think through the full Wheel of Influence. Each message that you put into the marketplace will impact a set of influencers, and each will have its own language. To break through the noise, each relevant party needs to be thoughtfully planned for. For any major announcements we make, we go around the wheel and assure ourselves that we have the right message and language for each constituency and the right way to reach them with the information. For example, when we introduce a new product, we look for how the GTM plan will be perceived for our partners, our customers, the press, and the analysts. We also recognize the influence that the players encircling IBM have on each other (such as analysts speaking to the press) and account for this when managing communication around the wheel. The application for your company would be to adapt the wheel to your company's influencers.

The Wheel of Influence must be made personal for your company as the audiences on the wheel can vary from those of IBMs. Also, the weights of each of the circle elements at different times will vary. Make sure you make this part of your planning and your sphere of influence.

The Jam: A Collaborative Platform to Leverage the Influencer's Ideas

Another best practice in breaking through the noise is around the Jam concept. Jams provide an Internet-based platform for innovation beyond the enterprise brainstorming, connecting across boundaries to develop actionable ideas around business-critical or urgent societal issues. Iwata described the initial concept as turning the Internet into a platform for collaboration and dialogue. IBM wanted to listen and collaborate with the influencers, not just "talk to" those on the Wheel of Influence. It was at that point that Iwata decided to leverage the wheel of influence strategically and initiate a series of conversations for specific and meaningful business outcomes.

First, IBM kicked off an internal ValueJam to involve the more than 300K workforce globally to redefine and shape IBM's core values for the first time in more than 100 years. The result? A set of core values—defined by IBMers for IBMers—that shape everything it does and every choice it makes on behalf of the company.

IBM'S SHARED VALUES FROM THE INTERNAL JAM

Dedication to Every Client's Success:
IBMers...

- Are passionate about building strong, long-lasting client relationships. This dedication spurs us to go "above and beyond" on our client's behalf.

- Are focused on outcomes. We sell products, services, and solutions, but all with the goal of helping our clients succeed regardless of how they measure success.

- Demonstrate this personal dedication to every client, from the largest corporation and government agency to the startup and neighborhood market.

- No matter where we work, we have a role in the client's success. It requires the full spectrum of IBM expertise.

Innovation that Matters for Our Company and the World:
IBMers...

- Be forward thinkers. We believe in progress and we believe that the application of intelligence, reason, and science can improve business, society, and the human condition.

- Love grand challenges and everyday improvements. Whatever the problem or the context, every IBMer seeks ways to tackle it creatively to be an innovator.

- Strive to be first in technology, in business, and in responsible policy. Take informed risks and champion new (sometimes unpopular) ideas.

Trust and Personal Responsibility in all Relationships:
IBMers...

■ Actively build relationships with all the constituencies of our business, including clients, partners, communities, investors, and fellow IBMers.

■ Build trust by listening, following through, and keeping our word.

■ Rely on our colleagues to do the right thing.

■ Preserve trust even when formal relationships end.

We followed up our significant internal Jam with a major external focus. Our external jam attracted more than 150,000 people (including 12,500 family members) from more than 104 countries and 67 companies came together online in the first InnovationJam. The goal was to innovate on some of the most important business and world issues and to place dollars behind solutions for the issues. The platform provided a facilitated, but not controlled, environment. It generated more than 46,000 new ideas for potential marketplace investments around a variety of topics. The topics were diverse and interesting. They consisted of ideas like these:

■ Transformation of travel, transportation, recreation, and entertainment

■ Transformation of global business and commerce

■ How to stay healthy and explore the state of well-being

■ How to balance economic and environmental priorities

The Jam took place in two parts: brainstorming and idea refinement of the best ideas. Despite the messiness of thousands of comments and the quasi-anarchy of an online collaboration, we could actually distill a clear set of takeaways that we then put into action. As a result, ten new IBM businesses were launched with a seed investment totaling $100 million. From www.ibm.com, the businesses were publicly named and shown to the vast community. The examples of the businesses that were seeded were Big Green Innovations, which was launching a new business unit in IBM that would focus on applying the company's advanced expertise and technologies to emerging environmental opportunities.

The value of the Jam was that it capitalized on the media and social networks with collaboration across the Wheel of Influence. It wasn't just that IBM listened; participants from many segments of the wheel took action, formed relationships, and capitalized on new opportunities. It took away the hierarchy inside and outside and focused instead on the ideas and the thoughts.

The process allowed for ideas to be evaluated based on their merits and not based on the person, his background, his perceived expertise, his longevity, his gender, or his part of the world.

Note: Jams are not restricted to business. They can also be used by governments or universities. For instance, the government of Canada, UN-HABITAT, and IBM hosted Habitat Jam. People from 158 countries registered for the Jam and shared their ideas for action to improve the environment, health, safety, and quality of life in the world's burgeoning cities.

FROM THE IBM JAM EXPERTS: PLANNING FOR YOUR OWN JAM!

From our team of experts who focus on Jams, here is how you can host your own Jam for marketing effectiveness! First start with the goals:

- What is the objective or the "intent" of the event?
- How are the results of the Jam going to be used?
- For example, the InnovationJam was to drive new business. IBM earmarked $100 million to develop the best ideas.
- Another example—the ValuesJam—the goal was to determine the values of an IBM employee. IBM redefined what it means to be an IBMer.
- What are we trying to learn? What are the top three issues or problems we want to address?
- If asked to describe this event in a sentence or two, what would it be? (As with InnovationJam, it was about "...discussing breakthrough innovations and ideas for emerging technologies." What is the essence of this Jam?)
- What is the size of the target population?

- If your total target population is 10,000 or fewer, a Jam is not a realistic option, both in terms of cost and validity of the outcomes.

- Are multiple time zones anticipated (for example, is this a global event)?

- Is this Jam internal, external, or both (for example, does the client plan to conduct the Jam internally only or will the client invite business partners)?

- Do you have executive sponsorship and commitment (CEO, board, business unit executive, and so on)?

- Do you have client commitment needed for the roles required; for example, do you have moderators, facilitators, subject matter experts (SME), communications people, and marketing for the event? Would you have the ability to tap into resources for these roles?

- What time frame are you looking to hold the event? (Note: Jam operations typically run 14 weeks leading up to actual live event.)

- What types of metrics are you seeking to track?

- Would you want to use a text-mining tool during and after event analysis?

- Do you have a way to track Web site traffic (hits, page views, and so on)?

Application to Your Company

Find a way to leverage the concept of a Jam in your environment. For example, we just completed a SOA Jam whose goal was to discover the top focus ways we can assist universities, customers, partners, and the analyst community in the marketplace. You can leverage a Jam internally for shaping your environment, externally with your customers, or even with family and friends to drive home innovation in your marketplace. It is easy to get started and test out the concept first internally, like IBM did, and then to take your Jam on the road in the marketplace. It will help you break through the noise because you are listening, acting, and forming relationships in the marketplace. It makes for a powerful way to go-to-market socially.

A first step might be to do a mini Jam. In Figure 9.2, you see that the mini Jam supports one step in the innovation process—the idea-finding step.

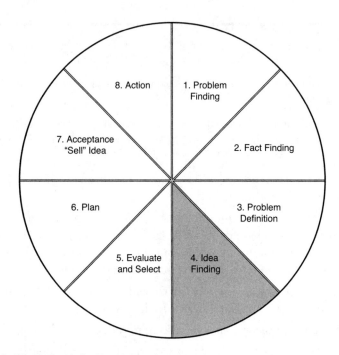

Figure 9.2   The Jam innovation idea plan.

Before you do a mini Jam, you must discover the problem and the root cause of the program. Then, run the mini Jam for new ideas and turn the ideas into action outside the Jam Session. Typically a mini Jam is based on the 6-5-3 idea—six participants, five minutes per each idea session, three ideas maximum to focus upon. You read the problem statement, write three ideas down, and reading and writing should take a maximum of five minutes. You can do this Jam either online or on paper! Whatever you do, involve the most relevant of your influencers from the Wheel of Influence.

Activation of the Internal Influencers

IBM was the first company to develop guidelines to activate the internal blogger influencers. The guidelines were initiated by IBM and developed by the bloggers on an internal Wiki in around ten days. Because IBM has around 390,000 employees, the goal of getting them all trained on how to use the new media tools was daunting. However, the impact could be phenomenal. According to blog-tracker Technorati, there are 9 million blogs. Forty thousand new blogs are added each day. The "blogosphere," or universe of blogs, is doubling every five months. Bloggers make six new posts per second. These numbers alone make these bloggers touch almost every aspect of the Wheel of Influence.

The goal that IBM set here was not to just permit or tolerate internal bloggers taking their opinions to the outside world, but to empower, enable, and encourage them. Iwata's vision was to have the employees and the partner network engage with these new media capabilities as a strategic advantage. To make them into an asset, he set out to have them create a set of guidelines and actively train them on the guidelines.

The bloggers came up with a set of guidelines that were complete, forward looking, thoughtful, and well written; when they were reviewed by the general council, the head of human resources and Iwata, none of the guidelines were edited. Iwata describes the guideline development: "I've been around corporate headquarters since 1989 and I've never seen anything go to me, the lawyer, and the head of HR and not be touched. The tower of collaborative thinking, as expressed in the blogging guidelines, was powerful. The guidelines themselves show IBM's great trust in our employees." IBM as a corporation wins by having its employees join the wider industry conversation of influence, either by creating its own external blogs, commenting on the blogs of others, or simply finding, reading, and passing along interesting blogs.

THE IBM BLOGGING GUIDELINES IN A NUTSHELL

- Understand and follow IBM's Business Conduct Guidelines.
- Bloggers speak for themselves, not for the company. Make that evident by using this disclaimer: "The postings on this site are my own and don't necessarily represent IBM's positions, strategies, or opinions."
- Respect copyright, fair use, and financial disclosure laws.
- Protect all confidential and proprietary information.
- Don't cite or reference clients, partners, or suppliers without their approval.
- Find out who else is blogging on the topic and cite them whenever appropriate.
- Don't be a stranger. Write in the first person and identify yourself by name and role when you blog about IBM or IBM-related matters.

- Protect your credibility. Try to be the first to correct your own mistakes, and don't alter previous posts without indicating that you have done so.
- Respect your audience. Lively discussions are always encouraged, but never resort to insults, slurs, or obscene language. Steer clear of unrelated topics that could be considered objectionable or inflammatory, such as politics and religion.

IBM's blogging guidelines are different and rather startling to some companies today. They are almost three years old. The preamble to the blogging guidelines encourages IBMers to engage in a blogosphere so that IBM can leverage the expertise of its people. IBM wants them to contribute and engage in the conversation and a dialogue around their fields of expertise, whether it's computer science, a product, communications, intellectual property, or whatever the area of specialty happens to be. For IBM to engage and be part of that conversation and dialogue is great for all areas of influence. However, you must also use thoughtfulness. For example, I blog as part of the blogosphere. When I speak as Sandy Carter, executive in a software group, a journalist can say that I am fair game if I blog on something that relates to my business. What I blog is on the record. The guidelines and policies were put in place to help IBMers to blog expertly. IBM has now gone beyond just the guidelines and focused on how to engage in a way that's more effective than its competitor's bloggers.

Application to Your Company

Your competitors are deploying large groups of people who are individuals of influence, and they are advancing their interests. Think through how you can impart your influence to win in the marketplace. You win by having a more-expert, better-trained, better-equipped, better-enabled group of people. Do you have a set of blogger guidelines? How about guidelines for other forms of social media such as Facebook? These can be powerful GTM elements or a weakness in your armor.

IBM Lessons Learned

In talking with Iwata, I asked him to articulate some of the most valuable lessons learned. Following are some of the top lessons he learned.

Constantly Modify Your View of the World

IBM always keeps an eye on where the influence is moving and shifting by using the Wheel of Influence. The size of the slice of the pie needs to be constantly reevaluated. A few years ago, IBM would have drawn that wheel with the biggest pie slices being customers, employees, and investors. However, now in a Web 2.0 world, the size of the slices for retirees and labor groups might cause us to redraw the wheel in terms of influence or at a minimum, resize the slices of the pie.

IBM is looking at 3D as well. Virtual worlds could end up being the future of the Internet. So, the 2D Internet becomes a 3D Internet. In the future, IBM.com might become a 3D IBM experience. When that change occurs, the wheel dramatically changes in terms of who has influence.

Power of influence has come to those who understand the fundamentals of Marketing 2.0. When you think through it, any influencer with a mastery over the use of Marketing 2.0 methods and the techniques can match a corporation's money, lawyers, brand presence, and lobbyist network because it knows how to take advantage of these asymmetrical tools. The wheel changes in that dimension, too. The magnitude or the significance of any one constituency's bearing on your business is not a matter of size, money, or skill. Those things are suddenly changed because of this new environment.

Food for Thought: The New Segmentation: Engagement?

We might have to rethink our capabilities of segmentation. We are used to segmenting based on the size of the customer, spend, demographics, or geography. However, for a successful GTM plan, do we now need to segment based on how a person wants to be engaged? There are people who are conversant and facile with Web 2.0 methods, and there are people who like to go to stores still and read traditional media. A new segmentation method we are experimenting with is segmenting by the nature of the engagement and the nature of the dialogue. This implies some change in the skills and analytics for those marketers focused on this important work. One of the great things about the online world is it offers the potential for cost-effective, real-time analytics.

Think Big

One of IBM's greatest accomplishments under Iwata's leadership was a concept called the Global Innovation Outlook (GIO). The goal was to leverage a huge network of influencers to set the course for the future. It began with the opening of the annual technology and business forecasting process to the world to discover opportunities for business and societal innovation.

This concept was another proof point of the CEO study where CEOs saw that innovation has changed and that now more innovation comes from outside a company's four walls. According to Iwata, "This shift means that the truly revolutionary innovations of our time—the ones that will create new markets, redefine old ones, and maybe even change the world for the better—require the participation and investment across multiple constituencies. The GIO challenges some of the brightest minds on the planet—from the worlds of business, politics, academia, and nonprofits—to collaboratively address some of the most vexing challenges on earth."

The concept is big in that there are open dialogues about a series of deep dives. These deep dives number more than 40 today, where dialogues of more than 550 influencers have engaged from 36 countries. In 2008, the areas of focus that represent trillions of dollars of investment include the following:

- The challenges every organization and individual faces resulting from the changing nature of security in an interdependent global society
- Social and economic implications of climate change and increasing pressures on water supplies and exploring the secrets of the deep ocean

Leveraging the dialogue, the findings will be available on the GIO blog and in a variety of printed means. The grand plan has been given to businesses, universities, and policy makers throughout the world, with more than 200,000 copies being distributed.

Conclusion

This IBM case study reinforces the notion that positioning for success is more than just differentiating and segmenting our market around customers. It is about enforcing the Wheel of Influence in the marketing success imperatives. Planning for successful enforcement through the Wheel of Influence provides a strong executable model for thinking through the targeting of the influencers in today's Marketing 2.0 environment.

For influencers, the best GTM strategy to break through the noise is to focus on the experience. It is not just a delivery of a message. It's a process. It's a whole series of things that have to be conceived, orchestrated, and synchronized. That means the online experience or the face-to-face experience is intentional and consistent with the brand promise. It means taking the relationship to a two-way, give-and-take relationship, and that is a different skill set than marketers who are used to controlling their message in PowerPoint or in advertising. In addition, marketers have to learn to leverage technology, especially Web 2.0, to join the conversation. Social computing needs to be thought through strategically, from setting guidelines, to unleashing employees into the domain, and to adjusting how and when the message is focused on what influencer. Success today and in the future requires that the Wheel of Influence becomes a part of the marketing planning and execution.

For additional content on SOA Jam, please visit ibmpressbooks.com/angels.

the Ecosystem and Market
- Social Networks & Communities
- Gaming
- Widgets and Wikis
- Blogging including Twitter
- RSS
- Podcasting and Videocasting
- Virtual Environments

10

The New Vessels

Today we are beginning to notice that the new media are not just mechanical gimmicks for creating worlds of illusion, but new languages with new and unique powers of expression.
—Marshall McLuh

As we look at the ways to drive success in business, the channel is a critical element and, therefore, needs to be energized around your portfolio. In Figure 10.1, you can see the energizing elements for the entire channel.

Energize the Ecosystem and Market
- Social Networks & Communities
- Gaming
- Widgets and Wikis
- Blogging including Twitter
- RSS
- Podcasting and Videocasting
- Virtual Environments

Figure 10.1 ANGELS framework—energize the ecosystem and market.

The channel is made up of your sales team, your partners, universities, and government agencies—basically your entire ecosystem of influencers. With all the competition in the market today, energizing your channel is an important driver of success. In this chapter, we talk about ways to energize and educate both your channel and marketplace. We focus on the newer techniques, or vessels, that should be used in tandem with traditional marketing methods. (Note: What is not included here are the basics in execution of your GTM plan with your channel. This could be a whole book on its own!) In Figure 10.2, we see IDC Research that shows the most popular forms of these new marketing types as vessels for energy.

Q. Please describe any online and interactive marketing initiatives that your marketing organization intends to deploy in the next 12 months.

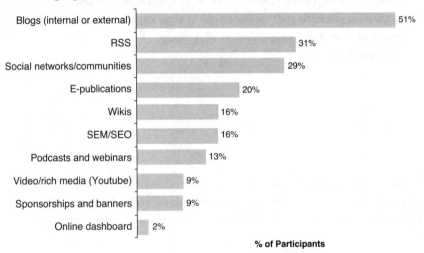

Source: IDC 2007 Tech Marketing Benchmarks Database (n = 45)

Figure 10.2   Interactive marketing or the new vessels.

Remember, interactive marketing is just the vessel for the content. What sets companies and marketing teams apart is the quality of the content and how effectively they use these vessels. The new vessels, which include blogs, games, social networks, and other Web 2.0 mechanisms, involve listening, cultivating, and participating in the continuous dialogue among customers and the entire ecosystem about issues relevant to the marketplace, either on or off a brand's digital properties.

Because we have covered how to drive the content through a focus obsession on the customer, we now talk about how to effectively use seven new digital vessels in the execution of your GTM plan for the channel, as shown in Figure 10.3.

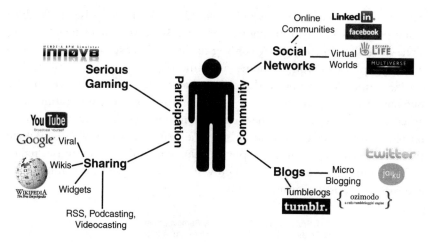

Figure 10.3   The new vessels linkage.

There are seven key new vessels to energize your channel that I will discuss in this book. While there are many more emerging (like Jellyvision and the like), this covers what my team and I have used and experimented with in the real world. Our Web site will have updates and results as we try out new media.

- Social networks with virtual environments, online communities including Facebook
- Participation with viral and serious gaming
- Sharing through widgets and wikis
- Blogging, including Twitter
- Really simple syndication (RSS)
- Podcasting
- Videocasting

The commonality among these seven areas is that they form a platform for social and emotional connection to energize the market and ecosystem. Let's explore how to leverage them.

Focus on Social Networks: Online Communities

People are social beings. Since the earliest of times, communities have been alive and active in the world. The importance of the emerging social networks that exist in our new online world should not surprise us. With so many people working from home, there is a societal shift of people being alone more than in the past. According to the U.S. Census Bureau, the number of people who work at home full time rose 23 percent from the last decade. Time alone while working from home and being connected online but not in person has changed society to crave more communication with others and has given way to new online communities. Even my dad who is retired spends much of his time online. The results shown in Figure 10.4 are that more than 70 percent of people participate in online communities today.

These numbers will continue to grow in the future as online communities and social networks continue to grow.

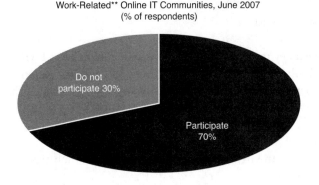

US IT Professionals Who Actively Participate* in
Work-Related** Online IT Communities, June 2007
(% of respondents)

Note: n=203; *by posting questions or contibuting to discussion;
**focused on systems of security management
Source: King Research, "The value of Online Communities: A Survey of Technology Professionals" commissioned by
KACE networks, June 2007 and eMarketer Inc.

Figure 10.4 Communities are growing in popularity.

People want to engage with others who have something in common with them, and the connections can be both personal and virtual. Remember high school, where kids grouped together by common interests? Even in the latest Disney movie, *High School Musical*, the kids sorted themselves by interests in sports, music, or science. People like to be a part of something, and they like to talk to others with whom they have something in common. This is one reason why communities are growing in their importance. Sharing commonalities and engaging in dialogue can be energizing and satisfying to the new-world customer. Communities bring to bear an engagement that causes customers to become passionate about your company and product.

What Is a Community?

A community is a group of people that has a shared interest. Communities can be two to three people or thousands; the people might connect in person, through electronic means, or both. Wikipedia, a community itself, defines community marketing as a strategy to engage an audience in an active, nonintrusive prospect and customer conversation.

Development of online communities has afforded us an opportunity to observe people interact with one another, express their own opinions, form relationships, and break relationships. These relationships might be with other consumers, with friends, with companies, or with products or logos; people form relationships with everything.

There are many ways to group communities. One classification is by who sponsors the community—a vendor company or a group of users. We will consider a classification by the common bond that causes the group to form and stay together.

Types of Communities

There are four major categories of communities: crowd sourcing, activity-based, obsession-based, and experience-based. Let's explore each type:

- **Crowd sourcing or definition communities:** These communities come together to design something, or they are created for the purpose of providing feedback to a company about its products or services. For example, Threadless is a community-based T-shirt company with an ongoing open call for shirt design submissions. If your design is chosen for print, you get paid for it. At IBM, we have communities that enable participants to input into the design of our products, such as our Project Zero. The company that produces WD-40, the lubricant used in thousands of households, formed an e-community for women, who were not buyers of its products. They formed this community to see what would inspire women to buy its product. They were told to make it into something women could carry in their purses, and so they did. Communities provide relevance in both B2B and B2C marketing as customers shape where the product and services will go or are going!

- **Activity-based communities:** These communities are brought together by a common love of an activity. It could be like Neopets.com, a community built around games, puzzles, and activities. Or it could be something like what IBM developed for a new business approach to technology, such as SOA. We developed SOA Space for an activity-based group of developers around best practices in architecture. In SOA Space, you can chat to an expert, share your activities, and progress in your deployments, all based on role.

- **Obsession-based:** These communities seem to be more passion-based. They form out of a strong love of an area. We will see a case study about Harley-Davidson in Chapter 11, "Energize the Channel with Communities: OMG, Adobe and Rubicon Consulting, and Harley-Davidson." However, other community groups exist, such as people who love Suduko, and Sears has an obsession-based community for people who love their lawn mowers and tractors!

- **Experience-based:** These communities come together around a shared experience. Bebopjeans.com has figured out a way to create an emotional connection. Its site is Flash-driven; as soon as you see the site, you can tell that it's oriented toward teenagers. It is relevant to its audience and includes splash screens and Facebook and MySpace tie-ins.

Communities also expand because of the capacity to create relationships with people in other countries. With globalization, being connected is not just about communities in your own country, but also those around the world. For example, for software developers in China, the best community is csdn.net. For general communities, MySpace is popular in China and for connections around the world. In China alone, the most popular local community is qq.com but it is for local Chinese, not for cross-language and cross-cultural groups.

An important choice as a marketer is to decide whether to start your own community or to influence and play in other communities that are of interest. If you choose to start your own community, it is critical that you start showing value to the larger group. In Figure 10.5, IDC shares three communities used to educate that are driven by the vendors. Quest leverages community sites by its product line; National has its own semi analog university. These vendor sites enable for tighter connection on content and for direct feedback that is trackable and usable by the company.

If you choose to play in other communities, you need to do so with care. You cannot dominate the community but listen and allow people to share their thoughts and ideas. In communities, people talk about the good and bad of your products; trying to "control" the conversation will be counterproductive and potentially harmful.

Figure 10.5   Building online communities to educate.

How do you find a community that might fit your needs? The answer is to use Google to research the topic and see if there are existing communities discussing your topic. For instance, if you Google the words dog and community, Dogster comes up. To use Google, be as specific with your query as possible. For example, if you were looking for SOA architects in Cincinnati, write a query like, "SOA architects Cincinnati." If you know there's some sort of community verbiage in the name, you can also include that.

If you can't find an existing community, work to create one. Create a blog and index it with Google. If the topic is of interest to others, they will come. To create your own online communities, you can use Google tools, such as Google Groups. A great example of this is www.idrinkyourmilkshake.com. This site is driven by the lovers of the movie *There Will Be Blood*, and the name of the site comes from the movie's famous line. It found a new audience of users interested in discussing the movie and the motivations of the main characters. It is truly a success story of communities rushing to join the discussions because they love the movie! Can you buy anything on the site? No, but it is driving movie tickets in an extremely clever way—through the community!

Top Five Lessons Learned for Communities

In working with communities over the years, the top five lessons learned for forming a community or social network range from getting started to whom to target. The list should provide a thought-provoking set of items for your formation or joining of the online community world:

1. **Know your communities:** Ensure you know which communities impact your company and influence your clients.
2. **Create communities for the long term:** If you have the time and patience for long-term results, sustained efforts in communities pay off. However, they are not a quick tactic. Communities are about energizing your ecosystem through stronger customer relationships created and engagement of active energy in your business.
3. **Communities can be internal as well:** Don't forget your own sales teams. Inside IBM, we view our sellers as a valuable community that we constantly dialogue with. As Lauren Flaherty, chief marketing officer at Nortel comments, "We look at our sales colleagues as a community. And we have learned what it takes to keep their interest in this new community portal and frankly they love the vessel. I've got a CNN crawl on the bottom of the portal so that we can tell them, 'Hey, here's what's fresh. Here's what's new, what's interesting, and what's funny. It's CNN.'"
4. **Start a dialogue:** Your dialogue can be about decisions you have to make on new products or features or just to provide an experience for your customers and ecosystem. Make sure you choose one or more ways to have the dialogue—the dialogue will continue with or without you!
5. **Great communities provide value:** Don't start a community just as a marketing tactic. Communities last because they provide real value, not just marketing messages. Make sure you have something they want and need.

Facebook

Because Facebook is such a popular and interesting community, this section is dedicated to this special community. According to Wikipedia, Facebook is a social networking Web site. It launched in 2004. The free-access Web site is privately owned and operated by Facebook, Inc. Users can join networks organized by city, workplace, school, and region to connect and interact with other people. People can also add friends, send them messages, and update their personal profile.

According to Forrester Research, there are between 40 to 50 million users today, with a growth of 134 percent to 200 percent or more in the last year. More than 40 percent of the users are more than the age of 35, and the average visitor stays about 20 minutes. The users are primarily in North America and the Middle East and are primarily college educated. Forrester says that Facebook could eclipse MySpace in the number of active users in early 2009.

To explore Facebook, I turned to Jeremiah Owyang, senior analyst at Forrester Research who is focused on social computing. Because the primary use of Facebook is for members to share what they are doing or working on, this community is ripe for a marketing dialogue. As Owyang said, "Facebook is a ready-made marketing platform, which offers a vast tool set (with challenges); but, to succeed, brands must develop a strategy. In fact, according to Forrester, the top three uses of Facebook are to see what friends are up to, send a message to someone, and to post or update a profile. "

Owyang provides these must knows about Facebook:

- **Invites via e-mail spur growth:** Invites arrive via e-mails. At one point, Owyang received dozens in one week; this is a sign of mass group of people using email to grow their base.

- **Discussions:** Within the groups sections, questions are posed, answered, and discussed. If you're a believer in the Cluetrain manifesto, this is a sign of a marketplace.

- **Business audience, not just college kids:** When Facebook opened up to the world, it extended its reach past college students. This might have been due to many of the original Facebook users graduating and moving into the workplace. Many of the contacts and friends within Facebook are senior managers, directors, VPs, and CEOs. Recent research indicated that the fastest growth segment is people more than 35 years of age.

- **Affinity groups:** Individuals with similar interests, problems, or traits are starting to self-assemble through their friend's network, or within the groups. All of these are opt-in, so these are engaged users who have self-selected: "Hey I belong here." These are communities and are microsegments of marketplaces.

- **Opt-in:** Unlike traditional forms of advertising and marketing, Facebook has many opt-in features that let users review, approve, and accept invites for friends, applications, groups, and other features.

- **Limited search crawling**—Facebook is a "closed" network, and you can see most data only if you are logged in. Most individuals' pages are somewhat private to nonfriends. As a result, this limits the capability of traditional search engines like Google, Yahoo, MSN, Ask, and others to crawl and index the data. This will prove to be an interesting dynamic in the next few years.

- **High growth**—Facebook has one of the fastest growth rates and could potentially overtake MySpace if these rates continue.

WAL-MART'S FACEBOOK PRESENCE TARGETS STUDENTS WELL

by Jeremiah Owyang

Wal-Mart launched a Facebook group targeting college students getting ready to going back to school. There are links to a supply checklist and links that go back to walmart.com's music, green shopping area, and information about its new "site to store" service.

But the killer "app" on the site is Roommate Style Match Quiz, which asks questions such as, "What is your favorite way to study?" and "If your life were a movie, what genre would it be?" I took the quiz and it turns out I'm a "Brain-Stormer." Wal-Mart did a good job pegging me! What was interesting was the picture of my "room" that does look like my room! Books are strewn all over the desk and floor.

I think that Wal-Mart does several things well here, which is a nice change of pace given its previous forays into social computing (consider the social networking site The Hub and blogging with Wal-Mart across America).

Most importantly, Wal-Mart understands the interactive, social nature of Facebook. The Style Match Quiz not only enables me to take the quiz, but I can also post it to my profile and send it to friends. Ideally, it would also allow me to plug in the profile of a friend automatically (I have to do this manually given the interface). I also noticed that I can't mix genders in the roommate matching, but I can't blame Wal-Mart for not wanting to go down that path!

I'm going to watch the Wall comments very closely; there will certainly be Wal-Mart fans who come to profess their fandom, as well as detractors. It's also an opportunity to see if students begin posting questions about dorm life. Will other students respond or will Wal-Mart step forward and help address some of those questions?

Something else to watch is how Wal-Mart evolves the group after the initial back-to-school rush, especially because the roommate-matching quiz is set to run only through October. This is a relationship that Wal-Mart now needs to think about nurturing, not a campaign that can be turned "off" at a specific date.

Wal-Mart has the opportunity to build a community with these students, but has to resist the temptation of treating this group as yet another marketing channel. For example, the members of the Apple Students Group routinely receive promotion (spam) messages in the Facebook Inbox (the latest one I received has the subject line, "Buy a Mac. Get a FREE iPod nano").

Top Five Tips for Facebook for Marketing

Facebook is an exciting new community for supplementing the traditional marketing mechanisms. As a new vessel, it is ripe for experimentation using the below tips for success:

1. **Use for Marketing 2.0 intelligence:** Owyang's view is that profiles, network information, and public groups provide a way to seek insight online.
2. **Use for advertising:** A variety of ways to leverage the power of this community exist, including banner ads, news feeds, social ads, and flyer ads.
3. **Attract a new audience:** Because we heard from Anne Holland at MarketingSherpa that neither those under 25 nor those more experienced use e-mail, leverage this new social networking tool in place of e-mail.
4. **Experiment with fan pages:** These fan pages can be used in place of sponsored groups.
5. **Not a standalone:** Integrate your Facebook tactics with your overall strategy. If this is the audience that you need for your product and offerings, leverage it as part of the overall go-to-market (GTM) plan.

Social Networks with Virtual Environments

Virtual environments are a powerful alternative reality online. It is a way to imagine a new digital world. Some of the popular virtual worlds are Second Life, OpenSim, ActiveWorlds, Whyville, and Entropia Universe. In fact, the Chinese government has invested a set of engineers to its claim for its own virtual world. Some of the differences in the worlds are their focus on games or business. For instance, Second Life has an economy for the business world and is trying to gear up for commerce.

When entering a virtual environment, you create an avatar for yourself. An avatar, as defined by Wikipedia, is a computer user's representation of herself in the form of a 3D model used in computer games. The term "avatar" can also refer to the personality connected with the screen name, or handle, of an Internet user. In Figure 10.6, you can see my avatar.

Figure 10.6   Soandy—my Second Life avatar!

I have made my avatar look like me, well kind of! Many people create an avatar that does not look like them; for example, if they have blonde hair in real life, they might choose dark for their virtual world. Active users on Second Life are around 50,000, which is up significantly from about 30,000 a few months ago. (Active is different from the millions that registered. With more than 4.8 million users existing in the digital network world, Second Life serves as a model for future online communities as they copy Second Life's formula for success!) Virtual environments are global. I have friends from all over the world, and we meet and talk in my SOA island.

What could you do in a virtual environment? Companies buy land, plan adventures, and participate in the economy. Digital characters walk, take vehicles, and even teleport. You can even start a church. Life Church, which has community church services, has planted swords around the virtual world, so that when you choose them, it sends you information about its church. (See Figure 10.7.)

Figure 10.7   Virtual life marketing—swords from Life Church.

Second Life also offers complete customization, providing the opportunity for users, businesses, and brands to completely reinvent themselves. Creating a corporate Second Life persona enables users to participate and contribute to your efforts, experience a brand-oriented journey through the metaverse, or provide the opportunity to reinvent or reshape your product to fit into the metaverse community.

What is the value in marketing from virtual environments? There are companies that have storefronts in the virtual world sites to try and seek revenue. The Coca Cola Company has an interactive site where customers go to help the company design new ideas for its products, and Cisco has experimented with selling and measuring results. I've also seen a Second Life

Chemistry Set. This is a box of chemicals. You give it commands, and it creates molecular structures that hover in the air over the box.

The marketing value of virtual environments is being tested now; however, I do believe that if you are a best-practice company, you should buy land in a virtual environment and experiment with what works. In our case studies on The Coca Cola Company and IBM in the following chapter, you will see some of what the leading edge companies are doing in this alternative universe.

Top Five Tips for Virtual Environments

Virtual environments are very new but worth the addition to the GTM execution for energizing the channel. Following are five tips to assist in the metaverse:

1. **Know your virtual environments:** Explore the 3D worlds that exist today to explore the options. Even kids are playing with Webkinz, Build a Bear, and Shining Star sites. These sites allow them to learn about a variety of topics such as art, math, and even commerce! See what the future holds for some of your potential buyers! For businesses, some of the top virtual environments are Second Life, OpenSim, and ActiveWorlds.

2. **Customize your avatar and play in the virtual world:** If you haven't been there, it is hard to describe the potential and the feel of the word. Words don't do it justice. You can host a staff meeting to get the feel for it or even host a customer focus group.

3. **Pilot with some of the primary successful uses of virtual environments today:** I've seen the most success in using virtual worlds to educate, to hold events, and to solicit input and ideas. Or use your innovation to drive you to be the first marketer with success in an area. Go ahead and invest in some land or an island. I believe this is the way of the future. I would invest early.

4. **Be active:** There is a common thread here to all the new vessels. If you invest to put them into action, you must be willing to continue active participation in them. Content is king. Ninety percent of the time spent on developing for virtual environments should be focused on the content upfront; as with a Web site, without a unique, rich experience, click outs are inevitable.

5. **Quality and visual continuity matter:** Just like a theme park, the visual impression is a major part of the experience. Your brand quality

and identity has to be maintained even in a virtual space. Make sure you don't forget that this vessel is just another element in your branding.

You can read "Zen and the Art of Social Media in Public Relations," by Kathleen Keating, Founder, FastStartPR, on the companion Web site at: ibmpressbooks.com/angels.

Focus on Participation with Viral

The term viral marketing has been used a lot, so I'd like to start with clarity around what I mean when I refer to viral. Viral is about leveraging either a preexisting social network or a set of friends to produce some sort of increase in brand awareness or demand generation through a self-replicating process. It exploits existing social networks by encouraging customers to share product information with their friends. There are lot of techniques and vehicles to produce exponential increases in brand awareness with viral processes.

Viral can be word of mouth delivered and enhanced online to reach a large number of people in a short term. The key intent is to create energy, intrigue, and curiosity. Most viral activities include video clips, interactive Flash games, images, and even text!

Viral marketing is more powerful than third-party advertising because it conveys an implied endorsement from a "friend." Why is viral marketing taking off today and why is it so successful? From IBM's recent market intelligence study, viral is a top influencer in the decision-making process.

There are four critical areas that are key influencers in B2B marketing. The first biggest influence is customer references or customer stories. The second is an external influencer such as an industry analyst or industry advisor. If you're B2C, think consumer reports; if you're B2B, think about some of the typical analysts such as an IDC or a Gartner. The next influencer of a sale is demo downloads, which include how you experience the product such as downloading some sort of simulation or code if you're in the IT space.

The biggest one, though, across every tier, is a colleague or a peer who recommends your particular product or service, and in fact, it's 40 percent of the influence regardless of who your customers are, regardless if they're B2C or B2B. This buzz factor or the friend factor can make a difference in the GTM plan. See Figure 10.8.

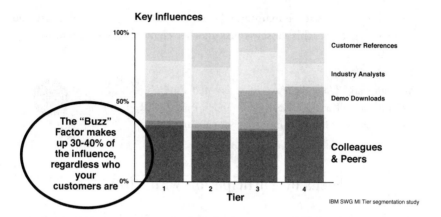

Figure 10.8   Why is viral marketing buzz so important?

When we think about some popular tactics used such as viral marketing to get that buzz factor, prioritization is needed. The latest MarketingSherpa report contains some nuggets to assist in prioritizing for your GTM execution. In its most recent study on viral marketing, MarketingSherpa found that the best viral tactics were microsites, which is not your own site but a separate site that is independent from your company. The second one is video clips, such as those that appear on YouTube. We saw an example of this viral video in Chapter 6, "Lightly Branded: EepyBird, The Coca-Cola Company, and Mentos." The third is online games, quizzes, or polls where you compete and manage the challenge back and forth. Now, the top three moderate results for viral marketing include

- Tell-a-friend boxes on the site
- Encouraging e-mail forwarding, such as, "Take a look at this and forward it on to your next best friend"
- Audio clips

The reason that viral is so effective in the channel is that you have a greater reach and a global reach. Viral breaks through the online and e-mail clutter, mostly because it's cool. The trick is to create viral marketing that is so fun, shocking, or provocative that the user will adopt the experience as his own and send it to a friend for bragging rights. You might be thinking that word of mouth has always been there. In fact, word of mouth has now moved from anecdotal to actionable because it is measurable in the marketplace.

In Figure 10.9, we see that viral marketing through friends and colleagues is the number one way that businesses use to decide who to purchase. "Word-of-mouth marketing is gaining more traction than ever before, and according to growth predictions, we're seeing just the beginning of a huge surge of both interest and word-of-mouth marketing activity," said Amanda Van Nuys, co-chair of WOMMA's Communications Council and vice president of Corporate Marketing at Organic Inc. "All this growth and increased curiosity makes a resource like WOMMA's Case Studies Library extremely valuable. So many marketers are looking for examples of how they can put this phenomenal thing called 'WOM' to work, and, of course, the Wommie winners stand out as the best of the best."

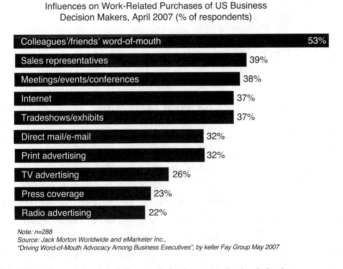

Figure 10.9 Word of mouth is a key influencer in business purchasing behavior.

Let's just talk about how a viral campaign might potentially work. At a highest level, you tell a story with strong content on the Web and include the opportunity to pass it along and share the Web site. So for instance, I do a lot of shopping on Bluefly.com, and I've watched little snippets about fashion on that Web site. The video at the end sometimes provides news of the opportunity to pass and share that video along, or you can do it with YouTube. My IBM team posted a set of "What is SOA?" videos on YouTube, and we used the mechanism there to pass that along. In this example, the Web is your organic interest, so someone has to find the video and then pass that video along. The best practice is combining viral with traditional marketing (as shown in Figure 10.10) to leads to greater success in doing one or other that's not integrated.

Figure 10.10   Enhancing the traditional approach with viral marketing.

Top Five Tips on Viral Marketing

Viral marketing is both agenda setting and cost effective. It provides the best of the goals of marketing. The following is a list of some of the top elements to drive through your viral strategy:

1. **Create something clever:** This should be something worthy of being passed and relevant. People will share good experience. Make it catchy; for example, use Flash in you Web banners and dynamic rotation.
2. **Use videos to tell your story:** This is a great medium if you can afford to use it and create fun videos. Videos can convey your marketing message by painting a video picture of the topic using humor or just grabbing the viewer's attention.
3. **Keep your offers simple and visible:** For example, for an e-mail signature, include a catchy tagline and a Web link. We are doing this now in every e-mail signature with IMPACT 2009. Use "Tell a Friend" with e-mail, Webcasts, and Web site visitors and let your prospects forward your marketing message.

4. **Participate in user forums:** This is free and you can touch people interested in your specific area. Forums are indexed by search engines and their posts increase exposure.
5. **Keyword buys with Google and Word Tracker:** Keep refining and optimizing your AdWord buys. If you can't afford to do word buys, submit your URLs to Google for search retrieval. It's free using Google Webmaster tools!

Focus on Participation with Serious Gaming

A shift in demographics has pushed a post-dot-com generation to seek an online experience with an emphasis on entertainment. Serious gaming is a new way to capture the channel for education and enablement. With the number of people growing up with gaming as part of their heritage, gaming can be a familiar way to teach new concepts.

Who is this gaming generation? According to the Entertainment Software Association, the average game player is 33 years old. Forty-seven percent of all gamers fall in the 18–49 age range. Twenty-four percent are more than 50 years old. The average age of MBA students varies by school, but they are generally in their late twenties for a full-time program and late thirties for an executive MBA program. There are already more Gen X and Gen Ys, where the primary thrust of the gaming generation exists, than there are baby boomers.

Author's John Beck and Mitchell Wade wrote a book called *The Kids Are Alright: How the Garner Industry is Changing the Workplace* about how gamers are impacted by games. A few leading-edge companies are using games for training. In the government market, we see examples, including training for military and first responders. Healthcare examples include Remission, a game designed to teach kids about cancer and simulators that teach surgeons how to perform a particular procedure. And one of my favorite places to eat ice cream, Cold Stone Creamery, has a retail service game to teach the retail fundamentals.

How does gaming translate to training? In Figure 10.11, we see why gaming matters.

How games are changing gamers	What games teach gamers
■ Gamers are **better at handling risk** and uncertainty.	■ **Be a hero.** The star's role is the best way to succeed or get satisfaction.
■ Gamers are **more creative** and have **better problem solving skills.**	■ **Be an expert.** Get really, really good so you can perform at your peak early and often.
■ Gamers are **more sociable** and have a greater need for human relationships.	■ **Failure isn't the end of the world.** Crashing and burning isn't so bad, and persistence pays off in the end.
■ Gamers think of themselves as **experts** and want to take problems head-on.	■ **Everything is possible.** You're capable of amazing things—you can defeat hundreds of bad guys single-handed or beat the best NBA team ever.
■ Gamers **aren't discouraged by failure** and believe each setback is just a chance to try again.	■ **Trial-and-error is almost always best.** The only way to advance in most games is to try new things and see if they work.
■ Gamers are **more flexible** about change. Gamers are better at seeing problems in a **deeper perspective.**	■ **Practice makes perfect.** Practice at something long enough, and you'll be ready for whatever comes your way in real life.
■ Gamers are great at **learning in informal ways.**	■ **Go global.** Bond with people who share your experience, not necessarily your national or cultural background.
■ Gamers are **more globally oriented** and outward-looking.	
■ Gamers are **more confident** and have amore **positive outlook** on life.	

Figure 10.11 How gamers are impacted by games.

According to *The Kids Are Alright: How the Garner Industry is Changing the Workplace*, to succeed in training gamers, one must create a curriculum which

- Aggressively ignores any hint of formal instruction
- Leans heavily on trial-and-error (after all, failure is nearly free, you just push "play again")
- Includes lots of learning from peers but virtually none from authority figures
- Is consumed in very small bits, exactly when the learner wants, which is usually just before the skill is needed
- Allows for people to take risks in a safe environment
- Allows for players to achieve a skill or talent that is not only meaningful but also perceived as having value

So gaming and marketing intersect in that marketing needs to enable and train the channel and ecosystem. Your channel and ecosystem is most valuable when they are knowledgeable and excited about your products and services. Serious gaming enables universities, partners, and your own sales team to learn the portfolio in an innovative yet valuable way. The unique platform facilitates the presentation of complicated material in a way that is engaging.

Before you start with a serious gaming effort, make sure you define your objectives. Are you going to use the game for teaching 101 fundamentals? Will an interactive learning-lab experience be included? From my experience, our complementing lab was a best bet for the success of our gaming solution. Also, you are probably currently doing traditional types of training. Make sure your gaming efforts are complementary to and incorporated within existing and institutional curricula. We also found the institutional groups helpful and, in fact, found gaming was most effective in conjunction with face-to-face classroom debriefs.

In addition, define your initial target audience. Will you target MBA, Executive MBA, or undergraduate business and information systems customers? Will you first go to partners and your ecosystem or to universities? Make sure you think through your planning in this area. Because serious gaming is new, read through, digest, and play the Innov8 game that is featured in my case study for IBM in Chapter 17, "Innovation, Engagement, and Business Results: adidas Group, ConAgra Foods, and Tellabs." For a sneak peek, see Figure 10.12!

Figure 10.12   Innov8! from IBM.

Top Five Lessons Learned for Serious Gaming

Serious gaming is an opportunity to teach, drive interest, and "show," not just tell your potential customers about your products. The focus here is new, so explore the following tips for serious gaming, but know that these will evolve with the market:

1. **Determine your demographics:** Does gaming fit your target audience? There is a generational divide that challenges marketers today. Selecting the right way to educate will be a combination of new techniques such as gaming with continued focus on traditional training like classroom and online. Gaming is for one of the segments of our society that likes to learn via activity.

2. **Pick core areas to focus on with your gaming training:** There are more natural areas to focus a gaming scenario. Make sure you are planning the areas of your business that work well in this Marketing 2.0 technique.

3. **Spend time on the teachable moments:** Think through your scenarios as teachable moments. For IBM's game, we spent more time in the scenarios and keypoints that gamers would have to grasp than on the actual development of the game. Leverage the teachable moments and the way to learn in bite-size chunks.

4. **Take the gaming concept to the limit:** Have a protagonist, hero, or heroine, and have the game in a competitive mode. Don't skip the cast, the story, and the theatrics. Have fun!

5. **Work with universities to understand how to train:** They add so much value to the thought process of your channel education plan.

Focus on Sharing with Widgets and Wikis

A widget is a mini-Web application that can be put onto a Web page, desktop, blog, or social profile that streams information in a more consumable fashion, usually containing some visual information. It is a dynamic, customizable, and convenient innovative medium. There are many possibilities for desktop widgets to assist a user in his area of work by delivering relevant, filtered information right on the user's desktop. A valuable widget is to present the most relevant information that someone uses daily. According to Niall Kennedy, "The Google gadget ecosystem received 960 million page views last week, a 36 percent jump from just one month ago." For some examples, see Figure 10.13.

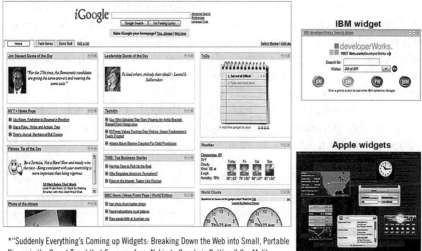

*"Suddenly Everything's Coming up Widgets: Breaking Down the Web into Small, Portable Pieces is the Smart Trend that Everyone from Nokia to Google is Betting," Om Malik, *Business 2.0 Magazine*, October 2, 2006.

Figure 10.13   The world of widgets

For a widget to be successful, it cannot just be an advertising mechanism; it needs to be a vessel to deliver your brand promise. For example, Shervin Pishevar, cofounder and CEO of Social Gaming Network (SGN) and board member of Free Webs, shares an example of Acura. Acura is commonly regarded among the autorati as having the best navigation systems on the market. It's developed the Acura RDX Traffic widget that delivers real-time traffic flow (and ebb) to a user's computer. It's a highly useful application, and because of Acura's positioning, it reaps more benefits from this widget than its competitors would. Shervin presents another great widget example from Amsterdam. The Rijksmuseum has developed a widget that is updated daily with a new picture from the world-famous museum's impressive collection. An icon on the picture spins it when clicked, revealing the piece's title, artist, date, some historical background, and a link back to the museum's Web site. Currently, the widget is just a desktop widget, but the fresh content it delivers each day would make it appealing to site owners and citizen publishers if it is ever available in that format.

With widgets, you need to ensure that you get it to your audience's desktop, and you need to ensure it stays there. To get the widget to someone's desktop means that the person has to want it there. Going to an already existing community to further inscribe your brand loyalty is a great way to leverage and use widgets. There are many examples of leveraging demand generation to get someone to use a widget. Jeremiah Owyang, senior analyst at Forrester Research: Social Computing, gives an example of Sony leveraging prizes for a widget, in this case, Rock You's vampire application. He writes, "Sony didn't beat the three million existing users with heavy advertising over the head, instead it offered value by giving away prizes and tied in a movie that already existed."

Getting the widget on the desktop is one thing, but then it was to provide value and be continuously updated with CNN-like tidbits of relevant and valued information. One of the things I learned doing our Smart SOA (trademarked) widget was to leverage a specialized firm that had experience with widgets. They provided me a great-looking widget (see Figure 10.13), and I provided the great content that I wanted to get out to my widget users.

Other uses for widgets that energize your market and channel include the following:

- **Customer support mechanism:** A widget can be designed in a manner so that the end user can ask a question or report an SOA problem, and the appropriate parties with the company can see that inquiry and respond accordingly, for example, putting a consultant in touch with the client or answering the question directly, and so on. Today, support chat rooms and e-mail question forms are often utilized, but this requires additional human effort to locate the appropriate division or person within a company to resolve the issue.

- **Document approval processes:** Often a presentation deck or other document needs to be reviewed, updated, and approved by various people located in various parts of the world. Today, Web applications, e-mail, and Lotus Notes® databases are leveraged to try to provide an approval hierarchy, but often the communication of key feedback and so on is lost or misconstrued along the way. The concept of a widget providing real-time information via RSS feeds can be leveraged to ensure everyone has access to the latest document of interest; additionally, the appropriate persons can provide feedback (written or verbal) that can then be tracked alongside that item's entry in the widget. Upon approval, the item and its feedback records are stored in a more permanent location (because most widgets are not designed as a long-term document reference repository).

The real beauty of widgets is that they narrow your scope of information and bring it to you rather than the other way around. It is so easy to become overwhelmed by all of the information out there. Strange as it might sound, sometimes going to a Web site is too much work. For example, take the blogs on my RSS feed. There's no way that I will go out and visit each of them once a day. I don't have that kind of time. However, if I take a quick look at my RSS widget, I can not only see the titles of any updated postings, but I can also read a selection from that posting, and then I decide if it is worth it for me to visit that Web page.

Companies should work with widgets to cut through the clutter of the marketplace and energize their channels.

The Collaborative Web Site: Wikis

Now let's turn our attention to wikis. A wiki is software that enables users to freely create and edit Web page content using any Web browser. Wikis enable you to create a place to store information. Wikis are special in that the organization and content can both be edited. Anyone can add, create, or edit a wiki page. Even nontechnical users can create their own information repositories. For internal use, wikis are an "interactive" repository of information, comments, and insights. They are a simple intranet that can be used by everybody in a simple way. Figure 10.14 features the IBM Super Women's Group for our group of outstanding female leaders in IBM. This internal wiki enables us to share information in a dynamic format.

Externally, wikis are like Web sites, but the interactivity makes the difference. On the outside, there is the risk that people can add content that is not useful or even inaccurate. It requires strong tracking and control. Wikipedia is one of the best-known wikis and has a great system to ensure the content is accurate and relevant.

Businesses install wikis to provide affordable and effective intranets and for knowledge management. Ward Cunningham, developer of the first wiki, WikiWikiWeb, originally described it as "the simplest online database that could possibly work." How might a wiki be used in marketing? To provide information to your sales team or your customers and ecosystem in a constant refresh state.

For example, I produce and publish to my internal and external community an award-winning newsletter. My editor, a brilliant woman by the name of Ally Jimenez Klopsch, sets up a set of links to the SOA wiki that my team manages. The newsletter has no bulk or size to it and is a brilliant piece of art going out the door. The wiki affords me the ability to have information sent without a huge size and to provide constantly updated data and information. I use the wiki for both my internal and external views of the data. In Figure 10.15, you can see the version of our newsletter that goes out to the distribution list of more than 100,000 people.

This newsletter and approach won a MarCom Award for Excellence in Marketing Communications from the Association of Marketing & Communications Professionals. This wiki keeps my ecosystem energized in that it always have access to the freshest content around!

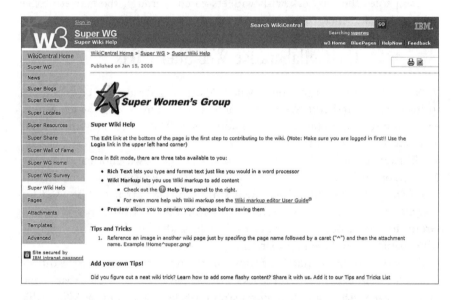

Figure 10.14   The Super Women's Group internal wiki.

Top Five Lessons Learned for Widgets and Wikis

I combined our top tips for both widgets and wikis as they tend to be similar in lessons learned to date. The following are the focus areas for success:

1. **Widgets are here to stay:** Pilot or play with a use now and learn from it. It can be a powerful extension of your brand and an energizer for your ecosystem.

Figure 10.15 The SOA Newsletter supported by a wiki

2. **Use a professional for widgets:** Focus on your core competency of marketing and the content that will entice the ecosystem to come back, and use a professional for the production of the actual widget application

3. **Brings information to the user:** If the widget merely contains a collection of titles and hyperlinks, it is really no more useful than a Web page. Things such as scrolling titles to breaking news, videos that play within the widget, and information tailored to the user are examples of valuable widget features. It should be something that a user can glance at and see that it is compelling.

4. **Be creative in your use of wikis:** Leveraging the power of constant updates and small file size is of value in newsletters and other interactive forms of communication with your audience. Wikis are powerful enough for both your core channels inside your company and outside your company.

5. **Content is king:** In both widgets and wikis, the value is in the content being fresh and new. Don't invest in this vessel for your ecosystem and not invest in the upkeep and passion for the content.

Blogging Including Twitter

Blogging is a Web-based discussion tool that enables individuals or groups to directly and easily communicate their thoughts, experience, opinions, feelings, and observations for all to see! Blogs espouse a worldview with the voice of the author reflecting her ideas (either knowledge or a unique perspective) that might influence perceptions and an overall position of those opinions in the marketplace. Blogs create great opportunities for shaping messages, but they also create risks if there is propagation of inaccurate or proprietary information. They foster discussion, debate, and even a sense of community.

Depending on the source, there are millions of bloggers throughout the world, although the number of active bloggers (those posting twice a week) has slowed a little with all the new choices of Web 2.0 technology available. (Remember that blogging actually began as Weblogs back in 1997.) For example, IBM's internal blogs have posting from those in more than 73 countries and saw 60,000 page views on the main blog story on IBM's intranet. IBM has more than 160 external blogs and group blogs. IBM blogging guidelines are well established across the business world (see Chapter 9, "Influencer Value: The IBM Case Study," for how the guidelines were created).

Blogs can create awareness and buzz. They can create positive word of mouth and interest in new products and establish interaction and relationships with customers or prospects.

They present a new way to frame and influence public discussion and form a new economic and social space for learning and collaboration. As blogs are text-heavy and frequently updated, they can be leveraged with search engine tools. For example, several blog search engines are used to search blog contents (also known as the blogosphere), such as Blogdigger, Feedster, and

Technorati. Technorati provides current information on both popular searches and tags used to categorize blog postings.

A tumblelog is a type of blog. It is focused on being simple and short versus some of the longer blogs that have become known in blogging. People who write tumblelogs use a lot of visualization, such as pictures, videos, audio, and links. The primary focus of tumblelogs is typically to share experiences and discoveries of the author, not as much to focus on a topic or area of interest. Often there are few words but lots of extras!

Microblogging is also a short form of a blog but more in text form. A lot of the content comes from instant messaging and mp3s or even texting. Often these blogs are restricted to a small set of friends.

The most popular service is called Twitter. Twitter is free social networking and microblogging site that enables users to post their latest updates. An update is limited by 140 characters and can be posted through three methods: Web form, text message, or instant message. Twitter is interesting in that the younger generation is enamored with it! A friend's son uses it as an "efficient" way to keep track of his "crew." They use Twitter to log what they do all day, and then instead of calling each other, they check out Twitter to keep up to date on their friends' lives.

The increase in the use of Twitter is amazing. Web visits have increased eight times in the last year. Compete shows about 900,000 U.S. monthly Web site visitors. Comscore puts the worldwide number at 1.3+ million unique monthly visitors. Twitter can be used to virally spread information to your intended audience and provide them with simple instructions about how to sign up for a free account and follow your stream. Customers, prospects, partners, and colleagues can view your updates. It is a good idea to follow those who follow you in turn because now that you have a portable broadcasting channel, you can do a variety of things.

For example, given the opt-in model Twitter uses, and because people choose to follow a Tweet stream based on the quality and relevance of its content, Twitter presents an ideal way to reach and foster a real-time community of brand evangelists and key influencers. Because IBM Lotus also drives to raise the brand's legitimacy and relevance in the world of Web 2.0—making the case that "IBM really gets it"—it is imperative that our efforts to market our own social software products embrace such emerging communities and channels.

A recent example is a trade show where Lotus Connections scored a big win with its customers. We were able to keep the chatter going and push the story to our fellow Tweeters, and the groundswell of follow on blogosphere and press activity served as a proof point to Twitter's capability to help us build a story's momentum. Lotus had about 350 followers on Twitter, with more following each day. As Jeff Schick, IBM's vice president of Social Software commented, "We have learned that Twitter can play an important part in our communications efforts and can be a keystone as we raise brand and product awareness/credibility in these nascent communities of purpose."

Goals of blogs vary for marketing purposes, as you see in Figure 10.16.

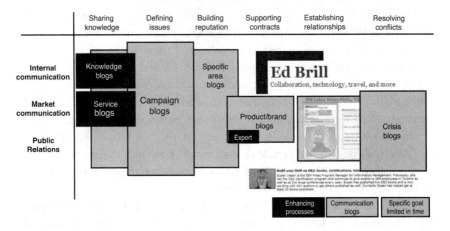

Figure 10.16   The range of options for bloggers.

Some blogs are used for sharing knowledge and to inform. Some blogs tee up key issues and discussion areas. Others are used for extending your brand reputation or, most importantly, to build relationships and put a face on your company. Subject-matter and product-expert blogs help drive traffic, product awareness, and brand loyalty. They can be used internally, for the market, or even drive public-relations activities. They serve as tools and extend networks to collaborate and share knowledge.

Blogs have an impact on businesses. They often beat the mainstream media to major stories and serve as corporate watchdogs and quality control. Overall, they serve as an alternative source of information and company viewpoints. For example, IBM started a group blog called HeathNex. It is a group of IBM healthcare and external experts discussing the transformation of medicine and human health. It is often covered in the news and has led to the awareness of IBM's significant involvement in healthcare technologies.

From my viewpoint, blogging is an innovative PR media with strong influence when the bloggers are part of the community/group you need to influence, inform, or seduce. In Figure 10.17, we see a sample from IBM

Lotus's blogger Ed Brill. Ed helps Lotus' 46,000 customers with their sense of community and commonality and refutes its competitor's fear, uncertainty, and doubt (FUD). He shares news and information about Lotus and has decreased the distance between IBM and its customers.

- Edbrill.com—one of IBM's top ranked/rated blogs and it has been operation more than five years running

- More than 3K entries and more than 30K valid comments

- 2,500+ readers daily, thousands more via RSS subscription feeds

- Spikes in traffic driven by key Lotus and industry announcements (Lotusphere, Collaboration Summit, and so on)

- Linked to by more than 7,000 other blogs, press, and websites

Figure 10.17 The IBM Lotus example.

The key challenges you face are similar to the other vessels we discuss. How do you get people to your blog? How do you keep your content fresh, relevant, and exciting by combining different techniques, methods, and vehicles? Creativity is again one of the secrets of success! One example of how to get your blog read is to subscribe your blog in different directories to help disseminate and improve search engines so that more people will get to your blog. I have been a blogger on IBM's blogsphere for about two years and still host one of the top ten blogs. I use it to share information with my readers and linkers. It is part of my marketing mix where I disseminate messages, especially where other bloggers link into my site. My channel loves my blog, and I receive e-mails from around the world about the topics that I choose to focus on.

Top Five Ideas for Better Blogging

The top tips for blogging can make the difference in your success in the marketplace in leveraging this area for better marketing gains.

1. **Identify your key bloggers inside and outside your company:** Work with the bloggers to influence the marketplace. Set up your own blog

through Wordpress, Typepad, Blogger, or other blog-hosting services. Setting up your own blog will teach you "on the job" how blogging works, the technology behind it, and get you involved in the community.

2. **Content is king:** Note this trend on a lot of the digital media types. This is one reason I have started hiring writers. The digital world needs great communication and creativity skills. If using Twitter, share bites of knowledge from events and receive other people's impressions.

3. **Use multimedia types:** Videos, links, and pictures make your blog more readable and fun. You can broadcast meet-up places on Twitter and provide an online streaming video or audio channel for those who are not on the ground to join you live. (This is a nice touch for customers.)

4. **Be personal:** Bloggers share personal tidbits about their lives. Remember that your blog gets you closer to your customer. It strengthens the relationship.

5. **Think through it:** Try out Twitter or just blog. Voice your opinion and participate in the conversation. You can't see the impact until you start, but make sure whatever you write is fit to go on the front page. Because anything out there could end up on the news, use it as a tool to gather feedback on your reports from the road by asking questions and interacting with your audience.

RSS

According to Wikipedia, RSS is a Web-feed format used to publish frequently updated content such as blogs, news, and podcasts in a standard format. An RSS document, also called a feed, contains a summary of content from an associated Web site or the full text. RSS makes it possible for people to keep up with Web sites in an automated manner that can be piped into special programs. RSS has been around for at least five years. It is one of the simplest technologies to date that enables users to keep tabs of the content they care about without the hassles of always browsing all the Web sites.

The value of RSS feeds for marketers is that they provide a way to keep up-to-date fresh content flowing to your customers. A global survey of internal and corporate communications professionals found that more than half use blogs, online video, and RSS or plan to do so in the next 12 months. Instead of holding off for another two to three weeks for the next e-mail blast, with RSS, marketers can post content instantly.

For example, at IBM, our developerWorks® site allows experts to create their content, relate their knowledge, keep others informed, and connect with the broader developerWorks community that share their interests. There has been more than 100 percent year-to-year growth in RSS feeds on developerWorks.

Top Five Lessons Learned for Success on RSS

RSS feeds are powerful ways to drive your message dynamically into the market. The following are the top five tips for your RSS strategy:

1. Determine the content to distribute with regularly updated content, customized feeds, notifications, and alerts.
2. Build the feeds.
3. Use feeds to expand market by making RSS links easily available and visible and enable one-click subscriptions to RSS aggregators.
4. Build promotional applications with feeds.
5. Measure the feeds and their impact.

Podcasts

According to Wikipedia, podcasting is defined as a series of digital media files distributed over the Internet for playback on portable media players and the computer. The term *podcast* can refer either to the series of content itself or to the method by which it is syndicated. Podcasting (think "iPod" and "broadcasting") is similar to a radio show transmitted over the Web. The advantage over radio is that anyone can make a podcast, and the people can listen to the episodes whenever they like. People who downloads the podcast can listen to it on their computers or transfer the files to a portable player (such as an iPod). Podcasts are presented in a series and often have a theme so that the subscribers have an idea about what to expect when they sign up to receive the podcasts. Videocasting is used for the online delivery of video clips.

There is a lot of value in podcasting for marketers. eMarketer estimates that there was a 285 percent increase in the size of the U.S. podcast audience in 2007, which was a growth to 18.5 million. Furthermore, that audience will increase to 65 million in 2012. Of those listeners, 25 million will be "active" users who tune in at least once a week. We have also seen this growth inside IBM; our podcast series targeting developers has grown more than 200 percent since 2007.

Capturing and disseminating conversations can be a powerful tool because the listener can hear the excitement. A marketer's opportunity is to share knowledge through a proven medium (audio recording) but in a new and more personal way (fast download to a personal audio player). Like e-mail, instant messaging, and blogging, podcasting can break down barriers and deliver a personal touch.

To launch a successful podcasting program, think of podcasts as well-crafted, engaging radio segments delivered through the Web. Using radio segments as the model, podcasts should be short, focused communications or small nuggets of learning for customers, clients, partners, and employees.

Top Five Lessons Learned on Podcasting

Podcasting is fun and is powerful as a marketing play. Here are the top five tips for your podcasting strategy from my discussion with IBM's podcasting experts:

1. **Plan your podcast:** Podcasts require planning to determine the audience, the purpose, the format, and whether the material is appropriate for audio only. Talking to the IBM podcast experts, they recommend ten minutes as a target. This can be hard to do when you work with interesting topics and engaging subjects. Seek the opinions of your colleagues when editing your content and edit aggressively. Brevity is a powerful tool when dealing in spoken-word audio recording.

2. **Stylize your podcast:** Decide whether you want to do an interview or a one-person presentation. IBM's podcast experts advise booking the most knowledgeable person you can find on your subject and making sure you have chosen someone who can speak intelligibly with clarity and warmth. If you or your guests simply read your messages, chances are you will not get much of an audience. On the other hand, if you and your guests improvise with authority and intelligence, you will have a winning program.

3. **Podcast in a series:** Why a series? Well, this is the hallmark of what makes a podcast a podcast. Podcast users expect a continuing series that they can follow, not just a one-off file.

4. **Combine with interactive blogs:** After the demand for podcasts expands and your experience deepens, consider combining podcasts with interactive blogs to get an even higher level of interaction with your audience.

5. Use for internal and external purposes: Remember, your employees are a key carrier of your brand. Consider a podcast series on your company's brand value!

Videocasting

Videocasting is used for the online delivery of video clips. It is basically video online. Probably the most popular videocasting example is YouTube. Anyone with a camera and a computer can begin his own videocast.

INFORMATION ON DEMAND'S YOUTUBE

by Nancy Pearson, Vice President of IBM Information on Demand

This is a best practice in Viral Videocasting from IBM's Data Management group. The purpose of the viral video project was to increase awareness of the Data Management segment of our IBM Information Management business, both in the market and internally. The video series highlights key segment messages in a storyline about a corporate video project gone awry. The story was delivered in a series of three videos, with each video showing the progression of the fictional project. The series was shared through social media venues, including YouTube and IBM TV Channel. The goal was to make these videos smart, entertaining, and creative to enable a viral effect.

Step-by-Step Process

The approach was to post the video and share it with internal and external audiences, leveraging the viral effect of social media sites to promote it further. The thought process for increasing awareness was to initially seed selected internal and external audiences; for example, if 100 people watched the video, they expected that those 100 people will tell 50 other people, and those 50 will tell 25, and so on. Each week a new video was released, continuing the story and creating anticipation of the next release.

The viral effect goal was to reach the "whitespace" audience. The IBM team did their homework. Although videos are important, fewer than 10 percent get more than 1,500 views, 3 percent of videos get more than

5,000 views, and 1 percent of videos get more than 500,000 views! To date, in the three weeks since release, the videos collectively in the series have been viewed more than 6,000 times.

Lessons Learned

Doing series of three videos rather than three separate videos gave the team a better chance to hook the audience and create something viral.

This storyline had to have the right tone to have a viral effect. In this case, the tone is dry and deadpan, and therefore, it's funny, as the tone highlights the absurdity of the discussion at hand (trying to find ways to "personify" corporate message points into some kind of dramatic narrative).

The media enables the team to come out and blatantly state the message points (as part of the brainstorming), yet then immediately juxtapose them with ironic counterpoint (a smart and self-deprecating move appreciated by the audience and showing that we don't take ourselves too seriously).

The series strategy provided the opportunity to create recurring characters that will resonate with the audience.

The agreed on storyline has potential for a longer shelf life and can be reused in the future to create new scenarios.

Results

The viral videos were posted to YouTube and ChannelDB2 on June 12, 2008. In a short three weeks, the following occurred:

- The videos in the series have been viewed collectively more than 6,000 times on YouTube
- Linked to by five other sites (viral growth)
- Listed as a "favorite" on YouTube 18 times
- Scored a content rating of 4.5 stars (out of 5)

Top Five Lessons Learned on Videocasting

A picture is worth a 1000 words, especially online. Videocasting as a new vessel is a powerful add to your GTM execution for energizing your channel. Below are five tips on how to be most successful in its usage:

1. **Have a script:** Make the script informative and entertaining, and make sure you connect with the audience. This might seem like Marketing 101, but sometimes when a camera is around, people forget to keep it simple and targeted. Remember, do not read from the script!

2. **Editing is crucial:** Editing software is inexpensive these days, and editing can make or break your video. Make sure you shoot some "B-Roll" without sound. The editor will use this footage to enhance the video and make it much easier to edit. Maybe it's your subject walking around the location, doing or demonstrating some task if appropriate; maybe show the person interacting with others (without sound).

3. **Make sure you tag it correctly to get picked up:** A feed needs to be created for each videocast series, enabling users to subscribe to it. This feed is then submitted or registered with sites such as iTunes or Yahoo, and it will show up in their listings and searches.

4. **Call to action:** Just because it is video doesn't mean you can skip this step. Your videocast needs to have clear direction at its closure.

5. **Make it an experience:** Video is different from podcasting. Make sure you maximize the use of pictures and imagery to make your story become an experience.

Putting It Together—The Marketing 2.0 Starter Set!

I highlighted seven of the new interactive vessels for brand and product content. As you can tell, there is a lot of learning, experimentation, and success occurring in the marketplace today. I recommend that with these new tools, you focus on the goal that you need to accomplish within your integrated plan of both traditional and nontraditional elements. Begin by educating yourself on the social tools and experiment with small projects. Also, observe how the community works and its rules. Then, incorporate a few elements into your overall plan, such as a Facebook fan group around a product or a widget to share new information with your partner community. Learn what makes sense for you to measure and track. Then advance to a point where you increase your funding, your participation, and your integration of the social aspects into your overall strategy. Although this is new, try it first, but don't wait too long to jump in with both feet.

Make sure you start social bookmarking. There are more than 15 billion Web sites on the Internet, so you need help to sort through all the information sources. Step into the new Marketing 2.0 world using social tagging. There are some great ways to help you organize all your social news. Dogear (aimed at businesses and enterprises), del.icio.us, Digg, reddit, and Newsvine offer a similar system for organization of "social news." Because this is social bookmarking, these are meant to be shared! Get started by signing up for a service (maybe de.licio.us), start bookmarking with tags, and finally, socialize your bookmarks and see what others are looking at!

As Daryl Plummer, managing VP and Gartner Fellow writes, "In SOA, the least important word is Service. With Web 2.0, the most important word is community. When the two come together and systems start delivering services to communities, real phenomena begin to emerge. Large numbers of people coming together to use services will generate the next innovations for new business. If you ask me, the way to the next billion-dollar company goes through figuring out how to let a community of customers serve themselves while you allow the community to grow and take your money from the people who want to deliver services to them. That is the essence of the emerging 'Cloud' and rising successes of MySpace, Flickr, and many others."

For my business at IBM, we set up starter kits to help our clients get started in an easy fashion. Because my IBM clients love the starter kits for technology, here is our virtual starter set for your new vessel approach to Marketing 2.0. It is just a suggested way to get you going on your journey. From the above chapter and previous chapters, the following is my recommended Marketing 2.0 Starter Set!

Go to ibmpressbooks.com/angels to get a look at the Starter Set.

- **Listening:** Google reader
- **Social networks:** Facebook
- **Virtual environments:** Second Life, OpenSim, and ActiveWorlds.
- **Widgets:** Google, Yahoo
- **Wiki hosting:** PBwiki
- **Microblogging:** Twitter
- **Blogging host:** Wordpress, Typepad, and Blogger
- **Mobile blogging:** Utterz
- **Linking and tagging (blogosphere):** Technorati, Google Blogsearch, and LinkedIn

- Audio hosting: iTunes
- Video hosting: YouTube

Conclusion

Today is an exciting time in the marketplace as new vessels invade the marketers' toolkit. These new tools invite the trusted customer to speak on our behalf and energize the customer to be our brand advocates. Leveraging the new vessels with the channel provides us a way to listen, respond, and leverage the power of the ecosystem.

However, it is also scary the number and choices of new media and interactive marketing. The vessels that we use to energize our channel are abundant and cost effective. The new digital age lets us network with virtual worlds and online communities, actively participate with viral techniques and serious gaming, share through widgets and wikis, and blog for top media coverage and brand extension. Vessel success is based on strong and relevant content and creativity. The goal is to leverage these vessels to energize your market and channel. It brings the customer and ecosystem closer to your company with a personal digital face. Try them for marketing value in your ecosystem but have a coordinated and integrated plan about how and when to leverage them. Now is the time to experiment to see what works in this Marketing 2.0 world.

The growth of new media vessels reflects large-scale changes in organizational structure and work styles, and these changes will impact the future of the enterprise. College students use MySpace, and this is how they expect to interact. Blogging and gaming has invoked a feeling that credibility is bestowed by the community, not by title or position. The bottom line is that this isn't just about seizing marketing opportunities, but it is about remaining relevant in a changing dynamic.

For an example of an SOA newsletter, additional content on widgets, Twitter linkage, Smart SOA Social network flash, and a Marketing 2.0 Starter Kit, go to ibmpressbooks.com/angels.

11

Energize the Channel with Communities: OMG, Adobe and Rubicon Consulting, and Harley-Davidson

Communities can build amazing things, but you have to be part of that community and you can't abuse them. You have to be very respectful of what their needs are.
—Jimmy Wales

I am dog lover. I actually love all animals. I have always had a dog, whether it was my mixed breed Queenie, who went on many adventures with me in my youth, or my current dog Scarlet, a purebred Maltese, dogs have always held a place in my heart.

There are many dog lovers out there like me; we have a shared view of dogs and an interest to see dog shows, puppies, and virtually anything dog-like. A community like that, whether in person or online, drives opinions, thoughts, and word of mouth stronger than ever before. For example, take dogster.com. Nilofer Merchant, the CEO of Rubicon, discussed this community site and comments, "The site features everything to do with dogs. They've found a way to communicate the love of dogs. You can post the picture of the dog; you can write blog entries for the dog; they have a dog of the day that you can vote on. All of their advertising is actually sponsored advertising. So they won't just do a Shutterfly ad, they'll do a Shutterfly ad that is focused on creating a dog book." (If you, too, are a dog lover, check out dogster.com!)

Consumers today are not passive. They are active and want to have a bidirectional conversation with those who are interested in similar topics and areas. Communities are powerful and growing more powerful. In Chapter 10, "The New Vessels," we learned that a variety of communities are centered on soliciting input from customers, an obsession or activity, or an experience. Let's look at several case studies about communities.

Focus on Object Management Group's (OMG) Activity-Based Communities

For this particular case study, I talked directly with Richard Soley, the chairman and chief executive officer (CEO) of Object Management Group (OMG) and the executive director of the SOA consortium. The OMG is a community around the support and creation of software standards. The value of its shared activity is that the members of the community and their companies get value from the openness of the standards. Soley has been working in communities and leading communities for more than 18 years!

The OMG Community Agenda

The OMG community is both online and in person. I visited one of the in-person meetings recently in California. It was one of the quarterly meetings, and there was a strong in-person showing. However, in addition to the in-person meetings, it is also an active online community. The community has roughly 100 megabytes of e-mail that go back and forth per month among about 5,000 members of the participants in the 100 standards.

In fact, this community is a strong online community and a strong face-to-face community. As Soley says, "There are few people who participate only face to face, and amazingly there are few people who participate only online. Online meetings and more generally online communities are great but to have activity-based communities be effective, you need people to meet. To get real agreement on things, people need to meet in person to form a great relationship, so that decisions can be made both online and face to face."

That is why, under Soley's leadership, the OMG gains its intimacy from meeting once quarterly. A lot of value is delivered in the meeting. There's so much going on that there is little time to sleep. I spoke at the OMG community meetings, and at the same time I was speaking, there were 42 meeting rooms in use simultaneously that morning. In addition to the face-to-face meetings, there is real value in the online portion of the community. OMG leverages e-mail, wikis, and blogs.

The OMG was one of the first communities to leverage e-mail. Successful communities are both face to face and online. From those communities that are activity-based, most have moved to a face-to-face meeting at least once a year. For OMG, its online strategy is still changing and after talking to Soley, I think it will always change. This is the nature of the online medium; it is continuously enhanced to enable growth and change. As Soley explains, "In 1989, when we pushed our community to use e-mail, that was actually a fairly new thing. In 1990, we added document repositories and…that document repository, by the way, currently has 30,000 to 40,000 documents in something like a 100 different formats growing since early 1990, and we have added new collaboration methodology online as they become available." (See Figure 11.1.)

Figure 11.1   OMG's wikis.

What Are the Secrets to OMG's Success?

Richard Soley has led OMG to success in its community for many years. The key points I took away from what OMG did as a best practice follow:

- **The community members share a common goal and make decisions:** OMG is around open standards for the marketplace. Soley told me this strong common goal is the number one reason the community is so successful. OMG is working on the capability for their working groups to progress their standards activities faster by picking up meeting the same way the members would be able to do if they were all in the same space at the same time, even though they are spread all over the world. For this activity-based community, its success is built on what decisions are made and how rapidly they are made.

- **Special interest subgroups are valuable:** OMG has subcommunities that form around different verticals and technologies. The healthcare group and the government groups use different approaches and digital tools. Of the 30 different vertical market groups, roughly half of them are using wikis as a way to share documents. In the healthcare group, though, they decided to leverage group network software instead of wikis.

- **Balance of in person and digital:** For example, OMG's government group leverages online white boards and wikis. However, it also gets together for in-person meetings.

- **Continuous improvement:** Soley is always looking for new ways to do things. OMG did a sneak preview of its new digital strategy for the international members. OMG is going to more online structures for participation in e-mail lists and wiki updates on voting status, which is a structure that enables it to build networks of participants online.

- **New members, new needs:** The new OMG members expect more instantaneous results. They want the ability to create instantaneous relationships that go anywhere from instant messaging to SMS messages on telephones. OMG wants to make more instant relationships and turn the community process into a much more rapid decision-making process. This will be taken into account in OMG's new generation strategy.

Application to Your Company

In forming communities, you need to look for a platform for social and emotional connection. Obviously, for activity-based communities, you need to progress the activities. Like OMG, this takes a lot of work and focus on both the online portion and the digital portion of the communities' interactions.

Make sure you are prepared for the effort in driving to rapid activity completion and decisions.

THE KEY ELEMENTS AND ACTIONS REQUIRED TO BUILD A STRATEGIC B2B COMMUNITY

Rod Baptie, CEO of Baptie Online LTD and Lisa Barnett, vice president of Communities, Baptie Online Ltd

Key Elements of the Community

To build a B2B community, you need to meet these three key goals:

- Build an understanding of the needs of the community and an in-depth understanding of which of those needs are provided by existing organizations and how this community can provide additional facilities, information, and interaction to make it a viable entity.
- Develop a trusted environment; this can be built by engaging with a senior-level group of individuals to form the core of the community.
- Work with the core group to begin to deliver the essential content that will draw members into the community.

Understanding Their Needs

You must understand what they want. What are the key things they require from the community? What membership benefits would they find appealing? What is the core content they would like to have available for the community? Where would this content come from? What restrictions would they like to place on who can become a member and what they can do?

Above all, you need to establish that there is a need and that you can provide compelling value not provided by the organizations already operating in this area.

All this work needs to be carried out in an environment that builds the belief, and indeed the reality, that this is their group, developed for them, and by them. A big step for any organization embarking on the process is that the organization needs to respect a number of key things:

- It has to be their community, not yours.
  - ◆ It needs to be independent. There is a massive difference between a company x user group and a community sponsored by company x.
  - ◆ It should have an independent chair recruited from the ranks of the community who is enabled to run the community.
  - ◆ Topics, discussions, and so on within the community must be driven by the members.
- You need to answer their needs, not yours.
  - ◆ It has to provide the information they want, not the information you want to give them.
  - ◆ It's not about your products or services, it's about building true business intelligence about your community.
- It must be a trusted environment.
  - ◆ It must be a trusted environment, a place where they feel comfortable and can share their issues with their peers in a closed environment. Most high-level B2B communities are restrictive on press and vendor access.
- B2B communities are about people, not technology.
  - ◆ One of the key differences between B2B and B2C communities are that B2B communities need to be driven; they don't tend to grow by osmosis, so they need dedicated people interacting with the community, creating content, making sure new things are happening, answering members' needs, and so on.
  - ◆ Don't get hung up on technology. Yes the platform is important, but a community with poorer technology driven by the right people with drive and empathy for the community will always be more successful than a community that is dependent on technology alone.

B2B Communities Succeed Because They Do a Number of Things

- The community empowers the members. The community must be run by the members to deliver the services they want.

- Communities give the members what they want. Above all, the compelling content will draw members into the community.
- Communities have passion.

The community manager needs to develop with the community a content schedule, conferences, events, panels, webinars, surveys, polls, and so on, both online and offline that cover the most important issues and generate the passion for the subject matter, the debate, and as a result, the community.

They Are for People Like Me

Our experience runs counter to the Web myth that you should make it as easy as possible to join a community. In our experience, members respect having to qualify and the fact that not everyone can join. In most of the communities in which we are involved more than 30 percent of applications to join are turned down.

This is essential. It says to the community: "This is your group, it is for people like you, and when you join, a significant part of the value is that only senior executives like you can participate." Community members want to be assured they are with people like them.

The Community Allows Members to Collaborate

One of the key benefits to members of the community is the ability to collaborate in three key ways:

- To resolve common issues. Typically, the core group will decide on a monthly basis what the key issues are that affect the community and ask small groups of people from within the group to collaborate to produce whitepapers addressing these issues.

  In this way, all the group members benefit. Not only do members receive help from like-minded executives in other organizations to address the issue most pressing for them, but they also receive the benefits of all the other whitepapers addressing key issues that are or probably will affect them. Because of this, their productivity is massively enhanced and their perceived ability in their own organization increases dramatically.

- To build business together, certain communities benefit enormously from the fact that the community gives them the opportunity and technology to enable them to discover and work in collaboration with other members of the community.
- Social networking is another important element in the success of a B2B community.

Communities Must Offer Multiple Ways to Interact

There is no such thing as an online community. As the group forms quickly, it will want to interact in multiple ways both online and offline. It is essential to the success of the community that this interaction is enabled and encouraged. The community must offer multiple ways to interact. Although the online element is the glue that sticks it all together, B2B communities are based on trust, and trust comes only after a face-to-face engagement, so regular meetings and events are vital to the success of a B2B community.

Focus on Adobe and Rubicon's Definition-Based Community

For this particular case study, I talked directly with Nilofer Merchant, the CEO of Rubicon, which is a consulting company that focuses on a multidisciplinary approach for assessing a business situation clearly by applying critical wisdom and defining a strategic direction. Merchant is an amazingly talented woman, and I gained a lot of insight in our conversation. Here I will focus on an engagement she did with Adobe.

The community that Adobe wanted to engage with was a targeted group focused on technical users at work specifically in the biomedical and nontraditional fields. It wanted to gain insight about why users liked the current product and also where it needed more help and direction. This community was focused on leveraging the customers to help define where they were headed in the marketplace. Adobe's second community goal was to have it become a set of enthusiasts who would then spread the word to others. In other words, the community would become the "tippers" in their fields. Rubicon had to develop a strategic plan to find and cultivate these users, while showing respect and appreciation for them. In essence, it had to build a community from scratch!

In previous examples, we looked at how the community expanded and made decisions. This example is about setting up a new community. Rubicon started by assisting Adobe with a small, in-person advisory group of customers in the biomedical field. Eventually Merchant moved the advisory group to a community model. The community was anxious to have its ideas listened to and willing to help Adobe with seeing the way to the future. The goal of this definition community was to test messages, get input on product features desired by the group, view the work done by the biomedical users, and obtain supportive quotes, video testimonials, and more.

A microsite was created on the client's Web site that targeted biomedical users. Merchant launched the site by providing relevant information to the new community. The material was geared to the language of the community. Rubicon helped document online what biomed users could do with the Adobe product and used the Internet to spread the word about usage. Users gained valuable information, including diagnostics, patient education, and colleague education. Procedures and outcomes were shared among the users. The community was effectively used to drive the market entry and manage how they talked to other community members. (See Figure 11.2.)

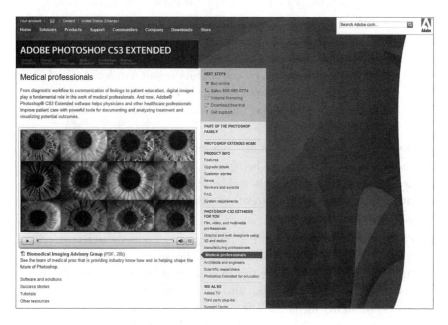

Figure 11.2   Rubicon and Adobe form a definition community.

The Secrets to Rubicon and Adobe's Success

Merchant is crisp and clear in her use of community in marketing. The following are insights derived from discussions about the successful use of communities in marketing:

- **Clearly know and state your goal for the community:** In Chapter 14, "Blogs: Midwest Airlines and IBM," we looked at the various types of communities. Clearly, if the goal of your community is to define a product or market, it will be different than an obsession-based community to further drive the passion and energy of your brand. Be sure you are clear in your goal. For example, "This community is being developed for users interested in your key subject." Make sure the goal of the group is specific to the needs of your users.

- **Low cost, big value:** Merchant relayed that Rubicon's success required reaching a vertical industry with a fraction of one head count. A traditional marketing program would require a company to hire several in-house, full-time people. Using the community approach, one that Merchant is personally sold on, enables the work to be accomplished with a small cost.

- **Ongoing effort:** A big recommendation that both Merchant and I discussed was how to begin such a community-building effort. We both agreed that cultivation of a new community requires experience and ongoing engagement. Without constant care, a nascent community dies. You need to touch online users, just as you would customers at a face-to-face (F2F) event.

- **Skills are critical:** To start a new community, you need a strong owner. The skills that work include being an extrovert, being a good listener, having strong follow-through, and being adept at using online communication tools. Knowing how to keep a small community of enthusiasts fed and happy is critical.

- **The recruitment strategy:** It is an interesting endeavor to recruit members to start a community. This is one of the keys to success and is also difficult. Merchant's strategy was to go after enthusiastic users and those who would provide insight but also who would like hosting events for other community members. She also looked for those who had big networks and were the "tippers" in the biomedical field.

In this example, Rubicon helped Adobe reach its verticals more effectively. It enabled Adobe to play a part in the conversation going on in the biomedical field. Its plans are now to take this community strategy to more communities in other verticals.

Application to Your Company

Beginning a new community is a big endeavor. Make sure you are up to the task in terms of time to provide relevant information. In addition, spend time determining the areas that provide value back to the community, whether it be growing their personal equity as thought leaders or gaining insight to take back into their companies.

Focus on Harley-Davidson's Obsession-Based Community: H.O.G.

Harley-Davidson is a global company that both sells and manufactures motorcycles and clothing, with a focus on the lifestyle of the open road and open spaces. It has consistently outpaced its record performance for 20 years. During the most recent 10-year period, compound annual growth rates for revenue and earnings have been better than 14 percent and 23 percent, respectively.

Harley's community, Harley Owners Group (H.O.G.®), is the largest of its kind with a global community. So, I wanted to go deeper and understand what drove the community. I spoke to a user-group leader for Harley, Ken Creary, an IBM employee but leader for the New Rochelle, New York H.O.G. Chapter and Dan Powers, an IBM executive, a proud Harley owner, and an active member of H.O.G. community.

The Harley Community Agenda

The Harley community is a fascinating one. Harley has had a viral social community since 1983. H.O.G. was started by the company as a way for riders to share the bonds between them and with the brand. Although it began in the United States, the first international group started in England in 1991 and global groups have only grown over time. The community is both online and in person with a focus on in-person meetings facilitated through events and the joy and passion of riding together and doing things together. All the groups exist around surrounding brick-and-mortar dealerships. Not all dealers sponsor H.O.G. chapters, but a H.O.G. chapter can exist only if a dealer sponsors it.

Harley's focus and philosophy for the groups is about interactions and obsession. In contrast are other communities that are about media plans and creative plans to sell things, but not about the aspect of the effect on people. The result is an increase in sales, but it comes secondarily. Its groups foster rich and deep social interactions. H.O.G. is probably the strongest social network of any company anywhere. There are more than a million members across the world.

Let's look at an example of Dan Powers. He joined the H.O.G. community in 2003 when he got his new Harley 2003 Road King. When you buy a bike from Harley, it gives you free membership to H.O.G. for one year. Powers comments, "After that timeframe, it is apparent this is a community you want to be in every year and you sign up for your yearly membership." You can also pay one price for a lifetime membership! A famous tagline from American Express is, "Membership has its privileges"; in Harley's case after you experience the community, you know membership is fun, and you can't imagine not being part of H.O.G. going forward.

Many times at motorcycle rallies, you see members proudly displaying H.O.G. patches on their jackets that go back many years. Some have chosen to be lifetime members. This is a badge of honor and branding all in one! Along with patches and membership pins, H.O.G. sends a travel guide and map that includes the location of all the dealers in the world. One of the reasons many H.O.G. members renew or become life members is the free towing to the nearest Harley-Davidson dealer should a member get stranded somewhere. This service is similar to AAA but for motorcycles. H.O.G. also has a terrific member magazine—*H.O.G. Tales*—complete with user-submitted content and pictures of their journeys. Many dealers also provide discounts for members of the local H.O.G. chapters. Although these rational benefits are powerful, arguably the social and emotional benefits of being in the community provide the most value.

The H.O.G. Web site focuses on what riders want and need such as mapping of routes and sharing those maps with other riders going on those routes. It also has a list of all riding events coming up for the year, including links to help ship your bike to the event, hotel arrangements you can make online, and links to others organizing the events for more information.

On the Harley-Davidson main Web site, it is hard to find a link to the H.O.G. Web site. Most Harley riders have already bookmarked it separately, or they click on "Riders" and find the site in addition to many other Harley happenings. Also, the H.O.G. Web site is tightly integrated into the entire

Harley-Davidson Web site to associate Harley from a look, feel, and experience perspective with the community. You are part of Harley and you are part of H.O.G. ; it is a seamless experience and a seamless community.

The H.O.G. community is a great example of not getting caught up in the buzzword of a community. Combining the power of in-person meetings with the Web creates a powerful community. In Figure 11.3, you see how the Web captures the essence of the community—"Express yourself in the company of others!"

Figure 11.3   The H.O.G. Web site.

In the end, H.O.G. is serious about its membership. You can't even join without a VIN number from your bike. Its members are serious, too, because they wouldn't have it any other way. The H.O.G. community charges a fee and does have groups with special interests such as the Ladies of Harley. They also have a membership guide explaining all the key and core concepts about the community.

The Secrets of Harley's Success

The following are the key points for an obsession-based community.

- **In-person meetings and events:** Harley has national, international, and local events. Every Harley executive attends the meetings to learn and listen.

- **Training for the H.O.G. leaders:** The training that is given to H.O.G. leaders in the community is the strongest that I have seen for a community. It truly is a best practice in the industry.

- **Membership is serious:** You can't join without owning a Harley or having a family member or friend to allow you to be an associate member with their full membership. This is similar to the OMG and your need for active participation, but many communities don't have this strict requirement. It does signal commitment.

- **A family value:** Above all, a local H.O.G. chapter is a family—a collection of diverse individuals united by a common passion.

- **Linked strongly to the channel:** Every H.O.G. chapter is sponsored by an authorized Harley-Davidson dealer. That allows strong linkage between the customers and the dealers. It is a strong value for the company. The channel looks for ways to help its members. For instance, it just completed a "ride planning" tool for members to assist them with their routes, restaurants, and hotels along their next trip.

Application to Your Company

When you think about communities, don't think about it just as a buzzword. Communities are serious business. They involve customers and channel partners. The community needs to be focused on them and for them. It cannot be just about selling. In addition, I learned from Harley the power of the in-person plus online linkage. Their organization and management, from training of the H.O.G. leaders to the special groups, such as Ladies of Harley, are truly a best practice. The number one thing Harley riders like to do is ride. So the number one focus for the community is to help riders find rides and other riders in their area, or to help them plan for rides and link with other riders on extended trips that they will take to new areas. Find that link for your community. The value is in the passion!

An online sidebar "Focus on the IBM SOA Society and Integrating Individual Communities" is available on the companion Web site at: ibmpressbooks.com/angels

Conclusion

Communities enable you to have conversations with your customers and tippers in your industry. Given the trends in the marketplace, communities are a cost-effective way to get close to your customers. Great ideas will create relevancy, so companies must be aware of and participate in the conversations. Communities are powerful in defining your market or products, leveraging passion around your products, or in getting activities done and decisions made. A combination of online and in-person meetings is the way to success. Develop a community plan, both with your own vendor communities and in determining what communities that exist in the market. Get in the conversation and be where your customer is!

12

Virtual Environments: The Coca-Cola Company and IBM

Virtual reality is like mainlining television.
—William Gibson

We discussed in Chapter 9, "Influencer Value: The IBM Case Study," the use of "Jams" to come up with new ideas for companies. IBM's focus on virtual environments was one of the top ten ideas from our InnovationJam. For IBM, it began in earnest when our chief executive and chairman, Sam Palmisano, stood outside the Forbidden City (see Figure 12.1), a space in the virtual environment created by IBM with the Chinese government. Through his avatar, he declared that $130 million of investment over the next two years would be made in virtual environments.

IBM works with many 3D Internet providers and platforms. Our work with clients focuses on understanding the business need, and then on determining the appropriate platform to ensure our clients realize true business value from their efforts. As of early 2008, IBM had more than 5,000 IBM employees involved in its virtual universe community exploring various 3D Internet technologies and business solutions. We use these virtual environments for a wide range of activities including virtual meetings, education and training, events, customer interactions, and product development.

In Second Life®, IBM operates a complex of islands where its growing ranks of virtual world innovators are working with clients, collaborating with the public and investigating how virtual environments can enable IBM to operate more productively.

Figure 12.1 IBM's CEO in Second Life.

The Coca-Cola Company also decided to enhance its investment in virtual environments by extending its brand into virtual worlds. It invests in Second Life, not by building islands, but with virtual Coca-Cola dispensers placed throughout the metaverse, an internal, 3D, collaborative environment managed by the CIO organization. It leverages Second Life to supplement work it did in other virtual environments—experiments on how to take its brand outside of the real world and into the metaverse.

In this chapter, we look at examples of virtual environment usage from IBM and The Coca-Cola Company within virtual environments. In this chapter, we explore three areas related to virtual environments. These include

- Education and training
- Events and collaboration
- Marketing and sales

I focus on those three types of uses for virtual environments and the results of experimenting with this new marketing concept, because these are the ones that seem to be the most common entry point for brands experimenting in the metaverse. Many view virtual environments as a potential next form of the Internet wave. Approaching and learning lessons from that Internet era can be invaluable. For instance, in the beginning of the Internet, everyone built Web sites and measured visitors. Back then, the initial set of metrics we used were about how many people came and how long they stayed. At IBM, we experiment with a wide range of virtual environments and tools, including Active Worlds, Forterra, Torque, and Second Life. One of IBM's past chief technologists and now MIT visiting professor, Dr Irving Wladawsky-Berger, acknowledges that this focus on virtual business is in the "experimental stage" for IBM.

Getting Started–An IBM Experience

We focus this IBM case study on some of IBM's early work in the virtual environment of Second Life, which is a 3D, online virtual world where a full economy exists. Virtual environments differ from a traditional Web site in that they enable the simultaneous connection of millions of users who can participate in a rich media collaborative experience. In a virtual world, users can play, work, talk, chat, and share content using Web-enabled graphic software. More than 13 million people worldwide have Second Life characters called avatars. Linden Lab has also called attention to the fact that a huge segment of the Second Life population is international: Approximately 70 percent hail from outside the United States.

> To get started on Second Life, see our online sidebar on the companion Web site at: ibmpressbooks.com/angels.

For this case study, I talked to some of the experts inside IBM and leveraged my own team's work in Second Life. One is British IBM software strategist Ian Hughes, avatar: ePredator Potato. He has been a gamer and a passionate fan of virtual worlds through his blog even before IBM began working in virtual environments. The second is retired IBM executive Dr. Irving Wladawsky-Berger, avatar: Irving Islander. (See Figure 12.2, in the Mets Jersey.)

He is now a professor at MIT and has been known at IBM as a visionary and leader in leveraging new technology. The third is a member of my team,

Georgina Castanon, who I (avatar: Soandy) tasked with getting our SOA Island functioning but more importantly, challenged her to become a part of the community on Second Life. Fourth, Max Andersen, a key IBM creative on my team for virtual worlds has worked tirelessly on the SOA implementation for our SOA Island.

Figure 12.2   Irving in Second Life.

The Marketing Best Practices

There are two best practices that I'd like to focus on to show how virtual environments can be used for marketing events and education:

- **Wimbledon tennis event hosted in Second Life**: We set up a simulation of the Wimbledon tennis tournament, using data that tracks the position of the ball to reenact points several seconds after they happen. This project demonstrates the power of the event experience beyond what happens in the real world.
- **The SOA Island**: Our SOA Island was designed to educate the market and enable visitors to try our products in a virtual world.

These are two of the many examples. We work with clients on a wide range of projects across multiple platforms. These activities include strategy and visioning workshops; hosting private education and training sessions; hosting collaboration activities and events; and customizing development and simulations.

You can find a sidebar "Other Glimpses of Second Life Use" on the companion Web site at ibmpressbooks.com/angels.

Wimbledon Tennis Event in Virtual Worlds

The Wimbledon tennis event has long been an IBM client hospitality event. Marketing and sales work together to invite customers and press to see the matches and go behind the scenes to check out the technology we use. In 2007, we decided to add a virtual world element to the traditional marketing approach. Using Second Life, we enhanced the experience using the rich information that we normally deliver to the regular Web, allowing people to experience the tennis match from a different viewpoint. (See Figure 12.3.)

In the real world, we host a client suite and network with our top customers. We show them the technology and answer questions on how we manage the scoring and host the event. And of course, we give away cool Wimbledon and IBM swag to make the moment last even longer.

Extending the real life experience
Staffed 12 hours a day

Figure 12.3   The Wimbledon Event in Second Life.

So what did we do in Second Life? Well, we hosted the event and invited press and customers to attend the event in the virtual world. The avatars were able to socialize and network. In addition, we conducted technology tours in Second Life and at Wimbledon. As you see in Figure 12.4, we showed off our technology and the work to support the event.

The same IBM messages as in Real Life, giving the same tour as customers see

Figure 12.4 The Technology Tour in Second Life.

And in the virtual world, we gave away goodies as well. What were the gifts? We gave away a 3D tennis racket and the official Wimbledon towel that works as a flying carpet.

What was better or different? Unlike in the real world, avatars were able to walk around the court and even take the position of one of the players to see what it was like on the court, while play was in progress. It allowed our customer avatars to pick the player's perspective and to socialize and meet just like in real life. In Figure 12.5, you see the side effect of the virtual event as well. The conversations continue long after the event itself!

In addition, the virtual environment enables you to have a more interactive discussion with your customers. For instance, unlike the Web, in a virtual environment we cannot just "tell," we must "show." One of the more interesting applications we see on the horizon is accelerated learning through simulations, which are proven to increase individual and team learning and drive innovative collaboration.

The use of this virtual environment has some unexpected benefits. On the first day, IBM had a press conference with 40 members of the press gathered inside Second Life. Now, normally we would not be able to fit 40 people in our data room down in the basement at Wimbledon in the physical world, so we expanded the IBM reach.

Figure 12.5 The virtual conversation.

Was it a success? We were able to interact with more people at the virtual event than we were able to host at the event itself. As Hughes comments, "We have had approximately 200 visitors a day and I have talked to most of them about so many varied subjects from 'What is Wimbledon?' 'What does IBM do?' to 'How does the script work?' This has been a tremendous success, with the customers on the tours enjoying what we have done and seeing our innovative side—even more answers to interesting questions that emerge for me when I am explaining what we do. Finally, the virtual implementation is a tremendous vehicle for showing what IBM does at the live Wimbledon event."

Application to Your Company

We have found that events can be successful inside virtual environments. They attract a large number of customers who are interested in engaging in conversations. The downside is qualifying with whom you are talking. For example, I was chatting with a CEO one minute and a college student the next. Given the power of virtual environments in the future, events are a great way to begin your exploration of how to leverage virtual environments for marketing.

The SOA Island Focus on Education

In November, 2006, my team and I decided to go with IBM into the 3D virtual environment. With Hughes's team setting the vision, we wanted to play with the concept around SOA. At first, the objective was simple—we wanted to translate our www.ibm.com/soa site into this 3D environment. We had just announced a set of ways for customers to begin with a new technology approach; however, the market needed more education. My team (Georgina Castanon, Lidia Gasparotto, and Max Anderson) and I plotted to make the education adventure fun and to bring a PowerPoint presentation used in classroom education to the 3D world.

The vision was simple. Our goal was to have people immerse into an experience and learn at the same time. We wanted to have our SOA hub designed in a way that people could live the SOA experience instead of only read the message. Avatars must experience SOA, not just read about it. First, we played off our hexagon-shaped education devices, turning them into 3D experiences. The shape of the building mapped into our famed hexagon shapes as well. To get around the building, we built a "teleport center," and the center takes you to the right location or floor.

We went further. The team created a cafeteria, an art gallery where art from famous artists in Second Life have been shown. Avatars can click on artistic pentagons to go directly to our podcasts. We created a library where you can click on the CDs and books to learn more. We have Web links to podcast downloads and a way to click on a virtual iPod to get the podcast. We even have a store where you can click and go to the obtain important pieces of code from our SOA business catalog or buy a construction hat with the information about up and coming architect summits or a briefcase with information about the executive summits. This hub of activity serves to host a press conference and also later university classes.

There were also a set of giveaways, just as we do in real-world education classes. We have Second Life bikes, jet cars, boats, and even an SOA reference architecture T-shirt. Our SOA sunglasses had built-in education on what SOA terminology is and where our upcoming events were located.

In that first experience with Second Life, we learned that as with every Web site (2D and 3D), there needs to be continuous updates to it to maintain top traffic. Also, the hub is a useful center of information but needed more of the 3D experience (less click and go to 2D Web site) to unleash the full potential of the experiential learning that an environment such as Second Life (SL) provides.

Taking those lessons learned, we decided to take the concept further and enable two of the most valuable elements that Second Life can bring to the table from a marketing standpoint: the community and the immersion of fantasy.

Five months later, we decided to create a full environment where people could experience our messaging without feeling that they were clicking and getting information about SOA, but like they were exploring. We made it an adventure—an SOA Adventure Island!

Imagine a small place in the Pacific Ocean, surrounded by water, with a huge volcano in the center that explodes on command. Different to our original objective where people were there finding information, here the information found them as they walked through the different places to explore. By now, we had learned that 56,000 people are active (online, not registered) on Second Life and many of them in the age group of 30–50—our target age group. Because of the way technology is deployed, these people do not come into SL to search for information. Instead, they come to play; they come to live in a fantasy community where they can live as a prince, a super model, a tiger, a scuba diver, even if in real life, their job is as an architect, a lawyer, a librarian, or an engineer. The way to attract users to come to these 3D Internet Web sites or islands in Second Life is different from what we learned through many years of delivering 2D content. We had to use the concept of making our learning more like entertainment.

People in SL are drawn to community activities—concerts, plays, dancing, shopping, art, exploration, and so on. Our island would involve them, but with a twist. Castanon then called on her SL friends, who fortunately are talented people in the community. Tayzia Abattoir (art promoter) helped by putting pieces of art all over the island where people could see the creativity of others, making SOA Adventure a branch of the oldest museum in SL, the Crescent Moon museum, which she curates. At the time, in SL there were few "corporate avatar wears" so Nicky Ree (famous designer) created the IBM dress and men's attire. Kaikou Splash (a fish expert who is now building the PADI island) created fishing rods that teach concepts while you are there sitting for hours trying to catch fish. Random Calliope (famous artist and jeweler) designed a piece of jewelry that was different to anything else that exists in Second Life "geek jewelry," as he calls it.

People go to SOA Adventure for entertainment reasons, but there is a lot of knowledge they take back as one of the visitors. Katicus Sparrow, an SL marketer, says in her blog, "Stop by IBM's SOA Island. There are some really fun things to do there: hang-gliding, drumming, hanging out on the beach. Plus, you can learn a little about SOA, if you're into that sort of thing."

The major areas that were successful were the breakthrough thinking around the delivery of content. What was different? The way the Second Life community was looking for content, what made it relevant to them, was that is was an experience, an experience of SOA—even if people were not specifically looking for SOA content! We leveraged the community at large; they have knowledge and skills and can make a huge difference for your marketing activities. My team, from Castanon as the executive lead down to each participant, became part of the community.

Our IBM SOA Adventure Island success resulted from obtaining about 800 unique visitors to events like the musical concert shown in Figure 12.6.

Figure 12.6 The musical experience linked to learning about SOA.

We hit traffic highs when we opened the island driven by our experiential butterfly hunt. We hosted our IMPACT 2007 event, streaming it live in Second Life, where the press was quoted as saying, "It was like a corporate

Woodstock." That Second Life event had more attendees than our live event with more than 4,300 attendees! Another great experiential example was a puzzle contest. We designed a binary puzzle necklace that avatars can solve and then wear—again allow learning to be an experience. We featured this at IMPACT 2007 and had an immediate and positive response!

Application to Your Company

One of the keys in Second Life is to become part of the community. There is a separate culture and accepted behaviors. From the previous example, you see that leveraging the community for its expertise gains you experience and acceptance for your concepts. Castanon and team were part of those early adopters. Even our CEO and I have avatars! Definitely become deeply involved in the community—the culture can easily pick out superficiality.

Second, because you can learn as you go, jump in and experiment early. Play with 3D now and learn. For example, we tried to execute in Phase I Second Life like a Web site. Second Life is 3D. You need to accept and leverage the power of 3D. It is becoming a power play in all industries from healthcare to computers. Imagine your next doctor's visit including your medical record as a walking, talking avatar with a 3D representation of the human body. Your doctor can "click" on a specific part of your avatar's body, such as the heart, and instantly see all the available related medical history, including text entries, lab results, and MRIs. The potential is unlimited. Think about customer service. Instead of trying to explain in a phone call how to unscrew your hard drive, someone in a more immersive 3D world could actually show you. Or with two in every five employees working part- or full-time offsite, imagine the vast power of education and meetings in a virtual meeting.

Third, content is king. Ninety percent of the time spent on developing for virtual worlds should be focused on the content. Just like on a Web site, without a unique, rich experience, click outs are inevitable.

Finally, as Andersen explained, focus on ease of use and access. Because a lot of time in virtual worlds is moving around your avatar, keeping relevant material in close proximity reduces wasted search time. There is nothing more frustrating than getting lost in a poorly planned 3D design or not being able to figure out how to use an information device.

The applications to your company in running virtual events or education are open and relatively inexpensive as part of an overall integrated marketing plan.

Focus on The Coca-Cola Company's
Second-Life Adventures

To understand what The Coca-Cola Company did in Second Life, I spoke to Michael Donnelly, director of Worldwide Interactive Marketing, who has a great job exploring and innovating around a number of social networking spaces. The Coca-Cola Company is the world's largest beverage company. Along with Coca-Cola, recognized as the world's most valuable brand, the company markets four of the world's top five nonalcoholic sparkling brands, including Diet Coca-Cola, Fanta, and Sprite, and a wide range of other beverages, including diet and light beverages, waters, juices and juice drinks, teas, coffees, and energy and sports drinks. Through the world's largest beverage distribution system, consumers in more than 200 countries enjoy the company's beverages at a rate exceeding 1.4 billion servings each day.

The Coca-Cola Company has been in virtual worlds for several years—from Coca-Cola Company Studios to World of Warcraft to CC Metro to Habbo Hotel. The Coca-Cola Company entered Second Life in 2007 with a special plan worked jointly with the community and to give back to that community. The approach that The Coca-Cola Company took in Second Life was different from that of other consumer-product companies. In 2007, about a dozen or so brands, including IBM, had begun to adventure into Second Life.

Therefore, The Coca-Cola Company entered Second Life a little differently than IBM. For example, IBM decided to build islands, such as the SOA Island discussed previously. As a result, IBM has to attract avatars to its islands. The Coca-Cola Company decided to take a different approach. Instead of building an island, it held a contest in Second Life where it asked avatars to help generate a virtual vending machine of the future that would dispense experiences rather than beverages. The vending machines would then be placed throughout Second Life, in multiple islands, similar to real vending machines are today. The vision was that The Coca-Cola Company machines would become ubiquitous throughout the metaverse just like they are in the real world. (See Figure 12.7.)

As Donnelly explains, "The test wasn't really just about Second Life. It was about learning to become better marketers in virtual worlds. We have virtual worlds that are moderated for teens in at least eight different countries. An example of our own is right here in the United States where we've got more than eight million registered users."

Figure 12.7   The Coca-Cola Company enters Second Life.

Before Donnelly and his team began, they worked to become part of the community. As they tested the idea, they did so in Second Life councils, ensuring that the early adopters would accept them into the community. The result was that they set out to create a contest to generate a virtual vending machine that they could leverage throughout all different virtual worlds. They accepted entries in YouTube, MySpace, Second Life, Virtual World Site, and via e-mail.

The contest was called VirtualThirst. (You can check it out on VirtualThirst.com.) It played off of the idea that "even avatars get thirsty." The contest was to create the virtual vending machine, and it would be judged on the following criteria: creativity (20 percent), cultural fit within Second Life (20 percent), consistency with the Coca-Cola brand (20 percent), potential value to Second Life residents (20 percent), and technical feasibility (20 percent). The prizes included 500,000 Linden dollars (the currency of Second Life) and a trip for two to San Francisco to participate with Second Life design company Millions of Us in the transformation of the winning design into a Second Life-ready vending machine. The VirtualThirst competition invited anyone to create a virtual vending machine that unleashed a refreshing and an attention-grabbing experience, on demand. The contest was judged by the Second Life Council. How did the team begin this adventure?

First, Donnelly and his team started the conversation. They convened an advisory board of residents who were early adopters, "influential in the community," as well as in-world companies and agencies. They carefully studied what and how other brands were entering Second Life. This board helped to decide on the contest and the rules. Next, they let everyone in the virtual world (and real world) know about the contest. They launched the event on April 16, 2007, to highlight the prototypes and announce the contest. Leveraging social media outreach gave the contest buzz through Second Life, YouTube, and MySpace as well as the traditional media.

They accepted submissions in-world and online for an eight-week period. The submissions submitted were anywhere from a sketch on a napkin, to a full-blown build. The Coca-Cola Company created an in-world pavilion (see Figure 12.8) to showcase the prototypes and generate submissions. They had over 12 events and most were sold-out affairs!

Figure 12.8 The Coca-Cola Company Pavilion and one location to submit ideas.

The contest drew a host of people in all virtual worlds. After the five finalists were selected and much review, the advisory board chose a winning entry—Magic Coke Bottles. The decision was announced via blogs on July 24, 2007. The winning concept wasn't a traditional vending machine but was in the shape of a bottle.

An avatar can go up and touch the bottle, and it presents you with a challenging Rubik's Cube-like puzzle. When you complete the puzzle, it gives you an experience. There are three experiences that embody the spirit of Coca-Cola's brand. There is a snow globe that your avatar can go inside and experience life with penguins, ice fishing, and even mountain climbing. You can control the intensity of the snowfall, and you can snap pictures of yourself. The second experience is a giant bubble ride in a Coke bottle. You can experience parachuting and becoming a carbonated bubble, floating all the way up through the bottle. At the top, your parachute opens and you fall to the ground. The third experience is a Second Life snowball fight. To have the brand extended even further, the virtual vending machines enable you to win transferable prizes. For instance, you can win a little polar bear that sits on your avatar's shoulders. In Second Life, avatars are transferring the polar bears to their friends, so you can get a glimpse of the The Coca-Cola Company polar bear throughout the world. Also, a Coca-Cola guitar gives you six different positions to play your guitar in and a virtual scooter that allows you to ride around the metaverse. As Donnelly comments, "Unlike an island, our brand is being taken wherever the avatars go. The scooter, in particular, as you ride around throughout the metaverse, leaves a trail that lasts for less than a half a second. It is lightly branding. It doesn't say Coca-Cola all over it. It just leaves a little Coke ribbon behind you."

On November 8, 2007, The Coca-Cola Company held a celebration party where the first viewing of the Magic Coke Bottle appeared. The winner was the first to solve the puzzle and launch an experience. It was a true event with live music while the avatars interacted with the puzzle bottles and prototypes.

Donnelly talked about his success this way, "We looked at the participation, engagement, and the response of the community. This enables us to begin the conversations that were valuable to our brand. We also saw huge blog volumes, with hundreds of posts 'linked to' over 33,000 times, plus 250+ photo posts (Flickr), 36,000+video views=180,000+ minutes, and extensive mainstream media. We produced a platform for ongoing conversation with consumers that resonated the brand promise in an intimate, long-tail way and embedded our brand where users are today." (See Figure 12.9.)

At the time of this writing, 25 virtual vending machines are spread throughout Second Life that dispense experiences and a prize.

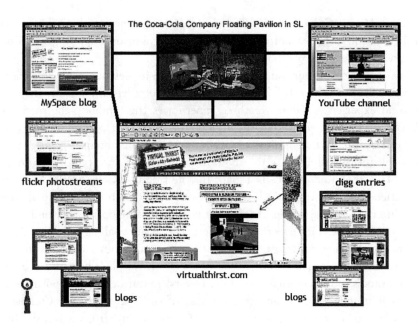

Figure 12.9 The social network created.

Virtual Environment Lessons Learned

From both The Coca-Cola Company and IBM, the following are the most valuable lessons learned:

- **Partner with professionals who know the virtual environment you choose:** The Coca-Cola Company partnered with Crayon, an agency that was actually launched in Second Life. IBM has partnered with many clients to help them understand virtual environments, Second Life, and how to connect into the community and culture.

- **Don't let someone just do it for you:** Experience the virtual environment yourself. In fact, if you are reading this without that experience, it is likely it will be hard for you to understand and follow the concepts and experience that I am describing. As Donnelly says, "I found myself at many a conference where I'd ask questions about what people were doing in Second Life and I found that they didn't know the answers. And my summation was because they hired somebody else to do it for them. And, in this case, we literally did everything ourselves." In the case of IBM, thousands of IBMers have been following the developments of virtual worlds for the past few years and working at the frontiers of the many technologies that have coalesced around virtual worlds. We have implemented an Intraverse, using Active Worlds, for collaboration and events taking place behind our corporate firewall. We have implemented a metaverse. As I mentioned earlier, we have an active virtual universe community working on a wide range of internal and client projects. From our CEO to myself, head of SOA marketing, and to others, we have avatars who participate in the experience so that we can make better decisions. We literally are there and converse with customers one on one.

- **Ask for advice, counsel, and permissions from these communities:** Both The Coca-Cola Company and IBM leveraged the community early adopters on their plans. We both held quite a few in-world focus groups with people where we brainstormed on the concepts. The biggest learning from both powerhouse brands was that you must stay close to the community and ask for that advice and counsel. Both truly listened.

- **Try some low hanging fruit first:** We have found with our two years of experience that collaboration and events, training and education, virtual commerce, and business process simulations are the easiest entry point for use of virtual environments. Experimenting in these areas enables your company to learn the ropes of virtual environments and gain a better understanding of the business value it will bring to your organization.

Application to Your Company

Where do you get started? What might work for your organization? As you think about the areas we discussed—commerce, education and training, and collaboration and events—think about your organization's own business objectives and evaluate how use of virtual environments can enhance the experiences you provide to your customers and your employees:

- **Commerce:** How can you improve customer satisfaction, enhance the customers initial (presales) or ongoing experience (post-sales) to tie them more strongly to your brand? What type of virtual tools (custom designs to see before you buy, for example) might assist customers in their purchasing decision?

- **Collaboration and events:** How can you use virtual collaboration and events to extend your reach, to find new customers, to create opportunities to bring existing customers together, and to enable virtual connections between you and your customers? What type of immersive experiences—re-creation of real-world destinations, immersion of spectators into real-world events—will connect you with your prospects and customers?

- **Education and training:** Virtual environments have great potential to create a highly compelling distance learning environment in support of both pre- and post-sales education. How can you use virtual environments and simulations to connect prospects and customers with experts from around the world, educate people on your products, simulate real-world environments for "walk-throughs" or reenactments or develop 3D models and immersive environments to simplify the complex ideas?

- **Process management and rehearsal:** This is an area where IBM is doing a lot of research, and in April, 2008, IBM Research announced that it had created a "rehearsal studio" that enables employees to rehearse their jobs and client engagement interactions in a virtual 3D world. IBM Research has specially designed a 3D environment to help IBM employees conduct more successful client engagements in diverse services such as implementing a software system in a constantly changing auto parts business and conducting crisis management. For example, in the rehearsal space, IBM Global Services teams can interact with avatars in real time and learn how to implement a successful services project. In one scenario, an IBM project manager tests out different auto parts production schedules—performing "what-if" analysis, such as creating excess inventory and sourcing different suppliers. The session can be recorded and replayed to identify key episodes and provide feedback.

Conclusion

IBM believes that virtual worlds will allow the deepening and enriching of a customer's product, service, or program experience—promoting and supporting commerce. In addition, these activities have the potential to increase individual and team learning capabilities. A significant number of enterprise, government, educational, and nonprofit entities are currently experimenting with new applications and services. These emerging applications can be loosely grouped into four functional categories: commerce, collaboration and events, training, and business process management. Given the high level of interest, any smart marketer should consider incorporating a trial run tactic using a virtual environment such as Second Life into its strategy. Innovative uses of technology will allow you to reach a new audience and capture customers around the world.

13

Widgets: The Use of Widgets at IBM

Science and technology multiply around us. To an increasing
extent they dictate the languages in which we speak and think.
Either we use those languages, or we remain mute.
–J. G. Ballard

Language in the marketplace is changing. There is more and more technology used everywhere. To cut through the clutter today, you need to think through how you get to the market in a different way, but one that is effective. IBM's sellers and ecosystem had a major complaint. We had so much information that they couldn't sort through the data for the nuggets that they needed. Information overload was in play, and as a result, our energy in the marketplace was not what it could be. So, we decided to leverage technology in the pursuit of sorting the information through widgets.

Focus on Widgets in Marketing

Widgets are miniature applications that can take a variety of forms. They can either sit on a Web page (such as igoogle.com's widgets) or on your hard drive (such as a desktop widget like a Yahoo! widget). Anything you can imagine, there is probably a widget out there for, although some are obviously more useful than others. Some widgets that I check out regularly tell me information; for example, the current weather, when my favorite TV shows are on, and even when my daughter's school events are. One of my favorites is Sticky Deluxe. This widget helps me organize my to-do list with a widget that is a cross-platform sticky note and memo taker, which is an electronic version of the venerable 3M Post-It® note. (See Figure 13.1.)

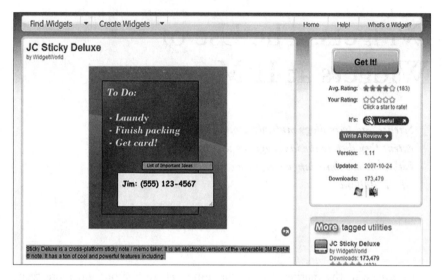

Figure 13.1   Sticky Deluxe.

The marketing value of widgets is that they narrow your scope of information and bring it to you rather than the other way around. Today, it is so easy to become overwhelmed by all of the information out there. Strange as it may sound, sometimes going to a Web site is too much work. For example, take the blogs on my RSS feed. There's no way that I will go out and visit each of them once a day. I don't have that kind of time. However, if I take a quick look at my RSS widget, I can not only see the titles of any updated postings, but I can also read a selection from that posting, and *then* I decide if it is worth it for me to visit that Web page.

Focus on IBM's Widget

For the SOA widget, I talked to my team that I tasked with figuring out how to leverage our content in a consumable fashion to our channel, sales team, and ecosystem. The team consisted of

■ Marcus Belvin, who currently handles the SOA widget tasks, such as content updates, technical support, and assisting in strategic direction for both the internal and external widgets.

- Jorli Baker ensured the design and launch of the widget was conducted on time, within budget, and in alignment with the customers' needs for real-time Smart SOA information.

- Deon Newman, executive in charge of the area of innovation for our integrated programs.

- Tami Cannizzaro, our resident expert on how we launch products into the marketplace leveraging innovation that matters.

What Is the Smart SOA Widget?

Our Smart SOA widget was used both internally and externally. We began first with the internal widget for our own sellers and then created a second widget for our external information. The widget is a personal assistant to our sellers and customers. It is a dynamic, miniature application with streaming RSS Feed to ensure our customers have the latest information. Continuously updated views and links are available directly to the desktop through a set of channels: presentations, collateral, videos, references, newsletters, events, and Webcasts. In addition, there is a featured area that shows the hottest information; in this case, our upcoming IMPACT event. It enables sellers and customers to quickly locate exactly what they need without wading through pages of unrelated content. The widget enables personalization by location and industry. As seen in Figure 13.2, the internal widget is compact and visual.

Why a Widget?

The clear challenge was to deliver valuable information to our sales force and to avoid bombarding them with all types of information every day. Because all the information they leverage was in different repositories around the company, we needed to provide access to the latest information that enabled them to better sell in the market. As Baker describes, "We were looking for a convenient way to deliver the right information in the right amounts, with proper version control, consumability, and relevance to them. We needed a vehicle to deliver that magic to our sellers." Cannizzaro further explains, "I was looking at an article on the top 25 innovations in viral marketing. And there was an article on widgets. Sandy had pushed us to find something that was kind of innovative and edgy and fitting the category of viral marketing that could benefit our sales team. And this was something in that category."

Figure 13.2   The Smart SOA widget.

Simply put, we decided on a widget because it enabled us to have channels suited to the top sellers' relevant information in a format that could leverage daily updates via RSS feeds. Thus, the internal Smart SOA widget was born.

Who Are the Users of the Widget?

The primary users of the internal SOA widgets today are both sellers and executives who frequently communicate with customers. The external widget is targeted at partners who depend on the latest information to drive their businesses and customer IT decision makers desiring to stay up-to-date on their SOA knowledge.

The Competition

The main competitors for widgets are existing sources of information: e-mail, Web sites, e-newsletters, phone calls, in-person meetings, and events. There are many other ways to get the information that can be found in a given widget. After we released the widget, many others internally and externally began copying the concept.

The Marketing Best Practice

For the Smart SOA widget, Belvin tells us that success can be measured in real results. "For the first 5 months after the initial launch, the results were more than 14,000 internal widget downloads and more than 2,400 external widget downloads. We have received feedback from passionate users requesting additional function and platform support, displaying a broader interest in the market to leverage the value the SOA widget offers.

In addition, we have a feature feed where we can highlight targeted messages on upcoming events, new content, or any sort of information we view as valuable to this target audience.

If copying is a form of flattery, the SOA widget is leading the charge there as well. We received a plethora of internal inquiries into how the widget was designed and created in an effort to create additional widgets with various informational focuses and we are now seeing competitors place similar 'SOA' widgets out in the market space." We are starting to explore the backend on the external widget for lead generation, complementing the information sharing.

The customer SOA widget enhances demand generation by decreasing the effort to locate new SOA messages and try out new frameworks and demos. For example, if a new whitepaper is added to a Web page, an e-mail can be sent to announce its presence to a prior group of recipients. In contrast, the widget leveraging RSS feeds automatically updates and alerts users of new items in various relevant content channels. This is analogous to a person having a team of people constantly searching and monitoring new announcements while consolidating them into a concise manner for consumption. These efficiencies correlate to less time ramping up on your knowledge of what ROI is offered by SOA solutions to more quickly reach the point of solution investigation.

The Widget Agenda at IBM SOA

Let's take a look at how the widget was created and deployed. For the internal widget, the team did a set of five steps in parallel. The first was working to design the look and feel of the widget. We approached a vendor who had experience in consumable widgets. The goal we discussed with the vendor was to focus on the look and feel so that it was easy to gain access to the information. We had all the channels— the categories— that the sellers would need. We also wanted to focus on the viral effect that we planned for the widget to have. As Newman comments, "For viral marketing methods, the look and feel is key; the capturing of user attention and getting that tool or information passed along is possible only if it has a coolness factor."

The second focus that went into the widget was the focus on the content. To say content is king is almost an understatement because if the information was not valuable, the sellers would not leverage it, regardless of the coolness factor. A massive amount of energy was spent with the customer—our sellers—assuring we had the latest and most appropriate content in the widget. The team sat down with a number of sellers and reviewed the key deliverables that they looked for, what they leveraged with their customers to understand what was critical. For example, they pushed on how the sellers used the case studies, what type of collateral they wanted at their fingertips, and whether a calendar of the latest events and Webcasts would be in the top priority items. As Newman explains, "We then created the major categories. We focused on the visualization of how to present the information and identified the gaps, what things they didn't have, and what the top priorities for them were when they went to market."

The third step was to determine the number of channels, what to name the channels, and where we would host them. The team wanted it to be more than just a redirect to a Web page, and so it spent time adding functionality such as screenshots of the video, descriptions, and other things that the widget technology supports. For example, the fact that featured items would change, scroll, and be dynamic and personal as opposed to just a static Web page that somebody had to go out and seek differentiated the widget further. The channels could be customized for the seller based on his interest in a specific industry for example.

The fourth focus of the widget was the actual functional design. The team worked hard to make the design tradeoffs on budget, and it rolled out the right amount of function that could be consumed at one time. As Belvin states, "We tabled the rest of the function that we thought would be good for later, either version 2 or based on what customers actually told us after we launched the widget. We didn't want to overload the sellers with too many things at once."

Finally, the team created a standard for the level of content, the amount, and a governance process to ensure the quality of standard around the widget. Governance was critical in constantly reassessing the value of what we placed on the widget. Cannizzaro comments "We continue the governance process today to ensure the quality and level of information. That has to be done for any successful widget." The team tracked the usage and what drove people to the widget—either to download or use the content. In Figure 13.3, you see some of the tracking that we did to ensure we had triggers to compel users to the widget. For us, events or new announcements had the greatest impact on the use.

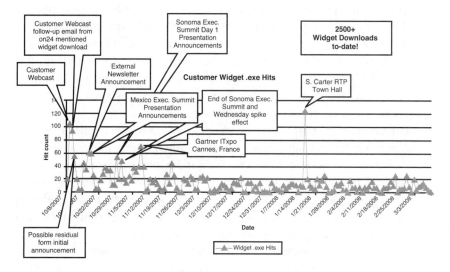

Figure 13.3 The initial Smart SOA widget metrics.

A few weeks later, the team launched the external widget, repeating the previous steps to ensure they had the customer's desire always in mind.

Top Five Applications for Your Company

Widgets are becoming a marketing tool for providing relevant information, targeted messaging, and education. Following is a list of the top tips for your company's trial of widgets:

1. **Brings information *to* the user:** If the widget merely contains a collection of titles and hyperlinks, it is no more useful than a Web page. Scrolling titles, breaking news, videos that play in the widget, and information tailored to the user are examples of valuable widget features. Something that a user can glance at to obtain the facts they need without having to click-through is also unique to widgets (changing colors or scroll-over commands, for example).

2. **2 Cs (Cool and Content):** Widgets that are easy to use and with an aesthetically appealing, useful, compact design will be selected more for download. But if the information on a widget is not relevant to the user,

then it doesn't matter how cool it looks; it won't be used. Cannizzaro said it best to "keep it simple, make it fun, keep it current, and make sure you don't overload it with information. Think MTV sound bite, generation type tool, and if you try to overload it or have it too much, I think it's less compelling and relevant." We had great pickup because everyone thought our Smart SOA widget was "cool." However, after the coolness factor wore off, the determinant of success was the fulfillment of a real business need. Specifically for widgets, the widget needs to provide consistently new, valuable information, and they need to save people time and effort for them to remain popular.

3. **Governance is critical:** Review your SOA widget on a regular schedule. Many widgets update their content at different frequencies. Per the design of the SOA widget, checking it for new content once a week tends to be enough. Schedule time periodically to read new content in the widget. Don't just rubber stamp what goes into the tool. It helps to have a number of constituents consistently reviewing content to help keep up the quality of standard required for success.

4. **Continuous feedback loop with your customers:** Despite the realization that every widget cannot provide everything desired by everyone, there is value in listening continuously to the feedback on the widget. For us, as the users got more mature, our delivery and content also had to adapt. Markets are constantly changing, and your end user insight into what the new market needs are invaluable to content creators and distributors.

5. **Metrics and good analyses:** It's important to keep track of which items are the most popular (via click-through rates, and so on) and to track who is using what to increase your market insight.

IBM Lessons Learned

This section discusses some of the most powerful lessons that we learned in this process. The biggest takeaway is that with the plethora of information available today internally and externally, the widget streamlines and focuses the user on the information most relevant to his role. In a world where information is power, this is a huge advantage to the user and the marketer who can filter the needed bytes of information.

1. **Education on "What is a widget?":** We found that a lot of customers and sellers didn't know what a widget was. The lesson learned here is that demonstrations and how-to videos are important. Setting expectations appropriately is also critical. The rule of thumb is to under promise and over deliver. Unmet expectations lead to lower customer satisfaction and lost interest in the widget.

2. **Be an explorer:** I am amazed at all the things my girls explore. They have the spirit inside of them to be curious. We need to do the same with widgets (and other new technologies that we as marketers can leverage). Don't be afraid to checkout the amazing widget content that is available today for free. A tip, though, because widgets are focused on the latest content, if you find something of value in a widget, makes sure you bookmark it for a later time. As Baker commented, "Widgets are designed to provide the *latest* content; subsequently older items are removed as newer ones are added. Book marking or downloading the item is the best way to ensure you will have access to it long term."

3. **Use the widget software for a feedback mechanism:** Much like with a normal product design, an FAQ can save you a lot of time assisting early adopters and general users with common problems.

4. **Make it easy for people to share the widget:** Word of mouth is a great way to distribute. A "shareable" widget that can be added to blogs or other Web pages is a wise next step.

5. **Don't skimp on the metrics:** Capture as much insight and information about your users. Think through how your sellers might be advantaged knowing that their customers just read three whitepapers on a certain topic!

6. **Understand what drives users to your widget:** Based on analysis of the download numbers, it appears the best method to drive demand for our widget is the face-to-face events with customers. We definitely saw spikes in the download after any events or Web casts. There were also spikes from e-mail blasts.

7. **Don't forget the backend:** You can use the widget as a lead-generation engine in addition to enabling your channel and ecosystem. As Newman comments, "The whole idea of the widget is its ability to key content, but that key content is such a valuable tool to us that we want to have some way of capturing a lead at the backend of it." Think through your backend process for capturing demand.

What Does the Future Hold?

Since we released our widget, there is a lot going on in this field. In the future, widgets will become more interactive, and there will be a time that they can accept transactions, especially those with social components to them. In addition, there are lots of standards being established. For example, today your MAC comes preloaded with widgets, but you can't use those widgets on a PC. So, a common set of standards are coming that will enable for sharing across systems.

Finally, because widgets are increasing in popularity, we may soon have a proliferation of widgets such that there is widget clutter just as there is information clutter today. We may end up in the future with a Super Widget to manage our key widgets!

Conclusion

Widgets are a great way to share information and to generate energy and demand for your product portfolio. They are cool, hip, and provide a consumable way to disseminate relevant information in a CNN-like format. Widgets can be personalized and that adds to the appeal of them in the marketplace. They enable information to be brought to you, not the other way around. Based on the tracking mechanisms that you use, you can build a strong demand generation engine on the backend that can become smarter based on who is downloading what information. In the future, we will see more widgets enter the marketplace, and a super widget to manage all our widgets might be on its way.

14

Blogs: Midwest Airlines and IBM

Change happens by listening and then starting a dialogue.
–Jane Goodall

I used to love my study groups at school. We'd debate issues, discuss case studies, and talk about what was happening in the world. Those who didn't come to study group not only missed what was discussed about school, but also the discussion about life issues that we exchanged. The conversation continued regardless of whether they attended. I did not want to miss study group for this reason! The same kind of vibrant conversation is going on in the world today.

Conversations are going on in the marketplace with or without our participation. If you don't recognize and acknowledge those conversations and actively participate in them, the dialogue will continue, but you will be left out of it.

A blog is comparable to an online newspaper or magazine column of opinions and interactive comments. It is a Web-based discussion tool on which individuals post their thoughts, experiences, opinions, feelings, and observations for anyone with an Internet connection to see. *The Cluetrain Manifesto: The End of Business As Usual* by Rick Levine, Christopher Locke, Doc Searls, David Weinberger *articulates* what blogging became. It states that markets *are* conversations and that transparency is critical to those conversations in a world where so many individuals are networked together via the Internet. That is why I have conversations with many people that I have never actually met. I record everything that I do, feel, and want to do on a set of subjects. I prioritize time for my blog at IBM, so that I can remain in the conversation.

Blogs Are Changing the Marketing Conversation

Marketers have long acknowledged that word of mouth is an important ingredient in marketing activities, but since the advent of early radio, television, and print advertising, the communication was always moving in one direction, and it never seemed to take the perspective of the end constituent in mind. Blogging (and the underlying technologies that enable it: cheap silicon, storage, processing power, and Internet access) have taken Gutenberg's one-way conversation of many-to-one and flipped it on its head. The blogger has an equal voice and has as much opportunity to be heard as the huge corporation or government institution.

What does that mean to the marketing equation? What does that new balance of power imply when an institution, which was able to create, convey, and tow a party line, is now (if it's smart) forced to *listen* to the marketplace, as well as scream out to it?

Blogging is important in marketing because it involves both listening and talking, and at the same time, it helps put a face on the large faceless mask of large institutions. Suddenly someone in the blogosphere can reach out and touch someone at IBM—me, you, Tish Robinson, Todd Watson, and others—and seek out that person's perspective and expertise, or just say, "Hello, thanks for being out here."

Let's explore the power of a corporate blog. I use Midwest Airlines as an example in this chapter, but I also inserted a lot of learning from IBM. A great marketing professional, Todd Watson, has a best-read blog at IBM, and I share his thoughts as well.

Focus on Midwest's Tish Robinson

Tish Robinson is a marketing writer and blogger. She created the Midwest Airlines blog for female travelers. She also writes electronic e-mail communications, Web site content, and other marketing materials. Through this blog, she is a key voice for Midwest Airlines in the market!

What Is Midwest Airlines?

Midwest Airlines is a U.S.-based airline that serves major destinations throughout the United States. The airline is known for its great customer service; its tagline is "The best care in the air." Midwest is a customer-service-oriented company and has won numerous awards for its outstanding customer service, including the World's Best Domestic Airline, 2007 from *Travel+Leisure's* World's Best Awards, among many others that are listed on its Web site.

Midwest Airlines is headquartered in Milwaukee, Wisconsin and employs approximately 3,000 employees.

The Customers

Midwest Airlines is primarily a consumer-based business, focusing on both business and leisure travelers. Its market consists of consumers who value good customer service and prefer nonstop routing to key destinations.

The Product

The technical product for Midwest Airlines is, of course, the flight. However, the airline differentiates itself through the high service level provided by its employees. Therefore, I would truly say that Midwest's product is defined by how well it takes care of you on the ground and in the sky. Midwest Airlines takes a commodity—a flight—and turns it into an experience. This will become important and will shape its blog story!

The Competition

Although Midwest does compete with most U.S. airlines and serves about 50 cities coast to coast, it is still somewhat viewed as a smaller carrier out of a Midwestern city in the United States.

The Marketing Best Practice

Corporate blogs are crucial to putting a face on a company and keeping it in the conversation. Tish's corporate blog does both; it is known affectionately as "Travels with Tish," incorporating and extending the company's commitment to service through the electronic media and community. The blog targets female leisure and business travelers. Take a peek as this award-winning corporate blog as shown in Figure 14.1.

Figure 14.1 Travel with Tish!

TURBO BLOG–TODD WATSON, TOP BLOGGER AT IBM

From the outset, Todd believed it was critically important that he set the tone and voice of the blog in a way that would establish his "creed" (having been on this e-business, ondemand journey since its inception). He also wanted it to be a two-way dialogue about anything and everything relevant to emerging technology, digital media, Web 2.0, and so on.

He wanted to establish his editorial and communications independence to indicate that this blog was not filtered by any editorial or corporate voice on behalf of IBM, but rather, that it was an independent voice. He wanted to show that the blog had a sense of humor and was beholden to no one, but a blog that demonstrated an understanding of the changing business and technology landscape and that he was willing to call it like he saw it.

One of his original posts said, "Blogs are the mavericks of the online world. Two of their greatest strengths are their ability to filter and disseminate information to a widely dispersed audience and their position outside the mainstream of mass media. Beholden to no one, blogs point to, comment on, and spread information according to their own quirky criteria."

He set that tone from the first post he made; one which he admitted could be his last if the IBM corporate communications funnel found what he said to be uncomfortable or unsettling. The following is a quote from that post to give a deeper sense of the tone and approach he took from the beginning:

> "Here's the deal: I'm your new IBM blogger. I know your purchase order didn't mention anything about getting a blogger, but one of our recent market research studies indicated that you wanted one, and I happened to be standing in a hallway in Armonk, apparently with a red target painted on my forehead.
>
> So, I'm it. Nice to meet you, virtually speaking. Of course, there will be plenty more where I came from. (Actually, there already are on other parts of the IBM Web...I'm just the first blogger on this particular area of our Web site. Over time, I'll be pointing you to other, more knowledgeable bloggers in given topic areas).
>
> Remember, this is IBM—we travel in large packs. I'm just here to help get the conversation going.

He has stayed true to that original post since the blog went live in June, 2005. Today, he has one of the top blogs at IBM, having been quoted in *The Wall Street Journal* and *The New York Times*. Todd is one influencer that marketers leverage in their conversation in the market.

More detail on Turbo Blog can be found on our companion Web site at ibmpressbooks.com/angels.

The Blogging Agenda at Midwest Airlines

For Midwest Airlines, the mission to start a blog began as a challenge. Blogging was becoming more popular, so Tish Robinson was asked to explore the possibility of creating a blog for Midwest Airlines. The type of blog was open for discussion, but as Tish explains, "The purpose that the blog would serve was important to me. I wanted to enhance our business. I wanted it to reflect our corporate philosophy of customer service." Her choice was an excellent one driven by a gap in the marketplace—female travelers— and it serves as a place in which she can speak from the heart and be authentic in an area about which she feels passionate. Called Travels with Tish (travelswithtish.com), this unique corporate blog features weekend getaway suggestions for women on the go! It recently won an award of excellence from Society for New Communications Research (SNCR).

Driven by Corporate Values and a Niche!

Given that Midwest Airlines had an intense focus on customer service, Tish wanted to serve the customer first. Through market research and in talking with Midwest customers, she uncovered a market that was not being served in the travel world for women. She discovered that baby boomer women have both time and money, but not enough expertise to try a weekend getaway with girlfriends. She found that a lot of woman wanted to travel with someone because the social interaction made it fun. As Tish explains, "Some women need to work up some courage to go away for a couple of days with girlfriends to a strange place. I found that this niche market wasn't being filled by other travel blogs out there. A travel blog aimed at these women would be a service we could offer. I have experience here because I love girlfriend getaways and have a long-time familiarity with how to make them work."

Midwest Airlines didn't start out by saying, "Let's do a travel blog." It started out by looking at the blogosphere and filling a need for discussion around a particular niche market. Again, in telling the story, the focus first was on the segmentation and meeting a need in the marketplace through a new media.

Tish is constantly looking ahead at what's next for her readers. She wants to add a forum for those who want to travel with their dog. This is another growing niche market in which Midwest Airlines is already an industry leader. Midwest has a premier pet program that is unique in the industry.

As Tish explains, "We take special care of pets that fly with us. We have a separate pet compartment and the person in charge of that program is a long-time dog show participant, judge, and pet lover. That's why our pet travel program is unique. So what I would like to do is introduce another segment that talks about pet travel, has a pet forum, and includes articles about traveling with pets and things that interest my readers."

As you can see, the blog extends Midwest Airlines' reputation for providing outstanding care for its customers and pets!

Application to Your Company

First, understand what needs exist and support your brand. I believe that corporate blogs should be in line with your corporate values. Two major applications here are to always be prepared to have whatever you wrote be published on the front page of *The New York Times*. Many bloggers are quoted in the media, such as in *The Wall Street Journal* and other major media, when all the blogger thought she was doing was writing an innocuous blog post. The major points should be in line with corporate values. For example, IBM has a strong set of corporate values based on three tenets:

- Dedication to every client's success
- Innovation that matters—for our company and the world
- Trust and personal responsibility in all relationships

As I blog for IBM, I do express my thoughts; however, I also ensure that I portray IBM's values as focused on client values and highlight our innovation. Of course, the rule of honesty must be adhered to on a blog! The same is true of "Turbo" Todd; above all else, honesty is his motto.

Second, be transparent about everything. There are plenty of incidents where a lack of transparency in even the most harmless situation still did great harm to the credibility of the individual blogger involved, often only because he wasn't upfront about something. For example, if an issue involves litigation, even if you're not officially speaking on behalf of the company, what you say might potentially be used as evidence in the litigation; don't ever lie in your blog. As a blogger, your reputation, truthfulness, and credibility are all that you have. You pay a high price for compromising them. For example, a major retailer had its PR agency underwrite a couple's cross-country trip in an RV where they blogged about their experiences. The couple that took the trip never identified that the large retailer sponsored their trip. When it was unearthed later, it damaged the credibility of the bloggers, the large retailer, and the PR firm. If they had just stated upfront that they were sponsored, it would have eliminated all the negative publicity. This is one part of marketing where hype does you more harm than good.

Get Personal!

With more value being placed on service, Tish wanted to have a blog targeted at this traveling population of women for getaways, but one that had a personal touch. On her blog, she features services that are of interest to women: travel information, details about destinations to where Midwest flies, costs, reviews of hotels, restaurants, and shops. Consideration for limited budgets is also part of the mix, such as finding decent hotels at a good value, bargain-shopping opportunities, using public transportation where feasible, and so on.

However, those aren't the reasons why Tish has a community willing to wear "Travel with Tish" T-shirts! The blog has a following because it is written from a personal point of view. For example, she told me that she includes items such as the amount of walking involved and recommendations for when to take a cab. She even does restaurant and shopping reviews based on the experiences she gains on trips with girlfriends to the featured destinations.

As Tish explains, "I primarily talk about my personal experiences in a variety of cities to which Midwest flies. I prefer to feature places and activities that are not necessarily commonly discovered by tourists. I single out shops, hotels, or dining places that I found especially good or interesting. If they're not good, I will comment on the fact that I wouldn't go there again. I can tactfully do that. So, I give Midwest a face—it's a personal blog in a lot of ways, but yet, it's corporate and cool."

I view blogging as a part of a company's personality. Marketing's job is to provide a lens for that personality, for the market to see the personality. The crucial part is to find someone who can make it personal, relevant, and true. In addition, it is crucial for relevance to the company that the blogger be connected! As Tish says, "I don't just find value hotels that are good. I take it to heart and personalize how to present the concept. And I try to engage people in reading and visualizing it. I don't want this to just be a review or a how-to. I want it to be personal and meaningful so that readers can take away useable information."

Tish herself regularly networks with other blog sites. A link to her blog appears on the Midwest Airlines Deals Web page and also appears in weekly customer e-mails and monthly newsletters to Midwest Miles members. Now others have asked to advertise on her site as well!

Application to Your Company

Blogs that are personal, such as Tish's, create a community. They enable you to gain insight into their attitudes and behaviors that might not have been possible before because these groups probably would have no interest in participating in market research, or if they did, they wouldn't be as open as in the blogosphere. Blogs can extend your corporate personality and can be a valuable source of information. Midwest is gaining insight into what one segment of its customers' needs.

Blogging implies you must write and read. Tish spends a lot of her time on other blogs, and reading about what is of interest in the market. One point Todd Watson made to me was not to be boring. With a few million active blogs in the world, never mind all the free IT media Web sites, newspapers, video content, and so on, people have plenty of content to keep them busy for a lifetime. Distinguish yourself by not being boring, but instead by writing with a unique voice that is fun and interesting while also informative.

Lightly Branded

Tish's blog is a low-profile corporate blog, but coded links to Midwest Airlines show a good return on investment in ticket sales. As Tish explains, "No goals based on financial return were set, but it was anticipated that some would occur. The effort was more of a service and networking opportunity for the airline brand. I tell them I work for Midwest, so it's transparent. But it's not an in-your-face marketing approach. I show them opportunities for sale fares and for group discounts. I also interact with other sites such as squidoo.com and judysbook.com on which I put airline offers that link back to my site. We can then see how those linked offers have driven revenue for Midwest."

The ROI has been excellent, providing approximately a 10:1 return, though much more return can be assumed that may have been triggered by the blog, but booked using alternative methods.

Application to Your Company

Blogging is an important element to your marketing mix. Try to measure it, but remember it is a relationship with your clients. The information and personalization are sometimes hard to measure, but they can be a good way to view the value of it in the market.

SANDY'S BLOGGING PHILOSOPHY!

I began my blog to experience the new world and to share with my customers. My blog, SOA off the Record, began with the following simple post:

> "Welcome to the blog where our community can exchange viewpoints, share its perspective to provide more insight around service oriented architecture solutions, and delve into a range of SOA-related subjects. We want you to speak out on SOA through comments in the blog—from where your organization stands on SOA adoption, to your challenges and experiences—to share with the larger community the impact of SOA on your marketplace. I am IBM's vice president of SOA & WebSphere Marketing, Strategy, and Channels. And I want to hear what you have to say!"

My view is that to capture attention, there are three primary ways to drive interest today. First, it is through a conversation or dialogue. My blog is now in the top ten most read blogs from IBMers in the blogosphere. The comments and opinions I receive are intriguing, helpful, and insightful to my marketing.

For example, this post tried to get a deeper conversation offering up a forum for brainstorming!

> Join IBM's SOA Jam, April 7–10!

> Great news—I found a way I can connect with all of you in the virtual world via the Web! Get ready for the upcoming SOA virtual jam.

> Join us online for IBM's upcoming SOA community exchange. Now you can join the SOA jam at IMPACT and let us know your thoughts on best practices as well as your questions and concerns.

> During next week's Impact Conference, you can join the 72-hour SOA jam, hosted on IBM ThinkPlace technology, and participate in

a global and local discussion about all things SOA. We'll have PCs available at the conference, so you can log on and network or you can log on from the convenience of your laptop.

Simply register at http://services.alphaworks.ibm.com/SOAJAM.

Second, the world today listens to entertainment. I try to entertain in my stories, in my video clips, or in my Second Life escapades. In the following blog post, I share my favorite places to shop in China!

SOA Contest in China!

China is a fabulous place—actually one of my favorite places to visit due to the energy and excitement in the Chinese people. I would recommend several key spots such as Xian where the terra cotta soldiers are—check out *this one!*

Because of the explosive growth in China, we designed a contest for Chinese university students. We asked them to build an SOA application using a virtual customer who is facing application integration problem with two legacy applications and wants to improve the operation process and increasing business flexibility. Five students can form a team and act as a solution team to design an SOA solution for the customer. The whole contest is to simulate a full selling cycle of an IT project: The first stage is collecting the proposal and the second is to have the top solutions (in this program, the top 15 teams) to do presentation and bidding and the top five solutions to enter the last phase—system implementation.

We already have more than 410 teams from 70 universities. Teams in the IBM China SOA Contest established more than 350 blogs such as *Leading Team*. They're the number one team in the first phase of the contest. The blog is in Chinese!

Third, I try to provide helpful advice or tools. I share customer best practices or even widgets with information to assist.

In this blog entry, I provided the link to our certification site and encouraged readers to become certified while sharing a little about my experience in downtown New York City during the July 4th fireworks!

Fireworks in NYC!

Happy Late 4th of July! Take a look at this exciting *fireworks video* that I shot in New York.

Also, note the electronic version of the July edition of *Certification Magazine* contains an article on our SOA certification. It hits the news on June 25.

Are you SOA certified?

For my personality and blog, those three things are required to have and drive that successful conversation in the market.

It is important to note that we have been able to close deals, see customers connect through the references I post, and have garnered a great deal of goodwill for IBM through my blog.

Midwest and IBM Lessons Learned

In talking with both Todd and Tish, I asked them to articulate some of their most valuable lessons learned. The following sections discuss what they believe to be those lessons.

It Takes Time!

For Tish, time was the biggest lesson she wanted to relate to others starting out on the path to a corporate blog. Developing, planning, and maintaining a good blog takes a great deal of time. She says that you must be realistic about the number of posts needed to keep the online relationship with readers alive. As Tish explains, "This is a commitment. You need to understand how much time it takes not only to set it up, but to keep it current and exciting. You must keep building your readership and online relationships. Plus, you have to keep yourself current by reading and participating in other blogs."

Todd agrees and adds, "Blogging implies you must write and read. I spend as much time reading other blogs and finding out what's going on in the blogosphere as I do writing on my own. To have something to say, you must know what's being said."

You have to be active in the blogosphere. You have to research what kind of sites exist. As Tish says, "I've got a whole list of RSS feeds that come in every day to me that are blogs that I like and that helps me determine where the market is going."

Follow the Golden Rule

Many heated opinions and perspectives exist in the blogosphere. You should treat others just as you would want to be treated, which means sometimes cooling down before hitting the Send button. As Tish says, "Midwest is a company that values people. We treat our employees the same way we treat our customers. It's a matter of caring. That corporate philosophy of honest caring just becomes the way you live and work when you're associated with Midwest Airlines. The same care needs to be taken with comments on the Web. Even when I critique a restaurant or hotel that I don't care for, I try to do it with style."

You Can't Fake Passion

I think this lesson is important. A blog is personal. It is not something you assign to a staff member who isn't interested in the topic. You have to understand with whom you are talking with and the value of talking to those people through a blog. As Tish comments, "You have to be passionate about the blog topic. If you just say to someone on staff 'I want to have a blog about travel' and that person is not passionate, she won't really put her all in it—it won't be as successful; it won't be a good communication piece. It will just be you talking at people, not talking with people. Everyone knows when you fake passion."

Again, Tish and Todd agree. If you want to be heard in the blogosphere, you must expend as much energy promoting your blog as you do writing it. Don't become a parallel to that "a tree falls in the forest and nobody was around to hear it" adage. It is most important that you write from the heart.

Learn the Basics

How do you find good blogs? You can find them through blog aggregators such as TechMeme, Technorati, Google Blog Search, and other aggregators. How do you promote your blog? You can comment on other blogs and include a link back to your own blog. You can also link on Facebook, LinkedIn, Plaxo, and others; however, tagging is the best way to promote your blog. Technorati tags get picked up and provide good promotion and coverage. After you have a readership, you will begin receiving comments and postings to your blog. A good commenter can add as much value as the original blog post writer. Research would suggest that in blogging the weakest link in the chain can be the most important voice in the chain. What does that mean? Never write off those who speak infrequently because they can carry a lot of weight!

It Is Beyond a U.S. Phenomena

English is no longer the most prominent blog language. If you review Technorati's latest report, 39 percent of blog posts were in English. In March 2007, only 33 percent were written in English. Japanese, Chinese, English, Spanish, Italian, Russian, French, Portuguese, Dutch, and German are the languages with the greatest number of posts tracked by Technorati.

It Is About the Conversation

Tish has the conversation in two ways. The first is through the blog itself where others can post comments and question her wisdom. Her blog is a conversation with the marketplace. The comments come in all flavors and shapes and are sometimes critical. The way a blogger responds to criticism is a key part of the community. Tagging can help because your tags get picked up by Technorati and other blog crawlers (including Google), so there is a contextual reference to an individual blog post. This technique enables other bloggers to discover your blog, which increases your propensity for linkbacks and more conversations. With respect to building linkbacks, it is a matter of which company you most like to keep. Remember, this is often a "you-scratch-my-back-I'll-scratch-yours" kind of scenario, so look first at other bloggers in similar spaces or complementary spaces. There are also other areas of influence.

The second way Tish has the conversation is in person. She goes on the trips with her community, thereby strengthening her voice in the market.

Conclusion

Blogging is about having a conversation in the market. Blogs with active contributors influence market perceptions and position their opinions in the marketplace.

Blogs create great opportunities for shaping messages and can be considered as viral marketing to create positive word of mouth. Some key actions from a marketing perspective include

- Identify your key bloggers (high permission inside and outside your company) and work with them to influence the marketplace.
- Create a corporate blog based on an area of strong interest from your clients.
- Reach out to the blog community. Sometimes the perfect person to write about a topic is not one in your company.

From my view, this is an innovative marketing media with strong influence when the bloggers are part of the community you want to influence, inform, and seduce. Some of the key challenges include getting people to your blog, keeping it fresh by combining different techniques and methods, and of course, using creativity.

As Todd comments, in the future, a blog might evolve to a more strategic focus. How? Well, we think that the blog will become the "business card" of the future. Everyone from executives to salespeople will leverage blogs as their primary calling card, using them to reach out to, interact with, and even sell to customers and prospects. Get involved now!

For Sandy and Todd's blogs, visit ibmpressbooks.com/angels. Online

15

Serious Gaming: IBM's Innov8

If you're trying to train a pilot, you can simulate almost the whole course. You don't have to get in an airplane until late in the process.
—Roy Romer

The old stereotype of the gamer no longer applies. According to the Entertainment Software Association (ESA), 63 percent of the U.S. population now plays video games, and this number is significantly higher in Asia. The average age of gamers is 35 years old, 40 percent are women, and half of them play games online one or more hours per week. Think about the success of Sony Corporation's PlayStation 3, Nintendo's Wii, Microsoft Corporation's Xbox 360, or the latest online game on which young people and adults play for hours on end. It was interesting to me, when during a college case competition where student teams compete to solve a business problem about how to reach the market on a new concept, that every case-competition team recommended games as the way to educate the market. Today's game players are acquiring the skills that companies increasingly value as the gaming generation enters the workforce.

Using games to market has a compelling value proposition. When well implemented, a game can virally target people in a specific demographic where they live in a medium they love and understand. The games can then be used to gather information about the player and even generate leads.

Almost every company will have to adapt to this new gaming generation as either customers or employees. Let's think through how to reach this segment of the market. The case study in this chapter is IBM's SOA team, the division where I manage an incredibly innovative yet results-driven marketing team. Let me share our story.

Focus on Serious Gaming in Marketing

To get a feel for the impact that gaming will have on how we market, I encourage you to read John C. Beck and Mitchell Wade's book, *The Kids Are Alright: How the Gamer Industry Is Changing the Workplace*, which is about how gamers are impacted by games. The authors discuss some interesting facts about this gaming generation. They are more creative and can solve problems better. Games teach about trial and error and experimenting to learn, and they even teach about the globalness of the world. In fact, the skills needed to succeed in gaming can help young people "to be more sociable, develop strategic thinking, and become better leaders in life," according to Beck and Mitchell. If you think through these facts, you will see what leads us to try serious gaming as an education means in a new category and to extend that concept to include how we enable sellers for a sales call.

Focus on IBM's Innvo8

Innvo8 is an innovative game to reach a new audience and to educate a market that is emerging. It leverages the concepts and energy of serious gaming to excite a passionate group of leaders around IBM's concept and view of the lifecycle. Innov8 is actually a serious game built for universities and training facilities to teach the concepts in a fun way. At IBM, we are trying to accelerate the understanding of business process management (BPM), which is the way a company manages its processes. Step 1 for us in gaining traction in this market category was to help the market understand what BPM is in an educational and informative way.

The IBM team that assisted me in completing the vision of leveraging Serious Gaming in a B2B world included

- David Lapp, IBM manager. He was the team lead with management responsibility for all day-to-day operational aspects of Innov8 project, including design, development, marketing, and support.
- Phaedra Boinodiris, Serious Games Designer and part of the university team who suggested gaming. She is a serious games expert, Innov8 game designer, development liaison, and evangelist.

Why is this part of marketing? As discussed earlier, segmenting and targeting your audience is crucial for your success. However, also critical is ensuring that these target markets understand the need and the solution to their problems. That's why we leverage the serious game for both education and selling in the steps of market creation.

The specific challenge presented at the case competition was to come up with a compelling way to evangelize BPM to non-IT executives. The original vision of the team that presented Innov8 was to create a simulation game that executives could use to simulate their own business process models, run it through a game scenario where you flood the process model with orders, and then use a dashboard to tweak the model to respond to game-initiated events so that you can either tank or save your business. All the while, the game can capture information on how the simulation is used and generates leads. In this way, the executives could fundamentally understand the value proposition to their businesses.

The Games Stigma

I had to argue until 1a.m. the night before our presentation because there was a student on my team who kept insisting that games were for kids and IBM was way too conservative to buy into the idea of using a game to sell to executives.
–Phaedra Boinodiris, student and currently an IBM employee

The university team lead pitching this idea realized the concept of point-of-sale games while watching a demo from a serious game studio in North Carolina that had made a simulation for generals to easily ascertain their troops' movements and strategies. Within a few scant minutes, the general could easily visualize where the bottlenecks were and where his attention was needed. When a company tries to sell something like a complex system, point-of-sale games are meant to enable the player to easily visualize the value proposition.

The team decided to alter this vision for the pilot and deliver a game that targeted MBA students. The learning points were broadened to include the anatomy of the technology, how to interpret it, how to use it in a business setting, and its value proposition through the "game play."

What Is Innov8?

Innov8 is a serious game. It has all the aspects of a game—joystick and villain included—with the goal of teaching basic concepts for an emerging category. In Figure 15.1, you see that the game was linked to our SOA movie (see Chapter 21, "End to End Example: IBM WebSphere and the SOA Agenda, Prolifics, Ascendant Technology"). It starts with a mission from your CEO Mike, a character in the game, and a learning journey that the user has to complete. We started with the objective of providing an immersive experience that simulates real life with key teaching moments. It is fundamentally different from traditional e-learning and needed for the gaming generation.

Opening Cinematic: Intro and Mission

- **Logan (protagonist) has been recruited to save AFTER Inc.**

- **Mike (AFTER Inc CEO) sets up situation...**

- **provides laptop...**
- **and gives Logan her mission:**

✓ **Investigate critical process**

✓ **"Find Sam Archer in IT"**

Figure 15.1 Innov8: The serious game for business.

In Figure 15.2, you see the goals and the three levels of Innvo8. The game begins with a normal movie-like introduction that accompanies all games on the market. It sets up a story and a challenge.

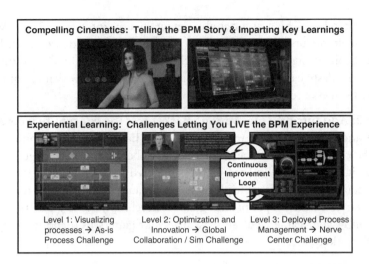

Figure 15.2 Innov8 high-level view.

Why Innov8?

There were two drivers of the creation of the game. First, we knew that there was a gap in understanding the marketplace. The game would generate attention and attract our targeted market to learn more. Second, we saw the shortage of required skills in the market as being a short- and long-term issue. Our survey revealed that 50 percent of our target market had less than 25 percent of the necessary skills, and 80 percent wanted ways to increase their skills in their companies. Given the skills required were solving complex problems involving both business and IT (68 percent said the ability to solve both sides of the equation was a prerequisite for hiring), a serious game, as suggested by our case-study competition, fit the needs.

Our Recipe for Serious Game Design

Because this is a new concept, the following steps will drive you to success in your entry into gaming:

Step 1: Start with what you are trying to teach and *know* your audience.

The first step our team took when designing Innov8 was to ask, "What is inherently *fun* about technology?" This is a critical question. After it was answered succinctly, the team matched its learning points to the right puzzle that fit the bill. This was, after all, a game, not an interactive demo. When we thought about what was fun about this IBM technology, we decided that there is something compelling about the idea of tweaking knobs and dials on a business dashboard and seeing from a bird's eye view how that can affect an entire business's ecosystem.

Step 2: Add intrinsic motivation, market test the concept to your audience and then choose your genre after you have done your homework.

The concept stage of the game is critical because making a good game takes significant time and money. A game used for marketing is the face of your brand and conveys multiple messages because it is a powerful marketing channel. With the proper planning and research upfront to guide the development of your game, you can maximize your game's ROI and its reception in the marketplace.

Step 3: Determine your platform choice.

Maintenance requirements, user-interface needs, and the community at large need to be carefully analyzed before choosing what game engine platform your game will reside on. Ask yourself the following questions:

Who is this game for? Is it for the general public?	Where is the audience?
How will you get the attention of the audience?	Are we planning to offer support?
Do we have the resources to build a community?	How will people get access to the game?
Will these players have accounts?	How often are updates needed?
Are we maintaining the game?	Are customization tools needed?
Are we locked into this vendor's platform if we want to expand later?	In essence, what fits the bill with regards to learning points, budget, maintenance and user interface needs, and availability of experts?

Step 4: Recruit a strong rollout team.

Choose partners with a proven track record in game development. The people designing a game from the corporate side should eat, drink, and breathe games in all genres because they are directing their vendor and must speak the same language and understand the complexities. The danger is that most people think they can honestly design a good game. Know what you do not know and retain experts when you can. Attend Game Developers Conferences (GDC) and the Serious Games Summit. Be on the Serious Games Listserv. Go to IGDA (International Game Developers) meetings. Be involved with the game community so that you are tapped into the latest technologies and best practices.

Who Are the Customers?

For our targeted segment, our audience was most typically from the gaming generation. This segment consists of both IT professionals and university students—both MBA students and students of technology given that this new category of BPM requires skills from both disciplines. How do we meet their needs in Innov8? Well, if we think back to Wade and Beck's book, to succeed in training this gaming generation, we must look at this gaming generation's characteristics, which include the following:

- Aggressively ignores any hint of formal instruction
- Leans heavily on trial-and-error (after all, failure is nearly free, you just push "play again")
- Includes lots of learning from peers but virtually none from authority figures
- Is consumed in small bits, exactly when the learner wants, which is usually just before the skill is needed
- Allows people to take risks in a safe environment
- Allows players to achieve a skill or talent that is not only meaningful but also perceived as having value

The Competition

Although Innov8 is unique in the marketplace, business schools have used simulators to teach concepts hands on. There is widespread, historical use of business simulators since the mid-1950s and used by 97.5 percent of business schools by 1998. There are uses in other industries, for instance, flight simulators to train pilots and government examples for training for military (America's Army is the most famous example) and first responders. In the healthcare area, games teach about illnesses, such as Remission, a game designed to teach kids about cancer, and simulators that teach surgeons how to perform a particular procedure.

A related article "Public Virtual Worlds: Ready for Corporate Prime Time?" by Scott Randall of BrandGames can be found on our companion Web site at ibmpressbooks.com/angels.

The Marketing Best Practice

With that in mind, thousands of universities around the world now have access to Innov8, IBM's new "serious game," available at no charge. We created the game to help university students and IT professionals develop a combination of business and information-IT skills, important attributes needed to compete in a global economy. My father is a pilot, and he learned to fly leveraging simulators. Here our game, or simulator, contains the benefit of enabling IT professionals and university students to engage in learning activities in the way they like to learn.

In the game, they can make decisions about real-life business situations, such as redesigning a call center process. They can see the immediate results of their decisions, and if they make a mistake, it's much more private than "failing" in front of a classroom of colleagues. Because a love of gaming is shared around the world, our current users have told us the game can help to bridge cultural barriers.

Skeptics reading this book might wonder if the practical, hard-nosed business world is ready for serious games. After all, do corporate fast-trackers and busy MBA students have time to play video games? This is where it's important to understand how serious games work and the segmentation we applied with Innov8. We targeted universities, executive MBA programs, and training groups like our partners, who wanted to provide an immersive, yet practical hands-on experience as part of their courses. By providing an innovative, educational game, our message became embedded at the center of many curricula. After the game becomes part of a course, student participation naturally follows. Similar to new recruits playing America's Army or pilots flying a flight simulator, students are often required to complete challenges in Innov8 as part of their coursework. Bottom line: Innov8 has proven to be an innovative marketing tactic to reach a particular market segment. It is successful because it is fun and illustrative of our products, while at the same time meeting the education needs and requirements of business and IT educators.

This is a marketing best practice in several areas. First, it reaches a new market on a global front which in many cases is "white space" or a new market for IBM. Second, it personalizes and creates a community around BPM. The game players related to the case are shown in Figure 15.3. The characters are specific roles in the company and, of course, develop their own personality:

- Stavros, the business analyst
- Sharon, the vice president of sales
- Logan, the protagonist hired to help the company
- Mike, the CEO
- Stella, the call-center maven
- Sam, the CIO

Figure 15.3 Innov8: the cast.

Through these characters, the game teaches skills. With skills being of the utmost importance in technology, this serious game is a best practice. According to The Apply Group, a marketing consultant, at least 100 of the Global Fortune 500 will use gaming to educate their employees by 2012, with the United States, the United Kingdom, and Germany leading the way.

INNVO8: THE JOURNEY BY SANDY CARTER

From the outset of our case competition between Duke University and the University of North Carolina at Chapel Hill, the game was born as a vision and passion of mine for my team. I am intrigued by the potential of gaming in the global world. It is a universally loved pastime.

As marketing professionals, we cannot ignore the changing group dynamics. In fact, we should tap into the most innovative ideas to redefine the fundamental nature of marketing. Just as games present us with situations that invite players to make choices, consider the advantage of using graphics and decision-making steps of games in business. By enabling decision makers to immerse themselves in the real-world simulations, judging cause and effect before making decisions, we free up out-of-the-box thinking.

The possibilities are huge and not just for business. That's why the journey here is equally important. My vision was made into a reality through a super team from several groups. The objectives I set out were to create a serious game to assist teaching BPM 101 fundamentals and to include a lab experience in the learning. I wanted it to be free to universities, which meant the budget had to be managed carefully. The initial target audience was MBA and executive MBA students as well as undergraduate business and information systems students. My partners were a key part of the plan for skills, so I wanted to pilot with them. In addition, I wanted to be able to take the game to an online position and to later serve a broader base of audiences such as provide customization for my large and small clients.

We leveraged a gaming engine, a great partner company Centerline, and a superb set of marketing professionals to make this a reality. It was a small off to the side project that reaped major benefits for IBM. My hat is off to the team!

Content providers:
Extended team: David Lapp, Dave Daniels, Kramer Reeves, Duke Chang, Phaedra Boinodiris, Angel Diaz, Kathy Keating, and Matt Berry as well as selected professors from the University of North Carolina, (especially Ron Williams) North Carolina State University, and Duke University.

The Serious Gaming Agenda at IBM

One of the most interesting things about serious games is watching them take hold and expand in multiple industries and genres. Companies are daring to use videogame technologies and lessons learned in new business models from corporate training to marketing. The primary focus is on games that face outward to the external world of the general public, clients, and business partners.

With the following, I have attempted to categorize the different genres of serious games for corporate use:

- Internal corporate training and collaboration
- Point-of-sale games (mini games that can teach value proposition to a client)
- Academic initiative (universities use game programs to boost retention)
- Games that extend brand reach

Internal Corporate Training and Collaboration

This internally facing genre of corporate serious games is the most well known. Companies have been using e-learning and simulations for years to train their employees on topics from management to diversity. More companies are adopting lessons learned from videogames to make these modules more engaging, more immersive, and more effective. Where I see the most potential here is in sales rep training. Currently IT and pharmaceutical companies invest heavily in training their sales reps in their latest technologies and products utilizing old-school techniques that are anything but engaging. There is a fine line between the creation of a corporate training game meant to train sales people on the power of their products and point-of-sale games as described in the following section.

Additionally, companies such as Cisco and IBM are investing in Virtual Worlds as a platform for both training and collaboration, bringing in critical components like application sharing, voice over IP, programmable bots, and social networking.

Point-of-Sale Games

When a company tries to sell something, such as a complex system, point-of-sale games are meant to enable the player to easily visualize the value proposition. Although I haven't seen this in action yet, my understanding is that the medical devices industry is already experimenting with this model—creating games to leave with surgeons—that they might see how the device can be used within a human body. My team is currently investigating ways in which IBM can use this same model so that it can generate leads from games and communicate our value proposition to nontechnical clients that might require customizable visualization tools to see how concepts such as SOA can help businesses. We are also investigating ways in which some of our tools can actually integrate on the backend to our games.

Games That Extend Brand Reach

Many companies have explored this territory not just through in-game advertising (such as the Coca-Cola ad in Grand Theft Auto) but also via mini-games that don't necessarily teach anything, but they do make the player more aware of brands. Mobile games are a great place to see more of these games because it is a perfect medium to explore this territory. Mobile games are less costly to create, and they have a growing following. (Forty percent of U.S. heads of households play mobile games.)

Academic Initiative

This is a venue for corporate serious games in which Innov8 resides. The pilot for the game was released to business schools as a way to evangelize BPM to MBA students in a facilitated medium. The academic community is a great place to spearhead a marketing strategy around games because you have your target audience of 20- to 30-year-olds who love games, you have a recruiting base you can then tap into because your company now has the elusive coolness factor, and there are so many opportunities for expansion and partnership.

Let's dissect the elements of the marketing best practice. Having customers and students learn that category by running a fictional company without major penalty teaches real-world skills that our customers have told us they value and are in short demand. In addition, it drives loyalty and passion in a personalized way. I'd like to share with you three specific areas that help to drive our success: our focus on skills, leveraging the press, and helping students grow up with IBM (a page from Apple's book).

The Game in Action, Building Key Skills

In this gaming scenario, the market was one where skills were in tight demand. A primary role for the game was the development of skills or enablement. Marketing needs to ensure that the right skills are ready for acceptance of new concepts. For the IBM game, we focused on education. In this serious game, learning occurs through dialogue with other characters in primarily peer roles and self-discovery. This learning from peers fits with the requirement that our clients gave us: They didn't really want to learn from authority but from their peers. Second, the development of skills occurs via trial-and-error and in the mini-games contained in the game. Each mini-game is preceded by a tutorial that explains how the game works, in a "just in time" manner. The experience is risk free as the user drives the fictional company.

In Level 1, we ground the user in the basics. This includes key BPM vocabulary, process steps, and details about how varied job roles contribute to the success of a BPM project. In Figure 15.4, you see a real-life lesson taught about how all processes might not work as documented. A peer, Sam the CIO, is instructing about how to get the task done through working and talking to those who actually do the task.

In Figure 15.5, you meet Stella, the call-center maven, and get a view of the product as you build your first business-process model. This enables over 2,000 universities around the world to teach about our product in a fun setting and with those who have real-world situations such as this one in the call center.

- Sam provides and explains modeling tooling...

- advises Logan to document and validate As-Is process model:

✓ "Look in Operations for existing process map

✓ "Make sure you validate with a process expert"

Sam - IT Director

Figure 15.4 Level 1: the basics.

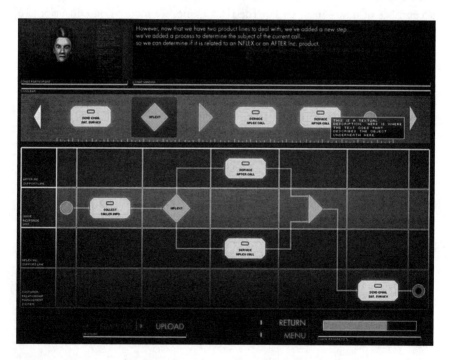

Figure 15.5 Stella teaches the product.

In Figure 15.6, you see an example of a miniature game in which Logan, the protagonist, has to complete a virtual scavenger hunt as she searches for the business data—the costs, call-type probabilities, and staffing levels—that she needs to optimize her call-center process.

Figure 15.6   Logan learns in a process scavenger hunt.

In Figure 15.7, we see the next level of challenges that the gamer has to go through. Mike, the CEO, asks for productivity improvements but not by adding people. Here, the gamer must further refine the process by running simulations, in a trial-and-error method, until key business performance goals are met. Throughout this level, the characters and cast push a set of global business challenges out to the gamer.

In Figure 15.8, you see the results that Logan has achieved after her business process is optimized and deployed. Here, she gets the experience of running the business with a new-and-improved process, using a futuristic dashboard interface. The dashboard is an essential element in the product portfolio and throughout you see how the gamer becomes familiar and comfortable with the IBM portfolio.

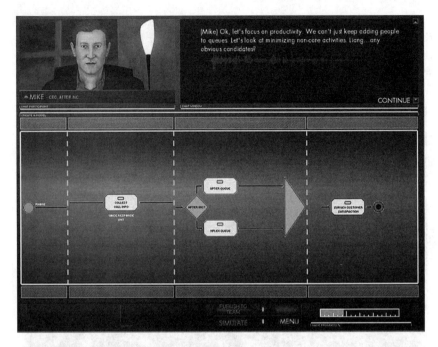

Figure 15.7   Mike, the CEO, issues a productivity challenge.

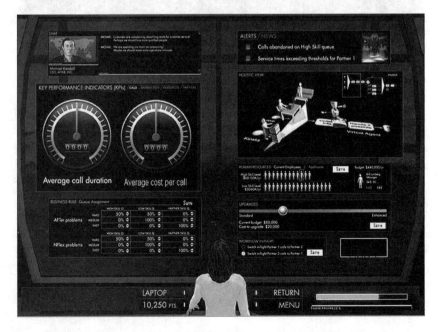

Figure 15.8   Logan reviews the dashboard based on IBM products to view her results.

I share these figures with you to demonstrate how the elements fit the needs of the gamer, and that during the fun, we never lost focus on the education. Our goal of growing skills has found that those students who play the game have a much higher retention rate than those in traditional education classes.

Application to Your Company

My challenge to you is to understand how gaming can work in your business. It is something that could be applied in B2C or as shown previously, B2B marketing. You might have to break out of your comfort zone, but there are serious gaming models for nearly every type of learning activity. Whether training technicians on a complex new product or teaching managers soft topics such as HR policy or management development, the critical step is defining your key learning points and picking an appropriate gaming metaphor to teach those points. You don't have to start with a full, 3D, immersive game; there are many ways to start small and build your expertise. If enablement on your product or service is critical, serious games are definitely something you should review and plan at least as a pilot.

Don't Forget the Buzz!

After we had the game and the elements to spur learning, we put a lot of effort in getting the story into the market. Because our goal was to get as many people trained as possible, we wanted to highlight the coolness of the game, but also its power. In Chapter 8, "Break Through the Noise," we discuss the key role influencers play, and we did our research. Universities read the key journals and with enough buzz, we could have not only a push strategy in the market but a pull as well.

We leveraged an event hosted by Brandeis University's International Business School that was focused on skills. They had about 100 attendees in the Boston area. That gave us our launching point of more than 20 press articles and television coverage. We followed that up with presentations to universities and major press at our IMPACT event of more than 4,300 attendees. The press response was more than 262 articles from *The Wall Street Journal*, *Business Week*, *USA Today*, and many other key and core influencers. Our momentum was sustained by our strategy to let the universities drive even more stories. By providing universities with a press kit that their PR departments could use to drive local coverage, we created another win-win. Universities adopting Innov8 were able to generate local coverage for their programs by highlighting a cool and progressive curriculum, while IBM word of mouth around BPM continued to build. In Figure 15.9, you see some of the examples of the press that the team worked with to generate the excitement in the market.

Figure 15.9 The buzz.

Application to Your Company

Leverage the press as a core part of your marketing. In today's market, public relations make a difference just as much as advertising and other marketing tactics. You need to be focused on both controlled media and uncontrolled media, so marketing and public relations have to work together. It's getting other people to tell your story for you. Leverage the power of public relations through third-party endorsement. Tooting your own horn about how great you are doesn't have the same effect as having other parties who are detached from the organization and have their own personal experiences, their own biases, and their own reason that people listen. Whether they are the ultimate thought leaders or whether they are just simply a significant other company, it can make a major difference in the market.

Growing Up Blue!

This game as you have seen has a short-term benefit. However, the marketing vision here is much broader. I wanted it to have a long-term impact on skills in the marketplace. A key element for Innvo8 was getting it into the hands of universities throughout the world. We began to leverage our contacts in key universities and to present the idea of a game included in a current course to drive home the key points. We prepared our targeted list of 100 universities and presented the story. Of course, because our design point was a free game to universities, we received a lot of interest. However, we also tried to go to the "tipper" universities. If you ever read the book *The Tipping Point: How Little Things Can Make a Difference* by Malcolm Gladwell, you understand the importance of recruiting those universities first, or if you haven't read it, tippers are those people and groups that influence others to try a new concept.

Most of the first to sign up were universities that were already seeing the trend around business processes, and they were going to use the serious game to assist teaching BPM 101 fundamentals. When coupled with the one-hour, interactive learning-lab experience, most universities were willing to try the game for an initial course. We have incorporated this into the existing IBM and institutional curricula.

Academic Initiative Next Steps

Not only has the game served as a great press magnet, it is also a fantastic recruiting tool (IBM makes cool 3D games), and it spurred something rather unexpected with universities. Three things began to happen:

1. MBA schools wanted to partner with IBM to help design scenarios for the next version of the game.
2. Engineering schools wanted to partner with IBM to build their game design and development degree programs so that they could recruit more computer science students.
3. Our customers began asking for custom versions of the game.

Partnering with IBM to use corporate serious games as a platform for learning would focus schools with multidisciplinary programs around one central program, an online network, bringing in schools of design, art, computer science, and business and have them collaborate in an online forum with independent game developers and innovative IBMers. In this way, we can tap into a creative low-cost game development machine, empower university students and professors, glean great press and visibility, and work with our partners and clients in a Wikipedia-blessed ecosystem.

Application to Your Company

Depending on the size of your company, thinking through the long-term aspects to win in the market will be crucial. Apple made headway with its systems because as students graduated, they were familiar with the Apple way. I wanted to replicate that best practice in the new world.

ROI

As described earlier, making a good game takes significant resources. From the corporate side, it takes time, money, and visionary people who can pull together the business messaging and communicate it to a stellar game studio vendor that can get the job done under a tight schedule. After that nontrivial feat is complete, you have to wrap it up into a campaign with legs that will be directed to your audience. How do you evangelize games in your organization and prove the case for ROI? For potential customers, the obvious golden egg here is to tie a game to a lead generation. In this way, you keep them engaged and give them tailored resources and a community with similar interests with which to collaborate. For training games, the goal is to tie the ROI to a monitored rise in productivity. Did the sales reps that played this game sell more widgets than those that didn't?

As Innov8 was our first real foray into games for marketing, we easily captured our ROI through press alone within the first month of the announcement. We are now getting ready to push the envelope further in terms of ROI and really test the market for the games channel.

IBM Lessons Learned

The following are some of the most powerful lessons that we learned in this process:

1. **Young Ideas.** This idea came from the Duke versus the University of North Carolina at Chapel Hill case competition. Not just one team, but 95 percent of the teams in the contest recommended a serious game. This idea is not the first from a case competition. Our CEO study showed that CEOs find that collaboration inside and outside their four walls brought in the best ideas. This is true at all levels of a business. I have run a case competition for four years, and each year, my eyes are opened to new and exciting activities that I can try inside my company. The cost is not that high, and you get not only great ideas, but also a good look at the talent in real-working conditions.

2. **Pick Your Partners Carefully!** Because gaming is not IBM's core competency, choosing the right game development company to partner with on the endeavor was important. We wanted to focus on the thought leadership and BPM content as our core and have those who know game development and game engine technologies focus on their core competencies. In a nutshell, we learned to leave the bleeding edge to entertainment games! In addition, we made sure we worked with the universities to shape the project because what we thought might work in a university was different than some of the advice we received from the professors. That being said, the team working with the game studio from the corporate side should eat, drink, and breathe games in all genres because it directs the vendor and must speak the same language and understand the ecosystem.

3. **Corporate serious games** for marketing have a short window of development compared to traditional games (a few months versus years), and it is typically a badly underestimated endeavor in terms of lower operating expenses and costs.

4. **Games are not interactive demos.** Games are games; they have elements of play. Always start with what makes what you are trying to teach fun and engaging, but do not fall into the trap of thinking you need to throw in a Pac-Man-like game to make your game fun. Don't waste your audience's time and think creatively.

5. You don't necessarily have to re-create the wheel! Look to the entertainment world to see how it incorporates concepts such as business management, supply chain, and complex systems.

6. **Build an ecosystem around the game.** Almost every corporate serious game would be more powerful if it was tied to a social network, enabling players to convene, compare scores, share best practices, collaborate, and so on. You have captured their interests; now capitalize on it and keep them coming back for more!

Conclusion

The term serious gaming is no longer an oxymoron. There is endless opportunity if you harness the power of games to get work done. Although it's too soon to measure the full implications, there's a new business environment emerging. If hundreds of thousands of players organize themselves to successfully complete specific endeavors during their "play" time, will they be content during work hours in organizational structures used since the Industrial Revolution with central command and control? Chances are, they're more likely to want to work on virtual teams distributed around the world, undertaking multiple endeavors, and taking advantage of the thought processes that succeeded for them in online gaming. Leadership marketing organizations will be on the forefront of this new technology applied to the new world.

To view the Innov8 trailer, go to ibmpressbooks.com/angels.

To access a view of the importance of Key Agility Indicators (KAI), visit ibmpressbooks.com/angels.

Leads and Revenue
- ■ In Process Metrics
- ■ Leads & VLR
- ■ Dashboards

16

Show Me the Money: A Discussion with Google, the Marketing Leadership Council, and MarketingNPV

The reason most people never reach their goals is that they don't define them, or ever seriously consider them as believable or achievable. Winners can tell you where they are going, what they plan to do along the way, and who will be sharing the adventure with them.
—Denis Watley

Where Are You Going?

Marketing metrics matter, and every marketer looks for the key metrics to drive business. Growing up, my dad always told me that you get what you measure. That fact has been articulated to me repeatedly in the business world. It is important for marketers to articulate achievement. The key is to set marketing metrics according to your specific overall business objectives. Especially in today's dynamic environment, showing value of marketing's outcomes is essential. In Figure 16.1, we see that the ANGELS framework would not be complete without the focus on the numbers.

and Revenue
- In Process Metrics
- Leads & VLR
- Dashboards

Figure 16.1 ANGELS framework—leads and revenue.

A dashboard is a great way to show your outcomes and determine your action plan. In your car, the dashboard contains gauges such as a speedometer and a fuel gauge. In addition, it has malfunction lights and even in most cars today, a navigation system to help you determine where you are going. The same is true in business. A dashboard is a set of metrics that enable you to see how your business is doing, where your marketing campaigns are on track, where they are malfunctioning, and how you keep an eye on the future.

However, unlike a car dashboard, your overall dashboard will be different than others because each organization has differences in their business goals, industry characteristics, and culture. There will be areas of commonality; however, an effective dashboard can uniquely tie to your company's balanced scorecard. Although metrics might be the same, variance based on your goals and what is going to drive your success is the key best practice. It is mandatory. For example, some businesses focus on being number one in a market niche, number one in a particular market, or a low-cost producer. Based on those business goals, your marketing objectives and tactics will vary in terms of how you generate demand, how you provide insight for new products, and even in the marketing mix. As you would imagine, these dashboards are different.

What is critical is that you set a dashboard of marketing metrics based on the objectives that your company is trying to achieve. It should be balanced between short-term objectives, such as measuring a specific campaign, and long-term view of your brand's image. Given the new world and the need to encompass a good mix of Web 2.0 plus traditional marketing methods, you need to reassess your key objectives and goals in today's context.

Why develop a dashboard? There are three primary reasons. The first is that a dashboard helps you improve and identify quickly where you have gaps so that you can take action. It assists in your planning to be a better marketing organization. Second, it can assist in showing value to the overall business. Your marketing metrics will reflect how well your company has leveraged each part of the ANGELS structure. These factors drive the level of marketing value. Finally, it can help you better integrate into the business by assisting in communications and shared goals, for instance, with your sales colleagues.

How Do You Develop a Dashboard?

In Figure 16.2, you can see a view of how to drive the process of building a dashboard. To begin a dashboard, an understanding of your company's financial and overall strategic objectives must be leveraged. Of course, the value proposition will also help to determine the marketing objectives and tactics. (The discussion of how to create a value propositions is found in Chapter 8, "Break Through the Noise.")

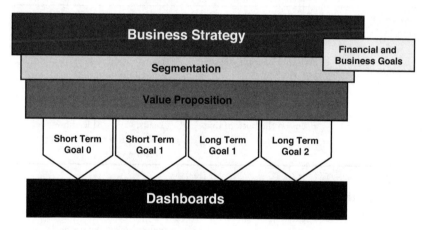

Figure 16.2 Simplistic marketing dashboard flow.

This simplistic marketing dashboard flow shows the firm linkage to the business objectives, as well as the focus on both short-term and long-term goals.

Let's now look at each of the ANGELS elements and show how they play a role in the dashboard and what can be measured at each step for success in our Web 2.0 world. Table 16.1 has a list of the goals and examples of what you can measure. Again, a precursor is that your metrics and views are linked to your company's balanced scorecard and goals.

Table 16.1 Angel View with Selected Example Metrics

	Goal	Example Metrics
Analyze the market.	Did you nail the market viewpoint?	Segment performance, new market growth, global skills on board, market share
Nail the strategy.	Is your value proposition, strategic roles, branding elements, and CSR focus showing progress?	Relevance of value proposition by role, success by role, green—carbon management, brand positioning, customer loyalty
Go-to-market.	Is your integrated campaign driving business and awareness in the market?	Pipeline contribution, campaign effectiveness, in-process metrics, integrated campaign results
Energize the channel.	Is your overall channel, both direct and indirect, driving business? Are your Web 2.0 activities making you more effective?	Customer engagement through communities, widget downloads, blog pickup in press, blog contribution to sales, gaming contribution to skill goals, buzz factors, internal enablement, employee engagement
Leverage leads and revenue.	Focus on the bottom line.	Leads, validated lead revenue and win revenue, customer lifetime value

Analyze the market and nail the strategy. Your metrics and success are driven by your strategy. The segmentation, positioning, and value propositions are the heart of how you perform in the marketplace. You need a strong product or offering that the market wants, and it needs to be positioned in the right way. I heard from Rackspace, Google, IBM, Nortel, and almost every company I talked to that you must nail the relevant value and positioning in the marketplace to win. As Klee Kleber, Vice President of Rackspace's Product Marketing says, "If you don't have the strategy and the right value proposition, I think all the rest of the marketing doesn't really matter." Those goals and strategies, such as having the best product with number share in a segment, are translated into the objectives needed to win. Then, you link in the appropriate marketing tactics to drive that overall strategy.

Determine what to measure. The three key areas are brand metrics, such as share of preference, share of voice, and of course, customer growth rate, preferably by role or segment. In this step, measurements of the relevance of your segmentation and success by segment can provide value into your personalized marketing plan by value segment. In addition, measurement of your global efforts, in breaking into new markets and your skills, can add value based on your company's goals. Also, consider the new metrics, such as carbon management, which might be one of your top 5–15 metrics based on your focus.

In Table 16.2, I include metrics for a segment. Customer loyalty by segment, share of wallet, and other key metrics might be on the top sheet of your scorecard or the deeper dive into the metrics. Also, in Chapter 19, "Screaming World Changes," we explore innovation metrics as well.

Table 16.2   Top Sheet for a Segment Example

Market Leadership in Brand

Targets	Year to Date (YTD) Results
Create awareness	Digital metrics Touch influencers Green relevance
Campaign success in segment	Integrated campaign effectiveness
Close near term opportunities	Develop sales plays Create telesales play Conversion to win

Go-to-market (GTM). If you do have a great strategy, innovative ways to go-to-market can make a difference in your results. For example, AFLAC was able to achieve stunning results with its introduction of the duck (AFLAC) campaign. The book *Bang! Getting Your Message Heard in a Noisy World* by Linda Kaplan Thaler, Robin Koval, and Delia Marsha explained that AFLAC's growth rate soared from 12 percent prior to the campaign to 28 percent following it. GTM metrics are typically the most measured area.

What do you measure? Campaign effectiveness, brand positioning, and integrated program results.

Energize the channel. The marketing mix, the combination of Web 2.0 and traditional elements can also drive strong results. At the program level, marketers can improve their effectiveness by better executing each of their marketing campaigns. Effectiveness can be improved by adding blogging, widgets, viral marketing, or even improving organic search results to drive the integrated program to higher revenue yields. Overall, externally, it is about customer engagement, and internally, it is about employee engagement.

What to measure: buzz factors, awareness, and sales from new Web 2.0 elements, customer engagement, employee engagement, customer satisfaction, and partner satisfaction

Leads and revenue are the ultimate end goal for the business. This chapter looks at how to leverage what you learn in this book and to articulate the value from marketing.

What do you measure? Leads, validated lead revenue, win revenue, and customer lifetime value.

Scream, of course, pulls in the technology to automate and amplifies your dashboards, ecommerce platform, Web analytics, search optimization, and more.

To put this altogether, one of my favorite pictures comes from MarketingNPV®. In Figure 16.3, you can see how the parts we have discussed have been pulled together in MarketingNPV's view of the dashboard flow.

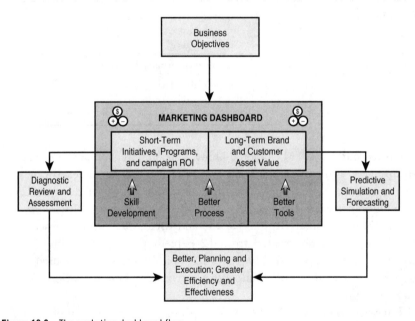

Figure 16.3   The marketing dashboard flow.

Caution!

The marketers I talk with are under pressure to add metrics. Too many metrics will not help articulate the value of the marketing organization. In fact, in this digital world, so many things are measurable that it can become overwhelming. Just because something is measurable, does not mean it should be measured or that it is valuable to measure. There is a risk that the measurable items can crowd out the immeasurable important items. For example, a risk exists that certain activities, such as branding, which do not have direct metrics tied to them, are receiving less focus. There are measures of awareness and consideration but not solid direct revenue impact metrics for brands. CFOs are starting to ask questions like, "I see that our consideration is up, but does that mean anything?" It is important for companies to keep focus on those critical marketing elements and not to ignore the immeasurable for the measurable.

Dashboards are most effective for C-level executives with between 5 to 15 metrics so that the focus is maintained. As a reminder, you can do deeper dives for specific marketing functions but the top line view must be understandable! Also, graphics do help. Finally, make sure you have the data refreshed based on the speed of the business.

What Should You Focus On?

To really understand where metrics are moving to in today's Web 2.0 world, I spoke with Molly Maycock, executive director, Marketing and Communications Practice at the Corporate Executive Board. She runs the Marketing Leadership Council and Chief Marketing Officer Programs that focus on advertising, marketing communications, market research, and corporate communications. I asked her, based on talking to multiple chief marketing officers (CMOs), which metrics should we focus on in today's world. Her major insight is that marketing metrics are moving beyond activity-based metrics, such as number of leads generated, to outcome-based metrics of leads converted to sales. The basic set of core metrics, again, prioritized based on what your objectives that we see as being on the rise, are the following:

- **Leads, validated lead revenue, and win:** The number of leads, the valid lead revenue, and the win revenue have been metrics tracked by marketing since the beginning. These are core metrics and ultimately tie into the value of our overall marketing strategy.

- **Brand metrics:** Even though brand metrics are under pressure right now, your brand is your critical asset. As Maycock advises, "Always have brand metrics. Ask yourself these questions: What is the specific objective of this branding campaign? Are we trying to take this specific target segment and increase our consideration with that target segment? Or are we trying to change their perception of the company? Focus in on the specific objective that you are trying to accomplish."

- **Customer metrics of loyalty and satisfaction:** Customer-focused metrics are some of your most powerful metrics. Maycock comments that the net promoter score (NPS) is on the rise in terms of CMO metrics. Because customer satisfaction does not equal loyalty, the NPS tries to get at what will drive business results. The NPS is usually obtained by asking customers, "How likely is it that you would recommend us to a friend or colleague?" The results categorize customers into three groups: promoters, passives, and detractors. In the analysis, promoters are viewed as valuable assets that drive profitable growth because of their repeat/increased purchases, longevity, and referrals, whereas detractors are seen as liabilities that destroy profitable growth because of their complaints, reduced purchases/defection, and negative word-of-mouth.

NET PROMOTER SCORES (NPS)

Interesting, in Wikipedia, I found research by Fred Reichheld, supported by independent research by Paul Marsden of the London School of Economics and Mark Ritson of Melbourne Business School, that claimed a positive correlation between NPS and growth of the company. General Electric (GE), for example, uses NPS to drive process excellence for its customers and plans to use NPS as a metric to decide the compensation of its leaders. Procter and Gamble uses NPS to measure the health of its brands. Allianz uses NPS to help it achieve what it calls "customer-centricity." Other companies using NPS include American Express, BearingPoint, The Carphone Warehouse, and Intuit. Verizon Wireless also uses NPS in all business channels including its call centers and retail stores.

- **Customer engagement:** In 2006, the Advertising Research Foundation (ARF) announced the first definition of customer engagement at the re:think! 52nd Annual ARF Convention and Expo as, "Engagement is turning on a prospect to a brand idea enhanced by the surrounding context." Engagement is not just about "Did you see this ad?" but "Were you engaged with it?" Companies are looking at engagement as the dialogue in the marketplace that is mostly driven outside the company's normal outreach. There are two primary ways that people are tracking the engagement with their brand. One is from Gallup and one is from IAG. There is not a common industry standard for the engagement with the brand metric as of yet. According to Bill Gassman, research director at Gartner, Inc, each organization's version of engagement will be unique. He says, "It will be derived from a number of root metrics, such as frequency, recency, length of visit, purchases, and lifetime value. User events, such as subscribing, downloading, or providing personal information and soft metrics, such as attitude, influence, and obsession may also be used in an engagement calculation. Metrics will come from multiple sources, including the Web analytics tool, call center, and physical store visits." After relevance, the ability to capture quality measurements are key factors in choosing root metrics. Look at Figure 16.4 for Forrester's view of the four components of engagement. It is the most comprehensive view that I have seen for the components that you need to review.

- **Employee engagement:** Happy employees make for better service people. Many companies measure this as part of their marketing efforts because better service comes from those who enjoy working for the company. The Marketing Leadership Council has a set of questions that they recommend including things like, "Are you willing to stay late and work hard for your boss?"

- **Integrated campaign metrics:** In an integrated campaign, marketers define the role of each channel. For example, "We want our television campaign to drive people to our Web site," or "We want this Internet campaign to drive people to this landing page." The integrated campaign moves people down a purchase funnel across a series of elements of the campaign. What is challenging is how to measure the success of that integrated campaign. Some companies measure different objectives for each of the different parts of the campaign. No longer would you look at your television campaign as driving people to buy, but driving people to your Web site. The way that you measure the integrated impact of tactics is difficult, in particular, how the channels are synergistically working

together is incredibly difficult. Neither Maycock nor I found a company
that had cracked this code yet.

■ **Digital metrics:** Most companies track the digitally related metrics.
Google, for instance, encourages its clients to filter, categorize, and rate,
that is, market its products. It realizes consumers are not only much more
adept at creating highly-targeted taxonomies given that they are more
adept at delineating the segment they constitute, but also that they are
willing to do so for free. Let's dive a little deeper in Google's views on the
new-world metrics.

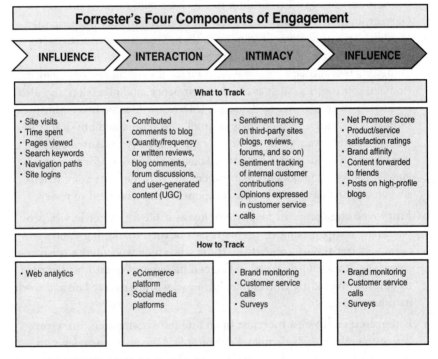

Source: August 2007 "Marketing's New Key Metric: Engagement."

Figure 16.4   Four components of engagement.

THOUGHTS ON HOW TO MEASURE ENGAGEMENT? MARKETINGNPV (WWW.MARKETINGNPV.COM) MARKETING^NPV ©2003–2008 MARKETINGNPV LLC., USED BY PERMISSION

Given this focus on collaboration with the customer and cocreation, how do you measure how you are doing? A lot of focus has been placed on engagement and how you measure it.

In MarketingNPV's recent article, "How Do You Measure Engagement?" they outline some simple rules of engagement in this new area.

1. Develop a vision. Don't attempt to measure engagement until determining the outcomes you want to achieve. The way you design your campaigns and make allocation decisions will be influenced by your objectives. Are you trying to sell more of Product X to Customer Segment A? Are you trying to retain more customers from Segment B? The narrower your initial focus, the less daunting the task will seem. With the objectives defined, map out the different components of the purchase funnel and the nonlinear pathways that customers or prospects may take to get to a point where economic value is created. How do customers find and enter your Web site? What steps do they take to download a whitepaper? At what point does your sales team interact directly or indirectly with customers or prospects? What role do channel partners play?

This exercise provides insight not only into the paths themselves; it will also begin to shed light on how different behaviors influence one another and create purchase opportunities or other value-creating activities. To probe more deeply into these drivers, your next step is to identify places on the map where you have good data and where you don't. Look beyond the traditional customer survey information, brand-tracking studies, and the CRM system. What Web analytics are you capturing? Do you have access to point-of-sale data or call-center transcripts?

2. Create a methodical testing process. For the areas in which you have little or no data, make assumptions based on experience—and then test your assumptions by constructing experimental designs. Understanding the chain better can provide insights into the value of specific activities. This enables you to begin validating previously fuzzy relationships between, for example, word-of-mouth referrals and cash-register sales. Focus these experiments on one or two areas at a time, replacing assumptions with facts as you go along to plug holes in the map. Applying more disciplined, scientific techniques will help marketers understand the net impact of specific interactions, and thereby determine which levers are the most beneficial to pull for a positive outcome.

3. Look for predictive validity of upstream behaviors. As you fill in the data gaps, you'll be in better position, through multivariate, linear, or nonlinear regression techniques, to add more rigor to your predictive modeling. For example, a customer who downloads a whitepaper gives us 80% confidence that she will speak positively to someone who's considering our brand. And if a customer speaks positively to three people, there's a 75 percent likelihood that one of those people will have a direct transaction with us.

Be careful not to blow your credibility by holding up small, isolated pieces of the puzzle as predictive. True predictive models encompass all the drivers of engagement and, importantly, the interrelations among them. Trying to draw a straight line between awareness, for example, and sales puts marketing in a vulnerable position and makes it easy for other stakeholders to question allocation decisions. Finance knows that awareness alone doesn't put food on the table.

4. Leverage your engagement drivers. After you find the correlations between upstream behaviors and economic value (such as transactional behavior), you can isolate the likely drivers of more economic behavior and begin focusing marketing activities on extending or leveraging those drivers. For example, if you see that word-of-mouth references actually make the referrer 60 percent more likely to repurchase, then you might want to invest more in promoting referrals among your current customer base. Alternatively, if you find that e-commerce activity at your site spikes when certain influential bloggers post news of your wonderful products, you may elect to increase the frequency of your news releases and provide those bloggers with advance release notice.

The goal is not just to find the engagement behaviors that are indicative of profitable economic outcomes, but then to build your marketing (and potentially selling) programs around the goal of stimulating more of those behaviors.

Enter the New World–Experimentation Required for a Lifetime!

I had the pleasure of speaking with Tony Fagan, the director of Quantitative Analysis at Google. We discussed the right ways to measure results in the new world. There are several current blogs that discuss the death of the page view and even the number of unique visitors. This "death" is the result of a shift to the new world, which simply cannot be measured using old world metrics. Fagan and I discussed how to measure in the new world for indications of successful Marketing 2.0. Here, Marketing 2.0 is defined as any activity intended to increase awareness, trial, or usage of a product or service, ranging from shaping brand perceptions to dynamically serving content on Web pages that will be most relevant to customers to direct response marketing.

We discussed two major areas: the value of randomized experiments and customer lifetime value. IBM and Google share a love of experimenting online. Because the cost of trying something out is low, the value of testing an ad in the morning and seeing the results and modifying them by noon, makes this media much more real-time than television advertising and the traditional methods. As such, all marketers should leverage the low cost of experimenting. Google always adheres to the low cost of experimenting online. They have created an online ad platform to provide an ability to run randomized experiments to help answer difficult advertising questions, such as:

- What's the optimal spend mix across media?
- How much of my marketing is incremental? For example, how many acquisitions would I have if I had not advertised?
- Is my advertising profitable?
- What's the impact of online advertising on offline sales?

The main objective of this work is to determine how much to spend on each media to maximize profit. So if you run television and online awareness campaigns, is there a bump you get from running them independently. Or do you get incremental value by combining different media, whether it's radio, print, television, or online and whether it's search or display, YouTube, or other social media opportunities. When you combine those in various ways, what is the incremental value that you see from them?

Experimentation is the number one opportunity for better understanding your marketing in the future. The online media enables a level of flexibility not previously granted to marketers. As Fagan explains, "For searching or for buying display advertising, you can turn things on and off quickly. You can vary how much you spend by geography. You can actually design experiments and implement them in a much easier and more flexible fashion than you could before online marketing existed."

Customer lifetime value is a metric that began a few years ago to gain some interest, but we can see it heating up in blogs and Twitter right now. What is the customer lifetime value metric? It involves measuring the value of acquiring and retaining customers over their lifetimes. In its simplest form, it is a calculation of cost versus overall value. For example, if you have ten loyal customers, they remain with your company for three years, and your profit from them is $7,000 collectively, your customer lifetime value is $7,000/10 = $700. This means that each new customer is worth about $700. It is becoming an important metric for understanding overall marketing ROI.

It can also help to determine values in the new Web 2.0 world. An example might be measuring the lifetime value of an influencer in your social network, which can be many times more than the lifetime value of an average customer. Looking at the lifetime value of a customer changes the way you think about marketing and the relationship you have with your customers. In our example of influencers, it might make more sense to spend $500 with each of your influencers to get them deeply engaged with your brand and products so that they will speak for you rather than doing a marketing campaign to your clients directly.

Throughout the book, we discuss the dialogue that marketing is now in with multiple touch points (in person, mobile, social, search, e-mail, and so on) with customers. These various online media techniques enable your company to approach its segments in relevant ways replacing screaming into the marketplace at everyone with everything.

Understanding and being able to measure how each customer should interact with the brand allows companies to generate better customer lifetime values. From a panel that I attended on customer lifetime value, one person in the audience said that "one customer may want to be contacted by mobile text message when a specific product is available, while another may want to be contacted by e-mail when the company is offering special promotions. If you can know and respond with what is relevant, you increase your value."

There are many tools to assist you in determining your customer lifetime value, such as the one from my alma mater, Harvard Business School, at http://www.harvardbusinessonline.com/flatmm/flashtools/cltv/.

A key metric to look at your marketing organization, in addition to these Key Performance Indicators, is Key Agility Indicators (KAIs). For a discussion of KAIs, please see the companion Web site at ibmpressbooks.com/angels.

Lessons Learned

In building your scorecard, consider a few simple best practices. It is important to focus on the right set of metrics of both qualitative and quantitative. Marketing is a science and an art, and as such, both are valid in viewing your success.

Build a marketing dashboard, not a single ROI calculation. This enables you to track along a series of metrics across the objectives that are right for your company. In Figure 16.5, you see a sample role-based dashboard. This includes in-process metrics such as response rates by role, a view by geography, pipeline contribution, and install-based reports by role. This dashboard provides a way to not just measure but to run your business and take action based on the data.

It sounds easy—link the marketing metrics to your corporate and marketing strategy. Metrics cascade from your corporate strategy and marketing strategy. For example, you should logically flow your metrics view from the overall business. These are different from company to company, depending upon the strategy and where your opportunities lie.

However, this is easier said than done. One area in marketing uses marketing metrics and "marketing speak" with business professionals who simply switch off because they do not understand the metric or see value in it. It is critical to select metrics that matter to your business. However, that is also the key challenge to develop a set of metrics that measure the impact of marketing activities against the goals of your company. Look at the business end game, not just marketing. CEOs and CFOs want to know how to grow, how to develop customer relationships, and other business outcomes not necessarily about the "marketing portion." Terms such as awareness, share of voice, and other marketing jargon are distracting and uninteresting to the untrained. Design your dashboard to be relative to the business and show linkage to the business and how well marketing is driving and supporting the clients' key needs.

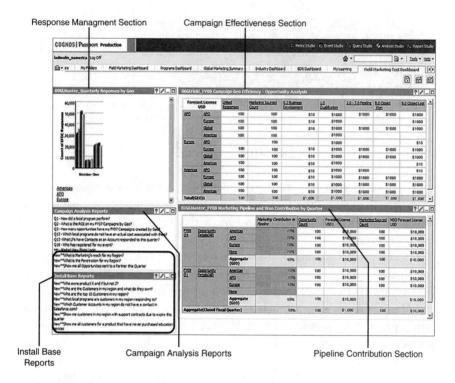

Figure 16.5 Role-based dashboard.

According to Harvard Business School's Gail J. McGovern, the dashboard that is aligned to support the CEO's office is structured to develop and track the following:

- **Business drivers:** Business conditions that, when manipulated or changed, affect performance directly and predictably. Business drivers are leading indicators of revenue growth.
- **Pipeline of growth ideas:** A set of future customer initiatives and innovations that translate into sustainable future growth.
- **Marketing talent pool:** The skills needed to facilitate the marketing function as well as a plan to address any gaps through staffing, training, and outsourcing.

At IBM, marketing is responsible for the full pipeline for its products and offerings. As such, finance and sales see value in the metrics because we created the measurement, the indictors of success, and use it to run the business.

At the end of 2007, the Australian School of Business conducted a survey of CEOs and CFOs and found that improving marketing efficiency is a great or critical concern for 44 percent of CEOs.

Track what's valuable not just what's measurable. Just because something is not measurable does not mean it is not valuable. When you take the customer-centric approach to your strategy, come up with a metric to try to see how effective it is, even if it is an intermediate set of metrics. Focus on what's important, not just on what you can measure. For example, we track "feelings" of our customers not just quantative things but how they feel about doing business with IBM. It is a set of quotes and views, not anything statistical but is a sign for us as we leverage our "tippers" or those influencers in the market to talk with.

There is a significant movement toward integrated campaigns and the focus on development of metrics to support that integration will help you measure the overall impact of integrated campaigns and the individual components.

Having the right marketing infrastructure helps to make your business more effective. Most of the best-practice companies have a technology-enabled dashboard that automates key metrics. If you don't leverage technology for effectiveness today, check out Chapter 21, "End-to-End Example: IBM WebSphere and the SOA Agenda, Prolifics, Ascendant Technology" on the power of dashboards.

Experiment and then experiment some more. As Fagan at Google noted, "The most successful companies are those that are experimenters by nature. They try things that others would not and end up with an optimized approach combing their online strategy and their traditional marketing."

Limit the number of metrics, but ensure you are looking at the most important ones, not forgetting that the 2.0 world influenced what those are. For instance, IBM's business of tracking carbon credits has gone up due to the green focus. Make sure you have between 5 and 15 top-line metrics for those C-level executives, including global, green, and interactive metrics that matter.

The Wrong Metrics

Beware of looking at the wrong metrics. For example, in Italy, people love to come to events. You can't announce an event in Italy without getting 50 people into a room who come for food and conversation. The "butts in seats" metrics don't convert to revenue at the right level, so we have to ensure that the teams are following through on validated lead revenue and not feeling successful until they get that revenue number, not a number of attendees.

In talking with John Gordon, director of IBM's WebSphere Channel Marketing, he relayed a story when he was invited to speak at an event in Rome. He says, "I was invited to be the main speaker on a Monday. The event was on Thursday. Somehow, the teams managed to get great audiences for both of these events on extremely short notice. Because they had filled the rooms, they considered this success. However, after a few weeks the revenue was not coming in and I had to focus with them to do the lead followup. The only way we could truly declare success was by measuring the right metric."

Typically when you look at metrics such as the number of influencers you touch or the number of business partners in a program, you shortchange the value of marketing. The value is not in the activity, but in the business outcome. For instance, it is more important that you have high-quality business partners who value your program than many partners who are not committed to your company or the program.

Conclusion

Metrics are required for marketing teams to reach their goals. They demonstrate the value of marketing to the organization, and they help the marketing leadership know when and how to change based on what is working in the marketplace. A key is making your dashboard unique to your business. Understanding your priorities and having the right linkage points can help you determine which metrics you want to track. Be selective. Less is definitely more when it comes to a great dashboard. Measuring costs time and money, so do not measure just because you can.

Ensure you are evaluating the new metrics that are rising in importance in the CMO community. And don't be afraid to experiment. Working online enables us to become risk takers and experimenters to determine the best marketing mix. Start experimenting with customer lifetime value metrics to determine how much time, effort, and money you can afford to invest to acquire that customer. These metrics and experiments can help you determine how much you need to spend on acquisition and how much you can focus on customer loyalty.

Regardless of the metrics you choose, make sure you put technology to work for your company with automated marketing dashboards. Driving your business through the metrics makes you more successful in the marketplace and internally, if you can link the marketing metrics to your overall business strategy.

17

Innovation, Engagement, and Business Results: adidas Group, ConAgra Foods, and Tellabs

Insanity: doing the same thing over and over again and
expecting different results.
—*Albert Einstein*

As you learned in Chapter 16, "Show Me the Money: A Discussion with Google, the Marketing Leadership Council, and MarketingNPV," dashboards have several goals. They typically serve to show value to the business, alert and help diagnose gaps, and better integrate marketing into other functions. For marketers, revenue and leads have to be a way of life, and in today's environment, doing the same thing we did last year just isn't going to cut it. Marketing today is focused on proving internal value too often. For true success, companies need to shift the focus from internal pressures to external pressures.

As seen in Figure 17.1, the dashboard goals are used to drive better results. In this chapter, we look at examples of companies using dashboards in different levels of maturity and how some leverage collaborative innovation to drive stronger results.

Innovation is about inventing new and better ideas to drive results. With the competitive pressures increasing due to advances in technology, the rapid advent of globalization, and the consequent flat world, revenue is even more serious as a mandate for marketers. Marketing needs to be a thought engine of innovation that drives revenue.

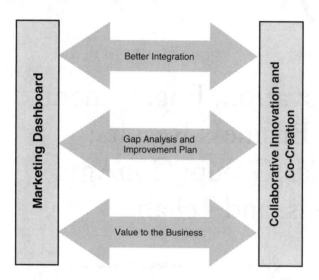

Figure 17.1   Dashboard results grow stronger with collaborative innovation and co-creation.

This chapter includes examples about how marketing organizations are maturing and using metrics to accomplish both the "value to organization" question and using dashboards to outperform competitors in the market. They are also driving greater customer value. Let's start with a view of one of the Marketing 2.0 metrics and that's innovation to drive better dashboard results in showing value to the business and in the market. This innovation through collaboration and co-creation will be explored as a way to drive greater external results from the gap analysis.

Focus on Innovation That Generates Revenue

What is innovation? The classic definitions of innovation include

- "The act of introducing something new: something newly introduced" (*The American Heritage Dictionary*).
- "The introduction of something new." (Merriam-Webster Online).
- "A new idea, method or device" (Merriam-Webster Online).

- "The successful exploitation of new ideas" (Department of Trade and Industry, United Kingdom).
- "Change that creates a new dimension of performance" (Peter Drucker).

One of the major goals of marketing is to drive the business's strategy into the market. As we reviewed earlier, IBM's Global CEO Study demonstrates that the pressures to achieve profitable growth have driven a new mandate around innovation. Two-thirds of the CEOs we spoke to believe their organizations will need to introduce fundamental, radical changes in the next two years to respond to competitive pressures and external forces.

Given that these changes have to occur through innovation, what do we see as drivers of innovation? There is a growing sophistication about how and where innovation occurs, especially regarding who is in the collaboration phase. Collaboration is critical within and beyond the organization. Best-practice companies are seeing their innovative ideas come from partners and clients in addition to their own employees. The phrase I love is innovation outside of your four walls or rather, to get ideas outside of your own company.

Among all the dimensions we examined, collaboration shows the clearest correlation with financial performance whatever the financial metric—revenue growth, operating margin growth, or average profitability over time. The innovation view has gone beyond just product or service innovation, and more CEOs are looking to business model innovation as a key differentiator. As one CEO put it, "Products and services can be copied. The business model is the differentiator." Couple that idea with an interesting fact that proclaims new product introductions get you one month of market exclusivity before your "innovation" is copied, and you see that innovation must be rapid and in nontraditional areas. The relationship between innovation and revenue is tied together in such a way that marketing has intrinsic value. This innovation driver can help marketing to view as a way to drive revenue not a cost center to be reduced. However, it requires the value to be framed in terms of innovative revenue growth.

The concept is twofold: First, innovation is needed to drive revenue in the new world, and second, the greatest correlation of innovation and revenue occurs when it is done collaboratively. This book has driven home the new points of Marketing 2.0 where marketing is done more collaboratively online. The goal is marketing-led actions to real businesses to create new revenue streams.

INNOVATION METRICS TO CONSIDER
BY: MARKETINGNPV (WWW.MARKETINGNPV.COM)
MARKETINGNPV ©2003–2008 MARKETINGNPV LLC.
USED BY PERMISSION

Without question, innovation is being asked to play a greater role in the CEO's organic growth strategy. Yet to date, innovation metrics have been vague at best and more often elusive. Some companies can calculate and track the value of their "innovation pipeline" in net present value terms, on a risk-adjusted basis. Their key metric is then expressed as the percentage of targeted innovation contribution realized compared to the pipeline forecast. Managers then focus their efforts on ensuring that there are a sufficient number and magnitude of innovations in the pipeline to hit the mid- and long-term corporate goals. This takes tremendous discipline in managing ideas through multi-gate commercialization processes and even greater forecasting acumen honed over several years.

For others lacking advanced pipeline management competencies, the most common approach to measuring innovation is stroke counting the number of "new ideas" brought to market. This methodology is not only prone to significant political manipulation (for example, what exactly constitutes a "new" idea and when exactly did it enter the market?), but it also fails to recognize the significant economic value differentials between various innovations. Those still on the innovation learning curve might find that a more pragmatic approach emphasizes the "actual" versus "targeted" percentage of revenue (or preferably profit or contribution margin) expected to be derived from new products monthly, quarterly, and yearly. In classic Ansoff Matrix format (see Figure 17.2), the company should be able to express its innovation goals in terms of the percentage of growth coming from new products and new markets from one period to the next. Performance metrics are then built around comparing the actual figures obtained versus the forecast, leaving the debate to focus on explaining any gap between the two.

It's certainly true that discontinuous innovation at the market level can wreak havoc with markets and forecasts. However, effective innovation measurement is less a function of being perfect than being generally correct within the current environment. Remember, the actual percentage of profits derived from "new" products isn't nearly as important as the performance versus expectations. Provided that the process for setting the expectations and targets is F rigorous and involves all key stakeholders, periodic recalibration will be seen as benefiting performance management, not circumventing it.

Ansoff Matrix Applied To Innovation		
	Existing Products	New Products
Existing Markets		Product development innovation
New Markets	Market development innovation	Diversification innovation

MARKETING**NPV**   www.MarketingNPV.com

© 2003–2008 MarketingNPV LLC., used by permission.

Figure 17.2   MarketingNPV® emerging metrics of relevance: innovation.

Collaboration for Results with adidas Group

The adidas Group is headquartered in Herzogenaurach, Germany. Also located in Herzogenaurach are the strategic business units for running, soccer, and tennis as well as the Research and Development Center. For more than 80 years, the adidas Group has been part of the world of sports on every level, delivering state-of-the-art sports footwear, apparel, and accessories. Today, the adidas Group is a global leader in the sporting goods industry and offers a broad portfolio of products. Products from the adidas Group are available in virtually every country of the world. Their strategy is simple: continuously strengthen its brands and products to improve its competitive position and financial performance. Its brands include adidas, Reebok, and Taylor Made-adidas Golf.

March 2, 2008 was the date for the applications for adidas' guerrilla marketing challenge for teams of three to five students to develop, in a contest format, the most innovative, creative, and authentic guerilla marketing tactics for EURO 2008. According to the Web site announcing the contest, the goal was to leverage inspiration from Jay C. Levinson, who coined marketing as an "unconventional system of promotions on a very low budget, by relying on time, energy, and imagination instead of big marketing budgets." adidas challenged the students to use their creativity on their Web site stating,

"Come up with smart, clever, funny, unconventional ideas, and show us how you would promote adidas with your guerrilla marketing concept. Outline your strategy, define your target group, and describe the activities and/or events of your concept. You have a fictional budget of 50,000 euro for the implementation of your strategy."

This particular innovative way to gain results bought adidas focus across Europe with the top 20 teams coming from schools throughout Europe and ideas that electrified and innovated above and beyond. I leverage this example as a way to collaborate both inside and outside your four walls.

Application for Your Business

Given collaboration is a way to drive revenue, using top talent through university contests expands your thoughts from product creation to advertising to Webcasts and events. Interaction is important because people can select how, where, and when they want to become aware of something. In this new world, where there are no boundaries, customers demand to be involved. In fact, because of the way and context in which people participate, we cannot just consider them customers but must think of them as part of our branding team. This adidas example shows that even a brand that people take personally can get closer by direct involvement. Co-creation helps to make brands more relevant in the marketplace and, therefore, increases loyalty and ultimately revenue. As the Society for New Communications Research wrote, "You will have a winner if customers always have the last word in positioning."

THE IMPORTANCE OF THE CO-CREATION MODEL FROM THE SOCIETY OF NEW COMMUNICATIONS RESEARCH BY KATHY KLOTZ-GUEST, SNCR FELLOW

What Do Companies Need to Do?

- Don't over engineer brand stories; but companies must facilitate and manage.
- You must position, but the brand story will develop organically based on customer feedback.
- New technologies facilitate these exchanges now in ways that are effective and viral.

- Companies must reintegrate customer insights into an evolving brand story.

  How the Coauthor Model Works and Leads to Co-creation

- You must do more than simply put customer stories on your Web site; take baby steps.

- Means 360 communications and open exchange with your customers.

- Requires reintegration of customers' stories into the company's branding and communications.

- Engages loyal customers to co-create: discover, develop, and deploy new products.

- This can be positive or negative, for example, Jet Blue's customers push for a bill of rights.

  A Few Models That Work—What Do You Think?

- Software models—Open-source (Linux®), Microsoft Developers' Forum, Adobe.

- Consumer products—Whole Foods, Lego, Saturn, Ikea, and Jones Soda.

- Tech—Yahoo! as case study: Where do you think Yahoo! should go in the future?

- What doesn't work—Over engineering, fake communications, lack of authenticity, over editing users, lack of relevance, co-opting dialogue for spin (such as Wal-Mart, Cadillac, and so on).

- Open question— How much control do you give consumers over the brand story?

  Co-authoring to Co-creating with New Technologies:

- Give customers new tools to create and share content with you and each other, such as dialoguing, gleaning insights, building trust, and co-creating stories and products to strengthen brand.

- Monitoring and reintegrating feedback into company positioning.

- Culling research for product ideas vetted by target.

How? Ways Include...

- Stories, peer tips, and creations with your products, contests, forums for user-generated content and product ideas, open dialogue with CEO, asking for feedback on business models, products, books (John Mackey of Whole Foods lets users became co-authors of his book).

What Keeps Companies from Implementing Despite Interest?

- They are not sure how to implement and are still learning how the new models work.

- Management support and internal processes remain issues and barriers.

How Do You Measure Success?

- Customers must be engaged; increase positive customer comments, loyalty, profitability, and trust.

- Product ideas are generated.

- The value of customer insights are gleaned, and critical market research is done.

Dashboards and Metrics

There are several case studies of companies in different phases of marketing dashboard deployment. These case studies show the overall view of the plans and how the innovative tactics are woven into their overall framework of value. We look at:

ConAgra Foods: Piloting a dashboard across ten of its brands

Tellabs: Focusing on a business driver for interactive metrics

ConAgra Foods

Who Are They?

ConAgra Foods is a leading branded, value-added food company focused on sustainable, profitable growth. The company is organized into four reporting segments: Consumer Foods, International Foods, Food and Ingredients, and Trading and Merchandising (also referred to as the ConAgra Trade Group). Based in Omaha, Nebraska, the company has 28,000 staff and annual revenues of around $15 billion. The company grew rapidly through acquisition. Household name brands include Banquet, Chef Boyardee, Healthy Choice, Hunt's, Jiffy, Orville Redenbacher's, PAM, Slim Jim, and Van Camp's.

What Do They Measure?

According to ConAgra Foods, it is just launching a companywide marketing dashboard initiative. It is currently being rolled out on a trial basis across ten brands and several operating groups, including frozen, grocery, and refrigerated. This rollout is under the direction of the interactive team. The team manages more than 30 brand Web sites and is responsible for online promotions, e-mail marketing, and customer relationship management (CRM) initiatives.

They began defining what the dashboard needed to measure. The plan was to begin with interviews with all the internal stakeholders including all marketing groups, procurement, and brand design teams. The results they collected include a long list of potential metrics that had to be pared down.

The overall dashboard effort is being led by Kevin Doohan, the director of Interactive Marketing at ConAgra Foods. Through his leadership, the metrics were pared down to those that mattered consistently across the company. This set of pared-down metrics will be used for the C-level reviews, recognizing that ad-hoc reports still have to be pulled at times.

Because the interactive team drives the effort, the dashboard is currently Web site-focused but will soon become experience-focused, based on Doohan's vision. The purpose of this initial version goal is to familiarize users with the basic concepts incorporated in a marketing dashboard, before they migrate to a more sophisticated, full-featured platform.

Benefits They Hope to See

Doohan believes the most important part of the marketing dashboard is the analysis of the "whys." For example, why do Web site visits go up at a certain time? What is the impact of this tactic on the end-to-end results? The goal of the initial deployment is education and a movement in culture. The cultural change is the measurement of results, not effort.

Tellabs

Who Are They?

Naperville, Illinois-based Tellabs provides telecommunications products and solutions to telecom service providers and others—including wireline, wireless, cable television companies worldwide, and government agencies—enabling it to deliver voice, video, and data services over wireline and wireless networks. The company had annual revenues of about $1.9 billion in 2007 and has about 3,000 employees. The innovative and results-oriented leader is Mike O'Malley, the director of External Marketing at Tellabs.

What Do They Measure?

Tellabs, a company of over 30 years, experienced its biggest success with a single product line in a single geography—North America. As O'Malley looked at assisting the business in growing the company beyond one major product and one geography, he and his team began an integrated campaign called "Inspire the New Life." This integrated campaign leveraged the next-generation consumers who demanded new products and services to meet their ever-increasing communication expectations and reliance on technology as a way of life. Tellabs' plan was simple: Use Marketing 2.0 tactics to provide thought leadership that helps telecom service providers better understand the needs of, and therefore, inspire this digital citizen with new services that are enabled by purchasing Tellabs solutions! One part of the Tellabs' campaign focused on educating its customers and others in the industry on its portfolio in a way that would drive confidence and enable it to see the future. In addition, given the target audience, it required innovative marketing with the new Marketing 2.0 methods, dictating both tactical methods of specific Marketing 2.0 tactic metrics and integrated end-to-end campaign metrics as well.

Tellabs implemented this campaign by launching an innovative video podcast series called "Get Schooled." The series aims to tout the Tellabs portfolio and move the company up the ladder as an industry leader, and Tellabs tracks the results closely to measure its success. (See Figure 17.3.)

In 2007, it launched 12 video podcasts that were each about six to eight minutes long. For each video in the series, you can download a "cheat sheet" from inspirethenewlife.com that provides key points about each subject covered and additional links for further reference. The series includes telecommunications topics ranging from quality of service to carrier Ethernet 101. According to Tellabs and MarketingProfs, the target audience consisted of senior-level engineers and decision makers, the Tellabs sales force, sales consultants, Tellabs partners, tech bloggers, and the industry media. One outcome of the videos was that they created subject matter expert "rock stars." In trade shows, these experts became a draw at the event because event goers interacted with them to seek expertise about this new world.

Figure 17.3 Tellabs' award-winning "Get Schooled" series.

Although Tellabs has a focus on measuring the specific tactic of its innovative "Get Schooled" video, this is not the only thing that it measures. As discussed, a great marketing metric system looks at an end-to-end view with areas of focus based on the business need. For O'Malley, this area of education in the market is a particular focus o the business. He says, "We started with the subject matter experts (SMEs), measured the number of downloads each month, and quickly saw an increase in the number of videos forwarded overall."

Thereafter, the videos were highlighted in HTML-based e-mails to the customer base and sales force. A typical Tellabs customer e-mail drop goes out to some 25,000 recipients globally and has a click-through rate (CTR) of 3.2 percent and an open rate of 28 percent. In the first week to ten days after a video podcast was highlighted in a mailing, O'Malley says, traffic to the videos would spike, as would the number of videos "forwarded to a friend."

Benefits They Have Seen

Initially, Tellabs hoped the video podcast series would generate at least 50,000 views. As of July, 2008, the campaign generated 68,500 views in the first 12 months. The Google paid search campaign delivered 47 million impressions and some 12,200 click-throughs in a six-month trial in 2007. The most-viewed podcast was titled "IPTV Market Drivers: The Evolution of

Video," which generated 7,582 views. The videos that generated the most views, not surprisingly, covered the hottest industry topics and those closely associated with Tellabs' known market strengths.

O'Malley says Tellabs viewed the videos with lower view rate as equally critical, because their topics represented features on leading-edge technologies that many in the industry might not yet be familiar. "This gives Tellabs an early opportunity to impress our thoughts on that target audience," he notes. The overall campaign "Inspire the New Life" has a microsite where all the digital content is housed that allows the team to track the end-to-end metrics.

In viewing the overall metrics, there is more business value as well. O'Malley is seeing positive impact on his brand and growth. As he comments, "Our Tellabs brand awareness has risen across all geographies and solution areas and the brand value has now been extended past one product. In addition, growth from creation of this new campaign has positively impacted customers' inclination to purchase from us, among other tangible and intangible business results."

Tellabs tracks not only the number of downloads or views each podcast receives, but also the length of time watching the podcast, whether it was forwarded to a friend and whether it was in response to a particular online ad or customer e-mail.

Tellabs incorporates a number of different statistical tools to track return on investment (ROI) including, but not limited to, Google Analytics, NetTracker, third-party reports (telecom specific online advertising), and mentions in the media and various industry blogs.

Innovation

The effort garnered a MarCom Platinum Creative Award in 2008. The competition (www.marcomawards.com) is administered and judged by the Association of Marketing & Communications Professionals. Tellabs also received a Silver Hermes Creative Award for Environmental Branding in its "Get Schooled" Customer Experience Showcase. The Inspire the New Life campaign overall has received more than 16 awards. The video podcast series has already been translated into Japanese and Korean; Tellabs plans to translate them into Chinese, Spanish, and Portuguese in 2008. Moreover, Tellabs has planned 20 new video podcasts for 2008.

IDC's View for the High-Tech Marketer

IDC's research on marketing ROI has consistently shown that tech marketing leaders tend to expand their budgets at a rate equal to or greater than their revenue growth rate. In Tables 17.1 and 17.2, we can get a view of IDC's research for 2007.

Table 17.1 Marketing Efficiency Scorecard

Attribute	Key Performance Indicator (KPI, Current FY)[1]	All Vendors	IDC Insight
Marketing Investment	Marketing budget ratio (marketing spend/revenue)	3.0 percent	Varies as a function of sector, size, and channel strategy
	Marketing investment change (mean, most recently closed to current fiscal year)	6.1 percent	Maintain MIC levels at or greater than revenue growth
	Awareness-Demand (A-D) Ratio	47.9 percent	Shifts with company size and channel strategy
Marketing Staff Efficiency	Program-to-People Ratio (program spend as a percent of total marketing spend)	62 percent	Increases with greater leverage of investment (for example, advertising and channel investment)
	Marketing staff throughput ratio (program spend per staff)	$284,000	
	Revenue per marketing staff in millions)	$15.3	Good check of staff levels, varies across sectors
	Marketing staff turnover	9.7 percent	Clarify roles and responsibilities, focus on professional development

[1] 2007 Tech Marketing Benchmarks Database (weighted average KPIs based upon current full year at survey completion unless stated otherwise).

Table 17.2 Marketing Efficiency Scorecard

Attribute	Key Performance Indicator (KPI, Current FY)[1]	All Vendors	IDC Insight
Global Alignment	Centralization ratio for program spend	60.7 percent	Few companies are able to demonstrate efficient and effective execution of market ing investment with a high level of decen- tralization
	Regional staff as a percent of total staff	45.5 percent	
Marketing Performance Measurement	Marketing operations (MO) ratio[2] (MO staff per total marketing staff)	4.1 percent	2 percent to 4 recommended

[1] 2007 Tech Marketing Benchmarks Database (weighted average KPIs based upon current FY at survey completion)

[2] Refer to "Marketing Operations: Is it Evolving Fast Enough?" December 2006, #204647

* Marketing dashboard refers to either a specific application or the capability to compile perform- ance metrics into an easy to use format/template (in use today or within 12 months : >12 months or no plans for availability)

For the average tech vendor, this investment change leads to an MBR (marketing spend as a percentage of revenue) of 3 percent of total annual revenue for 2007. Practitioners should note that these are the average investment and budget ratio changes and that both of these benchmarks vary *significantly* across the tech vendor community. Company size, sector, and sales model (such as direct versus indirect selling strategy) are all sig- nificant factors in expected investment profiles for different companies. Seventy percent of technology companies experienced a reduction in their MBR from 2006 to 2007 as a result of their marketing investment not growing as fast as revenue. Technology companies continue to struggle with the right mix of program spend and staff to optimize productivity and efficiency. IDC recommends two key performance indictors (KPIs) to track staff efficiency: marketing staff throughput that measures program execution per marketing employee and program-to-people ratio or pro- gram spends as a percent of total marketing investment.

Application to Your Company

- **One size does not fit all.** Based on your need, you might need to focus on a particular area and really dive deep into the metrics around it, not just numbers but qualitative as well. Your dashboard and metric strategy is uniquely yours. You can learn from others, but in the end, the dashboard will be linked to your own businesses goals. The objectives and tactics that you need to drive success will link marketing directly to the bottom line as shown in Figure 17.4.

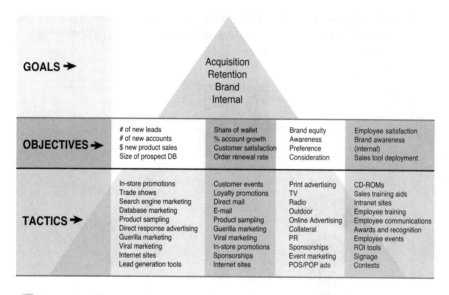

GOALS ➤	Acquisition Retention Brand Internal			
OBJECTIVES ➤	# of new leads # of new accounts $ new product sales Size of prospect DB	Share of wallet % account growth Customer satisfaction Order renewal rate	Brand equity Awareness Preference Consideration	Employee satisfaction Brand awareness (internal) Sales tool deployment
TACTICS ➤	In-store promotions Trade shows Search engine marketing Database marketing Product sampling Direct response advertising Guerilla marketing Viral marketing Internet sites Lead generation tools	Customer events Loyalty promotions Direct mail E-mail Product sampling Guerilla marketing Viral marketing In-store promotions Sponsorships Internet sites	Print advertising TV Radio Outdoor Online Advertising Collateral PR Sponsorships Event marketing POS/POP ads	CD-ROMs Sales training aids Intranet sites Employee training Employee communications Awards and recognition Employee events ROI tools Signage Contests

MARKETING^{NPV} www.MarketingNPV.com

© 2003-2008 MarketingNPV LLC., used by permission.

Figure 17.4 Sample linkage of business goals, objectives, and tactics.

- **Focus on the right metrics.** Time and time again, from every case study here to the thousands of articles, case studies, and lectures on marketing dashboard, there is one solid focus: Limit the number of metrics and ensure you can go deep enough on the ones that matter so that you can diagnose and fix them. The dashboard should not just show the problem but aid in determining why the gap exists so that you can address it.

- **Spotlight on value to the organization but heavy lifting goes on the external view.** This goal is one goal of your dashboard. It is important to articulate the value of marketing. Make sure that your dashboard not only provides you with the ability to demonstrate the value to the organization, but that is also focuses on the customer and the market. This view is the end game.

- **Update your metrics based on Marketing 2.0.** Throughout the book, you've seen new ways to market and new items of relevance. For instance, with green, marketing is the voice of the customer and should be responsible for measuring what is important to the customer. Innovation, Web 2.0 items, global metrics, and engagement are areas to ensure you are updating your view.

- **Start small and grow.** In Figure 17.5, you see that eventually we believe that marketing organizations will be driven by overarching dashboards. However, you can't get there overnight.

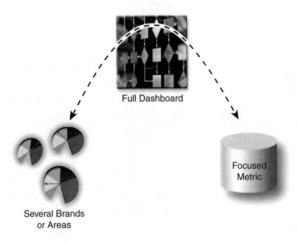

Full Dashboard

Several Brands
or Areas

Focused
Metric

Figure 17.5   Start small in your journey to the marketing dashboard—but start!

As Pat LaPointe wrote for MarketingNPV, "There's no longer much of an argument over the need to measure marketing performance. Face it, the left-brainers have won at least the battle, if not the war. How are chief marketing officers (CMOs) faring with their new measurement-driven agendas? The short answer is: So far, so good. Marketing leaders point to more focused initiatives, a better handle on their investments, improved relations with an old nemesis—finance—as a result of their marketing dashboard initiatives. However, they also admit that there's still much work to do, not just with what they're measuring, but also in how they're sharing those results with the rest of the organization."

Conclusion

From a report written by Clark, Abola, and Ambler, as many as 40 percent of U.S. and UK companies report substantial efforts in developing marketing dashboards. Dashboards serve many purposes. Many companies today focus on leveraging the dashboards to demonstrate marketing's value to the organization. One of the benefits of a dashboard is an understanding of what marketing is, the role it plays, and the end-to-end view of its impact on the organization. From the case studies, we can see a greater number of companies using the dashboard insight to more effectively compete and deliver value to their customers.

Whether you are measuring the organizational view, a few brands or areas, or just a focus on an area that is a gap, the act of measuring and analyzing enables your marketing organization to become more competitive. A simple dashboard could be a summary slide or a focused area of the business. A more complex dashboard would encompass more business intelligence and scope. Better metrics enable you to provide greater insight, effectiveness, and more value. In this chapter, we saw two companies and the value they are seeing from their deployments. And both companies have started their Marketing 2.0 metrics looking at experience, customer loyalty, and engagement. In fact, many companies that I interviewed who are measuring NPS and Customer Lifetime Value would not allow me to feature their stories yet because they consider this work a competitive advantage.

When you begin to focus on what differentiates you the most, the new marketing model becomes more open and porous. As companies begin to partner more extensively, they become more global and more competitive. That, of course, drives what we are after: more revenue done in a responsible way.

18

Marketing Dashboards: IBM Cognos

In the absence of clearly defined goals, we become strangely loyal
to performing daily trivia until ultimately we become enslaved
by it.
—Robert Heinlein

Just like the entry quote communicates, metrics in marketing are crucial. If you do not have the right goals in front of the team, there is so much happening in the world that the marketing organization could be stuck in daily trivia. The best-practice companies have solid metric systems and a culture that is incessant on the metric system.

In Chapter 16, "Show Me the Money: A Discussion with Google, the Marketing Leadership Council, and MarketingNPV," we discussed the importance of metrics and some best practices from the world's top chief marketing officers (CMO). In this chapter, we review the management system, a new metric, and a dashboard for best practice from IBM's Software Group, which is the world's largest infrastructure software company and second largest software business, driving over $20B in revenue and 40 percent of IBM's profits.

Management System and Vision

Objectives are important to business. Having a solid management system that drives your objectives enables you to determine where you are performing well and what changes need to be made. Beyond the management system, it is essential to have clear and precise metrics that can measure progress against objectives. They can serve as a great vehicle to communicate across the team. All of marketing's metrics should cascade from the overall business objectives.

IBM Software Group's CMO Buell Duncan takes this approach: "For the IBM software business, it is about delivering on both the revenue and the profit objectives for the company. To deliver those goals, it is absolutely critical that we build a strong opportunity pipeline. For our business, the key measures are the number of leads that are generated, the value of those leads, and the win rate or yield. Finally, we analyze the cost to generate and close them."

IBM Software Group leverages a four-prong approach:

1. **Conditioning the market.** Awareness through press and advertising as well as favorable analyst reports assist in conditioning the market for the channel. Press, analysts, and advertising are examples of awareness activities that assist in conditioning the market for sales. In the IBM Software Group, we track CARMA for press awareness indicators. The CARMA Favorability Rating and Media IQ score provide clients with objective metrics that evaluate the tone and potential impact of media coverage. CARMA uses these measures to provide detailed analysis of competitive share of voice; leading issues, products, and divisions; strongest positive and negative messages; positive and negative thought leaders and journalists; and top publications. Unlike computer software that uses keywords to determine quality, CARMA's custom analysis is powered by human-based research that enables a more complete and accurate understanding of your image in the media. For influencers, the number of positive analyst reports, blogs, quotes, and a rating system by key analysts and for advertising, we measure the share of voice and brand awareness.

2. **Marketing 2.0 Metrics.** SWG has begun to focus on the newer metrics like engagement, innovation, and NPS. We have found that those marketing programs that include Marketing 2.0 tactics are outperforming programs that do not include interactive tactics. One of the items that IBM tracks is the marketing mix of Marketing 2.0 to traditional tactics and has been ensuring that more interactive tactics, where appropriate are added into the entire program approach. The data demonstrates that a higher ROI will be achieved by adding interactive tactics to the program mix. In fact, this is true outside the United States even more than in the United States.

Transforming Marketing 2.0 tactics into a demand generation engine will allow companies to leverage the shifting customer evaluation and purchase behavior, provide a cost-effective way to reach new customers and drive an excellent ROI through scale and 2-way customer engagement.

3. **Leads and validated lead revenue.** The generation of leads and opportunities for the software sales force and business partners is a metric that we review weekly. The number of leads is an indictor of the health of our interactive Web 2.0 marketing and the revenue associated with them gives us insight into the revenue we hope to close. For each product family, the multiple is calculated, and a red or green score is given. For example, one product family in WebSphere needs three times the pipeline given the sales cycle, and another product family needs two times the pipeline for the targeted revenue. These multiples vary by geography. In Figure 18.1, there is a sample of the attainment to signal the focus areas.

	WW						
	90%	east	central	west	Canada	LA	federal
AG	72%	74%	120%	36%	39%	71%	51%
		CEMAAS	Germany	UKISA	Nordics		
NE	148%	145%	82%	141%	311%		
		BeNeLux	France	Italy	IGIT		
SW	123%	130%	138%	43%	225%		
		ANZ	GCG	ASEAN	Korea	India	
AP	82%	106%	43%	269%	40%	32%	
JPN	62%						

Figure 18.1 Example of a validated lead revenue scorecard.

4. **Progression and win.** After those leads are identified, marketing has a clear responsibility to ensure the quality of the leads and to help progress them through the sales cycle. We measure the time in the sales cycle, the win dollar amount, and the influence of marketing in closure.

Duncan commented that for IBM, 25 percent of the effort is around conditioning the market and creating a favorable selling environment. The remaining 75 percent is split equally between lead generation and progression. The goal is to increase the number of leads and lead revenue coming from Marketing 2.0 tactics. To do so, SWG has set into a play an aggressive plan of 7 steps:

1. **Planning**: Maintains Web content and offers calendars
2. **Content**: Refreshes with high-value news-worthy articles
3. **Solution Content**: Messaging Workshops need to include Web content by role on Web pages
4. **Offers**: Available for countries to translate in a timely manner
5. **Perpetual campaigns:** Links from demand generation emails and landing pages to related Web content
6. **Relationship marketing**: eNurture tactic plans created for programs
7. **Skills growth**: All marketers should engage in using social media tools

A key focus will be on better and better Marketing 2.0 metrics.

A New Metric: The "In-Process" Metric

A high-performance marketing organization is one that ensures that marketing and sales are tightly connected. The premise is that it is not enough for the seller to say, "I have responsibility for an account. Marketing is not my job." It is equally unproductive for marketing to say that they have completed their job because they helped create an ad or helped create a lead. Duncan and his team have innovated on a metric that helps to further tighten the sales and marketing relationship. The approach is called "in-process" metrics. This metric connects the role of sales in helping drive better attendance to events and faster follow-up to leads as they progress through the sales cycle.

In Figure 18.2, the in-process metrics show one example of the use of in-process metrics.

There are a few important areas to note here. First, these metrics are tracked by geographic region so that the local sales and marketing teams can relate to and respond to the tracking. Next, the metrics measure the number of attendees to the events. This drives teamwork and signals the importance of maximizing opportunities to drive demand. Both sales and marketing have a role to play in ensuring that this number is achieved against the goal that has been set. The cost is also measured and compared across the brands and regions to achieve best practices.

Finally, after the event is held, the most important action is the focused and timely lead follow-up. Specifically, these in-process metrics drive sales and marketing to work more closely together to drive the progression and closure of valuable leads. This scorecard is used at the highest levels of IBM and by the field sales organization. It signals a set of shared, common goals that both marketing and sales drive. Connecting sales and marketing with in-process metrics is an example of the strategic importance of both working together to grow IBM's business long term. Metrics that drive that type of behavior are critical.

02/01/08 - 03/31/08 Planned Events in EST		PRODUCTION			PROGRESSION	
REGION	# Events	Planned Attendance	Actual Registrations To Date	Projected Budget	Projected VL	Projected VLR

Source: 2008 Data from EST – 1/26/2008

Figure 18.2 Example "in-process" metrics.

As Duncan states, "I think the most important thing, the single most important thing is to better connect marketing with the organization's business goals. Marketing clearly has to be tightly connected to the company's overall business objectives, not just to create the brand image, not to just work on the brand value proposition, but most importantly, to generate demand to grow the business. It is not a Cost Center, but a driver of revenue."

Focus on IBM Cognos

Cognos was an independent software company when the analysis of its best practice began. It has now been acquired by IBM Software Group as the largest software acquisition by IBM to date. IBM purchased Cognos because of its great products, but also because of its world-class management system. That management system was a part of the entire marketing culture. Dave Laverty, VP of Worldwide Marketing at Cognos, was focused on ensuring that the marketing metrics at Cognos drove a culture of growth and linkage.

Cognos looks at three core dimensions in its overall marketing efforts: establishing a leadership position, demand management, and sales enablement and effectiveness. Market leadership focuses on elements of the marketing mix that help drive the overall market's agenda and IBM Cognos position within it. The elements of the marketing mix include press, industry analyst relations, and thought leadership. Demand management concentrates on pipeline building activities. Sales enablement focuses on equipping sellers with the tools they need to be as effective as possible in progressing sales opportunities. This includes detailed sales plays that document successful selling approaches with variants for competitive strategies, references and case studies, and vertical content. Metrics are applied and tracked across each dimension to ensure all elements of the execution strategy contribute.

In fact, Sirius Decisions, Inc., rates the best-of-breed companies and determines Cognos is one of the best. Sirius Decisions evaluated the best B2B companies in the world and found that most do not have a closed loop process for their management system around metrics. In Figure 18.3, Sirius Decisions shows the stages of maturity in metrics starting with a basic manual system to those that use customer relationship management (CRM) systems.

B-to-B Marketing Measurement

SiriusPerspective:
The majority of B-to-B marketers today do not have closed-loop marketing measurement systems in place.

Phase	Manual	CRM Centric	Analytics Engine	Integrated
Characteristics	• No SFA system or SFA adoption • eMail marketing system • Outsourced marketing database	• CRM system which is primarily an SFA system • Limited reporting • Central marketing database	• Business Intelligence Platform • Common reporting packages • Data integrated from multiple sources	• Hub and Spoke architecture is developed • Systems are updated close to real time • Dashboards are automated
Technology	• Spreadsheets • Ad hoc SFA system • Email Marketing tools	• CRM Application • Database cleansing tools • Spreadsheets for reporting	• CRM Application • Marketing Automation Platform (MAP) • Data quality Tools • BI tools in place	• CRM System is in place • Marketing Automation Platform (MAP) • Database cleaning tools • BI tools in place • EAI tools in place
Clients at each Stage	27%	57%	11%	5%

Source: Sirius Decisions, Inc.

Figure 18.3   Sirius Decisions, Inc. maturity model for metric drive B2B companies.

The majority (over 60 percent) of B2B companies, according to Sirius Decisions, are in this maturity stage. Although they leverage a CRM system, they draw from only one source of information, ignoring other sources of insight and still leveraging spreadsheets for reporting their dashboards.

More mature companies have progressed beyond the CRM stage, to leveraging business intelligence technology to assist them with more advanced analytics. IBM Cognos is one of the few companies that achieved an integrated view, where Sirius stated only 5 percent of B2B companies are today. Now IBM Cognos' business is in the business intelligence and corporate performance management space, so they "ate their own cooking!" In this section, we share how IBM Cognos leveraged the power and value of metrics for business growth.

Best Practices at IBM Cognos

In Figure 18.4, the management model for IBM Cognos is laid out for the key demand generation metrics. For this example from IBM Cognos, it lays out its metrics according to the typical marketing funnel. The funnel begins with databases of marketing responses that represent potential target segments and markets. This funnel is narrowed with techniques such as prospecting and targeted campaign tactics. The narrowing of the funnel does not end with the closing sale, but when it has concluded with a word-of-mouth reference, upsell opportunities, and cross-sell opportunities.

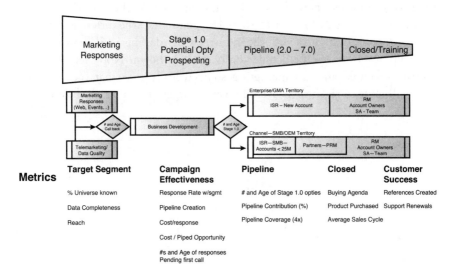

Figure 18.4   IBM Cognos key demand generation metrics.

IBM Cognos examines a set of metrics as leads progress through the pipeline. First, it measures the success of its target segments. The indicators it reviews are a percentage of the market known (% universe), how complete the information is on the clients (data completeness), and how far into their potential client base they can reach. IBM Cognos takes its lists from buys, events, the Web, and other marketing activities, and it runs campaigns on those clients targeted by the specific offer. In this phase, it measures campaign effectiveness. The indicators it uses are response rate with a particular segment, the dollar amount of the pipe created, and the cost for those responding. To judge how good of a job Cognos is doing on follow-up, you can look at the age of responses and hot leads that are pending first calls.

As the lead progresses, IBM Cognos looks at the pipeline coverage multiples or said another way, it calculates the value of leads it needs to reach its final revenue goals. It will need some multiplier like 2x or 3x because not all the leads will close. After the deal has closed, the buying agenda is evaluated. The buying agenda consists of the core topics that drove the closure of the sale. The average sales cycle is measured for best practices, which are fed back into the marketing team. Also, the team ensures that the wins turn into references and are followed up on for cross sells and upsells.

This entire management process is automated and done by role. We discussed in Chapter 4, "Fish Where the Fish Are and Use the Right Bait," and Chapter 5, "Relevance and Roles: Forrester Research," the importance of role-based marketing. This not only shows IBM Cognos' focus on role-based marketing, but also how it has taken the concept all the way through its measurement system. In Figures 18.5, 18.6, and 18.7, the different views by role are shown. In Figure 18.5, the industry seller dashboard is shown.

In Figure 18.6, the field seller dashboard is shown. Note here that the metrics reviewed are still marketing sourced leads and what they forecast they will close to reach their overall revenue target or win contribution.

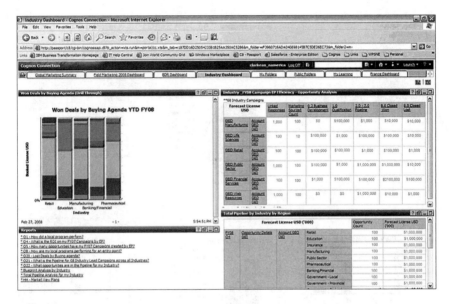

Figure 18.5 Industry view of the marketing dashboard.

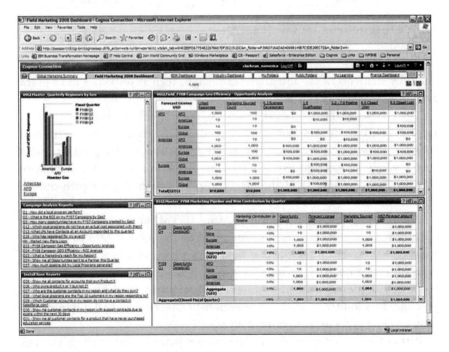

Figure 18.6 Field sales view of the dashboard.

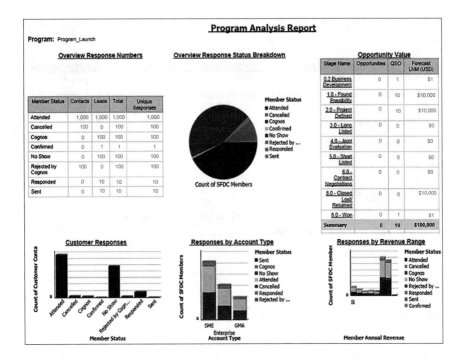

Figure 18.7   Marketing manager view of the dashboard.

In Figure 18.7, the marketing manager report is shown. Here, you can detail by elements of the integrated campaign, such as responses to an event and status by stage of the deal.

These views of the dashboard enable Cognos not only to demonstrate metrics by role, but also the power of its product. It becomes both an internal tool for growth and an external case study in how well a product and a methodology of metrics help to drive sales. It also allows IBM Cognos to start to show the impact of the Marketing 2.0 tactics that supplement the traditional tactics.

The full alignment of go-to-marketing (GTM) strategy by region and country is shown in this Cognos example. The dashboards help to drive the focus on the agreed on segments, field sales plays, solutions, partners, and capacities. The quarterly market view plan is the consistent framework that reinforces alignment with the strategy and resources to yield the increased pipeline. It is jointly created by the regional marketing and sales leaders and shows a few key focus management areas.

Part of the market view plan is the territory analysis. The territory analysis shows the priority segments, account targets identified for joint marketing and sales activity, and the pipeline goals established with the timely follow-up actions agreed upon, in addition, the regional priorities of the chosen key field plays and solutions along with those partners. Tactics also drive the pipeline. These consists of the campaign and regional program investments.

Figure 18.8 shows the gap analysis report that helps to drive focus on the gaps existing in the pipeline. It helps the teams to take corrective action based on the root of the problem. It is an elemental analysis used to correct items such as progression, deal size, or conversion rates. This level of analysis pinpoints the tactics that the teams need to take to correct gaps that will occur.

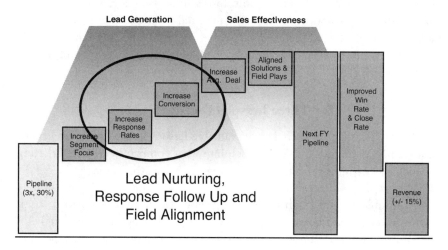

Figure 18.8 Gap analysis.

According to Sirius Decisions, Inc., the most appropriate candidates for nurturing will likely fall into the early stages of their buying cycles.

Here is an example of eNurturing—a Marketing 2.0 tactic—as an action from a gap. Targeted communication for downloads of key IT offers from cognos.com and other third-party sides are key to fixing the gap. The area noted in the gap analysis as a gap is diagnosed as needing more complementary offers for follow-up communications with the client. After interlocking with sales, it is decided that electronic mail that references the previous material the client downloaded would be the right personalized follow-up piece. IBM Cognos will not offer a piece if the person has previously downloaded it but will use intelligence to suggest the next offer in the buying cycle. IBM Cognos shows no landing page to the potential customer. The customer can download directly from email.

Then the leads and contacts separated into two tiers those that IBM Cognos should follow up in a targeted way and those that need to be removed from the lead-nurturing system. Note the value of the use of the technology. There is a low cost per opportunity as a result of automation in this example, both in terms of finances and human resources.

This example from IBM Cognos shows one example of an end-to-end metric system. It started with the objectives driven by the corporate goals that were translated into actionable metrics. These metrics were set at the regional level by both marketing and sales. The dashboards were customized by role, enabling each person to see his view of the world. But when a gap is discovered, sales and marketing join forces in a systematic way to discover why there is a gap and what actions to take and measure. Cognos' dashboards are automated, the data is cleansed with a set of business-driven rules, and the intelligence is leveraged throughout to make IBM Cognos' management system world class.

Top Three Lessons Learned

Laverty finished up with a set of valuable lessons learned from his experiences in IBM Cognos but also in helping other companies create marketing dashboards with his software. The top five lessons learned follow:

1. **Linkage to the business strategy is critical:** As Laverty said, "Our marketing dashboard is a strategy-management application that helps our organization measure and align the strategic and tactical aspects of the businesses, processes, and individuals via goals and targets. In addition to helping track the sales pipeline and marketing campaigns, our metric system enables Cognos executives and senior staff to chart progress against overall strategic objectives to help drive business growth." It is more than just a marketing dashboard. It is what binds marketing to the business and truly reflects the value of the function.

2. **Consumable dashboards enable actions to be taken:** To be effective, a marketing system or dashboard must enable management to drill into supporting details in related reports. In addition, to be consumable, the key is to determine why a metric is performing a certain way when targets, forecasts, or resource allocations are changed. This means marketing and sales staff at every level receive the information they need to help drive revenue and improve overall business performance.

3. **It is a journey:** Laverty points out that establishing this integrated marketing management system is a journey. It requires specific focus on data quality, systems to support campaign management, and the movement of data from the Web to sales automation systems, establishing consistent processes for lead management and integrating business intelligence tools to monitor results and plan appropriate actions.

Application to Your Company

Technology-led dashboards enable companies to drive the connection to their business strategies. Explore the elements of your dashboard and then begin the journey to test the metrics with your business leaders, examine the sources of data quality, and begin an implementation that places powers into your team's hands to address and move in a real-time fashion on gaps in your performance.

Conclusion

In this case study from IBM Software Group, we see several best practices in management system. First, for IBM, the culture of metrics and the teaming of sales and marketing is driven straight from the top. It involves a direct and tight linkage with the overall business goals. In addition, the innovation of new metrics, such as IBM's in-process metrics enable IBM to apply intelligence to its tight linkage of sales and marketing. We also saw how IBM is adding into its tracking the Marketing 2.0 tactics including drive-to-Web registration, links to Web sites, RSS feeds, and viral marketing. While things like the participation in continuing social media discussions, eNurturing, and repackaging and syndicating content is hard to measure, engagement metrics are being used. IBM Cognos leverages technology to drive its metrics including adding into the mix the Marketing 2.0 tactics. Through a best-practice process, an understanding of its strategy through metrics, and its tight linkage to sales, IBM Cognos is a best-practice example in its marketing effectiveness.

Scream
■ Technology
■ Digital Citizen
■ Timing

19

Screaming World Changes

Sometimes a scream is better than a thesis.
—Ralph Waldo Emerson, Journals (1836)

I tend to like screams. They are short, to the point, and full of energy. I scream for excitement when I see a friend that I haven't seen for a while, or when I am thrilled about the outcome of a ballgame—especially Duke playing basketball. A scream reflects the energy and the passion of the person's inner being. (We all know that screams can be made when you are scared or frightened, but let's focus here on the screams we make due to our energy and enthusiasm.) When I began this book, I wanted to focus on new techniques in the marketplace. As I interviewed more than 50 people, the common message from all of them was that you have to break through the noise. To me, this means companies need to learn how to embrace the energy of a scream in their marketing at the right time and to the right person. To be successful in attracting the right attention, a scream's essence must be short, to the point, and leveraging techniques that apply to today's customer in an agile fashion. And it must be a scream that is relevant to the time and the place of the product or service that you want to bring to and sell in the marketplace.

Three principles, shown in Figure 19.1, are needed to effectively get your message into the market, using the right tone and volume based on

- Technology
- The new digital citizen
- Timing

Figure 19.1   ANGELS framework—scream!

This chapter focuses on the use of technology to raise your voice, the emergence of the new digital citizen that you have to reach, and the timing of your marketing projects and campaigns. This chapter focuses on the who, when, and how:

- Who?—Digital citizen
- When?—Maturity of your company, market, and stage
- How?—Technology (Web 2.0)

The how is about technology, mainly Web 2.0. The who you scream to is determined by the degree of digital citizenship, and the when is determined by timing in the market, of your products, and your company's maturity. These principles provide the agility you need to respond and change the market as we know it.

These principles work hand-in-hand with Chapter 8, "Break Through the Noise," that addressed the "what." What you scream focuses on the message and the relevancy of the message that you scream with the what that completes the who, when, and how!

Technology

In today's world, technology matters. According to Patrick Quinn, president and CEO of PQ Media, "Marketers are seeking new strategies to connect with customers through engaging means in captive locations, while at the same time providing proof-of-performance metrics. These shifts in the marketplace should be apparent to every marketer but even today, some marketing professionals do not use technology to their advantage."

Technology is important in today's world where more than 1.2 billion people use the Internet and more use technology through mobile phones. IBM has identified a set of trends that it believes to be future change agents. For direct application to your business, explore these topics and how they can help your business gain a competitive advantage:

- Online customer experience
- Reach
- Integration of user content
- Virtual experience
- Agility
- Analytics

Online Customer Experience: Commerce and More

I had the opportunity to talk with Errol Denger, the senior strategist for IBM WebSphere Commerce. He is responsible for defining product and business strategy and works to develop strategies to harness the power of emerging technologies, such as Web 2.0, social commerce, and mobile commerce. In this role, he is fortunate to work with the world's leading retailers and businesses, helping them to embrace customer-centric retailing strategies to deliver a superior shopping experience.

Scream Enhancement

Today's most successful companies have redefined themselves to deliver more relevant brand experiences. They are utilizing customer-centric strategies to personalize the brand experience for each individual customer, his needs, and his lifestyle. Commerce technologies have followed a parallel evolutionary path going beyond simply presenting products, to placing the customers and their needs at the center of the experience. IBM's Institute of Business Value Studies has shown that these customer-centric commerce strategies create advocates or prosumers. Advocates spend 30 percent more annually and spend 25 percent more with their preferred vendor.

Creating a customer-centric experience begins by monitoring customer preferences and behavior during each interaction. Commerce technologies then make this insight actionable by translating these behaviors into roles to customize this experience. It electronically enables role-based marketing. This approach is often more effective than simple segmentation because it enables companies to tailor the experience to the specific buying occasion. This approach more closely aligns to our discussion of the segmentation of one found in Chapter 1 of this book. For example, when buying a printer, the consumer might fit into the "Ralph researcher" persona where the primary need is access to comprehensive product information and high-value solutions. However, when he returns to buy ink, he falls into the "Bill the bargain-hunter" persona whose priority is to find the best deal quickly. Advances in commerce technologies enable companies to recognize these behavioral shifts and appropriately modify the experience. These differences in role can be realized in the technology. Applying traditional segmentation techniques and static technologies to this same scenario would not address the customer's unique needs for these buying occasions like the use of technology does.

As Denger comments, "Today's leading brands have embraced customer-centric strategies, architecting the entire experience from the customer's perspective and adapting each interaction to the specific occasion. Every single time a customer interacts with your brand, there is an opportunity to learn and respond. The companies that drive the best results are those that respond in real time"

Application to Your Company

Exploration of your online experience can promote your brand in all channels. If your role-based approach is to be successful, technology enables your scream to be heard online in an automated fashion. Case studies in coming chapters illustrate this point.

Reach: Mobile Technology

Almost everyone has a mobile phone today. These devices are becoming more multi-usage–based and a prime candidate for better marketing. Knowing how to leverage this technology can serve your company well today and into the future.

Scream Enhancement

Business requirements and technology advances are driving tremendous change across the enterprise mobile space. In many regions, mobile devices are becoming an increasingly viable alternative to PCs. With the rapid rise of mobile business, companies can do more than just give their employees the option to access e-mail remotely. They can give them access to critical data and applications—when and where they need it—because the infrastructure and security features will be there to support them. Because consumers are multitaskers who can do business anywhere, anytime, a marketer's scream cannot be a one-channel campaign. It must span all the mediums and channels that match consumer behavior.

What was shocking to me was that according to Marketing Sherpa's research, more than 91.4 percent of marketers didn't think that mobile marketing applied to them! In the latest global survey commissioned by IBM, of more than 16,000 consumers, 66 percent of teenagers used their mobile device to text friends for buying advice while shopping, and 25 percent of teenagers accessed the Web from a mobile device while in a shop. Mobile computing is not a fad, but a trend that will continue far into the future!

Experiment with the technology. An example of a company that has leveraged this new mobile space is Moosejaw Mountaineering. According to its Web site, Moosejaw Mountaineering, Inc., is "one of the Midwest's leading outdoor-adventure retailers, offering the finest outdoor gear and apparel as well as some totally unnecessary nonsense guaranteed to make any day better." Based in Madison Heights, Michigan, the company operates six locations in Michigan and Chicago and six Web sites—Moosejaw.com, theJaw.com, thaLowdown.com, Moosejawrewards.com, Adventurewatches.com, and CampMoosejaw.com.

Moosejaw Mountaineering launched a text message campaign to its clients. The mass text message campaign yielded an impressive response rate. The retailer's text message to recipients reveals humor and playfulness that customers connect with: "Text me back with Rock, Paper, or Scissors. I already know what I'm throwing and if you beat me, I'll add 100 Moosejaw Points to your account now." The result was an astounding 66 percent response rate! Moosejaw continues to experiment with new marketing "screams" driving response as high as 70 percent.

Application to Your Company

In the application of your budget, analyze your spending in this mobile area. According to PQ Media, spending on online and mobile advertising, including search and lead generation, online classifieds and displays, e-media, online video and rich media, Internet yellow pages, consumer-generated ads, and mobile advertising, rose 29.1 percent to $29.94 billion in 2007 and increased at a compounded growth rate of 31.4 percent in the

2002–2007 period. Growth was driven by marketers shifting budgets out of traditional advertising to reach key demographics that have increased online and mobile usage due to improvements in online and wireless technology, particularly with wider adoption of broadband access.

Explore the global best practices. NTT published their view of the role of technology in Japan, where this mobile technology is positioned as a "lifestyle infrastructure." They view the role of the next generation cell phone as their ultimate screaming device.

I was with one of our Japanese colleagues and as you go walking down the street, every storefront sends you a mobile message that is integrated into their marketing. Ultimately, as you're walking by the storefront, it'll say, you know, "Hi Sandy; how are those jeans? We have a special on matching belts if you come in now." Japan is driving the use far above what we have seen in the United States.

Integration of User Content: Social Networking

Social networking was discussed in Chapter 10, "The New Vessels" as a technique to drive more relationship-centered marketing. According to Forrester Research., Enterprise spending on Web 2.0 technologies will grow strongly during the next five years, reaching $4.6 billion globally by 2013, with social networking, mashups, and RSS capturing the greatest share. The art of the technology to drive that effectiveness is discussed in the following paragraphs.

Scream Enhancement

Social networking platforms are the technology used to integrate user-generated content into the "marketers' scream." In today's marketplace, the most efficient means to grab a customer's attention is not heavy brand pushing, but rather to host or facilitate a community for people to actively engage with one another. Web 2.0 refers to the second generation of the Internet with Web-based communities and hosted services, such as social-networking sites, wikis, and folksonomies, which aim to facilitate collaboration and sharing between users, for example, by putting customer ratings and excerpts from reviews on in-store price tags, or even using customers as the voice of the brand through a series of blogs, Twitters, and other Web 2.0 techniques. (Twitter, Facebook, and mySpace have more than 40 million users!)

Community Web platforms have introduced new forms of content contribution, which has lead to more users because it's easier to share information and more data through these new tools because users are finding more value in collaboration. As these new business models evolve, additional capabilities will emerge to help sustain and grow the features and functionality that companies will require to take advantage of these new technologies.

VNUnet2 predicts that consumers will increasingly use their social networks to research prospective product purchases. The implications for marketers are that traditional market research tools such as focus groups and questionnaires will be superseded by data found on the social Web. Smaller, lesser-known brands will pick up loyal customers as a result of influence from within their networks. People expect their social networks to do more for them, such as finding jobs and getting advice. Official news will be increasingly personalized by consumer opinion, making it harder to distinguish real news from opinion.

For marketers, this means that social networks will become a bigger part of our lives. Pew's Research Center for People and the Press published a report titled "Internet's Broader Role in Campaign 2008." In this survey, a social networking site use was explored, with the researchers finding that 22 percent of Americans use social networks. Broken down by age range, 67 percent of people age 18–29, 21percent of people 30–39, and 6 percent of those 40 and older use social networking software.

Social networks have amazing potential. For instance, social networks will become a standard vehicle for channel enablement, relationship development, and communications. They have already grown in reseller communities and between some vendors and the channel, particularly over technical support issues. Some distributors are likely to charge vendors for access to their social networks.

Our research in the B2B space reveals that the two biggest complaints are that everyone wants to connect (which puts off the most senior people) and that the current networks require the release of too much information. In B2B, people want it to be highly targeted, and they want to choose who to network with directly. The most successful networks in the B2B space are those that enable B2B users to choose how they are contacted.

I predict that in the future, the rise and fall of highly targeted B2B social networks will have severe restrictions on who can join. The trend to selectively network is developing in the B2C space with invitation-only networks starting to appear and becoming more trusted as a result.

Application to Your Company
Earlier chapters discussed forming a community. If you take one thing away from this book, it should be the power of the social network now and in the future. Your community marketing plan should enable your team to

grow its skills in the platform itself and leverage and learn about the power of communities and the technology behind it. Social software provides businesses with means of innovating and executing more quickly by using dynamic networks of coworkers, partners, and customers. Leveraging this new technology as a marketer, you can build more responsive sales teams by enabling them to more quickly find needed experts and information, gain competitive advantage by involving customers and partners throughout the development process, and discover pockets of hidden expertise.

The types of capabilities you want to look for in your social networking software is the capability to do the following:

- **Profile:** Finds the people you need by searching their expertise, current projects (more B2B), and responsibilities or finds and interacts with people like me (more B2C)

- **Dogear:** Allows you to discover bookmarks that have been qualified by others with similar interests and expertise

- **Blogs:** Helps facilitate and unlock the expertise of individuals within an organization, internally or externally

- **Communities:** Helps organizations cultivate and build strong relationships by bringing people together with common interests

- **Activities:** Provides a way to organize your work and easily tap your expanding professional network to help execute tasks faster

- **Discussion forums:** Enables community members to discuss online key topics

Jimmy Wales, founder of Wikipedia, recently was at our **IBM IMPACT** conference and stated that since the launch in 2001, Wikipedia is the largest, fastest growing, and most popular Web 2.0 general reference site. As of April 2008, Wikipedia attracts 684 million visitors reading more than 10 million articles in 253 languages.

Internet 2D to 3D

The Internet is used by most companies in their marketing. The Internet is moving to 3D sooner than later. Following is a discussion of our leverage of this technology for better marketing.

Scream Enhancement

The 2D Internet is comprised of standardized features that yield many forms of content in a variety of formats, including HTML, dynamic HTML, video and audio streams, interactive widgets, and secure transaction. 3D Internet is a digital environment that enables people and organizations to gather, communicate, and work together in a collaborative, open forum.

With the success of 3D communities, such as Second Life, and Active World, there is a dramatic shift taking place in the way people see and navigate the Internet. The experience of interacting with another character in a 3D environment, as opposed to a screen name or a flat image, adds new appeal to the act of socializing on the Internet. As the users become more immersed in the environment, advertisers see better ways to market their products.

By the end of 2011, 80 percent of active Internet users (and Fortune 500 enterprises) will have a "second life," not necessarily in Second Life, but in the overall virtual environment according to Gartner, Inc. In April, 2008, IBM and Linden Lab, creator of Second Life, announced that it was working on adapting the popular virtual world technology for customized and secure collaboration in corporations. At the Virtual Worlds Conference in 2008, the two companies demonstrated the Second Life Grid, a platform that enables an organization to create a public or private virtual environment using Linden Lab's 3D online virtual world technology.

Application to Your Company

The 2D Internet is unarguably the largest source of information around the world, yet I still find marketers not leveraging it as they could. How do you combine this powerful technology engine for marketing with your traditional direct marketing? An award-winning example of leveraging technology for competitive advantage is a campaign that Mary Hall, on my team, developed. Hall is in charge of interactive marketing for the SOA and WebSphere Brand at IBM. We recently won a Gold Award from MarketingSherpa for the Best Opt-in Email Campaign. (See Figure 19.2.)

This award-winning campaign was a technology driven e-mailer with compelling offers to drive response with an automated ROI assessment that linked into a Micro Site. It achieved a click-through rate of 4.8 percent, which was well above industry average due to the technology-focused targeting that was done, leveraging our current 2D Internet interactive. We looked at the target customer who might be interested in receiving the mailer, and sorted the list appropriately to include that customer in the send. This 2DInternet campaign was a huge leverage of the technology to differentiate the interests of our buyers.

Figure 19.2   Use of technology to win.

We believe that this new 3D world is just around the corner. In 2010, it is estimated that more than 60 million users will be surfing, shopping, learning, working, designing, and creating new virtual real worlds in the 3D environment Internet space. In Chapter 20, "Technology Matters: IBM, Staples, Dell, and MyVirtualModel," see how virtual models in both the B2C and B2B worlds might be worth your investigation in the marketing realm.

Agility: Driving Sustainable Advantage Across the Enterprise with a Business Process Management Suite (BPMS)

Business Process Management Suites (BPMS) are in vogue today because of the competitive nature of a business's processes. Marketing has a set of processes that a BPMS could help drive more effectiveness. For example, a focus on the product launch process could lead to more consistent and innovative launches for a company.

Scream Enhancements

Traditional business process management (BPM) is a systematic approach to improve an organization's business processes. Companies today are increasingly realizing that their key differentiators and competitive advantages in the marketplace are contained in their business processes and not limited more narrowly to their discrete product or service offerings. If companies can quickly operationalize what-if scenarios and rapidly deploy new differentiated processes for specific audiences or channels, then they can exploit a new dimension of competitive advantage in the marketplace. If the organization's business process is something truly unique and revolutionary, there is the potential to leapfrog competitors or create a new business model altogether, as FedEx, Dell, and a whole host of other innovators did in a variety of industries. The point is that in today's rapidly changing business environment, treating your business processes as a key strategic asset that can be wielded as a competitive weapon can help you achieve sustainable growth or, in some cases, breakaway performance.

BPMS is the technology (software) to integrate and leverage knowledge, ways of executing business processes and islands of information across an enterprise. It is the connective tissue or neurons that drive the organization's operations and provides the visibility and feedback loop to sense and respond to change as it occurs within your processes or in the external market. Done right, BPMS can communicate or be the "scream" of the process owner, CEO, CMO, or other key stakeholder, rapidly conveying process changes and quickly aligning staff to new process goals and objectives.

Our business landscape contains many types of marketplace change and uncertainty. For many companies and industries, these changes are becoming more significant and more transformative in nature. This includes the effects of industry convergence or consolidation, aggressive low-cost global competitors, more complex regulatory requirements, and other market changes. Organizations must adapt and respond rapidly, capitalize on new opportunities, reduce their risk exposure, and outmaneuver their competition. BPMS plays a crucial role in enabling organizations to address these needs and succeed in today's marketplace.

BPMS represents a unique set of capabilities that are designed to support ongoing change and continuous process optimization. Core BPMS includes the following:

- Process-modeling tools and the ability to collaborate with stakeholders to design how you want your business processes to work.

- Comparing new processes with how the business runs today and recognize the changes you need to make to optimize further.

- Running a simulation before you make those changes to make sure the outcome is exactly what you want, and if it is, rapidly deploying the business process changes directly into your operational environment.

- Monitoring your existing processes and gaining greater insights into how they work.

- Tools to better analyze and understand areas where you can improve, elevate, and visualize key performance indicators that matter to you.

As Dianne Del Rosso, IBM BPM marketing manager, commented, "These capabilities can be applied across entire, end-to-end processes in an organization. However, they can also be deployed incrementally to specific pain points or areas of prioritization, especially for those marketers who want the best-of-breed learnings in all areas of their business."

Application to Your Company

BPMS can deliver significant agility by aligning your organization to your business process objectives and your changing business needs, no matter what marketing process you want to automate, correlate, or leverage for more insight. IBM believes that different types of process participants, from business leaders to marketing professionals, can collaborate together in managing and optimizing their processes. The goal of BPM is not restricted to simply building and running a good process, but also to create processes designed for continuous optimization, supported by a continuous feedback loop, and the tools/capabilities to collaborate across multiple stakeholders within your organization.

Geico Insurance is a real-life example. It has used this technology in its area of online marketing to dramatically ramp up its new customer capture rate from customers who visit its Web site and begin the process of applying for an insurance policy but not completing it.

In addition, this BPM capability helps marketers examine customers calling in to the call center and making inquiries about either an existing or a new product. These actions can be used to add the relevant prospects to the campaign management system or to activate a call to be made outbound from the call center or for someone in a physical brick-and-mortar office to call up to a customer to discuss certain policies or certain options.

The Digital Citizen

In addition to understanding the technology that exists, an important segmentation in engagement has emerged. For the first time in a long time, there exists two distinct marketplaces—those who grew up digital and those who did not. As you segment your market to make your points in the marketplace, you need to scream in the right way to each group. I call the new group of customers the digital citizen. Don Tapscott calls it the net-generation. Regardless of what you call this group, 88 million offspring produced by 85 million baby boomers have eclipsed their parents in size and impact. Tapscott reveals that the net-generation is most numerous in North America but also is seen in Europe and in Asia.

As Tapscott comments, "The net-generation has come of age. The children of the baby boom, aged 13–30, are not only the largest generation ever; they are the first generation to come of age in the digital age. The new digital media, particularly the Internet, are at the heart of a new youth culture and a new generation who, in profound and fundamental ways, learn, work, play, communicate, shop, and create communities differently than their parents. For the first time in human history, children are authorities on a central innovation. This generation lap is leading to far-reaching changes in commerce and in every institution in society. As this generation enters the marketplace they are changing many facets of retail and marketing from influence networks and the customer experience to advertising and the brand."

They are already affecting the way we market. According to PQ media, spending on branded entertainment marketing, including event sponsorship and marketing, paid product placement, and advergaming and webisodes, rose 14.7 percent to $22.30 billion in 2007, and climbed at a CAGR of 13.4 percent from 2002 to 2007. Growth was driven by deployment of media strategies aimed at being more interactive and entertaining than traditional media technology.

This generation—the digital citizen—is different from those in the past. It is not just age that makes this group different, but also the way the people in this generation have been surrounded by the digital media. Computers and other digital devices like cameras have taught them to think of the world differently. They work with them at home and in school, and they use them for entertainment. Constantly surrounded by technology, these digital citizens are different from their parents in the way they learn, think, work, play, and even interact. Tapscott calls them a "force for transformation." This makes the Internet fundamentally different from previous communications innovations such as the development of the printing press or the introduction of radio and television. These are hierarchical technologies—inflexible and centralized. By contrast, the new media is interactive, malleable, and distributed in control.

To reach the new world, there are a few things you must think through in your marketing plan. Note that this digital citizen will be harder to reach with conventional media marketing and formats!

Top Five Ideas for the Digital Citizen

This new bifurcation in the marketplace makes marketing both a challenge and an opportunity. Below are a set of learnings on how to be successful in this new setting.

1. **Focus on interactive:** The digital citizens are not just observers, they are participants. The new generation expects to have new media that is interactive and malleable. It wants to be in control of the dialogue, not a one-way communication.

2. **Focus on Immediacy:** Immediacy is important in this new world. What used to take days or weeks, now takes seconds, and the expectation has been set as such. For marketers, that means that your marketing plan must have an element of interactivity in them. Your marketing plan needs to be strong, inclusive, and innovative. Some of the best-practice plans include the exploration, discovery, and investigation stages so that there is an element of two-way communications. It's important to use the technology to develop a dialogue with end users.

   Also, given the immediacy factor, elements such as eNurturing should be enhanced so that the process can be accelerated and targeted to what is of most interest at the time. In Chapter 10, "The New Vessels" you see examples of both interactivity and use of urgency in enurturing. Often, a corporation's biggest issue is not building an interactive capability but responding quickly and intelligently when all these customers and prospects engage. You need to understand the back-end implications of interactivity, which is a bit like traditionally running a successful direct-mail campaign but not having enough people to answer the enquiries.

3. **Focus on edutainment:** What is edutainment? It is the combination of learning and being entertained. This new group of customers wants to be entertained. They are used to the CNN snippet and the visual experience. They want to be enthralled in all that they do. Advergaming has

become popular on Web sites, such as The Coca-Cola Company, one of the case studies in this book. The first interactive games on Web sites had a goal of driving product awareness. Now interactive games involve a sense of the experience of the brand and even education, for example, the recent 3D real-time advergame Auris Ice Experience developed for Toyota France and IBM's Innov8 game to help with product and concept understanding, education, and brand experience.

These digital citizens love interactive gaming, which can be used for awareness, learning, and experience. The advergame industry is expected to generate $312.2 million by 2009, up from $83.6 million in 2004, according to Boston research firm Yankee Group. In addition to gaming, webisodes have become more popular as an edutainment form of marketing. A webisode, according to Wikipedia, is simply a Web episode—collectively it is part of a Web series, a form of new media that characteristically features a dramatic, serial storyline, and where the primary method of viewership is streaming online over the Internet. Although there is no "set" standard for length, most webisodes are relatively short, ranging from 4 to 15 minutes in length. Marketing plans must now focus on how to entertain and get your message across. In our next chapters, we share some best practice ways to gain attention through the use of movies and events.

4. **Focus on authenticity:** Regardless of what you do in the market, the new millennium generation must also validate what it hears and sees. Authentication of everything is required to establish trust. People want openness and honesty. For example, on Facebook and Myspace, the audience is exposing its feelings, personal life, and insights that no generation before it has done. On the Internet, nobody judges soley based on cultural stereotypes. In some cases, it is truly the idea that matters. For instance, in our IBM "SOA Jam" (a virtual sharing of ideas and experiences), the person's idea is judged on its merit, not on what rank the person holds who introduced the idea. For marketers that means a true focus on word-of-mouth marketing and influential touch points.

At our recent IBM IMPACT conference, for instance, we encouraged a blogger who had as many good things as bad things to say about us to come and demonstrate his idea. It had a great effect in that the customers believed we wanted the truth, not just the good. In addition, another good best practice was around a track at the conference on customer feedback. The whole goal was to hear the good, the bad, and the ugly. This authenticity plan at IMPACT won us a gold award for our IMPACT

2007 show from the MarCom Awards, an international awards competition for marketing and communication professionals. (See Figure 19.3.)

MarCom Gold
Award for
IMPACT 2007

- Drove attendance with combination of new & traditional tactics:
  - SOA e-newsletter, e-mails, User Groups, webcasts
  - ibm.com, developerworks,
  - YouTube, Blogs, tradeshows, press
  - Viral email signature, "Tell a Friend"

"SOA comes of age' milestone gathering might not be Burning Man for CIOs, but it's as close as you can get with your clothes on." – ZDNet.com

2008 IMPACT
SMART SOA CONFERENCE
LAS   VEGAS,   NEVADA

April 6 – 11, 2008
Find out more at:
ibm.com/soa/impact2008

Figure 19.3 IMPACT 2007

The application to marketers today is to invest themselves in their own authenticity plan. One of my favorite quotes comes from Rohit Bhargava in his book *Personality Not Included: Why Companies Lose Their Authenticity and How Great Brands Get It Back*; he wrote, "Every product and company has a personality. The problem is that businesses today have gotten extremely good at hiding it behind carefully scripted disclaimers and processes." Make sure you have an authenticity plan, one that shares the values of your personality but also has a few personality flaws! We all have them.

5. **Focus on personalization:** This personalization will drive marketing into more fragmented, niche-interest markets. The digital citizens will be savvy, skilled buyers who place a high level of importance on individualism, self-fulfillment, and personal involvement in the creation process. They are willing to sacrifice privacy to ensure that everything is interconnected and available!

Digital Citizen: Application to Your Company

These four characteristics of digital citizens will change the way we look at buyers and the way that we dialogue and market to them. In fact, we will be marketing with them. Ensure your market intelligence looks at your segmentation through the lens of the digitalness of your buyer or consumer.

Timing

The way that your company screams in the marketplace will be based on the time and maturity of your portfolio. As your product, category, or offering changes over time, your marketing plan should adjust accordingly. In Geoffrey Moore's book *Crossing the Chasm: Marketing and Selling High-Tech Products to Mainstream Customer*, he outlined where markets are on a maturity curve. As Shown in Figure 19.4, the market will range from innovators to early maturity to late majority and laggards. Your marketing scream also needs to match where you are in relationship to the staging.

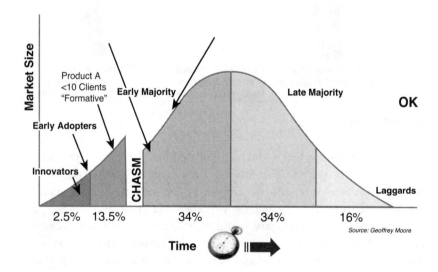

Figure 19.4   Build the playbook by time.

As a rough guide, if your market is in the innovation and early adapter stages, the focus needs to be on references, press, and the influencers in your industry, such as industry analysts. To cross the chasm, you need a broader scope of marketing and a broader marketing mix. Again, the mix will change as you move into late majority and laggards.

For example, in Figure 19.5, IBM's Tivoli® Brand wanted to introduce a new segment in the marketplace. The rollout began with the understanding of the marketplace and that it is an early adopter marketplace.

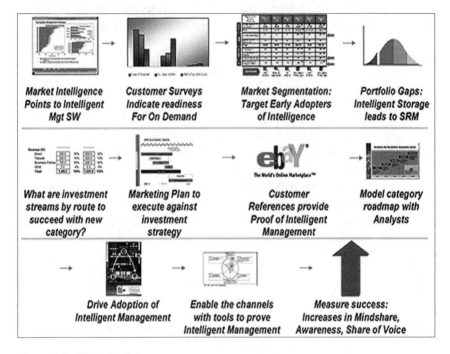

| Market Intelligence Points to Intelligent Mgt SW | Customer Surveys Indicate readiness For On Demand | Market Segmentation: Target Early Adopters of Intelligence | Portfolio Gaps: Intelligent Storage leads to SRM |

| What are investment streams by route to succeed with new category? | Marketing Plan to execute against investment strategy | Customer References provide Proof of Intelligent Management | Model category roadmap with Analysts |

| Drive Adoption of Intelligent Management | Enable the channels with tools to prove Intelligent Management | Measure success: Increases in Mindshare, Awareness, Share of Voice |

Figure 19.5 IBM Tivoli's timing.

Based on that knowledge, the team focused on references, press, and the analyst community first. This involved the creation of the category and working collaboratively with the influencer community. Then it expanded into more mass marketing with advertising and channels. In these later states (see Figure 19.6), advertising did the drive to the Web site to combine the technology approach with the traditional approach. After it was on the Web, the automation and personalization kicked in to take this particular project from early adopter to early majority in demand.

Companies need both agility and innovation for growth in today's dynamic economy. Traditional sources of growth through organic growth and acquisitions will create growth unquestionably, but the greatest amounts of growth against the competition will come from being agile and innovative in your company's understanding its changing customer and the use of technology over time. (See Figure 19.7.)

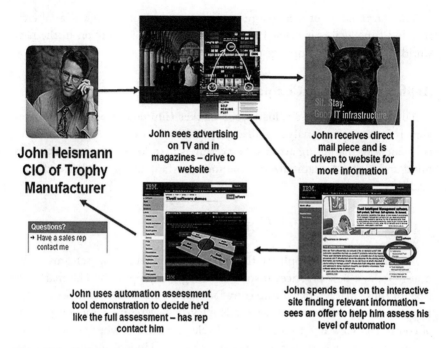

Figure 19.6 The integrated play.

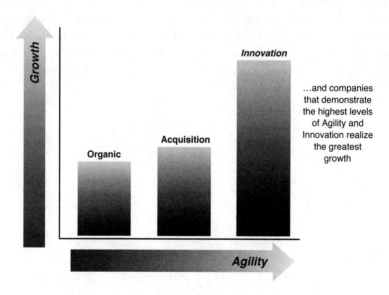

Figure 19.7 Agility is essential to any marketing growth strategy.

The combination of technology, an understanding of the new digital citizen, and time factors is needed to have your message acted upon in the new world, using the new language of technology.

Application to Your Company

Timing does matter. Evaluate your market timing and where your category is in maturity. Analyze your own portfolio and readiness to enter, and time out your marketing attacks. Marketing is best done with a timeframe in mind and a plan to capitalize on the moment best in the market and your readiness.

Conclusion

Technology is the amplifier that enables your marketing screams to be heard. Today's best practices involve an integrated approach. The market is ripe for those marketers who are truly tech savvy. This is only the beginning. Personal use of the Internet now rivals television-watching time: 66 percent of consumers view one to four hours of television a day, whereas 60 percent report the same quantity of personal Internet use. Understanding and leveraging Web 2.0 marketing technology changes the game. With the new digital citizen on the horizon and growth in the Internet-savvy buyer in all parts of the world, technology combined with the understanding of the new millennium client will yield the greatest and the fastest success in the marketplace. The time factor ensures that your choice of vehicle and integrated marketing plan will be effective for the maturity of the marketplace.

20

Technology Matters: IBM, Staples, Dell, and MyVirtualModel

Any sufficiently advanced technology is indistinguishable from magic.
—*Arthur C. Clarke*

Today's screams in the marketplace get amplified and more sophisticated with technology. It serves as an enabler to make the meeting of the needs of your customers much stronger. As Gartner Inc., a leading information technology research and advisory company, wrote, "All firms are undergoing dramatic changes as technology-enabled marketing emerges as the marketing model of the future. Companies run the risk of being swept aside if they fail to understand the shift."

Social media marketing involves listening, cultivating, and participating in the continuous dialogue among customers, partners, and stakeholders about issues relevant to the marketplace, either on or off a brand's digital properties. It assumes that marketers can speak the language of technology, and often, the technology leader, the marketing leader, and the business leader become melded into one person.

Today, an estimated 1.2 billion people or 1/5th of the world's population are online. There are few corners of the world without wi-fi hotspots, Internet cafés, or e-mail. The highest penetration is in North America where 70 percent of the population is connected. During the next few years, this number will explode as groups such as One Laptop per Child (OLPC) brings wi-fi-connected computers into classrooms in third-world countries.

One of the more amazing phenomena is the proliferation of social network-ing sites. If MySpace were a country, it would be the eleventh largest in the world (between Japan and Mexico). The average MySpace page is visited 30 times a day. What is even more amazing is that one out of eight couples married in the United States last year met online. It is safe to say that technol-ogy and social networking have changed human relationships and interactions.

Mobile phones have reached even higher penetrations than the Internet with more than 2.7 billion devices growing at a 15 percent compounded annual growth rate (CAGR). Let me put that number in perspective: That's three times the number of PCs, two times the number of credit cards, and two times the number of televisions. It is estimated that 84 percent of the U.S. population uses mobile phones, and the experts expect almost 100 per-cent of the U.S. young-adult and adult population to have mobile phones by 2015. In Europe, 80 percent of the total European population uses mobile phones and a recent statistic claimed that 96 percent of adults in Western Europe had mobile phones. Increasing functionality and improving wireless bandwidth and connectivity make the cell phone a device poised to disrupt all segments and verticals. And mobile phones aren't just used for talking. Texting or short message service (SMS) has become a favorite mode of com-munication among young adults with the number of text messages sent and received every day exceeding the total population of the planet!

Focus on Five Technology-Enabled Marketing Best Practices

To emphasize the role of technology in marketing, I highlight five best practices from five different companies. I chose these best practices because of the areas they represent:

1. **Incrementally leverage technology that every company has today—a Web site.** IBM's Online Chat takes advantage of one area that most companies have today, a Web presence, and incrementally takes it to the next level in a business-to-business (B2B) setting.
2. **Leverage technology to gain leads through the sales cycle.** IBM's eNurturing achieves this goal by leveraging technology to foster leads through their progression.
3. **Use customer-centric commerce.** Customer-centric commerce trans-lates into different strategies and capabilities depending on the segment.

At Staples, customer centricity is about being easy to do business with, whereas at Bass Pro Shops it is about becoming a rich destination featuring an active community.

4. **Use product promotions using Web 2.0 technology.** Dell Computer leverages and uses Twitter as a technology to drive product sales higher.

5. **Use next generation 3D technologies.** My Virtual Model is a company that leverages the digital citizen in business to consumer (B2C) spaces and in B2B markets.

Online Chat–IBM

Taking the Internet to the next level involves figuring out how to innovate from the basics. In this example, IBM borrows from a best practice used in the B2C world into the B2B world with an online chat to drive a personalized experience while a person is browsing your site!

The Leaders

Inside of IBM, we constantly look at incremental innovation. For this online chat best practice, I talked to Gina Poole, IBM vice president of social software programs and software Web marketing and sales. In addition, I highlighted our Service Oriented Architecture (SOA) usage of the online chat work led by Brian Adler who is on the SOA marketing team. Adler is responsible for the SOA interactive Web.

The Best Practice

The vision for this best practice was to take our Web marketing to the next level. By exploring real-time chat, there is more proactivity in answering questions and taking the customer further into the sales cycle directly on the Web site. Proactive chat takes the conversation to prospects at a time and place where they are more likely to appreciate it—when they're looking at the Web site and trying to find information about products and services. Customer-service representatives are trained to answer people's immediate questions while also asking questions that qualify them as a potential lead. In Figure 20.1, you can see the online chat window and how it works in a B2B setting.

- Proactive chat uses business rules to make efficient proactive approaches via the Website

  - Ex. Approach visitor after x minutes on launch page

- Puts us more in control of our rep resource deployment

  - Staff to opportunity vs. peak

- Improved customer experience and satisfaction

- Opportunity for accelerated lead identification and progression

- Pilot launched Nov 30 on all SOA pages, plus AIM/WebSphere product pages

Figure 20.1   Online chat—a proactive Web move.

Understanding the customers' behavior enables you to determine if you want to approach them and how you should approach them. Through real-time chat, you can determine if they need assistance or if they are focused on a particular topic. It offers an opportunity to interact with a person in a no-threat manner. During the process, there is an opportunity for a transformation to occur with the person—from information gatherer, shopper, potential prospect, and then ideally into a customer. A key piece of advice is to approach the person respecting their privacy throughout the process.

In addition, real-time chat enriches the customer experience. It provides assistance "just in time." As Adler comments, "Proactive chat gives us the ability to have a conversation with our prospects when they're most receptive—while they are on our Web site actively gathering information about our products."

The Technology

IBM leverages a hosted Application Service Provider (ASP) and real-time data mining with modeling, segmentation, metrics, and reporting. It combines technology with the human element. The technology helps identify the best customers to interact with based on the set of business rules defined.

One of the keys in using this advantaged technology involves the business rules. Business rules represent policies, procedures, and constraints regarding how a company conducts its business. The business rules are based on the customer's behavior and visiting process. For example, how did the customers arrive at your site, what search engine did they use, what search terms did they leverage, and what do they look at while they're on the site? In addition, how long the customers linger on a page and which pages they review in which order can impact how and what you communicate.

However, in addition to the technology, the online chat leverages the human telesales representatives. They engage in a relationship fashion. The technology increases their productivity. In the past, the telesales representatives would do call backs, for example, if someone clicked on the button on the Web site that said "call me back later." In that setting, you can talk to only one person at a time. However, with real-time proactive chat, they can chat with three people at a time. So it triples their productivity.

The Results

There were three major results. The first was increased leads. In the first three months of operation on the WebSphere and SOA sites, we had 2,845 chats, resulting in 182 validated leads for more than $5 million of potential revenue. The second was increased telesales productivity. As we discussed previously, their productivity increased threefold.

The third result was increased customer satisfaction. We received a lot of great feedback from potential customers. The visitors commented on the experience and the way they received almost instantaneous answers. In addition, because none of IBM's competitors have an online chat, the customers tended to view our customer service as more important to IBM. As Poole comments, "The results we've seen in terms of validated leads are phenomenal. This was more valuable than buying lists and cold calling. We were talking to people who we already knew were interested in what we had to sell."

Top Five Lessons Learned

Through the use of online chat to drive leads for the IBM WebSphere brand, several lessons were learned to make the technology combined with business a more powerful combination. To accelerate your venture into this online chat space, especially in the B2B world where it is not as prevalent as B2C, the following lessons should provide a basis for your experience to leapfrog ahead:

1. **Leverage the online chat part of your Web strategy:** Recognize the opportunity from an incremental investment in your current Web site. Real-time, online chat can take your Web site conversion rates up.
2. **Carefully choose and use the technology:** Choose carefully so that you have the right capability to interact and set up real-time data mining and modeling.

3. **Identify the right business rules:** Spend time understanding who your customers are, their personaes and profiles, and what type of things they might be looking for. The right rules ensure that you approach the right people at the right time and not just anyone online who might not exhibit prepurchase behaviors.

4. **Enable the telesales representatives:** Your telesales team is a critical part of the online chat success. The people on the team need to interact with the potential clients and respond to their clients. The more knowledgeable they are and the more they can help right on the spot versus saying, "I'll get back to you," the more positive experience for the online prospect.

5. **Segment your visitors:** All visitors to your Web site are not equal in terms of their potential to generate sales leads. That's why continual analysis of conversions (generating validated leads from chats) is essential. This analysis will determine which pages yield the most leads and which business rules are most effective in generating chats, which convert to validated leads. Invest wisely, even in B2B. The Web is a phenomenal resource for reaching out to prospects, and you need to use as much of it as you can. We have had phenomenal results out of the gate with IBM SOA because we started on day one by enabling proactive chats on every product-related page, and we started with sufficient representatives so that we maximize the number of potential hot leads that are getting invited to chat. In other words, we are not leaving money on the table by ignoring some parts of our Web site or by understaffing the reps.

eNurturing

Leveraging effective lead management is essential to turning your identified prospects into leads and clients. eNurturing is following up on those leads and contacts in an automated follow-process using technology to increase your efficiency and effectiveness.

The Leader

Virginia Sharma is the director of SOA Go-to-Market at IBM. She has had responsibilities running one of IBM's largest and most successful cross-IBM programs around SOA and is passionate about marketing.

The Best Practice

eNurturing is the ability to hold a sustained electronic conversation with your customer through a buying cycle. It is a sustained conversation because eNurturing is a two-way conversation. It can be as simple as, "Thanks for coming to our Webcast. Based on your question, we thought you could use this whitepaper" to begin the communications that go both ways.

Eighty percent of leads do not need the qualification right after a marketing tactic but need it after six to nine months. However, the customer is interested in ramping up and understanding the product and offerings so that when he is ready to buy, he has his vendor short list. eNurturing enables you to stay in the buying cycle on a continuous basis, instead of rejecting the lead right away because the customer did not state he wanted to buy within the next 60 days. If you do not continue the relationship with the customer, in six months when he can buy, your company will not be on that short list.

eNurturing enables us to nurture that lead with technology, and it enables an electronic conversation on a frequent basis. It is cost-effective because it does not require that the client show up again for another in-person event. IBM's best practice in eNurturing process is called 3-6-9. Every potential customer that comes to an event, in three months, six months, and nine months, is followed up with to continue the conversation. We cross-reference how many potential customers or prospects come to a Webcast and download a whitepaper on a particular topic. This view enables IBM to customize what the potential customers receive in the 3-6-9 plan based on their interest areas.

The Technology

Think back to every thank-you card you have written or received. The ones that stand out to you are the ones that are truly personalized. For example, "Thank you so much for the fondue set. Chocolate fondue is my favorite, but you already knew that! We will definitely have you over for our next fondue party!" Not only does this acknowledge what you gave them, but it also sets up the opportunity for the next meeting.

The same principle applies to B2B eNurturing. However, you are following up with thousands of prospects who have attended your Webcasts and events, visited your Web site, and registered for an offer. You are going to need more than a nice pen to help you follow up with so many prospects! That's where eNurturing technology comes into place. Here is how it works.

In today's world, technology prospects will use multiple mediums to learn, understand, and train on the available solutions. Some will use a combination of Webcasts, whitepapers, and events; others might speak to a representative and download a case study and a demo. In every one of these interactions, we collect the customer's information. Technology enables us to use this information to funnel these customers into interest areas (note: not tactic type). So someone who attends a connectivity Webcast, downloads a paper, and registers for a connectivity demo is in a different funnel from someone who registers for a governance technical briefing and downloads a customer-case study.

After your funnels are created, these interest groups are sent a trigger e-mail via the eNurturing application that highlights at least one and no more than three offers related to that interest area. These offers should acknowledge the prospects' interest areas and show how the highlighted offer helps them further their understanding of their interest area. It is also important for them to have a link to a landing page with live chat capability and other offers such as a customer widget that enables you to continuously deliver offers to the customers' desktops. Finally, be sure to integrate a viral element to the eNurture e-mails so that if a prospect would like to invite a peer or colleague to check out the offer, she can easily forward it. This enables you to build your contact database without executing any contact discovery tactics, which can be expensive.

Of course, you can still send a trigger e-mail after a single tactic, such as a Webcast or an event, but your click-through rates will increase if you can track all your customer interactions in one database. This is also more cost effective as you are sending out fewer, more targeted e-mails to the same customers. More importantly, it prevents e-mail fatigue because these trigger emails most likely feature the same offer regardless of tactic!

The Results

The Enabling Business Flexibility Program has the best performing eNurturing engine at IBM with a 24.8 percent click-through rate compared to an industry average of 1.6–8.7 percent (source: February, 2008 IBM e-marketing scorecard). These results were driven by the compelling e-book offers we created including the *Real-World SOA* e-book and the SOA assessment. In Table 20.1, you can see the results.

Table 20.1   eBooks Offered in February eNurture Transaction E-Mails

	Audience	Open Rate	Click-Through Rate (CTR)
SOA Assessment: SOA Technology eBook	125	45 percent	90 percent
SOA Web offers Touch 1: Real-World SOA Stories	3,385	35 percent	66 percent
SOA Web offers Touch 2: SOA Technology eBook	3,523	35 percent	87 percent

Top Five Lessons Learned

eNurturing with technology is new for many companies. Best practices can help accelerate your journey. The following are the top five lessons from our IBM case study:

1. Build nurturing streams by customer interest area, not by tactic or go-to-market vehicles. Keep eNurture e-mail offers compelling and relevant to the original offer registrations.
2. Think about your nurturing streams before your execution, not after.
3. Be sure to allow viral elements in your nurturing stream. A prospect should have the ability to virally invite peers into the nurturing conversation and say, "Hey, check this out. I attended this Webcast. I thought it was interesting. You might be interested in this, too." That is a great way for a company to extend its contact base and leverage word of mouth for better marketing.
4. Encourage adoption of customer-centric messaging techniques to build relationships and guide customer through the buy cycle with relevant and meaningful content.
5. Help newsletter owners clean subscriber data to remove bad addresses, which will improve delivery and click rates.

That Was Easy! Staple's Ease Drives Sales

eCommerce has been around for a while but this case study shows how Staples takes it to the next level around a set of services that are valued by customers to create stronger customer loyalty.

The Leader

Chris Madaus is the vice president of Marketing for Staples business delivery. Business delivery consists of Staples.com, the Private Web site business, and the catalog. In his three years at Staples, Madaus has helped to make Staples a market-driven company that listens to its customers and puts together its offers in a way that are for the most resounding with the customers. Staples' customers want to get a competitive price on product but in an "easy to shop and buy" way, receiving the product the next day without error with high reliability and with excellent customer service. That has been the way that Madaus drives business. That strategy has paid off to make Staples easy to do business with in all of its channels.

The Best Practice

Underpinning Staples' emerging vision was an awareness of a changing dynamic in the online office supply marketplace. For one, Staples saw customer retention becoming a higher strategic priority, largely because of the high cost of establishing new customer relationships. At the same time, it saw that its customer base was becoming increasingly pressed for time and demanding of speed and simplicity. To Staples' marketers and strategists, the new commerce solution helps meet this challenge by making it easier to bring groundbreaking capabilities to market more rapidly. In this way, the Web site supports Staples' "easy" brand promise. In Figure 20.2, you see that the strategy for marketing was driven by the brand promise.

With its online channel, a critical part of its growth strategy, Staples needed a commerce platform that would support and fuel its online business growth, not constrain it. Staples needed more flexibility to pursue creative, customer-centric business strategies. Some of the biggest improvements in online commerce practices have been in the area of multichannel integration, creative merchandising, product search, and the overall streamlining of the user experience. However, online retail is a perpetual work in progress, with the boundaries of the online purchasing experience continually being pushed by the retailers that have done much to shape it.

Staples, whose aggressive development of its Web channels has placed it among the top two eRetailer sites, is one such retailer. The growing volume of business generated by its two sites—Staples.com® (targeted to small businesses and home offices) and StaplesLink.com® (targeted to larger businesses)—has been a major factor in the company's overall top-line growth. Both channels figure prominently in the company's long-term growth strategy.

Figure 20.2 Staples! That was easy!

To better understand its customers' needs, Staples went straight to the source, conducting an extensive field study designed to gather fine-grained details of customer ordering behavior. One of its central findings was that customers needed a more organized way to inventory and order their office supplies. Staples responded by rolling out a service called Easy Reorder, which uses a customer's ordering history to calculate ordering patterns and create a comprehensive, pre-assembled list that is updated with each order.

With its research pinpointing the rebate submission process as another pain point for customers, Staples also introduced Easy Rebate, which enables customers to submit rebates online, with all supporting information automatically forwarded by Staples. These examples show how Staples is focusing its innovation efforts on creating a truly differentiated experience that makes life easier for its customers, encouraging more browsers to buy and more buyers to return.

The Technology

Staples rebased its technology completely around making it easy for the focused buyer to buy on its Web site. As Madaus explains, "Our Staples Web site is the Web site that the customer built. We did extensive usability to determine exactly what the customers wanted and what made it easy for them. Easy was our mantra—easy to find products, easy to buy them, check out, and get through the whole process quickly and efficiently. We also focused on making it easy when they came back with features such as easy reorder, order by catalog number, and favorites." The Staples ordering process was turned into an easy experience for customers who come back to the Web site frequently to buy. In addition, they added capability in a 2D format to drive customer satisfaction and conversion from search. Finally, Staples added in a comparison area so that the customers could compare products. The wizard technology was world class; for example, Staples added wizards for ink, toner, and batteries, so it is easy to find the ink and toner.

To achieve the high rate of growth it envisioned in the small-business/home-office segment, Staples realized it needed to realign the technology that powered Staples.com to make it better able to support the company's business strategies and meet the growing competitive demands of the market. Perhaps the most basic requirement was the capability of the Staples.com infrastructure to handle volume surges with no loss of performance or reliability, which customers have come to expect. However, although Staples viewed reliability and performance as foundational requirements, it also realized that the capability to execute business initiatives with speed and flexibility was increasingly essential to staying ahead of the competition and delivering an online experience that kept customers coming back.

The Results

Staples has seen a 60 percent increase in online conversion rate. In addition, its customer satisfaction has increased as more customers have seen the ease in buying from the Web. Also, the new Web-based platform has given Staples the capability to bring differentiating services and programs to market more rapidly and efficiently to support its rapid business growth.

Application to Your Company

The following are the areas of application to any business, whether B2C or B2B:

1. **Start with your company's vision:** With Staples, everything began with a simple promise of "easy." Its work in marketing supported that vision every step of the way.
2. **Focus on outside in:** Staples began its technology use with the customer's needs. It knew just where the most results would come from based on that intelligence.

3. **Start small:** Staples leveraged technology in a single area first. It began with the customer-order process, not all of the processes that were driving business.

4. **Blur the lines:** This story of Staples was told by Madaus but also by the CIO. In addition, the business leader played an active role. In the future, marketing and technology will become closer together. Prepare for it by learning about the new Web 2.0 world that exists today.

5. **Focus on the right metrics:** For Staples, this was the online conversion rate. For your company, it will be something different but make sure you are measuring it. It helps you to know what you've done right and where to improve.

Dell Uses Twitter to Drive Sales

When I was a little girl, I used to write in my diary every night. I used to document all the activities of my day and even focus in on key interactions with my friends and family. Well, today I keep a diary of sorts but everyone reads it. It is because my diary of all my activities, limited to 140 lines, is on Twitter!

Twitter is a free social networking and micro-blogging service that allows users to send "updates" (or "tweets," text-based posts up to 140 characters long) to the Twitter Web site, via SMS, instant messaging, or a third-party application such as Twitterrific or Facebook.

The Leaders

Ricardo Guerrero and Stefanie Nelson from Dell drove the vision to leverage Twitter as a tool to drive sales. Many thanks to my friends at the Society for New Communications Research for some of the details of this award-winning best practice.

For those of you who are not technology savvy, Twitter is a service for people to communicate and stay connected through the exchange of quick, frequent answers to one simple question: What are you doing? To me, it is like an online diary. Why do people Twitter? Well, as one of my friend's kids told me, I can start a Twitter group and know what all my friends are doing every day. It is much more efficient than calling them and finding out! Businesses like Dell (and IBM) are using Twitter in more corporate instances. Here is one best practice from Dell.

The vision for this idea came when Guerrero was reading an article from *The New York Times* where the author wrote, "It's one of the fastest-growing phenomena on the Internet." It got him thinking about Twitter, and he thought this technology might be one he would like to pilot.

According to Guerrero, "I was working with the Dell Outlet and exploring how we could do a better job moving the inventory of the returns that Dell receives. We do not usually know what is coming, so we can end up having small bubbles of inventory of a particular model. When it is a large bubble and we know far enough ahead, we can create an e-mail campaign around it. But e-mail takes longer so that by the time we design it and get it approved by our legal department, it is about a week-long process.

"So we can open up a truck-load of returns that come in—that arrive at the Dell Outlet—and we find out we have many more of model XYZ than we expected, and now we have an unanticipated situation of overstock of inventory on that model. So the key idea was to be able to promote quickly and easily that we had a deal on that model. Then, rather than having to decrease the price in order to make more sales, we might actually drive more demand to that model we had too many of. That was the key idea."

The Best Practice

Dell Outlet has inventory based only on the equipment that is returned to Dell, which therefore can fluctuate quite a bit. When there is a large inventory "bubble" of a particular model, there might be time to generate an e-mail campaign to promote that particular system and generate more demand. However, when the bubble is smaller, the major lever to drive sales has been to lower the price of the overstocked model. The challenge for Dell Outlet was to figure out a way to generate more traffic and greater demand for its products.

Dell Outlet came up with the idea that Twitter, a social networking and microblogging service, might be a solution to the challenges presented, by offering Twitter-specific promotions and featured products. The goals were

- To drive increased traffic, and thus increased demand for particular products for which Dell Outlet has inventory greater than desired levels

- To grow the pool of Dell Outlet's Twitter followers to the point where it is sizable enough to have an impact on specific demand-generation postings

■ To increase the visibility of Dell Outlet within the community of Twitter users and hence the share of mind and likelihood of Twitter users to consider Dell Outlet for their next technology purchase

By connecting with this group of potential customers that are likely to influence others who are not as technical or connected to social media, there might be a possibility of also influencing others beyond Twitter.

Dell Outlet's Twitter strategy revolves around regularly posting special Twitter-only offers or highlighting great deals currently available on www.twitter.com/delloutlet. (See Figure 20.3.)

Figure 20.3   Dell's special Twitter offer.

Launched in early June, 2007, Dell Outlet currently has nearly 1,300 individual subscribers (followers) and hopes to continue to expand that base. When a new tweet is posted, it generally provides followers a coupon code that can be used to obtain a discount on that particular model in the Dell Outlet. Typically, this coupon code is exclusive to Twitter, so Dell can measure the redemptions of the coupon and know that it was due to having been posted on Twitter. This way, Twitter followers can share the coupon code easily with their Twitter friends in a viral fashion, and those friends might decide to follow the Dell Outlet Twitter. Furthermore, on Dell Outlet's Home & Home Office customer homepage (at www.delloutlet.com/ home), an invitation to subscribe to Dell's Twitter postings is featured.

Top Three Lessons Learned

Guerrero shared his early experiences with Twitter and most importantly, the lessons he learned with the new technology:

1. **Use Twitter's vision:** A major lesson learned for Guerrero was the use of Twitter Vision, which is a public place where you can see everyone who is Twittering at any given time. Twitter Vision takes the public timeline, does a sample every two or three seconds, and plots it on a Google map, so you actually see where people are twittering worldwide. Dell leveraged the public timeline and sent out offers such as sales that expire within a certain timeframe. This method increased the demand.
2. **New customers:** For Dell, Twitter represented a new way to reach customers. Guerrero claims that per Dell's latest surveys, a significant portion of people who bought through Twitter were not aware of the Dell Outlet before Twitter.
3. **Combine Web 2.0 technologies:** Dell has now taken its blogs and RSS feeds and routed them into Twitter. From Twitter, you can subscribe to Direct2Dell, which syncs to the headlines of the day from Dell. (See Twitter.com/direct2dell.) This is a fully automated Twitter. There is no one who has to maintain posting the stories from the blog on to Twitter, which is a one-way communication. This provides an avenue for customers who want to talk to someone.

The Technology

The tools used for Dell Outlet's Twitter strategy are Dell Outlet's Web site and Twitter page. Guerrero led the development of strategy for Dell Outlet to use Twitter as a marketing vehicle and set up all the Web pages and Twitter presence, while his colleague Stefanie Nelson has been responsible for maintaining those pages and creating the actual tweets, with an attempt to post at least once every other week. Dell Outlet's Twitter has linked to all Dell's other Twitters, including the Twitter version of the Direct2Dell blog, other Dell blogs, and similar offer-based Twitters for Dell Home & Home Office (www.twitter.com/DellHomeOffers) and Dell Small &

Medium Business (www.twitter.com/DellSmBizOffers). By providing cross-linking among all its Twitter properties, Dell encourages people to follow any or all of the Dell Twitters in which they might have an interest. Additionally, each of Dell's Twitter properties follows the individual responsible for the property one is viewing. This provides an opportunity to communicate and converse directly with an individual, make suggestions, or ask questions.

The Results

For approximately the first month and a half of Dell Outlet's Twitter campaign, Dell Outlet tracked growth of followers as well as daily traffic metrics to the www.delloutlet.com/twitter page. Specifically, by tracking traffic to this page on the days that offers were posted to Twitter, a rough response rate to each posting could be calculated. Further, the actual utilization of each coupon code can also be tracked. In the first year since utilizing Twitter as a promotional tool, the Dell Outlet generated over $500,000 in revenue in sales of refurbished systems. Dell expects to continue to use this form of promotion in the future and expand it as appropriate throughout the company.

Application to Your Company

Twitter is a new technology. I spoke with Jennifer McClure, the executive director of the Society for New Communications Research, a think tank dedicated to studying the latest developments in new media and communications. The Society has been exploring the impact of new communications on business for the past few years. Here are the top tips for marketing using Twitter:

- **Increase sales by alerting followers about new deals:** This is how Dell uses Twitter, as we discussed previously, to send notifications and links about sale items. Dell also has several customer service representativess who are active on Twitter (see http://twitter.com/DellOutlet).

- **Put out fires with personal customer service:** Comcast is monitoring for mentions of its products and services and working quickly and diligently to resolve customer concerns. The Twitter profile is manned by Frank Eliason from Comcast Customer Outreach, who has already posted more than 700 public messages in less than two weeks and received praise from prominent blogger Michael Arrington of TechCrunch. (See http://twitter.com/comcastcares.)

- **Share and interact with your customers:** The CEO of online shoe store Zappos uses Twitter. Zappos also has built a Web site that explains Twitter to newcomers, shows off all of Zappos' employees' tweets, and every single tweet that mentions Zappos, no matter who it comes from. (See http://twitter.com/zappos and http://twitter.zappos.com.)

- **Other uses for Twitter:** Keep in touch with colleagues, bloggers, or reporters who cover your industry; post quick, live updates from company events or industry conferences; conduct an instant, informal focus group; build a community to answer your questions; share links and help brainstorm ideas; vent; tell jokes; and make friends.

The bottom line about Twitter was best expressed by Aaron Brazell, "Twitter's power is in authenticity and transparency. I've often said that brand is not something that can be controlled by companies. Brand is controlled by customers. Trust is controlled by companies. If customers don't trust a company, the brand is useless. If they do trust a company, that company has secured a marketer for life. Trust is built by authenticity, by transparency. It is the thing that allows companies to function in the twenty-first century." Twitter is an interesting hybrid communication. It is an interesting new communication channel full of immediacy.

Virtual Modeling

The 3D Internet is in use in some new areas. The following case study shows how an innovative company is leveraging 3D in B2C today and is expanding quickly into B2B usage. Watch carefully how the 3D Internet is forming. Its speed will be like that of the Internet!

The Leader

Louise Guay describes herself as a true visionary. She is the cofounder of My Virtual Model company, which she started with her partner Jean-François St-Arnaud in 2000. Her Ph.D. thesis was an essay on virtual identity. The context was museum collections. As museums and stores deal similarly with visual dynamics and acrobatics, it was natural to apply the virtual identity concept to the retail world. Guay is a customer advocate; she believes that each individual is responsible for her or his identity. In this way, the virtual model of people can be a personal agent of communication, an autonomous agent representing each user.

Guay holds a Ph.D. in Multimedia Communications from l'Université de Paris VIII. Her transcultural multimedia dissertation was the first ever presented on laserdisc. She received the Canadian Woman Entrepreneur of the Year Award (1996) from the University of Toronto.

The Best Practice

Guay advocates leveraging a virtual model to create a way to drive a stronger relationship and eventually drive more sales for retail companies. Her clients use virtual models to reach the digital natives and settlers by enabling them to become (not just create!) their own virtual model. The model enables you to become your own stylist, or even personal shopper. Extending the concept even further, you can connect your model to your Facebook entry or blog and have your friends dress you up.

The goal is to engage in a private and interactive conversation with the customer. Guay envisioned a world where fashion is transformed by the fact that people would express themselves, not just be dressed by designer likes and dislikes. Instead, she sees consumers focusing more on their style.

My Virtual Model provides a way to search, shop, and buy with your model, which goes beyond Google. Searching evolves from text to 3D. The customer dresses up her model with the styles she is looking for, just as if she were with her own personal shopper. Any search engine gives the results by matching real sellable items with the customer's query. This enables a discovery of products by personal style.

In Figure 20.4, you can see the virtual model in use at H&M.

The Technology

My Virtual Model's (MVM) environment is highly scalable and fully redundant. It is a hosted solution that is extremely secure. The custom application allows MVM to respond to peak traffic periods by scaling the application and instances rapidly over the Web of servers. MVM currently hosts more than 20 clients who cater to more than 1.5 million users a month performing more than 20 million try-ons per month.

Figure 20.4   Virtual Model in use at H&M.

The Results

Today, the virtual model allows users to display several brands in their virtual wardrobe and post them on their personal page where visitors can comment on them. My Virtual Model has clients in many fields including Sears, H&M, adidas, Speedo, Lands' End, and published on portals and virtual social networks such as Facebook, MySpace, iVillage.com, and gURL. (gURL.com is "a leading online community and content site for teenage girls. It contains stories, games and interactive content.")

A study conducted by Lands' End concluded that the conversion rate, the percentage of visitors who actually purchased, was 26 percent higher for shoppers who used the Virtual Model technology compared to the average shopper. The same study also concluded that the average order value was 13 percent higher for shoppers who used the virtual model technology than shoppers overall.

Application to Your Company

Guay has some great lessons for those companies ready to experiment with the 3D Internet in marketing. Her innovation is an interesting twist on forming and personalizing a relationship with customers.

- Support the **New World Motivation:** This technology enables users to follow their own models instead of following the fashion diktats. Brands and retailers using MVM virtual experiences (virtual models, virtual dressing rooms, and virtual homes) are enhancing the control of the user. This is truly customer-centric and is the direction of the future.

- **Provide the ultimate experience:** Shopping with My Virtual Model brings a high level of visual personalization to either your B2C or B2B world. When adding a picture of your face on the model, it becomes "you." In Figure 20.5, you see Guay shown as a Virtual Model.

Figure 20.5 Guay as her own virtual model.

When you search visually with the model trying on different styles, matching clothes and accessories with buyable products, it goes a step further than what is possible on the Web today. When you bring your model with a coupon from your cell phone into the store, it synchronizes with Radio-Frequency Identification (RFID) scanners and intelligent mirrors in the dressing room.

- **Don't stop at the 2D world:** Here comes the 3D world. The 2D Internet is a great first step, but keep your eyes open for the 3D world that is surely just around the corner. My Virtual Model uses 3D techniquest, e-commerce, social shopping, and networking. The virtual identity will allow circulation on the Web. In addition, Guay explained that you could send your virtual model on social sites, in 3D worlds or pictures of you in your new outfit to your friends!

- **Dream the future:** People who understand the implications of the new technology are the people who can exploit it most usefully and gain first-mover advantage. For example, the first people who understand the benefit of the new Sparkle technology of semantic Web searching will be the first to gain benefit. Then, others see it and think they can improve on that. There is a benefit seeing how to use it. There is also opportunity for those marketers who actually can see the leap.

Conclusion

Technology is powerful. Marketers need to understand how to harness the power and use it in their marketing plans. It is about picking a few technologies that apply to your business, not technology for technology sake. However, I predict in the future that the best marketers will be those who understand both technology and marketing. In this chapter, we saw some technology use that was incremental such as improvements to Web site conversion, better commerce capability, and eNurturing. We also explored some transformational technologies such as 3D technologies, virtual modeling, and Twitter. In each, they enabled companies to take their value proposition to the market in a more effective way. Technology can help you with the marketing magic.

To access a view of "how to create an experience" through technology, go to ibmpressbooks.com/angels.

Putting It All Together

21

End-to-End Example: IBM WebSphere and the SOA Agenda, Prolifics, and Ascendant Technology

As we saw in the last chapter, there are different ways to gain attention in the marketplace. The use of technology, the new digital citizen, and time are important in your plan for "screaming" in the marketplace. The IBM WebSphere brand is a true success story that can provide some insight in this regard. Starting as a dream by IBM's senior vice president Steve Mills, it was driven initially by Paraic Sweeney with some creative marketing techniques. I was privileged to be on that initial team and to spend seven of the ten years of IBM WebSphere's life personally working on the brand.

The reason I leveraged it as a case study is that it is the most powerful brand built at IBM and in the industry. The history of IBM WebSphere is one of applying the ANGELS framework. The strategy and analysis of the market over time is demonstrated over the brand's ten-year history and includes creation of market agendas. The go-to-market (GTM) for IBM WebSphere has combined both the traditional methods and award-winning Web Marketing 2.0 efforts. The energy that has been generated through the ecosystem and influencers has driven a strong community around the brand. And of course, the lead management system has driven the IBM WebSphere family to 15 consecutive quarters of growth at constant currency.

Most important, the marketing of IBM WebSphere has been an exciting case study in how business-to-business (B2B) marketing has evolved over time to People to People Marketing. As Dale Kutnick, Gartner's senior vice president of Executive Programs commented, "As the twenty-first century unfolds, a growing emphasis on business- and consumer-oriented services for all products will be key commercial drivers. IT-enabled services will increasingly bring efficiency, "life-support," and innovation to these offerings, which will ultimately become the embodiment of a company's market brand."

This case study is a way to tie together all of the ANGELS steps that we have discussed throughout the book, as shown in this list:

- 1998: IBM WebSphere vision/family announced.
- 2000: IBM WebSphere as a brand for the Internet.
- 2001: IBM WebSphere brand loyalty for developers.
- 2002: IBM WebSphere Application Server gets number one share.
- 2003: Innovate for IBM WebSphere Portals gets number one share.
- 2004: Extends to integration of people and information.
- 2005: Integration to ride the wave of Service Oriented Architecture (SOA).
  - Extends to appliances.
  - Extends to open source.
- 2007: Links to business-lead SOA.
- 2008: Powered by Smart SOA and Green.

The Story of the IBM WebSphere Brand from a Marketing Viewpoint

The IBM WebSphere brand story is a strong story showing how to leverage the Marketing 2.0 techniques in the marketplace coupled with the traditional methods. This case study brings to life the key concepts in the book.

1998–1999

When it was first conceived, IBM WebSphere was a bit of a different animal for IBM. The team saw a significant market opportunity for a segment of the software market; however, IBM had not perfected the technology necessary to seize this opportunity. So the company had to make a decision: Should

IBM enter the market with a new, unproven technology, or should the company wait for this technology to "harden?" We leveraged the questions we discussed in Chapter 4, "Fish Where the Fish Are and Use the Right Bait," about who we target and whether it is the right fit for the current master brand called IBM.

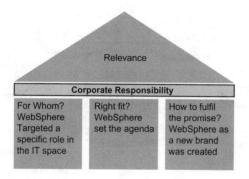

Figure 21.1 IBM WebSphere's birth: 1998–1999.

The final decision to enter the market was a significant departure from the traditional IBM approach. What's more, IBM didn't just want to enter the market with a product and merely survive. It wanted to become the company that was the number one brand powering the Internet with its software. Add to that the bigger challenge that at that time no one thought of IBM as a software company.

The marketing feat was to leverage our current strengths. IBM was known and respected in a similar technology area that was linked to the same buyers. The strategy was to take those concepts that IBM was successful in (if you are technical, IBM has been strong in transaction-processing technology) and move those concepts to the Web. Because of the maturity of the product and the market, the early marketing focus was around early customer references and word of mouth. Figure 21.2 shows that we purposely selected those influencers for this first round of introduction into the marketplace.

IBM focused on the "tippers" in the industry and worked to ensure its success with a new product. In addition, it focused on the influencer community. We sought advice and counsel on the priority and order of the product requirements and how to win in the marketplace. IBM determined that it wanted to be more than just "number one" in the market. Instead, it would be "number one" in people's minds, the first name that came to mind when talking about the software that supports the Internet. We wanted the IBM WebSphere brand to be synonymous with the term "e-business infrastructure" or *the* brand of the Internet! This was an exceedingly bold statement; we planned to go from being nothing in the market to being the "given" market leader.

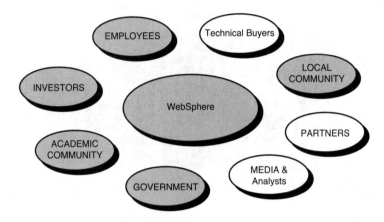

Figure 21.2   IBM WebSphere's circle of influence.

Application to Your Company

There are four major lessons from this brand and product introduction:

- **Segmentation is crucial.** To reach these goals, marketing needed to go back to basics to create a plan of attack. The team did an excellent job of market segmentation to articulate the value to the right audience and the right influencers to target first.
- **Branding.** IBM had to determine how to leverage what it stood for in the marketplace and build from its inherent value. For example, IBM was number one in hardware at the time, so leveraging that strength to win in the software market was an important success factor. To create a successful beachhead, this linkage and leverage turned out to be crucial.
- **Focus on the right influencers.** The focus in the beginning for IBM was on the wheel of influence and the most important influencers at this time yielded a focus on partners, media, analysts, and a segment of the customer set.

■ **Focus on the right time.** We discussed the value of understanding market and product timing. Given this was an early entry product, we saw
interest only from a few forward-thinking partners (such as Prolifics). We
could not use price as a differentiator in the market at the time because
the target audience was not price-sensitive for this type of product. The
only key element that we could leverage for success was promotion.

Make sure you understand the maturity of your product or offering to
determine a strategy and appropriate marketing mix. Also equally
important is to have a bold goal for your team. The skills and inspiration
for your team makes a difference, especially an inspirational goal of
becoming the market leader!

PROLIFICS: A GREAT PARTNER WITH GREAT MARKETING: A DISCUSSION WITH DEVI GUPTA AND ROBYN THOMAS

Part of the IBM WebSphere brand's success is a strong ecosystem and
community. Prolifics was one of the early partners for the IBM
Corporation. Founded in 1978 in New York City, Prolifics utilizes a
wealth of expertise to offer comprehensive business solutions and is the
two-year-running recipient of the IBM Award for Overall Technical
Excellence. Prolifics has also been honored with the IBM Business
Partner Leadership Award, the 5-Star Partner Award, the Best Portal
Solution Award, the Outstanding SOA Solution Beacon Award, and the
IMPACT SOA Solution Award. In short, they are one of IBM
WebSphere's key partners and influencers.

I spoke to Devi Gupta, vice president of Marketing for Prolifics, who
leverages her computer science background to shape Prolifics' marketing
efforts. In addition, Robyn Thomas, part of the Prolifics Business
Development team, joined us for the conversation.

Prolifics identifies many best practices that drive both the power of
IBM's WebSphere brand and its own:

■ **Referral marketing:** One of the critical factors to Prolifics'
longevity is the solid relationships it built in its ecosystem of partners and customers—the most strategic alliance today being with
IBM. Given the significant nature of that relationship, Prolifics felt

it was important to not only message to its customers, but also to the IBM community. A key approach was to leverage its past successes and client references for power. This concept led to the creation of a Prolifics "Win Flash," a monthly communication that primarily highlights recent, referenceable wins, while also sharing news, solution offerings, customer events, and more. The objective of the communication effort is to add value and grow the relationship through sharing resources that can be utilized by both partners. In addition, the Win Flash serves as a vehicle for communicating recently acquired skill sets, marketing tactics, and activities the firm is driving.

As Gupta explains, "At first, the Win Flash focused on one success story each month; however, as it evolved, we often had multiple wins we wanted to share. These frequently aligned with a particular focus area, resulting in a progression toward a topic-based communication that highlighted our efforts related to a theme. Given that much of the content is relevant to the IBM sales reps, Prolifics also created a partner extranet to directly link from the Win Flash to supplemental information that IBM could leverage with similar opportunities. For example, the focus of the communication can be competitive wins, and the extranet may host additional sales support like a calling guide, call to action, or a podcast."

Another key element Prolifics incorporated was to give the Win Flash a "face." It wanted the content to come from somebody who could offer a personal touch, respond to questions, and act as a liaison between the partners. Thomas became the author and "face" of the Win Flash. Having a dedicated contact has truly paid off, with the Flash generating a consistent number of leads through the IBM community. Thomas comments, "The Win Flash gets about a 50 percent open rate, and we can track the hotter topics, such as our record-setting SOA Win Flash! In addition, every Flash generates around five solid qualified leads back to the regions."

- **Agility tactics:** Gupta and Thomas also drive the brands through what I call agility tactics that provide a dynamic way to respond to what is happening in the marketplace. With customer face time being more and more limited, it's become increasingly important to engage customers in new and unique ways that differentiate the company from the competition and offer faster time-to-value.

- **Leverage the Web:** From YouTube to Second Life, the opportunities here are limited only by your imagination. For Gupta and the Prolifics team, they saw the need to provide targeted, business-level education to their customers and prospects in a "lightweight" fashion. Prolifics University was soon born. It offers a week-long online experience targeted at IT management and business leaders. The goal of the annual event is to bring solution information to customers who otherwise wouldn't have the time, focusing on best practices instead of being a commercial for products. During that week-long event, a Web site called prolificsuniversity.com comes alive with assets, live Webinars, blogs, call-to-actions, and Q&A sessions.

- **High-value events:** Highly focused, C-level events concentrated on a new offering, target market, or piece of news have shown Prolifics excellent returns. For example, working jointly with IBM, Prolifics hosted customers to a Boston Red Sox game where they had an opportunity to join batting practice, attend a VIP tour of the stadium, and were treated to great seats with full catering. Titled "Reverse the Curse" and conceived by Ayalla Goldschmidt, a manager on my IBM WebSphere SOA team, Prolifics and IBM invited BEA customers following Oracle's announcement of its intentions to buy BEA. Just a few months later, Prolifics had already closed a deal.

- **Search engine optimization:** Improving the volume and quality of traffic to your Web site will usually result in a greater number of opportunities. By considering how search algorithms work and what people search for, Prolifics has seen an increase in hits to its Web site resulting in a set of highly qualified leads.

Prolifics is a key influencer of the IBM WebSphere brand in the marketplace, and its early adoption of the IBM WebSphere Portfolio was the start of great success and a great partnership.

2000–2002

As IBM continued in the market, a few key decisions had a real impact on our future. From a marketing perspective, we invested in market research to understand the market perception of the product. At that time, we were viewed as complex and a set of "things," not as an integrated solution. Based on that feedback, we simplified the way we sold the offering. Initially, there were five separate pieces under one "umbrella." So, we decided to throw the "complexity" in a box and simplified the five into a solution for our clients. This new solution approach needed to be taken to the market globally, with a scream, and to the right set of roles.

Anatomy of a "Global Scream"

To proclaim the new solution, we held an announcement event at La Gare in Paris with customers and influencers. In Figure 21.3, the significance of both the location and the announcement came alive.

Figure 21.3   Solution launch in France.

First, we selected an anchor event to do the announcement, which was not in the United States. We were going global with our brand. This was purposely done, as we saw the growth occurring for our segment outside the United States. The selection made a statement that we are a global brand, not just a U.S.-based brand. This launch outside the United States was the first for a brand in IBM. Our audience choice was crucial as well. We mixed the audience of influencers—partners, analysts, media, and our customers—to generate excitement and to begin the "IBM WebSphere" community. But, it was not just an event. We leveraged an integrated approach with advertising, Web 2.0 marketing, and channel enablement to drive home the points about our new agenda in the marketplace. At this event, we took our brand and established it as the brand of the Internet through consistent advertising and messaging around the world. This demonstrated how complete a solution IBM WebSphere really was. And it showed the power of combining the marketing and communications functions together.

We also introduced to the market a commerce engine called IBM WebSphere Commerce. Because this was a visible offering, we made sure that we focused on the references and successes around this product. In particular, we launched an early project with L.L. Bean. Again, given this was an early market and product, it was important to have word of mouth to create the demand. During that time, growth of revenue for IBM's electronic commerce product and services grew 300 percent year to year (YTY), resulting in a number one market share in licenses per IDC, the premier global provider of market intelligence. We also leveraged this sexy product to create new markets in mobile commerce and digital content management.

Role-Based Approach

Another piece of feedback that we received from our initial customers was that to be successful we needed to focus on our partners and developers. Because we targeted all audiences, in essence we targeted none. We decided to focus on the role of the developers and our partner ecosystem in a targeted fashion. We learned what was important to this role, and even went as far as doing an open-source offering called Eclipse with our partners to meet the developers' needs. Eclipse was an early community of vendors who were "giving" away part of their code to the community. This open-source route was a challenge in and of itself. Trying to differentiate your marketing and offerings when they support standard approaches lends itself to the creativity needed to show differentiation through a sustainable value proposition and the resulting deliverables. For instance, we advertised our Eclipse membership with the other vendors in major print advertising.

A deep commitment to open standards continues to be critical to our IBM WebSphere brand strategy and our success. Today, much of our IBM WebSphere product marketing is led by Steve Mello, our director of Worldwide Product Marketing, who has said, "While fervent support of open standards levels the playing field a bit, it meets our clients' desires for ease, opens up opportunities, and still allows us plenty of room to innovate; we wouldn't have it any other way." In summary, our decision to support open standards has affected the way we market the IBM WebSphere portfolio, driven our brand differentiation, and enabled us to recognize the needs of our clients.

You can find a related article by Karla Norsworthy, "The Importance of the Open Standards Decision on Marketing WebSphere" at ibmpressbooks.com/angels.

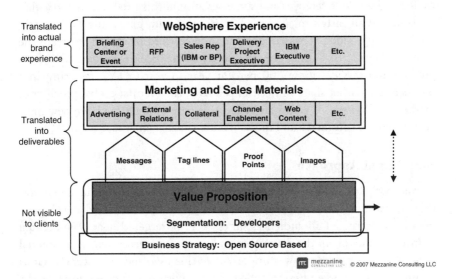

Figure 21.4   Value propositions were crucial for standard-based marketing!

In the Spring of 2001, we made progress in the Developer community at the Big IBM WebSphere Developer event. This event is where we launched our advertising campaign, which was more relevant and meaningful to developers. In Figure 21.5, you can see that we deliberately looked for a bold way to connect with this critical audience, and it was so effective that we expanded it across multiple software brands. The "codeanauts" were launched as the ambassadors for this role. The codeanauts were to symbolize developers. They showed up in all of our advertising.

Again, we focused on, developed, and enabled the channels to increase share in the medium-size customers. To drive this partner focus, we created and opened IBM WebSphere Innovation Centers throughout the world, enabling more than 150 new partners. These centers became a staple for IBM in future years. Many of the marketing initiatives started in IBM WebSphere became the foundation for broader IBM. For example, the IBM WebSphere Innovation Centers that we began later became popular for all IBM brands in Virtual Innovation Centers (VIC) located on the Web. These innovation centers were hubs for skills building in local regions, and they served as customer centers for demonstrations.

Figure 21.5 The developer focus with codeanauts.

We built our affinity with developers by launching a new product just for this developer role. These actions added to our brand image in that they showed how IBM WebSphere is the "real thing," the software of choice among the developer community. This effort increased unaided awareness in the market by 6 points, and the number of developers using IBM WebSphere by 150% to more than 1M developers. We drove a focused effort in emerging markets like India and China for our ecosystem and drove a redesign of our Web site resulting in a #1 hit Web page off of IBM.com, including more downloads of code more than all major competitors. These activities were all supplemented with building the team and consolidating marketing execution in anticipation of product integration. We made a conscientious focus on quality of execution worldwide—extending it just a focus in the United States to worldwide.

Application to Your Company

It was from this project that I learned the value of market intelligence through fact-based research methods. The next steps we took were guided by our user groups, our insight, and listening and learning in each step. In Chapter 1, "Listening and Analyzing in the Global World," we discussed the new hybrid market intelligence. This new way to listen to the market comes alive here as we combined classic uses of surveys and focus groups with the new modes of intelligence, such as our Board of Advisors (our top 24 most strategic customers), blogs, wikis, and jams. It is a great best practice that this combination empowers you to understand the market.

As the product and the market matured over time, you could see the marketing focus shift to the ecosystem to a focused, role-based approach, and to a focus on a visible portion of the portfolio—not all the products in the portfolio. Again, as you market, you need to balance your portfolio and where your offerings are in the maturity cycle. Strategies such as these turned into the initiatives that proved IBM WebSphere was more than a series of products; it was becoming a living, breathing, unstoppable, and growing brand.

2003–2004

From 2003–2004, the marketing story and approach was crafted. If you reflect on what the Allies did in World War II around the landing at Normandy, you will see many parallels to what is happening with the IBM WebSphere brand. The allies landed at many different places along the coast. Other Allied nations participated in the naval and air forces. After the beachheads were secured, a three-week military buildup occurred on the beaches before Operation Cobra, which was a predecessor to the actual Normandy beachhead attack began. Each one was required to hit certain objectives. When all of these beachheads met up, they had become such a dominating force, they could not be pushed back.

The marketing approach to IBM WebSphere is similar. We started with a first product that defined IBM WebSphere and expanded segments out from the base. This 2003–2004 timeframe moved us again into an additional segment, with the product plans, marketing, and sales always keeping attuned to the market. Each segment progressed at its rate and pace, building on the core base elements of what the IBM WebSphere brand stands for: innovation, scalability, and reliability. The IBM Websphere brand has a set of defined segments with slightly different roles—from developers, architects, business analysts, to Web commerce specialists and operations managers.

By this time, the keys to success in the marketplace were skills. IBM WebSphere became a part of college and university curriculum through the world. A key challenge in marketing during this era was finding the right balance of educating a marketplace and winning in the marketplace. For many of these early concepts, IBM was a first mover. Many customers did not even know what the technology could bring to them, and therefore, marketing had to focus on education of the market first. The correct balance of awareness, interest, desire, and action (AIDA) is important, as is shifting the balance when customers mature and change.

Application to Your Company

Marketing is broader than advertising. To scream in the market, marketing needs to identify what is important for success in the marketplace. In these years, it became a basis of skills. Placing IBM WebSphere in the university curriculum has paid off for years. As the students go out into the world, they take with them a comfort level with IBM WebSphere. You must constantly be in touch with your customer base, sometimes even before they become true customers. If you don't, you will soon lose some of your momentum.

2005–2006

In 2005, we focused on another next step for IBM WebSphere. We had driven the brand so that IBM WebSphere had become a household name in technology circles. However, as we did our next round of market research, we found that IBM WebSphere had become thought of as the "past" or "your father's brand of integration." It wasn't linked to anything exciting or new in the marketplace and more importantly, it was distanced from our customers' new challenges, such as aligning IT to the business and agility. In 2005, we set out to revitalize the IBM WebSphere brand to take it from being an application server brand and an integration brand to a brand that would stand for agility and business alignment.

Agenda Setting Moment

We held a strategic meeting to formulate a plan to play on our strength in core capabilities and to capture infantile thought of a new approach called Service Oriented Architecture (SOA). The key decision was that we would invest in SOA to drive the IBM WebSphere brand. It was not until we pulled the IBM WebSphere story and combined it with SOA that we unified the beachheads of strength. It is at this point that we became a dominant marketing force and leveraged the brand power of IBM WebSphere. The market research on the results support this agenda-setting moment.

We wanted to create a tidal wave of demand around the value that a flexible SOA business-driven approach could deliver to clients. When we looked at going after SOA, we debated whether we should create our own term. It was a key decision that we made to keep the market term because we had based the brand on an open approach. We did not want to go against our brand promise and have only a proprietary approach to SOA. We wanted to lead the market being true to our customers.

Educating the Market

The first thing we did was to educate the market. We found out quickly that the market didn't know what SOA was, so we decided to leverage technology to help them learn. We created three eclectic "What is SOA?" videos that were based on a set of simple analogies such as building blocks and music (see Figure 21.6).

We posted them on YouTube. One of my favorite press articles that came back on it was "IBM has posted three videos on Google's YouTube, which explain what SOA is in plain English. It truly looks like IBM is innovating on the marketing front. The cost involved in these must be tiny. What's the key takeaway for busy executives, even respectable companies? They can take advantage of the latest online technologies and trends." This, of course, was one of a few educational tactics, but it was the fire that ignited the interest. This education push was both internal and external.

Internally, we held sessions with everyone from administrative assistants to sellers to our top leaders. We didn't want this to be words on a chart, but the embodiment of the value in each employee. In fact, in a human resource survey, we asked, "Do you understand our strategy and our agenda-setting items?" Marketing lead the internal efforts as well as the external focus.

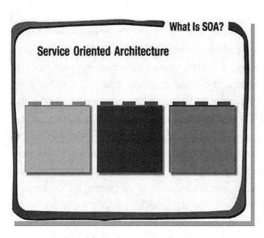

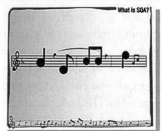

Figure 21.6 "What is SOA?" viral videos.

Why is this important? Think through the experience at Walt Disney. Disney's value proposition is about the experience of fun and great customer service. Each employee embodies what Disney positions as its value proposition. They are not just words, but they shine through in the employees. Most people learn about your brand from your employees; we wanted to make sure our IBM WebSphere brand and our agenda-setting category of SOA's value shone through each employee.

Our external education involved pumping up university programs with courses on SOA. We developed a strong and solid university curriculum that we gave away to colleges around the world with a set of university ambassadors. We created the Innov8 "serious" game (see Chapter 15, "Serious Gaming: IBM's Innov8") to reach not only the technical universities, but also the MBA programs. The focus shifted to the roles the agenda of SOA needed to reach to a new T-shaped skill. This T-shaped skill implies that a person's skills should be deep in technology and broad in the business process area (the horizontal part of the T). A new curriculum such as computer science was introduced; it was called Service Management.

Partner Skills

Our partner community joined in the work to drive skills into the marketplace. One of our key partners is Ascendant Technology. Its Zen Master series has been a three-year, branded series that has shown continuous growth (600 percent) over time. To break through the noise requires consistency. Striking the balance between changing dynamically to meet customer needs and maintaining consistency to build viral awareness are critical in your marketing mix. With so many businesses vying for your customers' attention, it can be hard to get noticed. In the Marketing 2.0 world, there are always new promotions, new ways of communicating, and new influencers. In fact, there are so many new ideas and messages appearing in front of potential customers that sometimes consistency is the key to being heard.

I spoke to Jim Deters, president of Ascendant Technology, and Liz Albert, Ascendant Technology's marketing director, about its Zen Master series of educational Webcasts. According to Jim, the series came out of a desire to help customers understand the latest technology innovations and the applications to their businesses. Each Webcast features real-world practitioners who provide tested insights on how to be successful.

Ascendant Technology has run these Webcasts under Albert's guidance for more than three years. Attendance has increased more than 600 percent as the series gains more popularity and is shared virally. The topics change and the speakers change, but the commitment to cutting edge, practical, business insights has remained consistent and has enabled the Zen Master series to capture and grow loyal audience bases in a market filled with competing noise.

Focus on Getting Started

After we helped educate the market about what SOA was, the next question was "How do we begin?" To simplify that, we determined from our customer base the five starting points. We set those up in packages and scenarios so that they were easily consumable, and then we leveraged technology again to have customers have the ability to play with the technology for free. We also published a whitepaper and Webcast on "The 5 Projects that Help You Get Started," which included another foray into putting metrics on business value into those projects. Under the leadership of Paul Brunet, our IBM SOA vice president of Product Marketing, we tried to find an easy way to begin. Bruner says, "Around the world, SOA became a hot topic. However, everyone wanted to know how to begin. Our focus on getting started was a key to our success."

The SOA Sandbox was born to assist in the simplicity play. We took this message of simplicity to our advertising campaigns online and in print, and we leveraged it as our rallying cry for our channel. This introduction of the positioning around the SOA entry points turned out to be one of our most enduring concepts. In Figure 21.7, you can see how we linked the simple positioning graphic to our advertising by entry point.

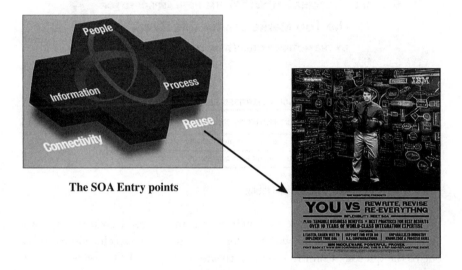

The SOA Entry points

Figure 21.7 The beginning of the SOA entry points.

Leveraging the New Vessels

Death by PowerPoint comes slowly. For our newfound audience, we found that going to another event to learn more just wasn't motivating enough. We decided to do an SOA movie both online and in movie theaters. We leveraged the digital citizen, who likes visuals and short takes on the message. Everyone loves movies and we wanted to leverage the entire format, from the trailer, to the theater, to outtakes, to interviews with the stars, and to the DVD version.

So what did we do? Well, we started out by first understanding what this new white space (for us—the new digital citizen!) needed and wanted. We found that the new digital citizens were interested in learning about our offerings, but they wanted us to do it in a fun, different way.

We felt that the film genre would burn the information into the audience's mind. It also would enable us the flexibility of going on the Web or going live and also providing the event in a set of other languages, because obviously all of us have seen foreign films that have subtitles.

We first focused on creating a preview that we had approved for customers' use for this event by the Motion Picture Association of IBM. (See Figure 21.8.)

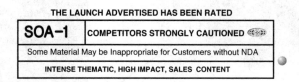

THE FOLLOWING **PREVIEW** HAS BEEN APPROVED FOR

The Top Marketers for this Event

BY THE MOTION PICTURE ASSOCIATION OF IBM

THE LAUNCH ADVERTISED HAS BEEN RATED

SOA–1	COMPETITORS STRONGLY CAUTIONED
Some Material May be Inappropriate for Customers without NDA	
INTENSE THEMATIC, HIGH IMPACT, SALES CONTENT	

Figure 21.8   The SOA movie preview and rating.

We also posted the movie on YouTube. Again, we got a great set of blogs and quotes from the press without doing any major outreach. Following is one of the quotes: "Coming soon to a theater near you, IBM service oriented architecture. Is video supposed to be viral? A strange idea, a movie trailer that advertises a new movie called launch, which seems to be about a returning executive who tried to implement SOA at this dress company, full of mystery. Is it just us or does anyone else wish that IBM actually made the full movie? It has a cult film written all over it and looks far more interesting than those Hollywood fares. They could do an online movie release whereby the SOA is used to conquer some pretty touch obstacles. Perhaps (seven) long-term employees supported by a mysterious union could try and sabotage the profits. Oh well, maybe it's just us. Nevertheless, [it's] good to see IBM trying new marketing techniques. We're giving it publicity at least." (See Figure 21.9).

Now, if you look at the posting of these YouTube trailers, we were actually number 16 for most discussed in science and technology. We were the top rated for science and technology, the most viewed, and the top favorite on YouTube. Now, why did we do this? Well, a lot of these folks weren't people that we would normally talk to or talk about. These bloggers and these articles that I just took you through are typically folks who would write about IBM. We started with our key audience takeaways, and we developed a screenplay to support it.

Figure 21.9   The movie trailer

We wanted to develop characters the various audience types would identify with, so we wanted someone who played the line of business view, someone who played the IT view, and someone who was at a C level in the corporation. We wanted to make it content full, but not too technology heavy, and we wanted to integrate some of the technical concept into natural dialogue. Sounding natural was the most challenging part. We also selected key scenes and we created behind-the-scene panel discussion guides, so after they watched this short movie, which was about 20 to 30 minutes long, there was a panel discussion to close out the event.

We started with a particular set of questions, and then we opened it up for customers to ask questions of us. After we created this movie, which is still available for viewing at the ibm.com/SOA Web site, we created an executable format for our geographies. It was created in both a Web and a live-event flow. We created complementary demand and deliverables, invitations, Web sites, e-mails, and posters and decided that we would view this in movie theaters to create the whole effect, provide popcorn, make it different, and set it up in local venues and local cities.

This was a true worldwide launch as we got our geographies to subtitle the movie immediately in 11 languages, including Spanish, French, German, Czech, Russian, Arabic, Brazilian, Portuguese, Chinese, Japanese, Korean, and of course, English. Our final step was to promote the live event shown in movie theaters, both virally and traditionally. We did a teaser and after the teaser, we did the trailer on YouTube, and then we did the movie. That three-step approach filled theaters.

We also did a viral approach, the teaser, and the trailer on YouTube, MySpace, Yahoo, in blogs, and in press articles. All included a send-to-a-friend option. We sent them to the movie microsite, which is called SOA launch.com. This microsite was critical to improving our organic search rankings because of the sheer volume of traffic we had to the site to view the teaser and the trailer. A critical business objective was to improve our organic search rankings so that when we do have new announcements, customers, and press, analysts can easily access this information on the Web. Before the movie, we consistently ranked in the top 10 or top 15, but we wanted to be in the top 3. The excitement around the movie teaser on YouTube drove a lot of people to click ibm.com/soa/launch, the site we promoted at the end of the teaser. As a result, this dramatically improved our organic search rankings without any significant investment in search optimization.

We combined the viral microsite with some of our traditional work. We had movie posters at all key customer briefing centers, demo centers, and at our partner facilities. We had third-party industry events where we advertised it. We did movie screenings in a number of locations.

Consider this: We showed the movie to customers who weren't typically customers. We wanted to make sure we had a way to follow up, and for that, we created a DVD much like you would a Hollywood movie. We created a DVD and had bonus features that would extend the life of the campaign. We gave out the DVD and took orders online. Again, what you see here is the combination of viral marketing and traditional marketing with a creative idea in the film festival, leveraging the new technology and desires of the new client.

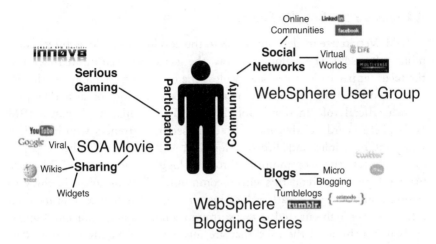

Figure 21.10 IBM WebSphere leveraged the new vessels for success.

We called this the continuous campaign, where our design was not only integrated, but it also leveraged technology to extend the life of the assets. (See Figure 21.11.)

Figure 21.11 The continuous campaign.

A Focus on the Loyalty Factor

IBM WebSphere made a big splash in the development and architect community, but somewhere along the way, the focus had been diluted. We lost the focus on particular roles, and we lost the focus on technology depth. We revitalized our IBM WebSphere user group communities because they play such a crucial role in our brand loyalty. To do this, we began a IBM WebSphere board of advisors, a strategic set of customers who helped to guide the principles and direction for IBM WebSphere. We also began to focus on a variety of communities through blogging and through SOA space for developers to extend this into a community. This use of technology to build community was greatly valued by our targeted audiences. Our focus on roles went through our soul in our surround sound strategy. Surround sound is about touching all the roles that are involved in a buying decision. (See Figure 21.12.)

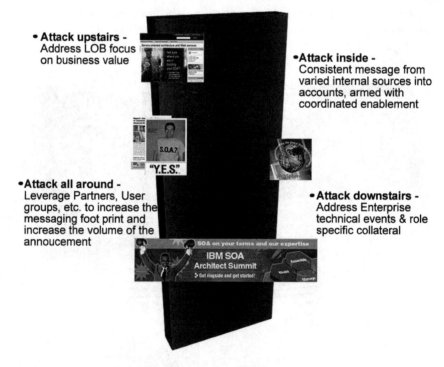

Figure 21.12 Surround sound based on a role-based focus.

Our SOA summits at first were IT-focused and intended to educate. The market transformed into SOA executive summits that focused on business value and alignment. SOA architect summits focused on IT execution. Running these in parallel helped in surrounding the client's key influencers based on roles and purpose.

One of the breakthroughs was in linking the roles together—thus showing how the roles fit together through the segments. Given we had begun a focus on "business processes," we tied the roles together across this perspective. It was also at this time we really pushed on the expertise thought. In fact, the tag line was SOA on your terms and our expertise. The competitive differentiation of skills and best practices through expertise became the heart of our value proposition.

Bring the Power of Your Whole Company to Bear on the Market

Before the IBM SOA effort, each brand inside of IBM was marketed on its own. SOA enabled us to pull together a broader marketing effort inside of IBM, gaining the combined might of IBM. Marketing truly lead and brought together the various business units and functions to think differently—from sales, to support, to development. Many things had to change to achieve success. For example, SOA marketing established change at IBM in the overall marketing program approach. Three years ago, everything was done by brand. Today, all marketing program initiatives are cross business unit views based on a business value proposition modeled after the SOA approach.

In addition, communications and press relations played an integral role. Joe Stunkard's team, led by Sara Peck for SOA analyst relations and Ron Favali and Matthew Berry for SOA press relations, worked seamlessly with marketing, a level of teamwork between the two functions that was unprecedented. PR is an indispensable tool. It can create the right atmosphere without seeming like a commercial. Here it led to terrific air cover in the form of a positive amount of press.

The results from 2005–2006, with this increasing focus on SOA, was that IBM WebSphere became the number one brand in SOA with a 53 percent market share according to Wintergreen Research. IBM WebSphere's brand loyalty increased as well, especially when used in SOA deployments. Mark Loughridge, who is IBM's CFO, addressed the financial analysts in the public third quarter 2006 review. He announced that the acceptance of service oriented architecture contributed to double-digit revenue growth in IBM

WebSphere each quarter. IBM's lead in SOA is well recognized; we're continuing to invest and extend our leadership position in both the digital world (see Figure 21.13) and beyond!

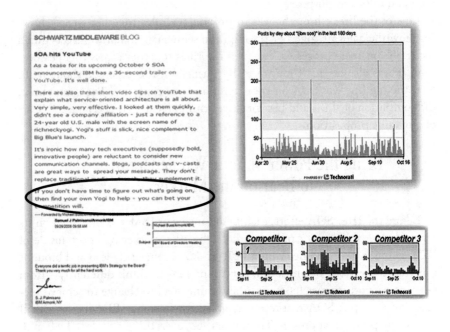

*Source: Technorati

Figure 21.13   IBM and SOA are number one in blogs!

Application to Your Company

To leverage the lessons learned from the IBM WebSphere Brand, these five areas are secrets to success.

- **Stay in touch with your market, constantly updating your strategy in relationship to your brand:** Throughout the IBM WebSphere journey, change is the only thing that is constant. The strategy was adjusted but kept true to the brand. The strategy was taking our core business as our strength and building from there. Make sure you know your core brand values. Listen to the market through the lens of your core brand values.

- **Take risks on how your GTM plan reaches new customers:** Our approach with the movie, starting with the trailer, sneak peeks, in-person theater show through the Web viewing also extended the time of the campaign in the digital world. It kept people interested and in-touch over time. The DVD enabled us to extend the life of the campaign, and the different media types enabled us to reach both digital citizens and traditional customers. Think about your customer and how to hold his attention over time.

  We followed the movie up with the "serious game" called Innov8. It enabled us to leverage the movie (much like *Spiderman* movies did with their Wii game) into the classroom to educate both university students and customers alike. It is geared for those digital citizens who learn from the gaming world that they grew up in!

- **Don't forget your channel and influencers:** Channel partners and influencers, like universities and analysts, have always played a key role in our success. The idea of surround sound helps you keep in touch with your wheel of influence.

- **Measure, measure, and measure!** Don't forget to measure the success of your new experiments in the Web 2.0 world!

- **A little bit of luck:** We were lucky that Google acquired YouTube about the time our movie came out. It drove up the traffic. We leveraged YouTube's key influencers and bloggers and the press to make this successful. The results were that we tripled the Webcast registration compared to what we had done in the past, leveraging these new technology tools.

A sidebar, "Marketing as a Change Agent: Working Across Multiple Disciplines and Divisions," can be found on our companion Web site at ibmpressbooks.com/angels.

2007–Today: Marketing 2.0

To extend the leadership and community of the IBM WebSphere brand, the next step in our march for success was to build a community around our efforts with SOA. With the growth in the overall opportunity, we decided to approach this in a set of steps. We wanted to host a major event with community as the theme and a set of local meetings to support each of the geography needs. In addition, to take the community concept online, we wanted to leverage the technology in the marketplace.

IBM IMPACT was a conference tour de force. For the first time, IBM created an event that had everything: customers, press, analysts, user groups, hands-on lab demos and a tradeshow exhibit area. It was a one-stop event for technical and business learning about current industry developments. It also became a way for customers to network with users from all over the world, IBM business partners, book authors, expert analysts (including Gartner Group, Forrester, and others), and superstars in the world of software development.

The conference offered something for everyone, and it showed in the attendance numbers. There were more than 4,200 attendees for this first event in 2007 and more than 6,000 for the second event in 2008. We followed the mega event with a series of localized events to carry the message out to every region of the world.

Top Five Lessons Learned

The lessons learned on the hybrid mix of activities have charged us into more innovation. This major event, IMPACT, has allowed us to create a community that has served to drive growth in our brand. We have accelerated our focus based on the following lessons learned.

1. **Word of mouth:** Our basic tenet for our event to foster the community feeling was that we wanted customers to tell the story. So, we focused on word of mouth and references. For our IMPACT 2007 event, we had more than 100 customer speakers. We topped that in IMPACT 2008 with more than 250 customer speakers. As Judith Hurwitz, a critical analyst influencer, wrote in her blog, "It's about the customer. IBM made it clear that it was putting its focus on customers at this meeting."

2. **Social network:** The SOA social network was also a focus at the event. The social network allowed the community to organize itself by roles, industry, or even geography. We started with the architect role and the developer role, but then added a business analyst role. We focused on reaching communities where these roles live, whether it was in Twitter, Facebook, blogs, or wherever they are most comfortable. We kicked it off with an SOA jam. More than 1,500 people participated from more than 29 countries to generate ideas for the community and social network.

3. **CSR and the Green Zone:** We also set a goal to show that SOA and IBM WebSphere could assist in the latest corporate responsibility areas such as Green. We set up a Green Zone and had a Green Day. Instead of water bottles, we gave out reusable containers. Most importantly, we showed how our portfolio helps in the Green battle. What resulted were quotes like this one about the power we put in the hands of our customers. Network World wrote, "Over time, there will be numerous approaches to applying green philosophies to SOA. Right now, the 'thunder' belongs to IBM from the IMPACT conference."

Jim Haney, Harley Executive, rides in on his Harley

Figure 21.14   Impact 2008!

4. **A mix of live plus virtual:** IMPACT was both a live event and a virtual event. For example, in our China Impact Event, we had more than 1,400 attendees; however, 20,000 attendees joined the event online. In our Paris Impact event, we held a live event in Paris, but broadcast the event in Paris to six other regions making up 52 percent of the opportunity in France. In addition, we added our ecosystem into driving the message through Impact Comes to You Events. This again allowed us to reach

our local audiences through global packaging into thousands of cities around the world.

5. **Business and industry focus:** Our focus on the business roles continued and grew in this time frame. From our IMPACT event, which had agendas for roles, tracks by industry, to individual events targeted by industry (like SOA for government), the focus is becoming increasingly on how to communicate the value of SOA to the business leaders. For example, we created the Business Value Assessment (BVA) tool, to help identify the starting point and but more importantly the value and ROI behind it. When IBM leverages the BVA tool, the closure rate of an SOA deal is 80%. These will continue to evolve to becoming more Industry-focused. For example, our IMPACT event in India led by Arwinder Caur, our SOA Indian Marketing Lead, consists of two days, the first evening for very high-level business executives followed by day two with the IT coming to hear the role-based relevant version for them.

The overall results from the IMPACT events were more than 10,000 attendees who provided millions of dollars in revenue. In addition, thousands of press articles were written about the event, the announcement, and even the innovations. But, most important are the results in market share. IBM is the number one market share leader in this space.

Application to Your Company

Your marketing strategy needs to grow incrementally. For example, in our event strategy, the role-based approach transformed the events. The use of Web 2.0 technology grew from its first use in 2006. In 2008, the social networking aspects made our earlier investments in technology and Web 2.0 pay off. Finally, as you read through this case study, you might have noticed an intersection of the product development plans and the way the market evolved. We went from commerce to portal, to integration, and to SOA. We infused marketing understanding into the product plans through a tight partnership and linkage. Focusing on your brand, such as IBM WebSphere, and a category that sets an industry agenda such as SOA, bring the force of the market into your marketing. It cannot be, however, just marketing. It must be marketing, sales, and development with the entire company to make an impact.

Conclusion

Screaming leverages all the marketing techniques in an integrated fashion. The IBM WebSphere case study shows the changes over time, based on the market maturity and the product. IBM WebSphere is now a household brand because while keeping to its brand promise, it morphed and grew as the market and customers' needs changed. From early 1998–2000, we caught the wave that was the Internet, but in 2001–2002, we kept the momentum going because we helped to solve problems that went beyond the hype. Many companies went under or disappeared, but we stayed true to our customers, the longer vision, and the brand promise. We grew again in 2005 with the introduction of a new category called SOA that truly served an unmet need in the marketplace.

This powerhouse brand was built by understanding the timing factors of the product and market and the powerful use of technology to drive awareness, education, and demand. IBM WebSphere focused on all the lessons we have discussed in this book with an emphasis on technology.

To view one of our tactics for the 10th anniversary WebSphere Video, go to ibmpressbooks.com/angels.

22

The Top 10 Don'ts and the Marketing Organization of the Future

Experience is the name everyone gives to their mistakes.
—Oscar Wilde

Throughout this book, there have been more than 55 best-practice case studies demonstrating the use of Marketing 2.0 techniques in the world today. The technology is changing so quickly and providing the platform for marketers to accelerate, personalize, and measure success in the marketplace. Web 2.0 has engaged customers in the dialogue and allowed the conversation to be dynamic and exposed on the Internet. Blogs, wikis, and social networking sites, such as Facebook, have now been added to the marketer's arsenal of tools. Social networking and collaboration tools are game changers—both from how marketing teams work internally and with customers and partners but also in terms of how consumers view companies.

However, marketing fundamentals still matter just as much as they always have and cannot be overlooked. Blocking and tackling, such as segmentation, branding, market research, and articulating a strong value position, are essential elements of success. We now have more resources to build on this foundation. As a result, our mindset has to be modified, tweaked, and changed. Press, analysts, and other influencers are playing a bigger role, and our wheel of influence must be reevaluated regularly. Social networking is becoming more pervasive, and there is no end in sight.

We have spent a lot of the book on the lessons learned and best practices on how to operate in this world; however, I learn from mistakes that I make as well. I dedicate this last chapter to those "Top 10 Don'ts" to enable us to learn from the "experiences" of others!

#1: Don't Forget About Office Politics

We didn't discuss the environment in this book, but I wanted to end with the point that you cannot forget office politics. In discussing marketing with Anne Holland, founder of Marketing Sherpa, Inc., she told me that one of the biggest disruptions for marketing professionals is in this area. Holland has been studying business-to-business (B2B) marketing for ten years, discovering best practices, and advising the best of the best marketers. In her view, when marketers fail, the #1 reason is that they did not pay attention to office politics. Holland comments, "Number one is office politics because if you cannot get the finance department and the IT department or legal department to agree to what you want to do, you have absolutely no power."

Marketing needs a seat at the table and to do so, it must be viewed as strategic, not tactical. Part of the chief marketing officer's (CMO) role is to convince his or her peers and executive team that marketing is essential. For the most part, this means leading without authority. For example, how do you get legal to let you make that offer or launch a blog? You need to internally market your ideas, marketing's value, and show the strategic nature of the discipline.

In the future, the value of collaboration will grow, which is why the need for collaboration, teaming, and an understanding that the business continues to grow for marketers. Marketers need to be self-aware and understand the environment in which they work. We need to do internal marketing on the value of what we do just as we do externally. As Holland says, "We have been studying this scientifically in addition to collecting lessons from marketers over the past ten years. It is the people skills and the office politics that are the number one critical thing that either made them a success or it was the number one lesson they learned in the past year." The bottom line: Prioritize the "marketing of your team's marketing" internally!

#2: Don't Take Your Eyes off Profit Generation

To show value and continuously improve, a grasp of the key metrics is a critical skill. In many companies, marketing is viewed as just art. However, the numbers provide a foundation of value. As Holland describes, "Determining a handful of metrics that your department can, to some degree, control is a critical task. Understanding and learning your trigger points so that you can take actions that will impact and move the bottom line of your business is now a mandatory skill. Marketing is seen as tactical instead of strategic. Marketers, especially in this recession, get laid off faster than any other type of senior executive because they're seen as a cost center and not a value center. Marketers need to be able to convince their peers and the management team that marketing is essential, as essential and important and critical as a CFO or a CIO. Understanding the numbers can demonstrate the value."

In the end, putting together a dashboard of essential metrics and learning how to ignore the rest is a key critical success factor. It is an exciting time because as a marketer, the Internet provides us with a great way to get numbers. You can get e-mail open rates, click-through rates, and so on. It is hard to know which to look at, which to react to, and which to completely ignore. As Holland says, "I see marketers walk in with their giant Web analytics report. They know it is valuable and they pay a lot of money for it, but they don't ever look at it because it's just a huge report full of numbers."

Don't spend your time on all the numbers, but pull out the handful of metrics that impact your business. You need to ensure those that you selected will move the bottom line when you take the appropriate marketing-driven actions. Your dashboard does not have to be fancy, but having that dashboard to show how well you are doing and what you need to quickly change because you're going to be in trouble is critical. The bottom line: the numbers do matter.

#3: Don't Ignore the Future

Alan Kay, a key computer scientist, says, "The best way to predict the future is to invent it." To drive the business, you cannot ignore the future trends in the market. If you do not segment the market and see how you can deliver on unmet customer needs or competitive trends, you will be vulnerable.

For instance, the rise of purchasing power in rapidly developing economies and prosperity in Western economies is driving a difference in the way marketers need to take their products to market. Another example is corporate social responsibility (CSR) and Green. As Yves Carcelle, the chairman and CEO of Louis Vuitton, said in our interviews for the IBM Global CEO Study: The Enterprise of the Future, IBM, 2008, "Our company is investing extensively in corporate social responsibility (CSR). We need to be a reference in this domain. As the leader of the luxury industry, we have to stay ahead." If you did not have your radar out, this trend might never have hit your line of sight!

Marketers need to track emerging profit pools and investigate the needs, trends, and policies demanded by society. The bottom line: Marketing's job is to develop insight about the future.

A sidebar, "Trend Spotting: How Do You Do It?" from The World Future Society in the *The Art of Foresight* publication. ©World Future Society, 7910 Woodmont Avenue, Suite 450, Bethesda, Maryland 20814, U.S.A. Telephone 1-301-656-8274. www.wfs.org can be found on our companion Web site at ibmpressbooks.com/angels

#4: Don't Forget That Marketing Is Not B2B or B2C, but P2P (People to People)

Given that marketing is about people to people relationships, we need to understand what makes a successful relationship work. First, all relationships require listening. Listening has become core to everything. Second, in the best relationships, there is a lot of active communication and dialogue. This dialogue is essential to growth in the relationship.

Third, a great relationship is one built on honesty. As I reviewed numerous books on relationships, the one thing the books and experts agreed on was that authenticity was at the heart of all successful relationships. Think long-term transactions, not short-term transactions. As many can attest, a long-lasting relationship without honesty is no relationship at all. Finally, great relationships are those where the parties know each other, and their hopes, dreams, and plans. They understand who they are.

For marketing to have a relationship with the customer, many things have to come together. Familiarize yourself with the new tools that are available so that the listening can begin. Dialogues and conversations are going on around us from our customers, our prospects, our competitors, our partners, and within our own organization. IBM has used our listening tools to restructure areas, such as customer service, marketing, and other areas based on feedback. Authenticity needs to be at the heart of all our actions from Green to product claims. "Knowing" your customer involves a combination of market research and a real humanization of their roles, pains, and dreams. I personally have a rolodex of my top customers who constantly provide me feedback and insight.

NINTENDO: BUILDING MARKET SHARE THROUGH CUSTOMER COLLABORATION AND RELATIONSHIP

In the early 1990s, Nintendo's share of the game console market was 61 percent, but by the mid-2000s, it had fallen to 22 percent.[1] To regain its leadership position, Nintendo needed to find new ways to delight gamers and to bring gaming to new audiences.

To do that, Nintendo went straight to the source—gamers themselves. The company established an online community by offering incentives in return for customer information. The company also selected a group of experienced gamers based on the value and frequency of their community contributions. These "sages," as they were named, were given exclusive rewards, such as previews of new games in exchange for helping new users and providing community support.[2]

Through this community, Nintendo has gained valuable insights into market needs and preferences. This has influenced everything from game offerings, such as an online library of "nostalgic" games that appeal to older gamers, to new product design such as the intuitive controls of the popular Nintendo Wii system, which helped attract new, casual gamers.[3]

By leveraging the loyalty and expertise of its core customer segment, Nintendo has successfully connected with two new ones—women and older men. This collaboration seems to have paid off: Nintendo is again ahead of its competitors, with 44 percent market share.[4]

As Dan Baum, CEO and creative director of DBC PR + New Media., comment about the new world, "The best way to communicate isn't about using new media types to fly around looking like an Italian hipster; it is about understanding your customers and how you can connect yourself into their conversation."

Sometimes that means figuring out what language and what value the market is looking for. Take the care and the time to structure a rigorous integrated process of informing your decisions and your thinking with customer insight from the beginning of your planning process, and you will yield much better outcomes. The bottom line: Marketing is about relationships and people. Keep this as top of mind as you plan your marketing not as B2B but as P2P.

#5: Don't Miss the Web 2.0 Power

The new world of Marketing 2.0 is happening now. I have heard many marketers say that they are waiting to see how it pans out. Don't be fooled by how frivolous some of the early uses of social and virtual worlds might seem. As Sam Palmisano, IBM's CEO comments, "The next phase of the Internet could have the same level of impact as the first Web explosion." Don't be left behind or playing catch up. The numbers and uses today are compelling and continue to grow, especially globally. The challenge is to determine when and how to use those powerful tools. See Figure 22.1.

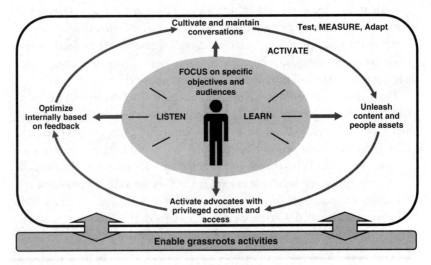

Figure 22.1   Marketing 2.0: Balance Listening, Learning, and Responding

As Rob Stone, the senior vice president at Market Strategies comments, "Technology itself is allowing us to collect data at an ever more granular and precise level." It is more than just for those deep insights. Technology is enabling better marketing.

This does not mean that marketers need to be technologists. However, they cannot be afraid of technology. Every marketer needs a set of skills as a user of technology and the new Web 2.0 ways of social networking. Blogging, podcasts, widgets, Twitter, and so on are part of the new technology trends that are boosting the marketing power in the marketplace. Add to that the power that the technology in the new mobile devices provides and you have a competitive advantage in the way you leverage the technology to expand your customer base. The spectrum of your Web 2.0 choices can help you choose the right vessel for your goal. See Figure 22.2.

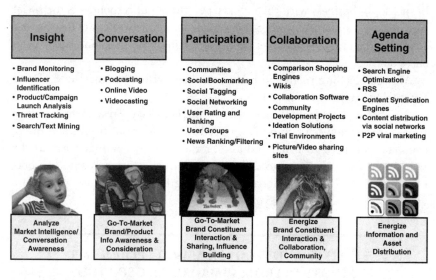

Insight	Conversation	Participation	Collaboration	Agenda Setting
• Brand Monitoring • Influencer Identification • Product/Campaign Launch Analysis • Threat Tracking • Search/Text Mining	• Blogging • Podcasting • Online Video • Videocasting	• Communities • Social Bookmarking • Social Tagging • Social Networking • User Rating and Ranking • User Groups • News Ranking/Filtering	• Comparison Shopping Engines • Wikis • Collaboration Software • Community Development Projects • Ideation Solutions • Trial Environments • Picture/Video sharing sites	• Search Engine Optimization • RSS • Content Syndication Engines • Content distribution via social networks • P2P viral marketing
Analyze Market Intelligence/ Conversation Awareness	Go-To-Market Brand/Product Info Awareness & Consideration	Go-To-Market Brand Constituent Interaction & Sharing, Influence Building	Energize Brand Constituent Interaction & Collaboration, Community	Energize Information and Asset Distribution

Figure 22.2 The Web 2.0 Marketing Spectrum.

Make sure that when you try out these new forms of Marketing 2.0, that you are prepared. As Dan Baum comments, "I continue to see a lot of companies using the new technology media types to be fashionable. Just yesterday, I saw a company that launched a YouTube channel with company produced videos. They posed their executives as newscasters except they weren't good newscasters. It just made them look out of touch, and they completely misunderstood the idea of viral video. There are many examples of the misuse of not understanding the differences among corporate video and viral video and community content."

Don't be one of those who doesn't get it. The bottom line: leverage the technology to impact each part of the ANGELS framework.

#6: Don't Forget the Value of the Influencer

This is an important don't. When I conducted my interviews, all the marketing experts agreed on this big one. According to Dan Baum, "Putting a focus on those online influencers should be at the top of a marketer's list." Jen McClure, executive director of Society for New Communications Research, agrees and sees the value of these influencers growing: "When it comes to the relationship between customer care and brand reputation, there is an enormous number of people using social media to research brands before doing business with them. Sixty percent of our respondents use social media to vent about a customer-care experience and what they're discovering about a company. This group of people is sharing both good and bad experiences online."

Are you reaching them and providing them with what they need? Don't ignore these influencers of your brand.

Partners are a critical influencer in the market today. Treat them as part of your company and your team. They need to provide you insight and direction, and you need to listen and ask for their input. Leverage them as the IBM WebSphere team did to drive innovation for your company. The bottom line: The Wheel of Influencer is growing in its importance. Make sure you know what is impacting your brand.

ELI LILLY AND ITS OPEN MARKETPLACE FOR INNOVATION FROM IBM GLOBAL CEO STUDY: THE ENTERPRISE OF THE FUTURE, IBM, 2008

To bring new medicines to market faster, U.S. pharmaceutical maker Eli Lilly and Company integrates an extensive network of external partners through its constantly evolving collaborative business models. In 2001, for example, Lilly launched InnoCentive, an open marketplace for innovation. On this Web site, "seeker" organizations anonymously submit scientific challenges to a diverse crowd of more than 140,000 "solvers" from 175 countries.[5] The best solutions can earn financial awards of up to U.S. $1 million. Lilly has since spun off InnoCentive and still retains partial ownership in the venture.

More recently, Lilly has embarked on another business model innovation—establishing itself as a Fully Integrated Pharmaceutical Network (FIPNet). The FIPNet model is based on pioneering risk-sharing relationships, such as its 2007 agreement with Nicholas Piramal India Limited (NPIL).[6] Under this contract, NPIL will develop one of Lilly's molecules at its own expense, from preclinical work to early clinical trials. If NPIL is successful and the compound reaches the second stage of human testing, Lilly can reacquire it in exchange for certain milestone payments and royalties.

These collaborative business models offer several benefits: reducing costs, increasing development capacity, accelerating the drug development process, and better leveraging not only Lilly's assets, but also those of its external partners. Lilly's results speak for themselves: from 2002 to 2007, sales have increased at a compound annual growth rate of 11 percent.[7]

#7: Don't Ignore Your Marketing Mix

Today, more than ever, the choices for your marketing mix can be overwhelming. There are many different media from YouTube videos to e-mail to television to radio to PR to online PR. Yet, the way that you combine the elements will determine your success. You can't depend on one medium because you don't know which one is not going to get through.

Richard Vancil, IDC's vice president of the Executive Advisory Group, reviews the marketing mix of marketing companies today. He discovered that in the current marketing mix, many companies were focusing on an "inside-out" approach. In other words, the mix focused more on outbound broadcast from a company to the customer, an "us–to-them" approach.

A company that allocates a marketing program investment by how *it* operates makes the mistake of having "the budget becoming the strategy." However, customers want an "outside-in" perspective because to them, the format is of little interest. (See Figure 22.3.)

Anne Holland agrees, "At least once a quarter, look at your mix and make sure you've got the right media mix." You need to focus on spending money on the media that is affecting your biggest buyers. It sounds basic but this is one of the problems in many B2B companies. Make sure you are asking the question, "Am I isolating my most valuable names and putting my money against the 20 percent who are going to give 80 percent of revenue in my marketing mix?"

Your marketing mix needs to analyze the impact of each element—both marketing 2.0 interactive forms and the traditional marketing. Both make a difference in your success. A guide to use is offered by IDC in Figure 22.4.

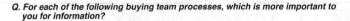

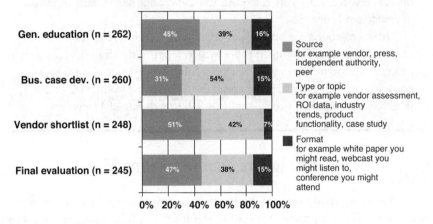

Source: IDC's *2007 Customer Experience Study*, n = 340

Figure 22.3   From the "outside-in," format or media factors are of least interest to buyers.

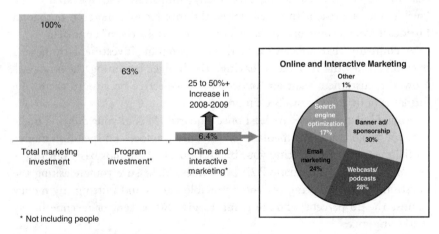

* Not including people

Source: IDC, 2007 Tech Marketing Benchmarks Database (n = 86)

Figure 22.4   Build the interactive marketing-mix—investment, operation, and processes.

The bottom line: Your marketing mix will never be all Marketing 2.0 tactics. The challenge is to constantly balance with your goals the right mix of elements.

#8: Don't Underestimate Change and the Prosumer

Change is coming from everywhere. The market, technology, geography, and skills are just some of the areas of change. You read in the preface about the IBM Global CEO Study: The Enterprise of the Future, IBM, 2008 and how more CEOs than ever before (more than 80 percent) anticipated turbulent change and plan bold moves in response over the next two years. Managing change needs to become a core competency for the marketing team.

What types of change should marketing lead on? As discussed earlier, a prosumer is a client who is a coproducer in your product or service. Marketers need the skills to understand the customers, to grant customers access to the brand, and to motivate them to be evangelists for the brand. These prosumers will become referral customers on steroids. In the "IBM Global CEO Study: The Enterprise of the Future, IBM, 2008" interview, Hartmut Jenner, CEO of Alfred Karcher GmbH, says, "In the future, we will be talking more about a prosumer—a consumer/producer who is even more extensively integrated into the value chain. As a consequence, production processes will be customized more precisely and individually."

Again, change occurs as we become a more global universe. In the "IBM Global CEO Study: The Enterprise of the Future, IBM, 2008," Jim Guyette, president and CEO of Rolls-Royce North America, said, "A few years ago, we were a national company; now we're a global company. Our integrated supply chain must adapt to meet demand in 50 countries."

LI & FUNG LIMITED'S CHANGE MACHINE FROM IBM GLOBAL CEO STUDY: THE ENTERPRISE OF THE FUTURE, IBM, 2008

With a network of 10,000 suppliers and staff in 40 different countries, Hong Kong-based Li & Fung Limited can source from virtually anywhere in the world and build customized solutions for its retail customers.[8] Cotton can be purchased from America, knit and dyed in Pakistan, and sewn into garments in Cambodia or in whatever configuration yields the best end result. Interestingly, the company orchestrates the supply chain for each of its customers without owning any piece of it.

Li & Fung has steadily moved up the value chain, changing its capability and asset mix to provide more sophisticated, and more profitable, services. To provide product design and brand development services in its largest market, the United States, the company has established a significant onshore presence. This move is just one more example of Li & Fung's capability to be both locally relevant and globally optimized.

Acquisitions, more than 20 in less than ten years, are a key way Li & Fung grows market share in target geographic markets.[9] Typically, it preserves the front-end customer interface, which is often the reason for the acquisition, but merges the back end with its own operation within 100 days of deal close.[10]

Li & Fung Limited's global integration formula certainly seems to work; between 1992 and 2006, revenues grew at a compound annual growth rate of more than 22 percent.[11]

The great thing about the new world is that testing your change concepts through experimentation is easier than before. Use the Web 2.0 tools available to shape, test, and drive your ideas. As Robert Painter, IBM vice president of SOA Programs, comments, "Embrace change. Invent it. Test it. Try it. The next generation of marketing is being shaped now; don't wait—jump in!" The bottom line: Change will occur even faster than before. Make sure your marketing is agile enough to handle the new prosumer.

#9: Don't Disinvest in Skills and Human Capital Management

To develop the marketing function that is sustainable, an area to focus on is twenty-first century talent. What is talent? In Hollywood, talent is the focus of your onscreen potential. Here, talent is that focus on potential and ability to execute in the new world of Marketing 2.0. More companies compete on brainpower, not on geography or product. A talent-centric marketing organization focuses on continuing to encourage and empower its people to experiment and grow their skills.

To continue to be competitive, marketers must identify and focus on the development of skills and expertise in the most critical areas in the marketplace. Cultivating these "market-valued skills" ensures you have the right expertise at the right time. Marketing is changing everyday. As such, a focus on the skills you need to succeed need to be refreshed regularly.

For example, because the world is turning into the "CNN sound bite" world, all marketers need to understand the basics of presentations, writing, and videos or have people on their teams who do. Developing your brand's recall messaging strategy is an art. Key to success for marketers is the skill to simplify and clarify your customers' value. In today's market, that skittering eye or that busy ear can hear only a few things. At most, you get 20 seconds. Are your team's skills up to the challenge of that new world? Bottom line: Your talent will make a difference in your success. Make sure you invest wisely in training.

#10: Don't Neglect Organization Transformation

Simply getting the best people is not enough. You need the organization systems and practices to get a competitive advantage from your human capital. Marketing organizations are transforming on many fronts.

For example, PR, communications, and marketing are becoming one. As Jen McClure comments, "We are intrigued and studying the new trend in Web-based press rooms, as opposed to traditional wire services. What we have discovered is that there are just as many marketing professionals using press releases as there are PR professionals using these new online channels. There is a blurring of the line as marketers are using them to reach customers and consumers, by actually creating their own media as opposed to just using them to reach the press. This is just one example where we see the marketing and PR function blending, converging, and changing."

Searching for an optimal marketing organization structure is tough and involves experimentation and a heavy view of what is important to your company. Richard Vancil, IDC's vice president of the Executive Advisory Group, projects that best-practice marketing organizations of the future will increase its investment in sales, channel enablement, and customer-segment marketing while decreasing its spending in the corporate area. (See Table 22.1.)

Table 22.1 Marketing Organization Transformation

Today		Tomorrow	
Name	Total P+P Resource	Name	Total P+P Resource
Corporate Marketing	45%	Marketing Shared Services	20%
Field Marketing	25%	Sales and & Channel Enablement	40%
Product Marketing	30%	Customer Segments Marketing	40%

The Marketing Function of the Future: A Framework

Marketing is the heart of a company. It is even more important in today's Web 2.0 world than ever before. The ANGELS framework that we began with is not a stiff, nonflexible, or sequential view of the world but a dynamic guideline to assist you through the new challenges. For instance, in Table 22.2, we can see through the ANGELS framework a way to address the trends we have discussed throughout this book on globalization, CSR, technology advances, and the accelerated rate of change.

Table 22.2 ANGELS Addressing the Trends

Trend	A N G E LS	Brand New	Traditional Made Better
Globalization	Analyze, GTM, energizing leads		Segmentation and market intelligence
Changing customer	Analyze	Online groups to learn segmentation	
Corporate responsibility	Nail the strategy	Green marketing	
Technology advances including social, experience, personalization	GTM, energizing, leads	Blogs, podcasts, virtual worlds, gaming, widgets, Twitter, online chat, social networks, communities, Mobile	Commerce and dashboards
Accelerated change	Leads, revenue, and metrics	Key agility indicators	Dashboards and skills

The framework has no beginning and no end. It encourages a continuous form of listening:

- Analyzing the market should constantly be done as an obsession. Great input comes from everywhere—employees, partners, customers, social networks, other industries, analysts, advocates, and even that last demonstration you did in a trade show. Deep customer insight still is at the top of the list for marketers and always will be. It helps determine which themes will resonate next.

- Nail the strategy and the story is equally as important. The strategy and story need to be constantly reviewed and evaluated. Themes and agendas are formed to enable clients to lead in their industries and open up new markets and opportunities. Differentiation stems not just from the product or offering but also from everything surrounding it—the place it is sold, the first person who talks about it (a call center representative for instance), the communication, the salesperson, and so on. The aspiration of the story must meet a need in the customer's heart. It must allow for profit generation to your company. However, in the end game, we saw that the value proposition of the product or service offering is what drives success. It is not the only variable. If that's the case, why do we use VHS tapes instead of Sony Beta tapes? The Beta was superior technically, but it's now gone. What wins in marketing is a great product or offering, strategy to reach the marketing, and story. The right strategy can win the hearts and souls of your employees.

- Go-to-market (GTM) plans are the way the story is brought to market. It allows us to work with sales to create client experiences that are a competitive advantage and to bring to market leading edge policies. It can help drive through entire countries' innovation and growth. It helps us to plan a surround-sound strategy to bring a message to market, have our customers experience the story, and form a relationship with them. For example, a supply chain officer could read an industry point of view on our Web site, then attend an event to experience the IBM value proposition first hand, and form a relationship through one of our strategic boards on supply chain leadership. GTM is about the integrated plan that leads to a long-term relationship with clients.

- Energizing the channel with the new Web 2.0 methods combined with traditional means really makes a difference in the market. Although the Web 2.0 methods are cool, sometimes the traditional methods serve us best. Holland and I again discussed the "VIP"-customer set and the best way to reach them. Holland comments, "In B2B areas, I run into marketers who say, 'Hey, print costs too much, so viral and e-mail's cooler; I am going to switch over to that.' And they switched everything over to only the new media, but they fail to remember that they have two generations not paying attention to e-mail or viral. In particular, the under-25 don't check e-mail, and the more experienced people don't have time to answer the 97 e-mails they have gotten that day. What's wrong with using a high-end direct mail piece to reach the important customer versus viral? It's not as cool, but it could be much more effective."

- Leveraging leads and revenue is a requirement. Leveraging the numbers helps to guide decisions, identify opportunity, and track meaningful progress for a path to profitable growth. Whether you use a fancy auto-mated dashboard or a Lotus 1-2-3® file, it is essential inside and outside your company to accomplish your goals. Maximizing the results from segmentation, targeting, role-based marketing, and value propositions demand generation results in leading edge practice.

- Screaming in the marketplace to break through the noise when today's client is overwhelmed is required. Knowing the timing of the scream and the target audience is essential. In addition, technology helps. It is not the answer, but as an enabler, nothing is more powerful.

Marketing is truly a passion. It is about an embodiment of the value proposition into the soul of your company. In every one of these areas of marketing, Marketing 2.0 plays a role. (See Figure 22.5.) Living it and breathing it in all that you do is what makes the good companies great. That's our marketing mission: to instill that value into every client experience, every influencer, and every employee that we connect with in the world and in virtual environments.

Build the marketing organization in your company that is not only producing results today, but also is driving to greater heights in the future. In Figure 22.5, there is a Maturity Model and a set of questions that you can begin to ask yourself about your readiness for the future!

I hope that this book provides a framework that you can use in this new Marketing 2.0 world. In writing this book, I was humbled by the great work from marketers around the world and the willingness of so many to share their experiences. That kind of collaboration and genuineness is unheard of in other fields.

I'd like to keep collecting the best practices and sharing those with you on my Web site, BooksBySandy.com. Continued success to each of you, and if I might personally add to your success, then you have made my day!

Bonus content on how to apply to win a marketing award can be found on our companion Web site at ibmpressbooks.com/angels.

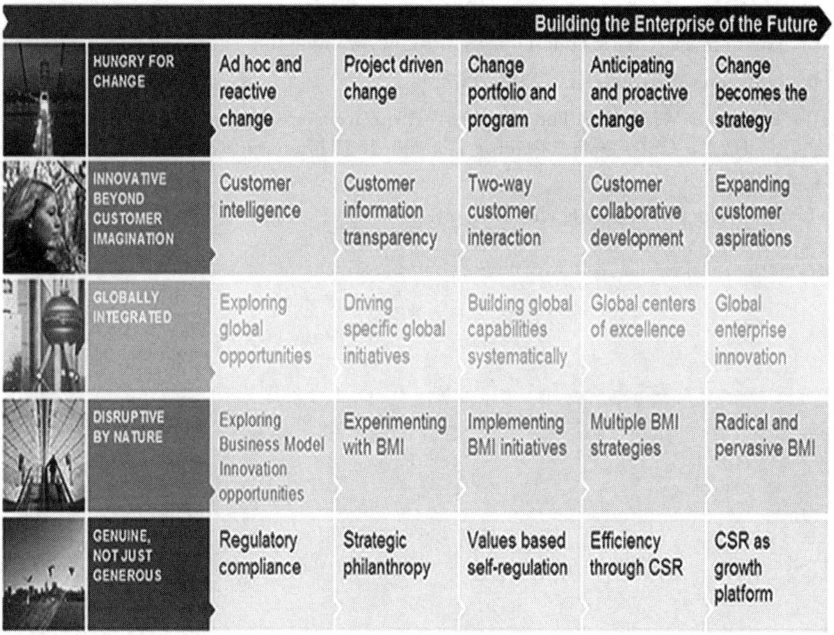

	Building the Enterprise of the Future				
HUNGRY FOR CHANGE	Ad hoc and reactive change	Project driven change	Change portfolio and program	Anticipating and proactive change	Change becomes the strategy
INNOVATIVE BEYOND CUSTOMER IMAGINATION	Customer intelligence	Customer information transparency	Two-way customer interaction	Customer collaborative development	Expanding customer aspirations
GLOBALLY INTEGRATED	Exploring global opportunities	Driving specific global initiatives	Building global capabilities systematically	Global centers of excellence	Global enterprise innovation
DISRUPTIVE BY NATURE	Exploring Business Model Innovation opportunities	Experimenting with BMI	Implementing BMI initiatives	Multiple BMI strategies	Radical and pervasive BMI
GENUINE, NOT JUST GENEROUS	Regulatory compliance	Strategic philanthropy	Values based self-regulation	Efficiency through CSR	CSR as growth platform

*Source: IBM Global CEO Study: The Enterprise of the Future, IBM, 2008.

Figure 22.5   Are you building your marketing function of the future?

Endnotes

1. IBM analysis.

2. "Nintendo Rewards Its Customers with New Loyalty Program." Xbox Solution. December 11, 2003. http://talk.xboxsolution.com/showthread.php?t=1088.

3. "Casual Gamers Help Nintendo Wii Take Lead in 2008, says iSuppli." Tekrati. February 14, 2008. http://ce.tekrati.com/research/10080/.

4. "Worldwide Hardware Shipments." VGChartz.com, accessed March 27, 2008.

5. The InnoCentive Web site, http://www.innocentive.com/.

6. "Nicholas Piramal Announces Drug Development Agreement with Eli Lilly and Company: Collaboration Represents a New Clinical Development Model." Nicholas Piramal India Limited Press release. January 12, 2007. http://www.nicholaspiramal.com/media_pr40.htm.

7. Eli Lilly and Company 2002 and 2007 annual reports.

8. Li & Fung Group Web site. http://www.lifunggroup.com/front.html; "Global Reach, Local Presence." Li & Fung Limited. http://www.lifung.com/eng/network/map.php.

9. Li & Fung Press Releases, 1999–2007.

10. Voxant FD Wire. "Li & Fung Limited—Acquisition of KarstadtQuelle Sourcing Arm—Conference Call—Final." October 2, 2006; IBM interview with Victor Fung, March 2008.

11. Li & Fung Limited 2006 annual report.

Index

Page numbers preceded by Web: indicate topics found in the online chapters at ibmpressbooks.com/angels

BONUS CONTENT
Available Online

This book provides additional chapters, case studies, examples, and resources available through the book's companion site.

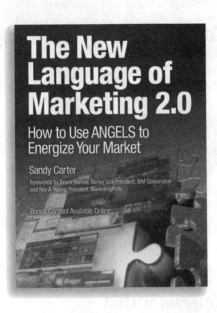

 FREE Online Edition

Your purchase of **The New Language of Marketing 2.0: How to Use ANGELS to Energize Your Market** includes access to a free online edition for 45 days through the Safari Books Online subscription service. Nearly every IBM book is available online through Safari Books Online, along with more than 5,000 other technical books and videos from publishers such as Addison-Wesley Professional, Cisco Press, Exam Cram, O'Reilly, Prentice Hall, Que, and Sams.

SAFARI BOOKS ONLINE allows you to search for a specific answer, cut and paste code, download chapters, and stay current with emerging technologies.

Activate your FREE Online Edition at www.informit.com/safarifree

> **STEP 1:** Enter the coupon code: HWFAQWA.

> **STEP 2:** New Safari users, complete the brief registration form.
> Safari subscribers, just log in.

If you have difficulty registering on Safari or accessing the online edition, please e-mail customer-service@safaribooksonline.com